IMPRESSUM
IMPRINT

Herausgeber *Editor* iF International Forum Design GmbH, Bahnhofstrasse 8, 30159 Hannover, Germany, www.ifdesign.de, phone +49.511.54224-0, fax +49.511.54224-100, info@ifdesign.de
▪ **iF Geschäftsführung** *iF Managing Director* Ralph Wiegmann ▪ **iF design awards 2013** Anja Kirschning, Rylana Kossol, Carmen Wille, Frank Zierenberg ▪ **iF yearbooks 2013** Korinna Braun, Heike Meier, Charity Sala Lirazan ▪ **iF Team** Dirk Bartelsmeier, Gabriele Bertemann, Sandra Fischer, Birgit Kölsch, Andrea Schewior, Andrea Schmidt, Rainer Schwarz, Annegret Wulf-Pippig ▪ **iF Branch Office Hamburg** Silke Hartung, Hans Pflueg, Anna Reissert, Hongkongstrasse 6, 20457 Hamburg, Germany ▪ **iF Branch Office Munich** Louisa Erbguth, Petra Nordmeier, Schleißheimer Straße 4, 80333 Munich, Germany ▪ **iF Branch Office Taiwan** Sean C.K. Lee, Tobie Lee, Kimberly Liu, Joan Wu, 3F., No. 133, Guangfu S. Rd., Xinyi Dist., Taipei 110, Taiwan ▪ **iF Representative Office Brasil** Juliana Buso, Centro de Design Paraná, Av. Comendador Franco, 1341 - Jardim Botânico, CEP: 80215-090 Curitiba - Paraná, Brasil ▪ **iF Representative Office Korea** Ji Hwan Lee, Designhouse Inc., Taekwang Building, 162-1 Jangchung-Dong 2-GA, Jung-Gu, Seoul 100-855, Korea ▪ **iF Representative Office Poland** Agnieszka Pagels, Äußere Oybiner Str. 14-16, 02763 Zittau, Germany ▪ **iF Representative Office Turkey** Sinem Kocayas, Cihan Sirolu, dDf // dream dream design factory, Eski Şapka Fabrikası, Kumbarahane Cad. No: 22, Haskoy, İstanbul, Turkey ▪ **iF Press Office** Claudia Neumann Communication GmbH, Silke Gehrmann-Becker, Kevin MacArthur, Eigelstein 103-113, 50668 Köln, Germany, phone +49.221.9139490, fax +49.221.91394919, iF@neumann-luz.de ▪ **iF DESIGN MEDIA GmbH** Ramona Rockel, phone +49.721.35455800, ramona.rockel@ifdesign.de ▪ **Textredaktion** *Copy Editing* Kristina Irmler, Großburgwedel, Germany; Dr. Tuuli Tietze, Winsen, Germany ▪ **Corporate Design** helke brandt communication, Hannover, Germany ▪ **Übersetzung** *Translation* Lennon.de Language Services, Münster, Germany ▪ **Fotografie Jury** *Jury Photography* Roman Thomas, Celle, Germany; Bernd Schönberger, Berlin, Germany; Euromediahouse GmbH, Hannover, Germany ▪ **Satz und Lithographie** *Typesetting and Lithograph* oeding print GmbH, Braunschweig, Germany ▪ **Druck** *Print* Offizin Andersen Nexö Leipzig GmbH, Leipzig, Germany

Bibliographic information published by the Deutsche Nationalbibliothek. The Deutsche Nationalbibliothek lists this publication in the Deutsche Nationalbibliografie; detailed bibliografic data are available on the internet at http://dnb.d-nb.de

© 2013 iF International Forum Design GmbH

Verlag *Publisher*

iF DESIGN MEDIA GmbH

Bahnhofstrasse 8

30159 Hannover

Germany

www.ifdesign.de

Printed in Germany

ISBN 978-3-7913-4810-0

iF DESIGN AWARDS
product 2013, vol. 2

INHALT
CONTENT

vol. 2

LIGHTING

JAMES AUGER
FRANZISKA KOWALEWSKI
OSCAR PEÑA

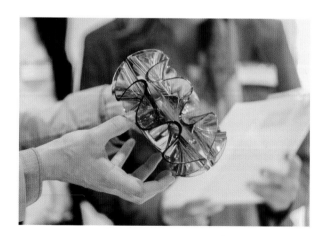

PRODUCT
IN-EI ISSEY MIYAKE
Leuchtenfamilie
Lighting family

DESIGN
MIYAKE DESIGN STUDIO
Issey Miyake
Reality Lab
Tokyo, Japan

MANUFACTURER
Artemide S. p. A.
Pregnana Milanese, Italy

Die Kollektion IN-EI ISSEY MIYAKE, von Issey Miyake und dem Reality Lab. entwickelt, umfasst Steh-, Tisch- und Pendelleuchten, die vollständig aus recyceltem Material hergestellt werden und das Licht auf äußerst interessante Weise abgeben. Die Faser der Leuchten- körper wird aus PET-Flaschen gewonnen. Diese innova- tive Herstellungstechnik reduziert den Energieverbrauch und die CO_2 -Emission um bis zu 40 % gegenüber der Herstellung neuer Materialien. Issey Miyakes künstlerische Vision verbindet japanische Lichttradition mit seiner ein- zigartigen Fähigkeit, Tradition in Moderne zu verwandeln. Artemide belebt diese nachhaltigen Formen mit LED- Technologie.

IN-EI ISSEY MIYAKE by Issey Miyake and Reality Lab. is a collection of floor, table and hanging lights. The project revolves around a fabric derived from entirely recycled materials, diffusing light in extremely interesting ways; it is a re-treated fiber made using PET bottles. The bottles are processed using an innovative technology that reduc- es both energy consumption and CO_2 emissions up to 40 % when compared to the production of new materials. Issey Miyake's artistic vision combines the Japanese tra- dition of light with Miyake's unique ability to translate tradition into modernity. Artemide animates these sus- tainable shapes using LEDs.

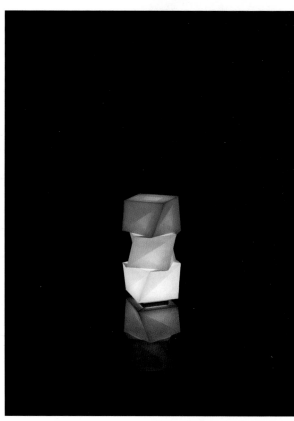

product
design award

2013 GOLD

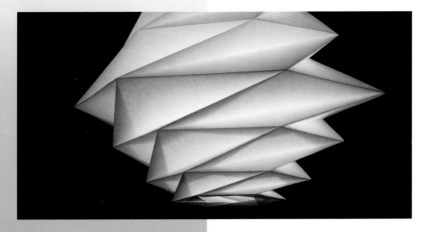 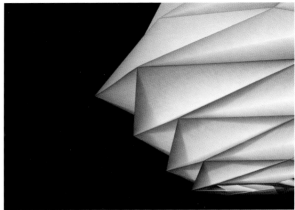

„Die Lichtqualität der Lampe ist überragend, was nicht zuletzt ihrem eleganten, vollständig recycelbaren Material aus PET-Flaschen geschuldet ist. Der Körper aus den Fasern der Flaschen wirkt zwar fragil, ist aber sehr robust und die flexible Konstruktion ermöglicht es, die Form frei zu verändern. Es ist eine sehr traditionell japanische und dennoch moderne Leuchte entstanden, die mit einem iF gold award zu belohnen ist!"

"The quality of light from the lamp is outstanding, which is due not least to the elegant, entirely recyclable materials used in its construction, obtained from PET bottles. The body, made from the fibers of the bottles, appears fragile but is in fact highly robust, while the flexible construction means that the shape can be changed freely. The company has come up with a very traditional Japanese lamp that is nevertheless highly modern, something that deserves an iF gold award!"

JURYSTATEMENT

PRODUCT

LDAHV6L27CGE,LDA6L/C

LED-Glühlampe, glasklar

LED light bulb, glass clear

DESIGN

Panasonic Corporation

Design Company

Nobuyuki Mase

Tokyo, Japan

MANUFACTURER

Panasonic Corporation

Osaka, Japan

Eine LED-Lampe, die nicht nur wie eine klassische Glüh-
lampe mit Glühfaden leuchtet, sondern auch genau so
hell macht. Sie liefert eine Helligkeit, die mit der einer
40-W-Glühfadenlampe vergleichbar ist, und bietet dabei
eine Nennlebensdauer von 40.000 Stunden. Konzipiert
wurde sie für den Gebrauch mit standardmäßigen Lam-
peninstallationen, einschließlich geschlossener Modelle.
Die Erweiterung des Produktangebots, das bislang das
ursprüngliche 20-W-Modell umfasste, um ein 40-W-
Modell wird den Übergang von herkömmlichen Glüh-
fadenlampen zu LED-Lampen weiter fördern.

*An LED light bulb that glows as if it was an incandescent
light bulb with a filament, and illuminates like one as well.
Delivers light equivalent to that of a 40-W incandescent
light bulb, but with a rated lifespan of 40,000 hours.
Designed for use in standard light fixtures, including those
that are enclosed. The addition of a 40-W-type product to
the original 20-W-type will further encourage the changeover to LED from incandescent light bulbs.*

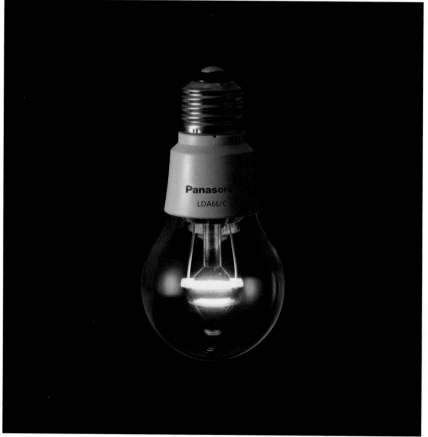

product
design award

2013 GOLD

„Die LED-Lampe zelebriert geradezu die Form von Edisons Glühbirne. Dies geschieht jedoch nicht aus Nostalgie. Denn das Leuchtmittel führt dem Benutzer seine moderne LED-Technik klar vor Augen: Ein in seiner Formgebung sehr gut durchdachtes und modernes Produkt im Bereich von 40W und einer Lebensdauer von ca. 40.000 Stunden. Schlicht eine neue Stufe im LED-Bereich."

"The LED light bulb pays direct homage to the shape of Edison's original light bulb. This is not for nostalgic reasons, however, because the lamp wears its modern LED technology proudly for all to see. In terms of design, this is a very well-thought-out, modern product in the 40 W range with a useful life of approx. 40,000 hours, setting a new standard among LED lamps."

JURYSTATEMENT

PRODUCT
Ledino Outdoor Dunetop range
Weg-Beleuchtung
Pathway lighting

DESIGN
Philips Design
Eindhoven, Netherlands

MANUFACTURER
Royal Philips Electronics
Eindhoven, Netherlands

Die Philips Ledino Outdoor Dunetop-Palette verneigt
sich vor Passanten, wenn sie ihren Weg beleuchtet. Die
schlichte Aluminium-Produktpalette wirft ein diffuses
Licht und ist konzipiert eine dezente Wegebeleuchtung
zu schaffen, die sich auf subtile Weise hervorhebt. Die
qualitativ hochwertige, designorientierte Kollektion ist
erhältlich als Außenpfosten, in grau oder anthrazit, und
als Wandleuchte, in hellgrau und hell-anthrazit. Das integrierte schlanke weiße LED-Lichtmodul spart Energie
und hält 20.000 Stunden.

*The Philips Ledino Outdoor Dunetop range bows its
head to passers-by as it lights their way. Casting a diffuse
light, the humble aluminum range is designed to create
unobtrusive pathway lighting that stands out in a subtle
way. The high-quality, design-driven collection is available
as an outdoor post, in gray or anthracite, and as a wall
light, in light gray and light anthracite. The integrated
slim warm white LED light module saves energy and lasts
20,000 hours.*

product
design award

2013 GOLD

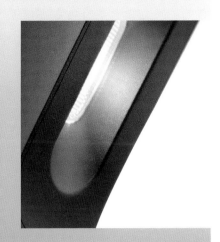

„Diese Outdoor-Lampe verkörpert Eleganz in einfachster und zugleich bester Form. Sie ist fein in ihrer Haptik, zugleich aber robust. Mit ihrem angenehmen Licht ist sie eine Bereicherung für die Umgebung, in der sie eingesetzt wird und beweist auf hervorragende Weise, dass gut gestaltete und technologisch perfekt umgesetzte LED-Technik in der heutigen Zeit angekommen ist."

"This outdoor lamp embodies elegance at its simplest yet best. The surface feel is refined, but also robust. The pleasant light means that the lamp enhances any setting in which it is placed and provides excellent evidence that well-designed and perfectly implemented LED technology is a reality."

JURYSTATEMENT

PRODUCT
Solar Mobile Light
LED-Taschenlampe
LED mobile light

DESIGN
MIYAKE Design Office
Kazushige Miyake
Tokyo, Japan

MANUFACTURER
Ryohin Keikaku Co., Ltd.
MUJI Design & Planning Office
Tokyo, Japan

Solar-LED-Taschenlampe mit Akku – Wenn man mit der Solarzelle Strom erzeugt und damit den eingebauten Akku auflädt, liefert diese Taschenlampe für bis zu vier Stunden Licht. Sie kann auch mit einer USB-Stromquelle aufgeladen und betrieben werden. Auch kann man sie kompakt zusammenklappen und auf Reisen benutzen.

Rechargeable solar LED Mobile Light – A mobile light that can be used for up to four hours when the built-in rechargeable battery is charged using electricity generated by the solar panel. It can also be lit by charging it from a USB power source. Since it can be folded up into a compact size, it can also be used when traveling.

product
design award

2013 GOLD

„Exzellentes Design ist für jedermann zu haben und Produkte von iF gold award Gewinnern müssen nicht kostspielig sein! Das zeigt diese Solar-LED-Taschenlampe mit Akku, an der man ihre einzelnen Funktionen klar ablesen kann. In ausgeklapptem Zustand wirkt die Taschenlampe beinah wie eine kleine aber großartig gestaltete Tischleuchte, die zudem an einer USB-Quelle aufgeladen und betrieben werden kann."

"Excellent design is available to all, and products by iF gold award winners do not have to be expensive! This solar LED pocket lamp with additional battery is the perfect example. The lamp's individual functions are clear: when unfolded, the pocket lamp operates like a small but superbly designed desk lamp that can also be charged and powered via a USB port."

JURYSTATEMENT

PRODUCT

Quadraled
Wandleuchte
Wall luminaire

DESIGN

RZB Rudolf Zimmermann, Bamberg GmbH
Helmut Heinrich
Bamberg, Germany

MANUFACTURER

RZB Rudolf Zimmermann, Bamberg GmbH
Bamberg, Germany

Quadraled macht uns deutlich, welch unbeschreibliche Anziehungskraft eine an und für sich simple grafische Form entwickeln kann. Alle Aufmerksamkeit gilt der Schönheit des Glaskörpers, kein Beiwerk lenkt von seiner Anmut ab, kein Kalkül verstellt den Blick. Berechnendes Denken erforderten jedoch die folgenden Fragen: Wie reduziert und integriert man Technik derart zukunftsweisend, dass sie dem Glaskörper diesen Solitärstatus überhaupt erst ermöglicht? Wie setzt man zeitgleich Meilensteine an Lichtgüte, Effizienz und Wertbeständigkeit? Die Antworten liegen in dieser Symbiose aus Anmut und Innovation namens Quadraled.

Quadraled states, which indescribable gravity an actually simple graphic shape can develop. All attention is drawn to the beauty of the glass corpus, no accessories draw the attention off its grace, no calculation blocks the vision. Yet the following questions required calculated thinking: how can you reduce and integrate technology in such a trendsetting way, that it allows the glass corpus this solitary status in the first place? How can you set milestones in light quality, efficiency and lasting value at the same time? The answers can be found in this symbiosis of grace and innovation named Quadraled.

product
design award

2013 GOLD

 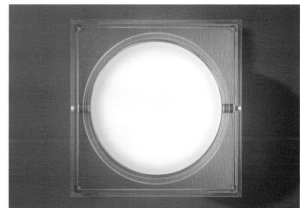

„Die Wandleuchte überzeugt durch ihre schlichte, klare Formgebung, die zugleich einen Eindruck vom handwerklichen Können des Unternehmens gibt. Die Lichtqualität ist absolut außergewöhnlich. Es handelt sich um ein insgesamt stimmiges und sehr gelungenes Produkt mit grafischem Anspruch, der in der Leuchte umgesetzt wurde."

"The strength of these wall lamps lies in their sleek, pure shape that at the same time provides a clear impression of the manufacturer's technical expertise. The quality of the light is absolutely exceptional. This is a highly coherent and successful product with design aspirations that have been perfectly implemented in the light."

JURYSTATEMENT

PRODUCT
DISCUS EVOLUTION
LED-Strahlersystem
LED spotlight system

DESIGN
EOOS Design GmbH
Wien, Austria

MANUFACTURER
Zumtobel Lighting GmbH
Dornbirn, Austria

Eine archaische Sonnenscheibe mit LED-Kreisring bildet den Grundkörper des Strahlersystems DISCUS EVOLUTION. Das flache Erscheinungsbild, samt effizienter Reflektortechnologie und 30-W-LED-Leuchtmittel, aber auch seine hervorragende Abstrahlcharakteristik und Farbwiedergabe von RA 90 zeichnen DISCUS als hochmodernen Shop-Strahler aus. Das neu entwickelte LED-Board-Design ermöglicht Lichtströme von bis zu 2000 lm bei über 65 lm / W Leuchteneffizienz. Mit passivem Kühlsystem und Dimmbarkeit direkt am Strahler oder per DALI verbessert DISCUS die Möglichkeiten eines niedrigen Energieeinsatzes bei bester Lichtqualität und langer Lebensdauer.

The basic structure of the DISCUS EVOLUTION spotlight system is a solar disc which is reminiscent of the ancient symbol for the sun. With its flat look, efficient reflector technology, 30 W light source and excellent beam pattern and color rendering (RA 90), DISCUS is an ultramodern shop spotlight. Its newly developed LED board design allows luminous flux levels of up to 2000 lm with luminaire efficiency in excess of 65 lm / W. With its passive cooling system and dimmability directly on the spotlight or via DALI, Discus provides more scope for using less energy, perfect lighting quality and a long service life.

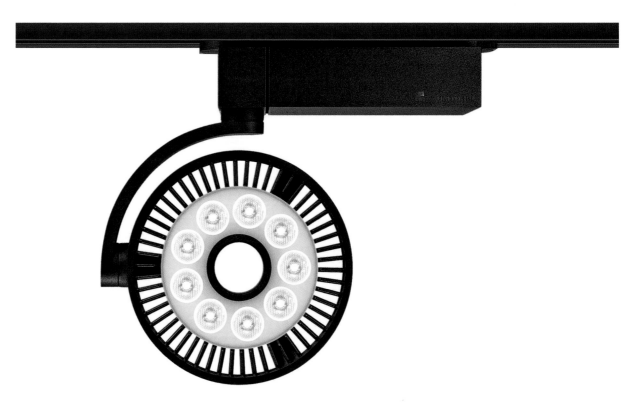

product
design award

2013 GOLD

„LED-Lichtquelle und Leuchtkörper sind bei diesem Strahlersystem perfekt aufeinander abgestimmt. Ihre ausgereifte minimalistische, schlichte Form macht das Produkt zu einem unauffälligen zugleich hervorragend gestalteten Lichtgeber. Alle technischen und gestalterischen Aspekte wie Energieeffizienz, lange Lebensdauer, Lichtqualität und Farbwiedergabe verbinden sich zu einem großartigen Strahlersystem, das unbedingt mit einem iF gold award ausgezeichnet werden muss."

"The LED luminaires and light fixture come together in perfect harmony in this spotlight system. The well-engineered, minimalist, sleek form makes the product both an inconspicuous yet outstandingly designed light source. All of the technical and design aspects such as energy efficiency, long useful life, quality of light and color reproduction are joined in an excellent spotlight system that simply has to receive an iF gold award."

JURYSTATEMENT

PRODUCT
Couche 60
Pendelleuchte
Pendant

DESIGN
Art Maison
Fernando Bernucci
São Paulo, Brazil

MANUFACTURER
Art Maison
São Paulo, Brazil

Couche 60 hat sich überlappende Schichten, die für eine weiche Ausleuchtung sorgen. Die Pendelleuchte bringt optische Effekte von Licht und Tiefe. Die Verwendung von Verbundsicherheitsglas, rustikalem Stoff und die Herstellung mittels Laserschneiden und -veredelung verleihen dem Produkt ein kühnes Design und Unvergleichlichkeit. Die Lampen verfügen über eine leichte Struktur aus Aluminium, die die Installation und einfache Handhabung ermöglicht. Geeignet für intime Momente, Heimkino- und Esszimmer, sind die Couche 60-Zielgruppen Architekten und Designer sowie all jene, die sich mit effizienter Beleuchtung befassen.

The Couche 60 is made of overlapping layers that provides a soft illumination. The pendant light operates optical effects of light and depth. The use of rustic fabric and laser cutting finishing, gives the product a bold design, unmatched in the market. It features lightweight structure made of aluminum, which makes the installation and handling easy. Suitable for intimate settings, home-theater and dining rooms, the Couche 60 target audiences are architects, interior designers and all those that seek to design and efficient lighting.

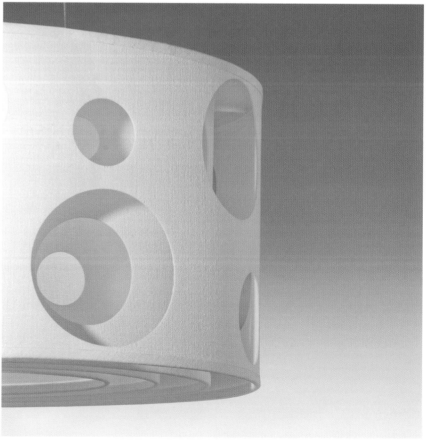

PRODUCT
Cata
LED-Strahler
LED spot

DESIGN
Studio Carlotta de Bevilacqua
Carlotta de Bevilacqua
Milan, Italy

MANUFACTURER
Artemide S. p. A.
Pregnana Milanese, Italy

Dieser LED-Strahler resultiert aus sorgfältiger Forschungsarbeit zum Thema Akzentbeleuchtung. Cata verfügt über eine innovative Kollimationsoptik und besteht aus drei Komponenten: dem Gehäuse aus Methacrylat mit austauschbarer Optik, dem Kühlkörper aus Aluminium und dem Betriebsgerät, das über einen Twist- & Lock-Mechanismus befestigt wird. Durch den Einsatz transparenter Materialien und reflektierender Oberflächen wird der Strahler im Raum entmaterialisiert. Durch die zwei Watt-Optionen (12,5 und 25 W) und die hohe Farbwiedergabe (CRI ≥ 90), konkurriert Cata hinsichtlich Lichtleistung und Lichtqualität mit den besten professionellen Lichtquellen.

A LED projector that comes from careful research for accent lighting, Cata features an innovative light beam collimation system, and is composed of three elements: the body in methacrylate with interchangeable optic, heatsink in extruded aluminum and dedicated power feed unit secured by means of a twist & lock mechanism. Thanks to the use of transparent materials combined with reflecting surfaces, the spotlight dematerializes its presence in the room. Designed with two power options (12.5 and 25 W), with CRI ≥ 90, the spotlight competes with the best professional light sources, in terms of lighting performance and quality.

lighting

PRODUCT
Ontero EC
Aufbaustrahler
Surface-mounted luminaire

DESIGN
brains4design GmbH
München, Germany

MANUFACTURER
BÄRO GmbH & Co. KG
Leichlingen, Germany

Gestalterischer Grundgedanke der gemeinsam mit dem
Münchner Designer Jens Pattberg entwickelten Ontero
EC ist der fließende Übergang von runden zu eckigen
Elementen. Die Leuchte besteht aus pulverbeschichtetem
Aluminium-Druckguss und wurde speziell für neueste
LED-Lichtquellen konstruiert. Integrierte Kühlrippen
ermöglichen ein exzellentes Thermomanagement und
damit den effizienten Betrieb. Die Leuchtenfamilie be-
steht aus einer aktiv gekühlten LED-Version mit DALI-
Steuerung sowie einer Ausführung mit passiver LED-
Kühlung und einem Modell für Halogen-Metalldampf-
lampen. Alle Leuchten können mit drei Reflektortypen
ausgestattet werden.

*The Ontero EC luminaire family is designed in coopera-
tion with the Munich designer Jens Pattberg. The basic
design concept behind the luminaires is the flowing transition from round to angular elements. The luminaire is
made from powder-coated die-cast aluminum and has
been specially designed to meet the demands of modern
LED light sources. Integrated cooling fins facilitate excellent thermal management and therefore they are efficient
to run. The luminaire family comprises an actively cooled
LED-version that also allows DALI control, a luminaire
with passive cooling and a type for metal halide lamps.
Three types of reflector are on offer.*

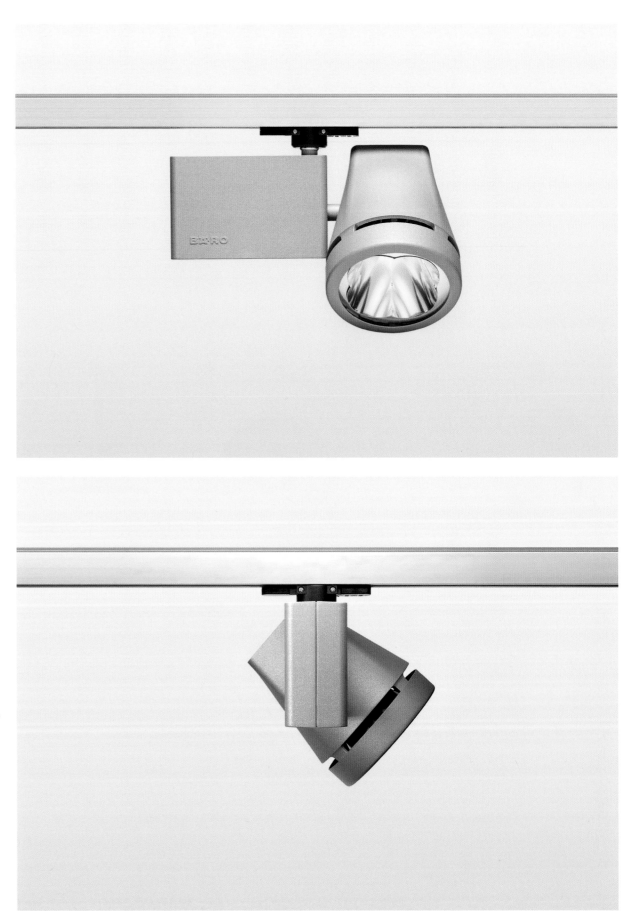

PRODUCT
VL-100
Selbstaufladendes Blitzlicht
Self-generating flash light

DESIGN
Brother Industries, Ltd.
Yosuke Mase
Nagoya, Japan

MANUFACTURER
Brother Industries, Ltd.
Nagoya, Japan

Die VL-100 ist eine selbst aufladbare LED-Taschenlampe mit Technologie zur Stromerzeugung durch Vibration. Selbst nach längerer Zeit ohne Gebrauch, genügt im Notfall ein einfaches Schütteln mit der Hand, um die Lampe wieder funktionstüchtig zu machen. Im Weiteren ist der eingebaute Dynamo weder ein Wegwerfprodukt noch kann er auslaufen und entspricht so den ökologischen Anforderungen unserer Zeit. Durch die Verjüngung der Taille und die handgerechte Form wird das sichere Greifen und Schütteln erleichtert und eine Gestaltung geschaffen, die sich an jeden Ort anpasst.

The VL-100 is a self-rechargeable LED-flashlight using a technology of power generation by vibrations. Even after a longer period without use, in time of emergency a simple shaking with the hand is enough to make the torch functional again. Furthermore, the installed dynamo is neither a disposal product nor in danger of leaking out and meet so the ecological requirements of our present time. The slimmer waist creates a hand-fitting shape to support a secure grip and shake, resulting in an overall design that fits easily to every place.

lighting

PRODUCT
Lamp E
Lampe
Luminaire

DESIGN
Kako ko design studio
Vesna Pejovic
Belgrade, Serbia

MANUFACTURER
BUCK
Belgrade, Serbia

Lamp E ist ein einfaches und skulpturales Lichtobjekt. Das Design nutzt vorhandene Al-Profile die geometrisch platziert die Form eines offenen Würfels bilden. Die Innovation ist nicht technisch, sondern eine klare geometrische Applikation. Absicht war, ein einfaches Erscheinungsbild zu bieten, das den Beobachter als Symbol anzieht. E verleitet zum Spielen, umgedreht kann man sie als Schreibtisch- oder Ambienteleuchte benutzen. AL-Profile und LED reduzieren die Produktions- und Nutzungskosten auf ein Minimum. Das geometrische Design wird in allen Teilen der Welt verstanden und durchzieht sich auch in der Entwicklung einer ganzen Familie von Produkten (E2, E3).

Lamp E is a simple and sculptural light object. The design uses existing Al profiles, placed in geometrical spatial form of open cube sides. The innovation is not technological, but a clear application of geometry. The intention was to make object simple in its appearance, that people relate to and want as a symbol. E invites the user to play with it, turn it around and set it as a desk or ambience lamp. Using existing Al profiles and LED sources reduces the production and exploitation costs to minimum. Universality of the design lies in geometry of lamp which is understood in all parts of the world, and in the development of the whole family of products (E2, E3).

PRODUCT
LEDICUS FLAT
Deckenleuchte
Ceiling lamp

DESIGN
Dieter K. Weis
Dreieich, Germany

MANUFACTURER
Casablanca Leuchten GmbH
Offenbach, Germany

Konsequente Gradlinigkeit, klare geometrische Formen und kompromisslose Reduktion sind die Gestaltungsgrundlagen von LEDICUS FLAT. Durch die flache Form des Leuchtenkorpus sowie vertikale Ausführung des Netzteilgehäuses entsteht trotz dem für Wärmeableitung notwendigen Flächenbedarf eine elegante, leichte Anmutung. Aluminium als sortenreines recycelbares Material dient zur Herstellung des Gehäuses und ist gleichzeitig Garant für optimale Wärmeableitung und lange LED-Lebensdauer. LEDICUS FLAT ist mittels verdeckt angeordneter Bewegungsteile in der Lage in jede gewünschte Richtung im Raum Licht abzustrahlen.

Reduction, clear geometry and rectilinear shapes are the design principles of LEDICUS FLAT. The flat shape of the luminaire body and the vertical design of the ceiling box enable an elegant and light impression despite the required surface for dissipation of heat. The use of recyclable aluminum for the body guarantees an optimal heat management and long lifetime of the LED. Due to hidden rotatable parts LEDICUS FLAT has the capability to illuminate its light in any direction of the interior.

lighting

PRODUCT
Spot 4SD
LED-Beleuchtung
LED lighting

DESIGN
Vimal J. Soni
Mumbai, India

MANUFACTURER
Corvi
Mumbai, India

Der dimmbare 4SD leistet bis zu 120 Lumen pro Watt.
Bei 7,5 Watt leistet diese kompakte LED beeindruckende
900 Lumen. Das einzigartige „Swivel Feature" ermöglicht das Neigen der Leuchte in unterschiedliche Winkel.
Der 4SD lässt sich einfach mit einem Schnappverschluss
installieren und hat eine Lebensdauer von über 75.000
Stunden. Das Produkt hat innovative Funktionen wie
einen eingebauten Treiber und ein unsichtbares Thermal Management System. Der 4SD bietet Sicherheit bei
Stromschwankungen, da er von 85 V bis 285 V arbeiten
kann und dadurch einen universellen Einsatz erlaubt.

*The dimmable 4SD gives an output of up to 120 lumens
per watt. At 7.5 watt, this compact LED luminaire gives
an impressive output of 900 lumens. The unique "Swivel
feature" allows you to tilt the light through a range of
desired angles due to the provision of multidirectional
tilting. The product which is easy to install with a snap fit
function, has a life of over 75,000 hours. The 4SD contains
innovative features such as an inbuilt driver and invisible
thermal management system. This product is fluctuation
proof as it can function from 85 V to 285 V, which also
makes its usage universal.*

PRODUCT
Mohow
Innenbeleuchtung
Interior lighting

DESIGN
DELTA LIGHT N. V.
Wevelgem, Belgium

MANUFACTURER
DELTA LIGHT N. V.
Wevelgem, Belgium

Mit einem Neigungswinkel von 90° und einer Rotation von 360° wird Mohow allen möglichen Beleuchtungs-bedürfnissen gerecht. Der weiß lackierte bewegliche Kopf verläuft leicht konisch hin zu den drei zentralen Power-LEDs, die für eine maximale Lichtausbeute konzi-piert wurden. Dank des Einsatzes der einzigartigen „Equalising Filter Technology" von DELTA LIGHT kann der Nutzer nicht nur einen maximalen Lichtwirkungs-grad, sondern auch eine sehr homogene und qualitativ hochwertige Beleuchtung ohne Mosaik- oder mehrfa-chen Schatteneffekt erwarten. Die Mohow ist in den Ausführungen spot, flood oder wide flood erhältlich und bietet starke Beleuchtungslösungen.

Tiltable up to 90° and rotating 360°, Mohow answers ev-ery possible lighting need. The white lacquered moving head has a slightly conical shape towards the three central power LEDs, designed to provide maximal light output. Using Delta Light's unique "Equalising Filter Technology", the user can expect not only maximum efficiency, but also very homogeneous and high quality illumination, without pixilation or multiple shadow effect. Respecting DELTA LIGHT's detailed finishing, no screws are visible. Available in spot, flood or wide flood, the Mohow provides a strong lighting solution for stores, showrooms, galleries or other professional environments.

PRODUCT
Boxter
Innenbeleuchtung
Interior lighting

DESIGN
DELTA LIGHT N. V.
Wevelgem, Belgium

MANUFACTURER
DELTA LIGHT N. V.
Wevelgem, Belgium

Neben dem funktionellen Zweck, der Aufnahme des
Vorschaltgeräts, ermöglicht die Asymmetrie dieser
Leuchte eine lineare Installation, die Räumen Richtung
und Eleganz verleiht. Durch die Unterbringung des Vorschaltgeräts neben den Lampen anstatt darüber, war es
möglich, eine bemerkenswert niedrige und kompakte
Deckenaufbauleuchte zu entwickeln. Die Boxter ist sowohl in der einlampigen als auch in der zweilampigen
Ausführung entweder mit Halogenlampe oder Hoch-
leistungs-LEDs erhältlich. Dank der LED-Array-Technolo-
gie von DELTA LIGHT stellt die LED-Version eine perfekte Alternative für herkömmliche Lichtquellen mit allen
LED-Vorteilen dar.

A distinctive feature of the Boxter is the asymmetrical
design. In addition to its functional purpose to store the
control gear, the asymmetry of this fixture facilitates a
linear installation, providing direction and elegance to
the room. By storing the control gear next to the lamps
instead of on top, DELTA LIGHT was able to come up with
a remarkably low and compact surface mounted fixture.
Both the single and double lamp version are available
with halogen or high performance power LEDs. Featur-
ing DELTA LIGHT's led array technology, the LED version
provides a perfect alternative for classic light sources,
with all the benefits of LED.

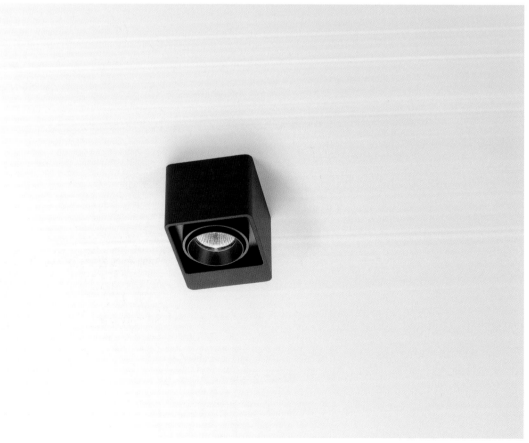

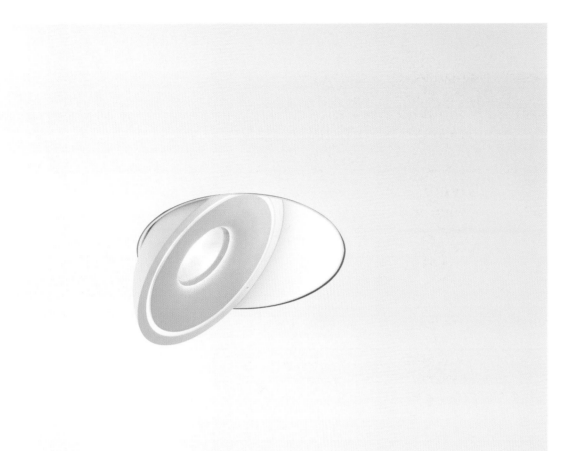

PRODUCT
Tweeter
Innenbeleuchtung
Interior lighting

DESIGN
DELTA LIGHT N. V.
Wevelgem, Belgium

MANUFACTURER
DELTA LIGHT N. V.
Wevelgem, Belgium

Mit der Tweeter-Leuchte bringt DELTA LIGHT das ERS (Excentric Rotation System (angemeldetes Patent) auf den Markt. Beide Ausführungen kennzeichnen sich durch eine asymmetrische Scharnieraufhängung, die es ermöglicht, extreme Rotationen und Kippfähigkeiten in einer einzigen schnellen Wirbelbewegung zu vereinen. Die Deckeneinbaumodelle ermöglichen eine optimale Verschmelzung von Licht und Architektur. Die Spots stimmen mit der Deckenaufbauinstallation überein und das Handling ist einfach und bequem. Das zweischalige Design verhindert Einblicke in die Decke, während die flexible Innenschale allen Beleuchtungsbedürfnissen gerecht wird.

Tweeter introduces new levels in flexibility, both in movement as in lighting application. With Tweeter DELTA LIGHT introduces the ERS – Excentric Rotation System (patent pending). Tweeter On and Tweeter Trimless are characterized by an asymmetrical hinge joint, combining extreme rotation and tilting abilities, all in one swift whirling motion. The recessed Tweeter versions enable a maximum fusing of light and architecture. The spotlight heads are identical to the surface mounted installation and handling is simple and convenient. The double shell design prevents ceiling exposure, while the flexible inner shell tailors for any lighting need.

PRODUCT
U7
LED-Einbauleuchte
Recessed LED luminaire

DESIGN
eer architectural design
Overijse, Belgium

MANUFACTURER
ETAP NV
Malle, Belgium

U7 sind quadratische oder rechteckige Einbauleuchten auf Basis der LED+LENS™-Technologie. Die U7-Reihe bietet normgerechte (UGR < 19) Lösungen für alle Arten von Büro-Bereichen (vom Einzel- bis zum Großraum-büro), für Schulen und öffentliche Bereiche. U7-Leuchten zeichnen sich durch ihr einzigartiges Design und ihre hochwertige Verarbeitung aus. Die Einbautiefe liegt bei nur 50 mm (100 mm bei Einbau in Gipskarton-Decken). Gehäuse-Material: Stahl; Farben: Strukturlack weiß (RAL 9003). Grau (RAL 9006) auf Anfrage; Farbtempe-ratur: 3000 K oder 4000 K; Lichtstrom: 2500 bis 5000 lm; Lichtausbeute: 85 lm / W.

U7 is a series of square and rectangular recessed lumi-naires on the basis of LED+LENS™ technology. U7 provides solutions for all types of office spaces (from individual office to office landscape), schools and public spaces. U7 boasts unique design, is perfectly finished and fits into any decor. The luminaires take up a mounting depth of only 50 mm (100 mm for integration into plasterboard ceilings); material: steel plate; color: white structure paint (RAL 9003). Gray (RAL 9006) upon request; color temperature: 3000 K or 4000 K; luminous flux: 2500 to 5000 lm; luminous efficacy: 85 lm / W.

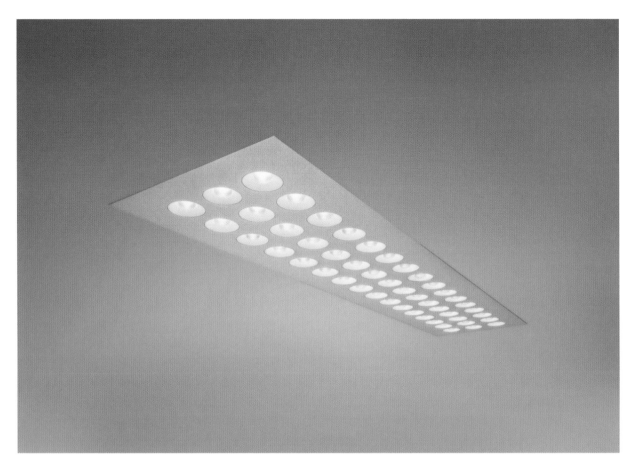

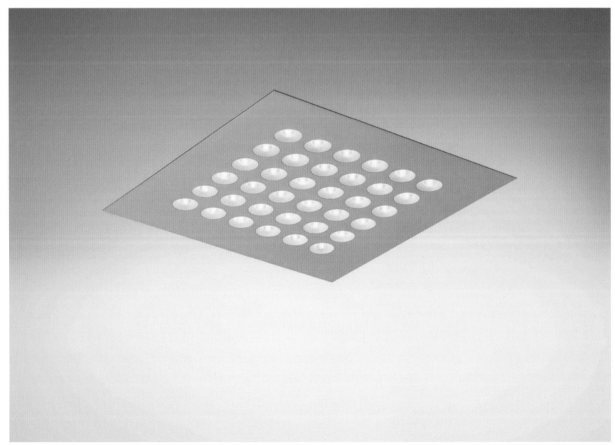

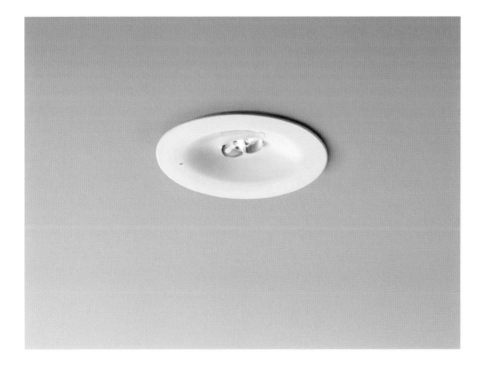

PRODUCT
K9
Anti-Panik-Fluchtweg-Leuchte
Escape route luminaire

DESIGN
Stefan Schöning Studio
Antwerpen, Belgium

MANUFACTURER
ETAP NV
Produktentwicklung
Malle, Belgium

K9-LED-Sicherheitsleuchten für alle Anwendungsbereiche: Antipanik-, Fluchtweg- und Rettungszeichen-Leuchten. Flexibel: Einbau und Anbau in Decke oder Wand, abgependelt oder als Leuchten-Einbau-Modul. Lichttechnik: Nur eine Hochleistungs-LED nötig. Anti-Panik-Version: Licht wird von Linse extrem breit gestreut; Fluchtweg-Leuchte: Linse sorgt für Bündelung des Lichts auf der Fluchtwegachse. Gehäuse: Aluminium-Spritzguss, Weiß (RAL9003) oder Weißaluminium (RAL9006), lackiert oder unlackiert. Maße: L x B x H in mm: 152 x 152 x 30 mit Zwischenabständen, Anti-Panik: 13 m (0,5 lux, Montagehöhe 2,8 m), Fluchtweg: 19 m (1 lux, Montagehöhe 2,8 m).

K9 LED emergency lighting for all applications: anti-panic-, escape route-, and illuminated safety signs. Flexible: recessed, surface, in ceiling or wall, suspended, or as luminaire built-in module. Photometry: only one high-power LED necessary. Anti-panic version: light is scattered extremely wide by lens, escape route version: lens focuses the light on the escape route axis. Housing: die-cast aluminum, white (RAL9003) or white aluminum (RAL9006), painted or unpainted measurements: L x W x H in mm: 152 x 152 x 30 interdistances, anti-panic: 13 m (0.5 lux, mounting height 2.8 m), escape route: 19 m (1 lux, mounting height 2.8 m).

lighting

PRODUCT

R7
LED-Anbau- und Pendelleuchte
LED luminaire

DESIGN

eer architectural design
Overijse, Belgium

MANUFACTURER

ETAP NV
Malle, Belgium

Die R7 ist eine Produktreihe extrem flacher Anbau- und Pendel-Leuchten auf Basis der LED+LENS™-Technologie mit direktem und indirektem Lichtanteil. Sie sind als Einzel- oder als Lichtband-Leuchten mit einem UGR <19 lieferbar. Ihr Einsatzbereich ist die Allgemein-Beleuchtung in den unterschiedlichsten Anwendungen. Die Pendel-Leuchte hat standardmäßig einen Uplight-Anteil von 30 %. Gehäuse-Material: Stahl; Farben: RAL 9003 Weiß; (RAL 9006 Grau; RAL 9005 Schwarz auf Anfrage); Farbtemperatur: 3000 K oder 4000 K; Lichtstrom: von 2500 bis 5000 lm, Lichtausbeute: 85 lm / W.

R7 is a series of ultra slim surface-mounted and suspended luminaires, which provide both direct and indirect light (in suspended version) on the basis of LED+LENS™ technology. R7 is available as individual or line luminaire. Area of application: general lighting in highly diverse environments. The suspended version comes with a 30 % uplight as standard. Material: steel plate; color: white RAL 9003; (gray RAL 9006; black RAL 9005 upon request); color temperature: 3000 K or 4000 K; luminous flux: from 2500 to 5000 lm; luminous efficacy: 85 lm / W.

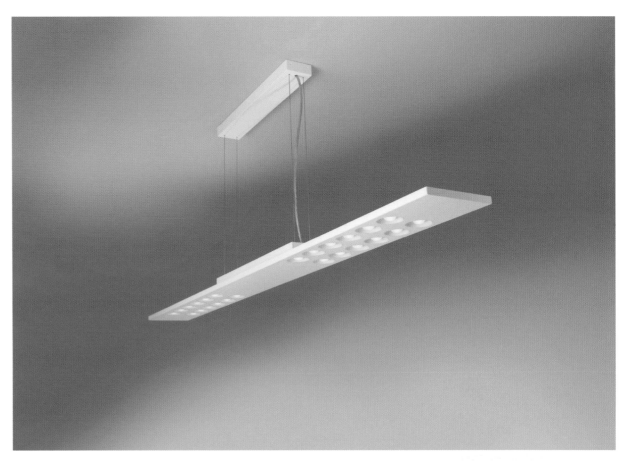

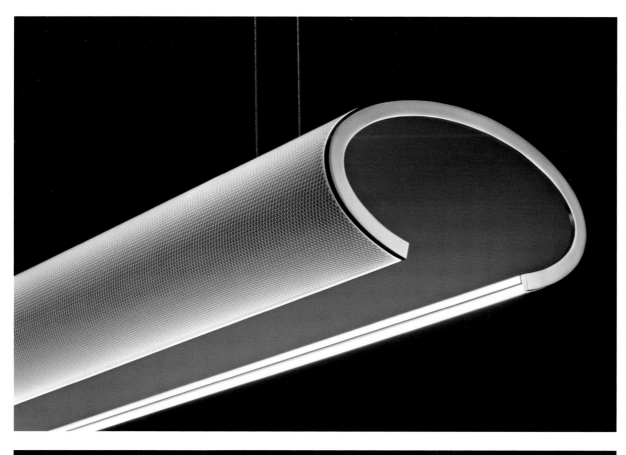

PRODUCT
Theory
LED-Pendelleuchte
LED pendant

DESIGN
Focal Point LLC
Graeme Watt
Chicago, IL, United States of America

MANUFACTURER
Focal Point LLC
Chicago, IL, United States of America

Das Konzept der Pendelleuchte Theory bedient sich des Miniaturmaßstabs der eingesetzten LED-Lichtquellen, um einen Leuchtkörper zu bilden, dessen Gestalt mit traditionellen Leuchtmitteln niemals darstellbar wäre. Der Innen- und Außenteil der Form besteht jeweils aus einem Diffusionskörper, der mittels LEDs homogen illuminiert wird. Die Seilabhängung dient auch der Stromzuführung vom in der Decke untergebrachten EVG zu den LED-Modulen. Eine durch den Nutzer einstellbare, individuelle Dimmung beider Kanäle ermöglicht unterschiedliche Lichtverteilungen und gleichzeitig eine faszinierende Variation des Erscheinungsbilds von Theory.

Focal Point is proud to introduce a remarkable luminaire that artfully exhibits the design possibilities of LED. Within a striking curved body, Theory uses the miniature scale of the LED to achieve a lit form that would be impossible with other sources. Power is fed via the suspension cables to separate circuits – one illuminating the exterior of the form, the other the interior. The ability to independently light the crisp white form inside and the precision textured acrylic outside with no obvious light source creates a sense of mystery. Drivers are concealed above the ceiling. Various ceiling types are accommodated.

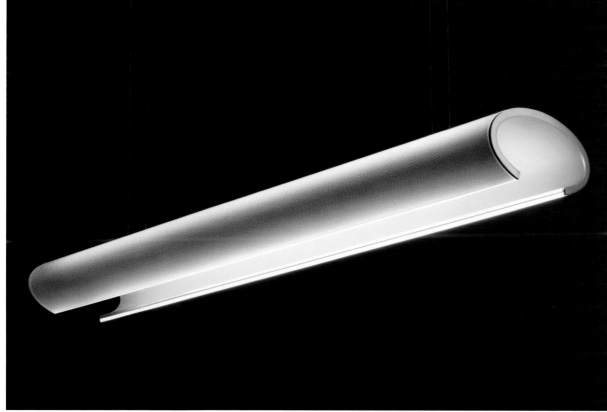

PRODUCT

A9 pure crystal
Wandschalter
Wall switch

DESIGN

Feidiao Electric Appliance Group Co.
Yizhong Xu, Jijian Ji, Baishuang Chen,
Xiufeng He, Zhicheng Ceng
Shanghai, China

MANUFACTURER

Feidiao Electric Appliance Group Co.
Shanghai, China

Wandschalter-Serie aus reinem Platin-Kristall, ultra-
dünn und ganz flach, einfach und elegant. Ein Gefühl
von Luxus, Lebensqualität, Philosophie, Wissenschaft
und Technik kommt beim Berühren des Schalters auf.
Der Körper des Schalters besteht aus importiertem
Bayer-PC-Material, hat hervorragende feuerhemmende
Eigenschaften und Schlagzähigkeit. Dadurch ist er viel
robuster und langlebiger als andere Produkte. Das Panel
mit Doppelschicht macht es einfacher, den Schalter an
die Wand zu installieren. Mittels LED-Anzeige bleibt der
Stromverbrauch sehr gering, etwa ein Zehntel gegenüber
anderen Neonleuchten. Der Schalter wird nicht warm,
hat eine lange Lebensdauer und ist nicht vom Typ der
Lichtquelle abhängig. In ihm sind Schönheit und Energieeinsparung in einem vereint.

The appearance of this series is thin, flat and fashion and highlights the distinguished luxury. Touching the reset switch and experiencing the interpretation of the quality of life, the interpretation of the science and technology concepts. The whole body plastic uses imported Bayer PC material. The PC material has higher flame redundancy and impact resistance and it makes our products more rugged and more durable. The panel uses a two-tier design; it makes our wall switch easier to fit the wall, and enhances the overall strength of the switch. LED lights indicate power consumption is very low, about one tenth of the ordinary neon. And it can be used longer time free from the light source type limit, not blinking. It makes our life more beautiful and energy saving.

PRODUCT
Feidiao the A9 Code
Wandschalter
Wall switch

DESIGN
Feidiao Electric Appliance Group Co.
Yizhong Xu, Jijian Ji, Baishuang Chen,
Xiufeng He, Zhicheng Ceng
Shanghai, China

MANUFACTURER
Feidiao Electric Appliance Group Co.
Shanghai, China

Glänzendes Aussehen dank IMR-Form-Übertragungs-technik. Die A9-Maserung ist frischer und heller, der Rand ist mit einer speziellen Technologie bearbeitet, so-dass ein metallischer Glanz entsteht. Unter Licht ver-stärkt sich die glänzende und reflektierende Wirkung. Besonders flexibel ist die große Drucktaste. Die Schalt-tafel und die internen Komponenten des Feidiao A9-Wandschalters sind mit Verriegelungs-Spleiß sowie dem importierten Bayer-PC-Material gefertigt. Das macht die Produkte robust und elastisch. Die Oberflä-che ist mit Einbrennlack bearbeitet, im Gegensatz zur allgemein verwendeten Spritzlackierung. Auch wenn die Produkte lange Zeit nicht verwendet werden, ver-färben sie sich nicht. Die Anschlüsse des Verriegelungs-Spleiß sind dicht, nicht wackelig, sicher und langfristig. Die Kupferteile sind aus hochwertigen Kupfer-Materia-lien gestanzt, im Gegensatz zum allgemein üblichen Schweißen. Daher sind die Teile fest verbunden, ange-nehm zu handhaben und langlebig. Auch rein silberne Kontaktpunkte werden verwendet. Silber ist der beste Leiter, kann Strom von 16 Ampere standhalten, wo-durch der Sicherheitsfaktor sich weiter verbessert.

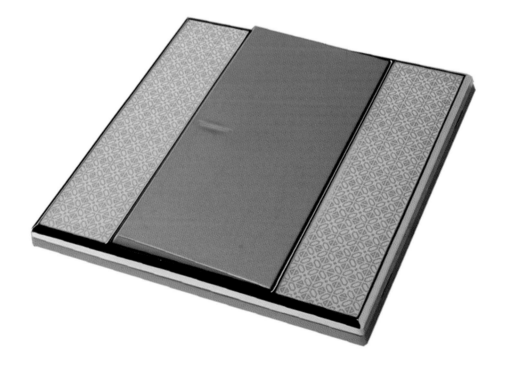

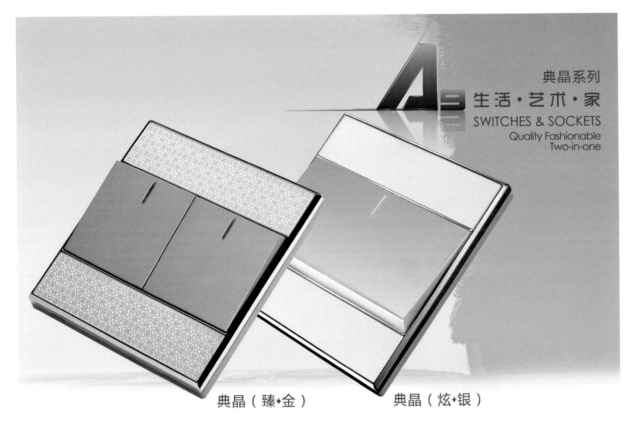

典晶系列

生活·艺术·家

SWITCHES & SOCKETS
Quality Fashionable
Two-in-one

典晶（臻·金）　　　典晶（炫·银）

Glossy appearance IMR mold transfer technology. The use of the IMR mold transfer technology to the typical crystal makes the A9 flower patterns more fresh and bright. Edge distribution uses metallic plating technology. With light irradiation, the crystal reflections match the edge of the chrome-plated each other. The button is large and flexible. The panel and the internal components of Feidiao the A9 Code crystal switch used in all lock-type stitching, imported Bayer PC material. So that the product has excellent elasticity, and the surface uses paint handling, different from the general switch paint, which avoids the problem of fade after prolonged use. Lock-type stitching connection close, it is not easy to loosen and uses safer and more permanent. Switch inside the copper all used the high quality copper material stamping, unlike the general switch welding the copper material firmly. This contact made the parts more solid, convenient and durable. Contacts used sterling silver, silver is the best conductor; it guarantees the 16 A current through and further improve the safety factor.

lighting

PRODUCT

H – motion

Scheinwerfer

Floodlights

DESIGN

Hansol

Lighting

Chungbuk, South Korea

MANUFACTURER

Hansol

Lighting

Chungbuk, South Korea

Das Produkt zeigt seine Unmittelbarkeit durch griffiges Design für effektive Strahlung. Seine quadratische Form bietet visuelle Stabilität mit elegantem Image. Mit dem Designmotive „Rad für industrielle Materialien" wurde die organische Kurve verwendet. Es ist ein erfolgreiches Produkt durch Kombination mit der funktionalen Seite der LED-Beleuchtung und durch Benutzerfreundlichkeit beim Transport, Transfer und bei der Einstellung.

The product is designed with heat radiation. Both side parts shaped like a steering wheel convey sense of immediacy. Sophisticated image from square shape provides users with a visual sense of stability. It is designed as an organic curve design inspired from steering wheel of industrial equipment. Finally, the excellent result was born in combination with both LED lighting's natural function and work convenience for transport, delivery and installation.

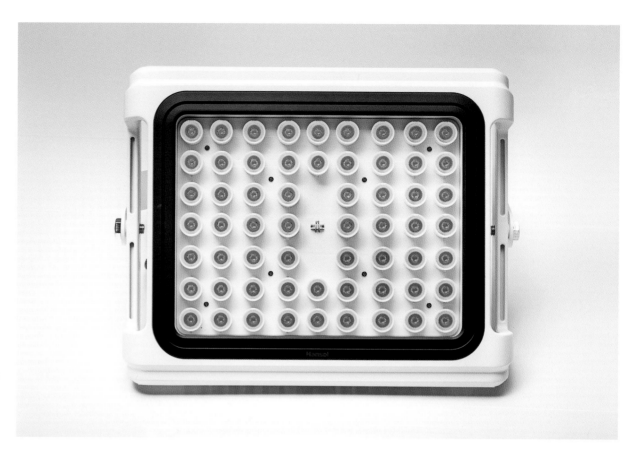

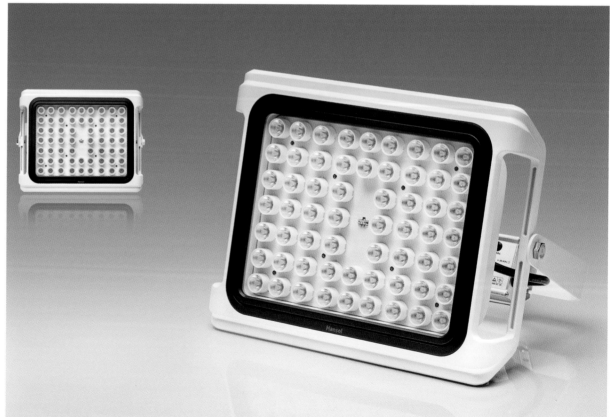

PRODUCT
H – eyes
Scheinwerfer
Floodlights

DESIGN
Hansol
Lighting
Chungbuk, South Korea

MANUFACTURER
Hansol
Lighting
Chungbuk, South Korea

„Dreiecksegel" – Das Produkt ist wohlgestaltet wie ein Dreiecksegel in erfrischender Meeresbrise. Wie ein Zitat von Louis Sullivan „Die Form leitet sich von seiner Funktion ab", hat das Produkt auch gut passende Funktionen. Der Winkel kann kontrolliert oder eingestellt werden, je nach dem, was Benutzer wollen. Daher kann man das Produkt für verschiedene Zwecke einsetzen. Durch Verbindung mit LED-COB-Modulen und „Heatsink" als einzelne Module ist die LED wasserdicht und strahlt Wärme ab.

The product presents a smooth and a slender curve just like a staysail sailing through a sea breeze. It fulfills the famous saying of Louis Sullivan, "Form follows Function". It radiates the heat effectively by designing the heat sink pin to get longer as it gets near to the heatsink element. Angle can be easily controlled and fixed to be applied at various environments, and LED COB and the Heat sink are designed as a single module in order to enhance waterproof and make an initial heat radiation from the LED unit.

lighting

PRODUCT
H – spin
Scheinwerfer
Floodlights

DESIGN
Hansol
Lighting
Chungbuk, South Korea

MANUFACTURER
Hansol
Lighting
Chungbuk, South Korea

Das Produkt hat ein stromlinienförmiges Design – wie
das Designmotive „Rad für industrielle Materialien". Die
Rundform bietet ein stabiles Griffgefühl beim Transport,
Transfer und bei der Einstellung. Sie ist auch optimal bei
der Installation in E-Base. Das kurvige Design von „Heatsink" ist für effektive Ausstrahlung konzipiert. Das Gewicht des Produkts wurde durch Metallvermischung
um 30 % reduziert. Damit sind die Schwächen von LED
beseitigt.

*The product is designed as streamlined shape inspired
from steering wheel of industrial equipment. Circle
shape giving softness provides users with stable grip. It is
optimized to transport and install into E39 base fixture.
Heat sink with streamlined shape, just like a sense of
gentle wave is designed to radiate heat as much as possible. Magnesium alloy allows reducing 30 % of weight
and it can make up for LED lighting's weak point. (weight
and heat dissipation).Warm gray color provide sense of
placidity and luxury, it shows a high level of satisfaction.*

PRODUCT
BE Light Floor
LED-Bodenlampe
LED floor light

DESIGN
Qisda Creative Design Center
Qisda Corporation
Taipei, Taiwan

MANUFACTURER
Qisda Corporation
Taipei, Taiwan

Die Idee für BE Light kam vom Origami, bei dem auch 2D in 3D umgewandelt wird. Die Lampe kann platz-sparend flach zusammengefaltet werden. Der schlanke Ständer lässt sich in der Länge verstellen, um eine opti-male Lichtquelle zu bieten. Zur Sicherheit gibt es an den Verbindungstücken einen Riegel. Die Lampe wurde mit Techniken der Aluminiumextrusion und dem Druckguss gefertigt. Das Gestell ist schlank und robust und wirkt sehr metallisch. Die Verwendung von LED-Licht und Light Guide Technologie ermöglicht eine gleichmäßige Verbreitung von Licht und Intensität, um Blenden zu vermeiden. BE Light ist ein umweltfreundliches Kunst-objekt.

BE Light is inspired from origami, transforming a 2D sur-face into a 3D presentation. The lamp can be folded flat, as a space-saving home deco. The slender lamp post has adjustable height to provide the best reading light. To ensure safety, a latch is installed at the connecting junc-ture. The lamp is mainly made of Aluminum Extrusion and Die-Casting techniques. The body is slim yet sturdy, with a distinguished metallic feature. Using the energy saving LED light and Light Guide technology, light and intensity are evenly distributed to prevent glare, and more suitable for reading. BE Light is eco-friendly and a vibrant work of art.

PRODUCT
Matrix LED
Strahler
Spotlight

DESIGN
Regent Beleuchtungskörper AG
Basel, Switzerland

MANUFACTURER
Regent Beleuchtungskörper AG
Basel, Switzerland

Ob Design, Technologie oder Produktion – der Strahler
Matrix LED vom Schweizer Unternehmen Regent Lighting
setzt neue Zeichen. Sein sehr modernes und doch zeitloses Design ordnet sich der Funktionalität unter, ohne
zu verzichten. So garantiert die ausgeklügelte Konstruktion größtmögliche Dreh- und Schwenkbarkeit. Trotz
markantem Design verschwindet Matrix LED im alltäglichen Einsatz dezent im Hintergrund. Hier werden
höchste Lichtströme passiv gekühlt und auf Effizienz optimiert. Ob im Schaufenster, über der Auslage oder zum
Setzen einzelner Lichtakzente – Matrix LED rückt jedes
Produkt oder Ausstellungsobjekt perfekt ins richtige
Licht.

*The luminaire Matrix LED made by the Swiss company
Regent Lighting sets new standards in terms of design,
technology and production. Its modern yet timeless design
is driven by functionality – not allowing any compromises.
The sophisticated construction guarantees a high level of
tilt and swivel alignment options. Despite its distinctive
design the Matrix LED remains understated. High luminous
flux is passively cooled to guarantee an optimized efficiency. Matrix LED sets a perfect spot on every product or
exhibit – whether used in store windows, to display goods
or accentuate special lighting features.*

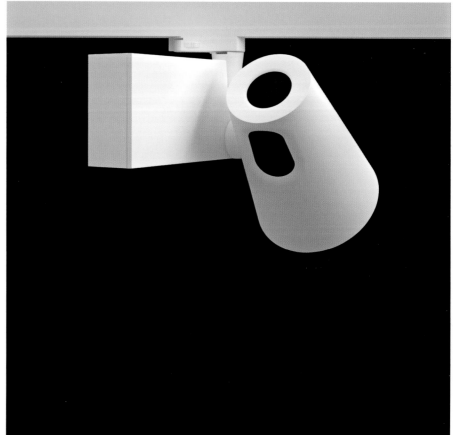

PRODUCT
LivingColors Aura range
LED-Beleuchtung
LED lighting

DESIGN
Philips Design
Eindhoven, Netherlands

MANUFACTURER
Royal Philips Electronics
Eindhoven, Netherlands

Dank der Umarbeitung des klassischen LivingColors-Designs war es niemals erschwinglicher, ihre Umgebung mit Licht farbig zu gestalten. Die Philips Living-Colors Aura ähnelt ihren Vorgängern mit ihrer weit-geöffneten Oberfläche, die den Fokus klar auf das far-bige ausgestrahlte Licht legt. Das neue Design wurde für den Verkauf zu einem geringeren Preis überarbeitet und macht das LivingColors-Erlebnis einem größeren Publikum zugänglich. Die Aura liegt leicht in der Hand und verfügt über eine runde Fernbedienung mit Farb-auswahltaster. Die Aura ist Teil einer neuen Reihe von fünf LivingColors Designs mit den Namen Iris, Aura, Bloom, Mini und Micro.

Coloring the world with light has never been more affordable thanks to this reworking of the classic LivingColors Conic design. The Philips LivingColors Aura resembles its predecessor with its wide open face that put the focus firmly on the colored light emitted. Crucially, the new design has been reengineered to retail at a much lower price point, making the LivingColors experience available to a wider audience. The Aura comes with a new circular remote control that fits easily in the hand and features a tactile color selection button. The Aura is part of a new family of five LivingColors designs dubbed the Iris, Aura, Bloom, Mini, and Micro.

PRODUCT
Lirio by Philips Eron range
LED-Lampen
LED lamps

DESIGN
Philips Design
Eindhoven, Netherlands

MANUFACTURER
Royal Philips Electronics
Eindhoven, Netherlands

Lirio by Philips Eron ist eine Reihe eleganter Steh- und Tischlampen, die leicht jeder Inneneinrichtung angepasst werden können. Die klaren, einfachen Linien der blendfreien, flachen Scheiben-LED wiederholen sich im Design, das keine sichtbaren technischen Details aufweist. Die Lampen sind vollständig dimmbar und können Dank eines flexiblen und noch dazu diskreten Scharniers, mit dem der Leuchtenkopf horizontal und vertikal bewegt werden kann, in jede benötigte Richtung gedreht werden. Die Lirio by Philips-Kollektion ist eine Familie ausgezeichneter Leuchten mit innovativem und stylischem Charakter.

The Lirio by Philips Eron is a range of elegant floor and table lamps that can be added to every interior with ease. The clear and simple lines of the glare-free, flat disc LED are repeated throughout the design, which features no visible technical details. The lamps, which are fully dimmable, can still be directed wherever they are needed thanks to a flexible but discreet hinge that allows the head to move around the horizontal and vertical axes. The Lirio by Philips collection is a family of award-winning luminaires with innovative and stylish characters.

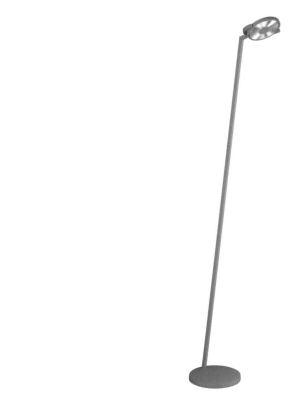

PRODUCT
LED spot range
LED-Spots
LED spots

DESIGN
Philips Design
Eindhoven, Netherlands

MANUFACTURER
Royal Philips Electronics
Eindhoven, Netherlands

Die Stärke dieses Designs liegt in der Einfachheit. Jedes Teil der Philips LED-Spot-Palette wurde optimiert, um ein attraktives Produkt zu einem bezahlbaren Preis zu entwickeln. Ziel des Projekts war die Entwicklung eines LED-Spots mit adäquater Lichtleistung, der für weniger als 20 € verkauft werden kann. Hierfür hat Philips alle Komponenten von Grund auf neu gestaltet. Für die Sockel wurde pulverbeschichteter Pressstahl verwendet, während das Drehgelenk aus Chromstahl besteht. Der Leuchtenkopf ist aus pulverbeschichtetem Aluminium-Druckguss gefertigt, um eine angemessene Abkühlung der LEDs sowie ein hochwertiges Aussehen zu garantieren.

The power of this design is in the simplicity. Every component of the Philips LED spot range has been optimized to create an attractive product for an affordable price. The goal of the project was to create an LED spot with adequate light output that can be retailed at less than € 20. To do so, Philips created all the components from scratch. In terms of materials used, the bases are powder coated, pressed steel, while the swivel is chromed steel. The spot head is made out of powder coated, die-cast aluminum, to ensure adequate cooling of the LEDs, as well as a high quality look and feel.

PRODUCT
Ecomoods Drop Pendants
Deckenleuchten
Ceiling lights

DESIGN
Philips Design
Eindhoven, Netherlands

MANUFACTURER
Royal Philips Electronics
Eindhoven, Netherlands

Stark als Gruppe, ikonisch wie ein einzelnes Stück, bieten die Philips Ecomoods-Pendelleuchten energiesparende Beleuchtung mit starker visueller Signatur. Durch die markante aber natürliche Silhouette gleicht die Pendelleuchte einem Tropfen, der aus dem Kabel, an dem sie hängt, entsteht. Sie besteht aus einer Kombination aus Plastik und Metall. Die plastischen Modelle haben keine sichtbaren Verbindungen oder Konstruktionen und verstärken das Gefühl der Einfachheit. Die Pendellampen gibt es in kleinen, mittleren und großen Größen in vier verschiedenen Farben. Sie sind Teil der stylischen, energiesparenden und bezahlbaren Ecomoods-Kollektion.

Strong as a group, iconic as a single piece, the Philips Ecomoods Drop Pendants offer energy-saving lighting with a strong visual signature. The striking yet natural silhouette makes the pendants look like they are drops that emerge from the wire they are suspended on. Made from a combination of plastic and metal, the highly graphic designs are made without any visual connections or construction marks to enhance the feeling of simplicity. The pendants come in small, medium, and large sizes in a choice of up to four colors. They are part of the Ecomoods collection, which is designed to be stylish, energy-saving, and affordable.

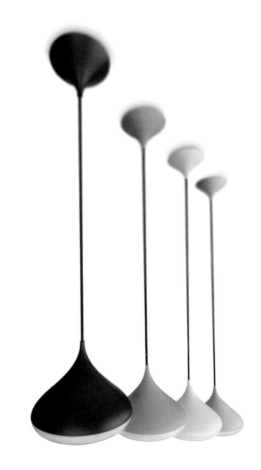

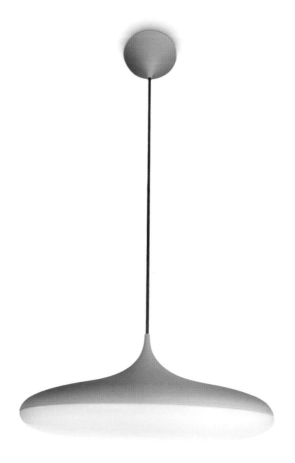

PRODUCT

Lirio by Philips Ecliptic range
LED-Licht
LED lighting

DESIGN

Philips Design
Eindhoven, Netherlands

MANUFACTURER

Royal Philips Electronics
Eindhoven, Netherlands

Die Lirio by Philips Ecliptic ist eine ideenreiche Pendelleuchte, die mit den neuen Formen und Effekten der LED-Technik spielt. Eine fortschrittliche Optik in der Ecliptic, die von traditionelleren Lichtquellen nicht geschaffen werden kann, reflektiert das indirekte LED-Licht und schafft ein vollständig dimmbares diffuses Leuchten. Die neue, verbesserte Form der Pendelleuchte ohne sichtbare technische Details, macht sie zu einem geheimnisvollen, ansprechenden Blickfang in Ihrem modernen Heim. Die Lirio by Philips-Kollektion ist eine Familie ausgezeichneter Leuchten mit innovativem und stylischem Charakter.

The Lirio by Philips Ecliptic is an imaginative pendant light that plays with the new shapes and effects that are made possible by LED technology. Advanced optics within the Ecliptic, which could not be created by more traditional light sources, reflect the indirect LED light and distribute it into a diffuse glow that is fully dimmable. The pendant's new form factor, which is enhanced by the lack of visible technical details, makes it a mysterious and appealing centerpiece for the contemporary home. The Lirio by Philips collection is a family of award-winning luminaires with innovative and stylish characters.

PRODUCT
CoreLine Recessed LED Luminaires range
LED-Leuchte
LED luminaires

DESIGN
Philips Design
Eindhoven, Netherlands

MANUFACTURER
Royal Philips Electronics
Eindhoven, Netherlands

Die Philips CoreLine Recessed LED-Leuchte ist ein dis-
tinktives aber reduziertes Beleuchtungssystem, mit inspi-
rierendem Lichteffekt für preiswerte Büroanwendungen.
Das System verwendet die neueste LED-Technik und
verfügt über saubere Oberflächen mit klar gerahmten
Lichtfenstern, die einen 3-D-Signatureffekt erzeugen.
Die Designer haben Materialien bis in den Kern abgetra-
gen, um sie leichtgewichtig, kompakt und leicht recycelbar zu machen. Das Produkt verfügt über farbcodierte
Touch-Points, um die Benutzer durch die Installations-
schritte zu leiten. Alles ist von außen zugänglich, wodurch
ein Öffnen des Gehäuses überflüssig wird.

*The Philips CoreLine Recessed LED Luminaire is a distinc-
tive yet stripped-down lighting system which offers an
inspiring light effect for low-budget office applications.
Using the latest LED technology, the system features
clean surfaces with sharp-framed light windows that
generate a signature 3D effect. Its designers stripped
materials down to the core, making it light-weight,
compact, and easy to recycle. The product comes with
color-coded touch points to guide people through the
installation steps. Everything is accessible from the outside, eliminating the need to open the product housing.*

lighting

PRODUCT
Laputa
LED-Leuchte
LED bulb

DESIGN
SAMSUNG Electronics Co., Ltd.
Seoul, South Korea

MANUFACTURER
SAMSUNG Electronics Co., Ltd.
Seoul, South Korea

Diese AC-LED-Leuchte bietet Komfort und überzeugendes Design. Ausgestattet mit unserem HV-AC-Chip, dem Marktführer bei hochwertigen AC-LED-Produkten, benötigt diese Leuchte kein separates Vorschaltgerät, was bei anderen LED-Leuchten so oft zu Ärgernissen führt. Durch innovative Bauteilminimierung entsteht ein größerer lichtverströmender Bereich als bei herkömmlichen Glühbirnen. Trotz der ausgestrahlten Lichtmenge verströmt Laputa ein angenehm weiches Licht. Die hier gezeigte neue Technologie ist mit Blick auf gute Lichtqualität, Verringerung des Gewichts und unsere emotionale Bindung an Licht ein großer Fortschritt.

This AC LED light delivers both convenience and a compelling design. Our HV-AC chip, the world's leading high quality AC LED package, has also been integrated. The light doesn't require a separate power supply, something that is so often a nuisance with other LED lights. The innovative reduction in the number of parts means that the light-emitting area is larger than conventional bulbs. Despite the amount of light that is emitted, the Laputa's light still remains soft. The new technology showcased here represents a major step forward in light quality, weight reduction and our emotional bond with light.

PRODUCT
Essence
LED-Nachrüstlampe
LED retrofit bulb

DESIGN
SAMSUNG Electronics Co., Ltd.
Seoul, South Korea

MANUFACTURER
SAMSUNG Electronics Co., Ltd.
Seoul, South Korea

Diese AC-LED-Lampe hat eine ikonische Form und eine 4-mm-Platine. Genau wie eine Glühbirne liefert sie eine omnidirektionale Lichtverteilung. Ausgestattet mit unserem HV-AC-Chip, dem Marktführer hochwertiger AC-LED-Produkte, benötigt diese Lampe kein separates PSU (Vorschaltgerät), was bei anderen LED-Lampen so oft zu Ärgernissen führt. Die Silhouette der Essence zeigt je nach Winkel des Kühlkörpers völlig verschiedenen Formen. Werden die AC-LEDs einander gegenüberliegend angeordnet, ist die Lichtverteilung wie bei einer Glühbirne omnidirektional. Durch den Wegfall der PSU ist die Essence ultraschlank und ultraleicht.

This AC LED bulb has an iconic form and 4 mm plated body shape. It provides omni-directional light distribution just like an incandescent bulb. Our company's HV-AC chip, the world's leading high-quality AC LED package, has been integrated. It does not require a PSU (power supply unit) that is so often a nuisance with other LED bulbs. The Essence's silhouette changes into completely different shapes depending on the angle of the heat sink plate. By arranging the AC LEDs opposite each other, light distribution is omni-directional like an incandescent bulb. The removal of the PSU has made the Essence ultra-slim and ultra-lightweight.

PRODUCT
Modify Bulb
LED-Leuchte
LED bulb

DESIGN
SAMSUNG Electronics Co., Ltd.
Seoul, South Korea

MANUFACTURER
SAMSUNG Electronics Co., Ltd.
Seoul, South Korea

Diese AC-LED-Leuchte besteht aus einem Lämpchen und mehreren austauschbaren Abdeckungen. Ausgestattet mit dem HV-AC Chip, dem Marktführer bei hochwertigen AC-LED-Produkten, braucht diese Leuchte kein Vorschaltgerät, was bei anderen LED-Leuchten oft zu Ärgernissen führt. Dieser Vorzug wurde beim Design gut genutzt: Es entstand ein transparentes, zylindrisches Gehäuse, 45 mm hoch (ohne Fassung) und 25 mm im Durchmesser. Mehrere Reflektoren und Diffuser wurden kombiniert, um vielfältige Bedürfnisse des Benutzers zu befriedigen. Die Birne passt sich verschiedenen Räumen an. Lampenkörper werden damit überflüssig – ein Mehrwert für das Licht.

This AC LED light consists of a small bulb and various replaceable covers. Our HV-AC chip, the world's leading high-quality AC LED package, has also been integrated. The light doesn't require a separate power supply, something that is so often a nuisance with other LED lights. This merit was made effective use of in the design, resulting in a transparent, cylindrical lamp body with a height of 45 mm (excluding the socket) and a diameter of 25 mm. Various reflectors and diffusers have been combined to satisfy various users' needs and make the bulb suitable for a range of different spaces. This removes the need for lighting fixtures, which creates additional value for the light.

PRODUCT

TZ-X-LED
Leuchtensystem
Lighting system

DESIGN

Serge Cornelissen BVBA
Roeselare, Belgium

MANUFACTURER

Schmitz-Leuchten GmbH & Co. KG
Arnsberg, Germany

TZ-X-System-Module sind für die Beleuchtung von Büro-
und Verkaufsräumen, Flurbereichen, Theken und Be-
sprechungsräumen konzipiert. Das X-förmige LED-
Leuchtenmodul besticht durch sein schlichtes Design,
das sich stilübergreifend einsetzen lässt. Einzelne TZ-X-
Leuchtenmodule können durch einen Linienverbinder
zu einem System verlängert werden. Modernste effiziente LED-Technik bietet eine klar strukturierte lineare
direkte / indirekte Raumaufhellung.

*TZ-X system modules are designed for the lighting of of-
fice- and sales areas, hallway areas, counters and meeting
tables. The X- shaped LED lighting module is impressive
with its simple design which allows it to be used anywhere.
Individual TZ-X light modules can be extended to one
system using a line connector. State-of-the-art, efficient
LED technology offers clearly-structured, linear direct / indirect room lighting.*

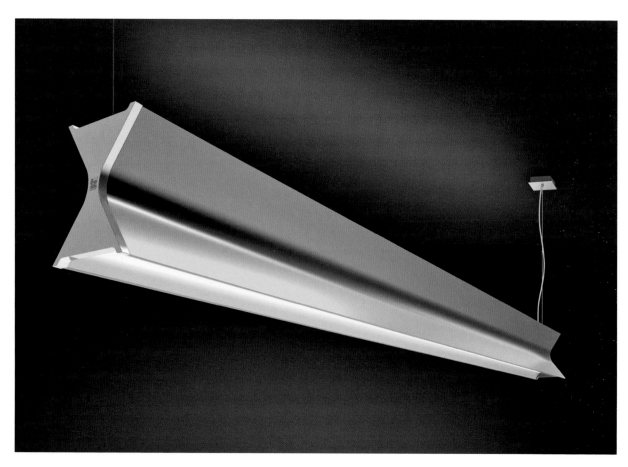

PRODUCT
TZ-V LED
Leuchtensystem
Lighting system

DESIGN
Hans W. Hegger
Korschenbroich, Germany

MANUFACTURER
Schmitz-Leuchten GmbH & Co. KG
Arnsberg, Germany

Das System TZ-V ist für die Wand- und Deckenbeleuch-
tung von Verkaufsräumen, Fluren, Treppenhäusern, an
Säulen oder zur Spiegelbeleuchtung geeignet. Die
schlanken, flachen LED-Module mit zwei Lichtlinien aus
weißem Acryl wirken architektonisch besonders reizvoll.
Die insgesamt sehr niedrige Aufbauhöhe der Module
ist durch das Verbauen des Konverters in der Wand oder
der Decke möglich. Einzelne TZ-V Leuchtenmodule
können durch einen Linienverbinder zu einem System
verlängert werden.

*TZ-V LED. The TZ-V system is suitable for wall-mounted
and ceiling lighting in sales areas, corridors, stairwells,
on columns or for mirror lighting. The slim, flat LED modules with two lines of lights made of white acrylic have
an especially attractive architectural effect. The very low
overall structural height of the modules is possible by the
installation of the converter in the wall or the ceiling.
Individual TZ-V light modules can be extended to one
system using a line connector.*

PRODUCT

Multifunctional lamp
Multifunktionale Induktionslampe
Multifunctional induction lamp

DESIGN

Shenzhen CIGA Design Co., Ltd.
Shenzhen, China

MANUFACTURER

Shenzhen CIGA Design Co., Ltd.
Shenzhen, China

Die multifunktionale Induktionslampe vereint vier nützliche Funktionen – ein Induktionsnachtlicht, ein Notlicht, eine aufladbare Stablampe und ein USB-Ladegerät. Das Produkt lässt sich in zwei Teile zerlegen – in die Haupteinheit (unten) und die Teileinheit (oben). (a) Nachts leuchtet sie bei ausreichend dunkler Umgebung automatisch auf, wenn sich eine Person innerhalb von 7 m befindet. (b) Ist die Steckdose ohne Strom, leuchtet die Teileinheit als Notlicht auf. (c) Nach vollständiger Aufladung kann die Teileinheit von der Haupteinheit entfernt und als Stablampe verwendet werden. (d) Der USB-Port an der Haupteinheit dient als Ladegerät.

This multifunctional induction lamp combines four useful functions – an induction nightlight, an emergency light, a rechargeable flashlight and a USB charging adaptor. The product can be separated in two parts - the main unit (lower part) and the sub-unit (upper). (a) At night, when conditions are dark enough, it will light up automatically when a person is within 7 m. (b) When the outlet has run out of power, the sub-unit will light up as an emergency light. (c) After it is fully charged, the sub-unit can be removed from the main unit to be used as a flashlight. (d) There is a USB port on the main unit which serves as a USB charging adapter.

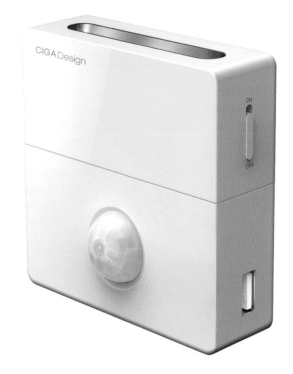

PRODUCT
DELTA arina
Schalter und Steckdosen
Switches and socket outlets

DESIGN
IDEO Shanghai
Shanghai, China

MANUFACTURER
Siemens Ltd., China
Shanghai Branch
Shanghai, China

Die Produktfamilie Siemens-Delta arina, die basierend auf nutzerzentrierten Erkenntnissen entwickelt wurde, bringt Schönheit sowohl in Hotels als auch in private Haushalte. Die Produktreihe umfasst Lichtschalter, Steckdosen und Türklingeln. Die Designsprache besticht durch Eleganz, Harmonie und nahtlose Integration in den Lebensraum. Solide, schlank und einfach zu verwenden: Diese Linie von Siemens verbindet technische Innovationen mit einer unverkennbaren Designsprache. Eine versteckte LED-Lichtquelle sorgt für weiche Ausleuchtung. Glänzende und matte Kontraste visualisieren unterschiedliche Funktionen.

Siemens Delta arina is a family of products that leverages human-centered design insights to create beauty and impact in hotels and households alike. The product suite includes light switches, sockets, and doorbells. The design language is defined by elegance, harmony, and seamless integration with the living space. Solid, sleek, and easy-to-use, the Siemens line marries engineering innovations with a signature industrial design language. A hidden LED light provides soft illumination. Gloss and matte contrasts visually illustrate functions.

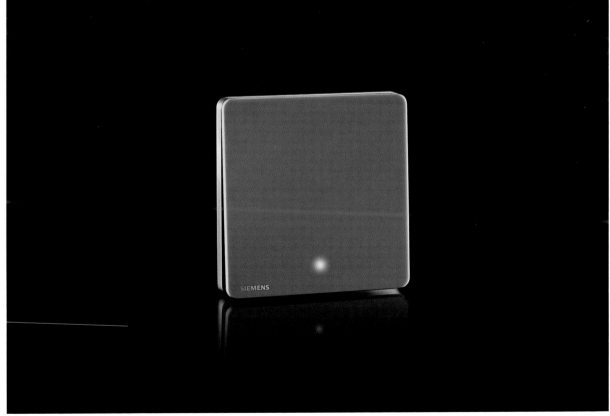

PRODUCT

SWAROSPHERE
LED-Leuchtenserie
LED luminaire series

DESIGN

Swareflex GmbH
Vomp, Austria

MANUFACTURER

Swareflex GmbH
Vomp, Austria

SWAROSPHERE vereint das Erscheinungsbild einer repräsentativen Leuchte mit der Funktionalität technischer Beleuchtungslösungen. Die lichtlenkende Kristallglaslinse erzeugt eine hohe Lichtbrillanz mit gleichzeitig weichen Schattenverläufen und homogener Lichtverteilung. Dabei hat sie eine filigrane Bauhöhe von nur 38 mm. Durch das Prinzip der Lichtpunktzerlegung schafft die präzise Facettenstruktur absolute Blendungsfreiheit bei einem sehr guten UGR-Wert. Die bionisch inspirierte hochwertige Kristallglaslinse dient als widerstandsfähige Funktionshülle und verstärkt dabei die hohe Produktanmutung.

SWAROSPHERE unites the appearance of a representative luminaire with the functionality of technical lighting solutions. The light directing crystal glass lens creates a highly brilliant light but also soft shadows and a homogeneous distribution of light, maintaining a flat construction height of 38 mm. The faceted structure that is designed on the principle of light point resolution provides a glare-free lighting with best UGR values. The bionically inspired high-quality crystal glass lens also serves as a resistant casing while conveying a sense of value.

PRODUCT
LED LENSER® M14X
LED-Taschenlampe
LED torch

DESIGN
Zweibrüder Optoelectronics GmbH & Co. KG
Andre Kunzendorf, Rainer Opolka
Solingen, Germany

MANUFACTURER
Zweibrüder Optoelectronics GmbH & Co. KG
Solingen, Germany

Die LED LENSER® M14X ist die hellste Lampe der M-Serie. Besonders auffallend ist die neue Lichtkegelcharakteristik, die auf die größere Leuchtfläche der Xtreme-Power-LED zurückzuführen ist. Im Nahbereich punktet die LED LENSER® M14X durch ein homogeneres Lichtbild im Spot und darüber hinaus. Im fokussierten Zustand erreicht sie, wie ihre Vorgängerin, eine beeindruckende Leuchtweite, hat aber zusätzlich mehr als genug Leuchtkraft, um auch außerhalb des Lichtfokus die Landschaft zu erhellen.

The LED LENSER® M14X is the brightest lamp of the M series. The character of the light cone is particularly remarkable, due to the large illuminated area of the extreme power chip. At close range, the LED LENSER® M14X scores with a homogeneous lit area and a larger angle of reflected beam. In the focused position it reaches the same impressive beam distance as its predecessor. In addition, it has more than enough lighting power to generously illuminate the landscape outside the focused area.

PRODUCT
LED LENSER® M7RX
LED-Taschenlampe
LED torch

DESIGN
Zweibrüder Optoelectronics GmbH & Co. KG
Andre Kunzendorf, Rainer Opolka
Solingen, Germany

MANUFACTURER
Zweibrüder Optoelectronics GmbH & Co. KG
Solingen, Germany

Die LED LENSER® M7RX erreicht durch einen neuen
LED-Chip ein Vielfaches der Lichtleistung der LED LENSER®
M7R. Während die LED LENSER® M7R nahezu sämtliches
Licht im Fokus bündelt, steht bei diesem Kraftpaket auch
jenseits des fokussierten Spots Licht zur Verfügung. In
Punkto Funktionalität steht sie ihrer Vorgängerin jedoch
in nichts nach: mittels Microcontroller gesteuerte Licht-
funktionen, eines der wohl weltbesten Fokussiersysteme
(Advanced Focus System). Einhandfokussierung (Speed
Focus) und eine Ladetechnik (Floating Charge System),
die kaum komfortabler sein kann, runden das Leistungs-
portfolio ab.

*Due to a new LED chip, the LED LENSER® M7RX achieves a
multitude of the lighting performance of the LED LENSER®
M7R. While the LED LENSER® M7R bundles almost all
focused light, this powerhouse emits enough light to illuminate the surrounding area of the focused spot as well.
Regarding functionality it is not inferior to its predecessor: microcontroller-operated light functions, one of the
world's best focusing systems (Advanced Focus System)
one-hand focusing (Speed Focus) and a charging method
(Floating Charge System), which could not be more comfortable complete the performance portfolio.*

FURNITURE / HOME TEXTILES

FRANCO CLIVIO
CARL GUSTAV MAGNUSSON
JOHN SMALL

PRODUCT
November
Esszimmerstuhl
Dining room chair

DESIGN
Veryday
Peter Ejvinsson, Emmy Larsson
Bromma, Sweden

MANUFACTURER
Artipelag
Gustavsberg, Sweden

Der Stuhl wurde für Artipelag entwickelt, eine neu er-
öffnete Kunstgalerie in Stockholm Archipelago. Das
Design wird durch das gedämpfte Licht der tiefstehenden
November-Sonne mit ihren langen Schatten und Streif-
licht inspiriert und wurde von Hand geformt. Die Designer
wollten den reibungslosen, kontrollierten Übergang
zwischen den Formen und Winkeln des Stuhls erreichen. Alle Seiten des Stuhls sind wichtig, nicht zuletzt
der Rücken. November ist ergonomisch, komfortabel
und komplett aus Holz. Die Tischlerei mit 100 Jahren
Erfahrung arbeitet mit der neuesten Technologie, um
hervorragende Qualität und lange Lebensdauer zu gewährleisten.

*The chair was designed for Artipelag, a newly opened
art gallery in Stockholm Archipelago. The design was inspired by the muted light of the low November sun with
its long shadows and raking light. The design has been
sculpted by hand. The designers wanted to dictate the
smooth transition between the shapes and angles of the
chair with full control. All sides of the chair are important.
Not least the back. November is ergonomically designed
for comfort and made entirely of wood. The chairs are
created in a joinery, where chair production dates back
100 years, using the latest technology to guarantee superb
quality and long life.*

„Dieser Stuhl ist fantastisch ergonomisch gestaltet und verliert dennoch nichts von seiner skulpturalen Anmutung. Er ist das perfekte Sinnbild großartigen skandinavischen Designs und seiner Tradition, Stühle in Handarbeit zu fertigen – und bringt mit November einen Esszimmerstuhl, gefertigt von einer Maschine hervor. Applaus und einen iF gold award!"

"This chair has a great ergonomic shape while still retaining all of its sculptural look and feel. It perfectly sums up excellent Scandinavian design and the Nordic tradition of handmade chairs, yet November is a dining room chair made by a machine. A round of applause and an iF gold award!"

JURYSTATEMENT

PRODUCT

Hosu
Arbeits-Lounge-Möbel
Work lounge furniture

DESIGN

Studio Urquiola
Patricia Urquiola
Milano, Italy
Coalesse Design Center
San Francisco, CA, United States of America

MANUFACTURER

Coalesse Design Center
San Francisco, CA, United States of America

Inspiriert von unseren Beobachtungen, wie der Boden als endlose Arbeitsfläche genutzt werden kann, ermuntert Hosu dazu sich auszubreiten. Diese einzigartige Arbeits-Lounge, designt von Patricia Urquiola, schafft eine beruhigend wirkende Privatsphäre zum Entspannen und Arbeiten. Die Einzelsitz-Lounge kann als ausklappbarer Liegesessel bestellt werden. Das Zweisitzer-Sofa führt zwei Personen zusammen, auch wenn sie sich jeweils auf verschiedene Aufgaben konzentrieren. Hosu ist hinten und an den Seiten mit praktischen Ablagetaschen ausgestattet. Hosus einzigartig strukturiertes Gewebe wurde auch von Urquiola entworfen und wird in sechs exklusiven Farben angeboten. Für den Europäischen Markt wird Hosu in Europa gefertigt.

Inspired by our observations about the use of the floor as an endless worksurface, Hosu encourages spreading out. Designed by Patricia Urquiola, this unique work lounge creates a comforting personal space to relax and get things done. The single seat lounge can be ordered with a convertible chaise foldout. The two-seat sofa brings two people together even if they are focused on different tasks. Hosu features convenient rear and side storage pockets and cord pass-through. Its unique textured fabric, also designed by Urquiola, is offered in six exclusive colors. For the European market Hosu is manufactured in Europe.

„Dieser Lounge Chair und dieses Sofa sind unglaublich. Der Einzelsitz ist ergonomisch genug geformt, um eine äußerst bequeme Sitz- und Loungehaltung einzunehmen und dennoch bis ins Detail ein Möbel, das ein neuer Designklassiker von morgen werden könnte. Das Ausklappen des Fußteils geht so leicht von der Hand, der Bezug ist perfekt verarbeitet und einladend, das Zweier-Sofa macht aus Arbeit auch Spaß – ein würdiger, großartiger iF gold award."

"This lounge chair and sofa are incredible. The individual chair is ergonomic enough to be extremely comfortable both when sitting upright and lounging, and yet down to the last detail is still an item of furniture that could become one of the design classics of the future. The fold-out footrest is so easy to use, the cover is perfectly crafted and inviting, and the two-seater even makes work seem fun – a well-deserved, excellent iF gold award."

JURYSTATEMENT

PRODUCT
da caster
Rollfuß
Caster

DESIGN
hozmi design
Kobe-City, Hyogo, Japan
SIMIZ Technik
Osaka, Japan

MANUFACTURER
HAMMER CASTER Co., Ltd.
Osaka, Japan

Das Konzept des da caster soll mit dem Design von Möbel oder Zubehör harmonisieren und zugleich seine unterscheidbare Präsenz als Rollfuß bewahren. Im Gegensatz zu konventionellen Rollfüßen mit "Kugellager-Struktur", bestehend aus Achse und Lager, zeichnet sich da caster durch eine "Gleitlager-Struktur" aus, die weder Achse noch Lager verwendet. Die da caster Struktur besteht aus einer Aluminium-Hülle, einer Rolle und einem inneren Ring aus speziellem Harz, die ein ringförmiges Rad mit einem Loch in der Mitte ermöglichen – ein Orbitalrollfuß der genügend Stärke und Festigkeit hat und dennoch zu treiben scheint.

The concept of da caster is to smoothly harmonize with the design of furniture or fittings, while maintaining a distinct presence as a caster. Rather than a "ball bearing configuration" comprising an axle and bearing, which is the basic structure of a conventional caster, it is characterized by a "sliding configuration" that does not use an axle or bearing. The da caster structure comprises an aluminum shell, a roller, and an internal ring made of special resin, enabling a ring-shaped wheel with a central hole – a hubless caster that possesses sufficient strength and solidity, yet seems to float.

product
design award

2013 GOLD ▪

„Ein eleganter, hochwertiger Rollfuß, der sich dem jeweiligen Möbel unterordnet und trotzdem einen eigenen Charakter hat. Mit seiner Gleitlager-Struktur scheint er fast zu schweben und behält jederzeit seine Standfestigkeit, auch visuell. Ein tolles Designstück, das mit einem iF gold award belohnt wird."

"An elegant, high-quality caster that can be integrated into any item of furniture yet still has its own character. Its bearing system means it seems almost to float, while maintaining its stability (including visual stability) at all times. A great piece of design that deserves an iF gold award."

JURYSTATEMENT

PRODUCT
Allsteel Clarity
Stuhl
Chair

DESIGN
BMW Group DesignworksUSA
Newbury Park, CA, United States of America

MANUFACTURER
Allsteel Inc.
Muscatine, IA, United States of America

BMW Group DesignworksUSA schuf für Allsteel eine Sitzlösung, die für moderne Arbeitsräume von heute die nötige Schönheit, Leistungsfähigkeit und Wandelbarkeit bietet. Dafür konzentrierte sich das Designteam in seiner Sprache auf Schlüsseleigenschaften wie Einfachheit, intuitive Begreifbarkeit, Integrität und Energie. Das endgültige Design sollte möglichst schlank sein und folgte daher der Philosophie „Design durch Reduzierung", deren Fokus allein auf den wesentlichen Elementen Funktion und Form liegt. Neben der reinen Ästhetik ergibt der minimale Einsatz von Teilen einen leichten Stuhl, den man überall im Büro einsetzen kann.

Allsteel assigned BMW Group DesignworksUSA with the task of creating a seating solution that would deliver all of the beauty, performance, and versatility needed in today's modern workspaces. The design team created a design language focused on key attributes such as simplicity, intuitiveness, integrity and energy to create a new seating solution. The team pushed for the final design to be as lean as possible, following the philosophy of "design by reduction" focusing solely on function and form. In addition to creating a pure aesthetic, the minimal use of parts results in a lightweight chair that can be moved anyway in the office.

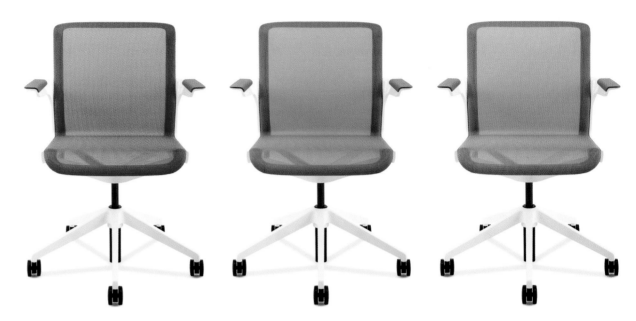

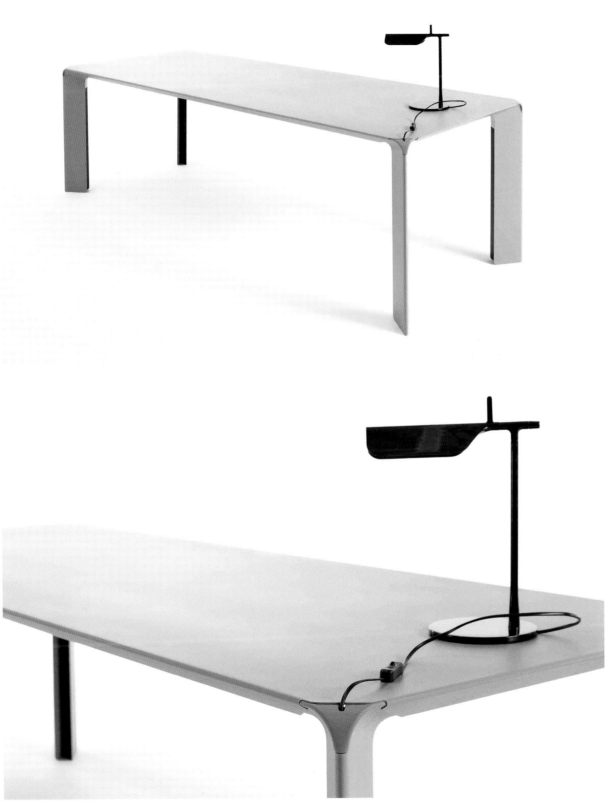

PRODUCT
Steel Table
Tisch
Table

DESIGN
Arco Contemporary Furniture
Jorre van Ast
Winterswijk, Netherlands

MANUFACTURER
Arco Contemporary Furniture
Winterswijk, Netherlands

Ein unkonventioneller Tisch, bei dem neue Techniken und Materialverwendung eine wichtige Rolle spielen. Der Tisch hat einen industriellen Charakter sowie eine feine und handwerkliche Verarbeitung, die für Arco so bezeichnend ist. Der Tisch kann ausgezeichnet in Wohn- und Geschäftsumgebungen eingesetzt werden.

An unconventional table that combines new technology with ingenious use of materials. The table has an industrial feel yet it also has the refined craftsmanship and elegant finish traditionally associated with Arco. The table is suitable for both residential and business environments.

PRODUCT
Deskbox
Tisch
Table

DESIGN
Arco Contemporary Furniture
Yael Mer, Shay Alkalay
Winterswijk, Netherlands

MANUFACTURER
Arco Contemporary Furniture
Winterswijk, Netherlands

Die Deskbox ist ein praktischer kleiner Tisch / Schrank,
der an der Wand hängt. Ausgeschoben ist es ein eleganter kleiner Arbeitsplatz, der sich nachher wieder zu
einer geschlossenen Schachtel zusammenschieben lässt
– halb so groß wie das Tischblatt.

*A surprising and practical hanging cabinet / table. When
extended it forms an elegant small work place, which
can be pushed right back when you are done to form a
closed box, half the size of the table top.*

PRODUCT
JUNO
System von Plastikstühlen
System of chairs in plastic

DESIGN
James Irvine S. R. L.
Milano, Italy

MANUFACTURER
Arper S. p. A.
Monastier di Treviso, Italy

Mit Juno ist der Kunststoffstuhl erwachsen geworden: aus einem Guss, fließende Linien, ein Leichtgewicht in puncto Silhouette, Gewicht. Juno versieht die Vorteile von Schlichtheit und Gleichförmigkeit mit einem cleveren Dreh und vereint Effizienz und Vielseitigkeit – ganz nach Kundenwunsch. Die schlichte, einzigartige Form gibt es in fünf Farben, in zwei Lehnenformen sowie mit Armlehnen und ist auf Wunsch auch mit eleganter gepolsterter Sitzfläche und Rückenlehne lieferbar.

With Juno, plastic chair has come of age. Cast in a single form, it has fluid lines and a light profile, in silhouette and weight. It enjoys all the benefits of simplicity and uniformity but with a clever twist. Juno brings efficiency and customization together in unique combination. This singular, simple shape available in five colors with closed or open back and arm rests can also be customized with sleek upholstered seat and back rests.

PRODUCT
KENT
Sessel
Armchair

DESIGN
Andreas Weber
Architektur und Design
Herrsching / Ammersee, Germany

MANUFACTURER
BW Bielefelder Werkstätten
Bielefeld, Germany

Das sportlich-maskuline Design des großzügigen Sessels KENT von Andreas Weber erfüllt jedes Zimmer mit Stil. Seine hohe Rückenlehne bietet einen erstklassigen Sitzkomfort und viel Raum zum Entspannen. Durch den gerundeten Boden wirkt KENT auf dem edel verchromten Kreuzfuß geradezu schwebend. Der formschöne Sessel überzeugt mit seiner handwerklichen Verarbeitung und eleganten Details. Noch entspannter wird das Sitzen mit dem passenden Hocker. Optional wird KENT auch mit einer bequemen Neigungsfunktion angeboten.

The sportive masculine design of the generous swivel chair KENT, designed by Andreas Weber, fills every room with style. Its high back offers a perfect seating comfort and space for relaxing and with its rounded seat plate on the elegant chromed star base it seems floating. This beautiful swivel chair convinces with its elegant details. The perfect relaxed setting to sit is the suitable stool. You can choose between a swivel chair without function or with a comfortable tilt function.

PRODUCT
SOSIA
Sofa

DESIGN
Maginidesign Studio
Emanuele Magini
Milano, Italy

MANUFACTURER
Campeggi S. R. L.
Anzano del Parco, Italy

Zwei Sessel, ein Sofa, ein überdachtes Bett und auch ein Wohnzimmer. SOSIA ist all diese Dinge und noch mehr. Ein mutierendes Objekt, dynamisch und gemütlich, bereit für verschiedene Alltagssituationen.

Two armchairs, one sofa, a sheltered bed but also a living room. SOSIA is all those things and even more. A mutant object, dynamic and snug, ready to fit with different everyday life situations.

PRODUCT

Sofá PEDRA
Couch

DESIGN

Decameron Design
Marcus Ferreira
São Paulo, Brazil

MANUFACTURER

Decameron Design
São Paulo, Brazil

Die Herausforderung bei diesem Produkt – in diesem Fall eine Couch für ihn zu schaffen – wurde in einer beispiellosen Weise aus Gestein umgesetzt. Hierbei sollte das Möbel auf der einen Seite die Charakteristiken von Gestein haben, das den Nutzer neugierig macht, und gleichzeitig sollte es auch einen entsprechenden Komfort bietet. Wir haben uns mit diesem Produkt einer ökologischen Herausforderung gestellt: Für den Prozess der Herstellung schneiden wir Fackeln in einer Dicke von 5 mm. Sie werden mit einer Struktur aus Glasfaser, Harz und Polycarbonat befestigt. Das bietet mehr Widerstandsfähigkeit und Leichtigkeit und verringert die Belastung der Natur.

The challenge posed by this product – in this case, to make a couch for him – was overcome by using stone in an unprecedented way. The furniture should have the character of stone, which makes the user curious, while at the same time providing comfort. We posed a challenge to ourselves with this product: for the manufacturing process we cut torches 5 mm in thickness. These are attached using a mixture of fiberglass, resin and polycarbonate. This reduces weight, provides more durability and minimizes the impact on the environment.

PRODUCT
PRO
Stuhl
Chair

DESIGN
Konstantin Grcic Industrial Design
München, Germany

MANUFACTURER
FLÖTOTTO Systemmöbel GmbH
Rietberg, Germany

Das Unternehmen FLÖTOTTO hat gemeinsam mit
Konstantin Grcic einen innovativen Stuhl entwickelt,
mit dem es an eine erfolgreiche Tradition in der Herstellung von Schulmöbeln anknüpft. Dabei ist mit PRO eine
Stuhl-Kollektion entstanden, die außer in Schulen auch
in anderen Objekten sowie im privaten Umfeld einsetzbar ist. Die Sitzschale von PRO verfügt über eine
sehr prägnante Form, die einerseits einen besonderen
Komfort bietet und dem Stuhl andererseits seine charakteristische Optik verleiht. Grundlage für die spezielle
Gestaltung der Sitzschale waren wissenschaftliche Studien
der vergangenen Jahre zum Thema „Aktives Sitzen" in
Schulen.

*Together with Konstantin Grcic, the German manufac-
turer FLÖTOTTO has developed an innovative chair that
continues the company's successful tradition of producing school furniture. The new PRO line of chairs can also
be used for other contract areas and for domestic interiors.
PRO's seat pan has a distinctive shape, allowing a very
comfortable seating experience and giving the chair its
specific esthetics. The design of the seat pan is based on
several studies into the area of "active seating" in schools.
PRO has a lightweight and welcoming appearance and is
available in six attractive colors.*

PRODUCT
FLIP for kids
Kindermöbel
Children's furniture

DESIGN
MARCO HEMMERLING
Studio for Spatial Design
Prof. Marco Hemmerling
Köln, Germany

MANUFACTURER
Foamshop
Geschäftsbereich: FLIP for kids
Gemert, Netherlands

Das kinderleichte Spielmöbel FLIP integriert vielfältige Sitzpositionen in einer geschwungenen Form und unterstützt Fantasie und Bewegungsdrang der Kinder. Das Möbel lässt sich vielfach kombinieren und zu individuellen Sitz- und Spiellandschaften erweitern. FLIP ist aus einem besonders belastbaren Schaumstoff gefertigt und daher sehr leicht, stabil und strapazierfähig. Durch die hochwertige Beschichtung ist FLIP zudem gesundheitlich unbedenklich, schmutzabweisend und leicht zu reinigen. Das komfortable Kindersitzmöbel kann im Innen- und Außenbereich eingesetzt werden und ist in sechs fröhlichen Farben erhältlich.

The playful furniture FLIP for kids is designed to support children's creativity and activity. By flipping and turning the exceptionally light chair, it changes its appearance and unfolds many different sitting positions. The curvy seating element has been manufactured from durable and cushy foam that boasts a coating of elastic, breathable and hypoallergenic plastic. FLIP comes in six vivid hues and can be used indoors and out.

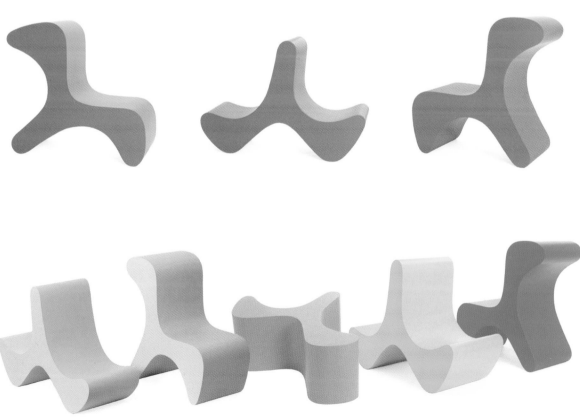

PRODUCT
OCTO
Hocker
Stool

DESIGN
Stefano Sandonà
Selvazzano Dentro (PD), Italy

MANUFACTURER
Gaber
Caselle di Altivole (Treviso), Italy

Die mystische Zahl Acht und das Symbol der Unendlichkeit inspirieren diesen Hocker mit einer wesentlichen und ständigen Erneuerung beim Blick in jeden Raum. Gefertigt wurde der Hocker aus stark belastbarem verschiedenfarbigem Polymer und verchromtem Gestell.

The mystic number eight symbol of boundless and have inspired this stool with an essential and continuous, capable of renewing the look of each type of space. It is made in high strength techno polymer and steel main frame. It is available in different colors.

PRODUCT
Climatex Dualcycle
Möbelbezugsstoff
Upholstery fabric

DESIGN
Gessner AG
Wädenswil, Switzerland

MANUFACTURER
Gessner AG
Wädenswil, Switzerland

Ökologischer und ökonomischer Möbelbezugsstoff mit funktionalen Eigenschaften. Die Kombination natürlicher und technischer Rohstoffe bewirkt passive Sitzklimatisierung. Die Dualcycle-Technik absorbiert, puffert und verdunstet, dosiert Feuchte und bewirkt extreme Atmungsaktivität. Die spezielle Webtechnik vereint kreislauffähige Materialien des biologischen und technischen Kreislaufs zu einem Gebrauchshybrid mit extremer Leistungsstärke. Die Verhältnisse kostenintensiver Funktionsfasern werden zugunsten ökologischer und ökonomischer Vorteile stark optimiert.

Environmentally sustainable and economical upholstery fabric with functional properties. The combination of natural and technological raw materials result in climatized seating. Dualcycle technology absorbs, buffers and evaporates moisture and triggers exceptional breathability. Proprietary weaving techniques combine recyclable materials from both the biological and technical cycles into a hybrid textile with extraordinary performance. The settings of cost-intensive function fibers become optimized in favor of ecological and economical advantages.

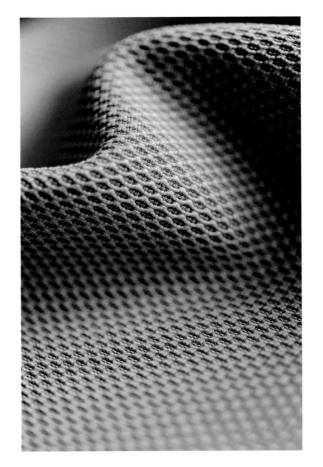

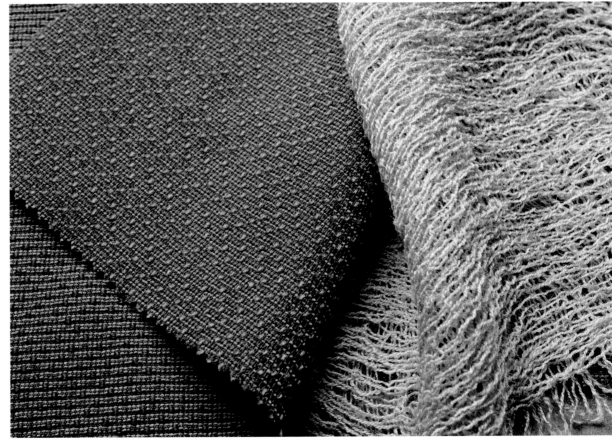

PRODUCT
Diamond Window Blind
Jalousie
Window blind

DESIGN
Golden Champion Ind.
Kaohsiung, Taiwan

MANUFACTURER
Golden Champion Ind.
Kaohsiung, Taiwan

Die Diamant-Plissee erzeugt einen einzigartigen, aber klassisch eleganten ersten Eindruck durch den innovativen Gebrauch eines neuen Schlitzvorgangs. Zusätzlich zu ihrer Energiesparfunktion ermöglicht die zellförmige Blende eine intuitive, kindersichere, schnurlose Bedienung, die mittels einer in der Oberleiste verborgenen Federspannvorrichtung erfolgt. Die zelluläre Diamant-Plissee erzeugt einen auffälligen 3-D-Effekt, der einerseits modern ist, andererseits an eine einfache Laterne erinnert und der Funktionalität auf diese Weise Attraktivität verleiht.

The Diamond Window Blind gives off a unique yet classically stylish first impression by making innovative use of a new slitting process. In addition to its energy saving capability, the cellular shade offers an intuitive, child-safe cordless operation by means of a spring-tension device hidden inside the head rail. The Diamond cellular shade creates an eye-catching 3D effect that is both modern yet reminiscent of a simple lantern, thus adding attractiveness to functionality.

PRODUCT
statthocker
Hocker
Stool

DESIGN
Beierarbeit GmbH
Bielefeld, Germany
phantastischlerei
Oliver Bahr, Bastian Demmer
Herford, Germany

MANUFACTURER
Identity Group
Bielefeld, Germany

Der statthocker ist eine ehemalige Straßenlaterne. Die seit Jahrzehnten bekannten „Pilzkopflampen" werden bundesweit durch energiesparende Diodenlampen ersetzt. Somit verschwindet ein Stück Kindheitserinnerung und Heimat. Wer erinnert sich nicht an die Zeitangabe der Eltern: Wenn die Laternen angehen, kommst Du nach Hause. Die Wiederverwendung als Hocker schont Ressourcen, bewahrt Stadt- und Designgeschichte. Der Hocker ist stapelbar, stabil und wasserresistent. Der Deckel aus Mineralstoff auf der ehemaligen Montageöffnung ist in diversen Farben wählbar.

The statthocker is a former street lamp. The well-known for decades "mushroom lamps" are replaced by nationwide energy-saving lamps diodes. Thus disappears a piece of childhood memory and home. Who does not remember the time shown by the parents, if the lanterns tackle, you get home. Reuse as a stool saves resources, preserved city and design history. The stool is stackable, sturdy and water-resistant. The lid is made of minerals on the former installation opening can be selected in various colors.

PRODUCT
ARC
Stuhl
Chair

DESIGN
Yonoh estudio creativo
Clara del Portillo, Alex Selma
Valencia, Spain

MANUFACTURER
Inclass Mobles S. L.
Crevillente, Spain

Der Stuhl ARC, mit seinem kurvigen und eleganten Design, wurde für vielseitige Gebrauchszwecke entwickelt und findet sowohl in Auftragsprojekten als auch im Wohnbereich Verwendung. Seine Lehne ist der Form des Rückens ergonomisch angepasst und bildet einen Bogen, der den Benutzer stützend umfasst. Die Struktur des Stuhles aus Stahlstäben ist in vielen verschiedenen Farben oder in verchromter Ausfertigung erhältlich, um sich den ästhetischen Anforderungen jedes beliebigen Projekts anzupassen. Der Sitz und die Rückenlehne bestehen aus stabverleimtem Holz und können in Naturholz, lackiert oder gepolstert geliefert werden.

With a sinuous and elegant design, the ARC chair is designed for versatile use in home and contract projects. Its backrest is based on the ergonomics of the back which is molded into an arc that embraces us. The structure, made of steel rod, is offered finished in a multitude of colors or chrome to match the aesthetics of each project. The seat and backrest are molded in plywood and can be finished in natural wood, lacquer or upholstered.

PRODUCT
CASTOR CHAIR
Stapelstuhl
Stackable chair

DESIGN
Big Game
Augustin Scott de Martinville, Elric Petit,
Grégoire Jeanmonod
Lausanne, Switzerland

MANUFACTURER
Karimoku Furniture Inc.
Chitagun, Aichi, Japan

Die CASTOR-Serie besteht aus einer Familie von funktionalen, zierlichen Möbeln aus massivem japanischem Eichenholz. Der Name CASTOR (engl. f. Bieber) ist abgeleitet von einem gemeinsamen Detail, welches an die Spuren eines Bibers an einem Baum erinnert. CASTOR CHAIR ist ein charmanter, kompakter Stapelstuhl, der mit seiner charakteristischen weit geschwungenen Rückenlehne außerdem überraschenden Sitzkomfort bietet. Der Stuhl ist erhältlich in einem matt-transparenten Finish in den Farben Schwarz, Grau und Natur.

The CASTOR series consists of a family of basic, functional and elegant objects made of solid japanese oak wood. The name CASTOR derives from a carved detail that reminds of the traces left by beavers on trees. CASTOR CHAIR is a charming, compact chair, that offers stackability and surprising sitting comfort through its distinct, widely curved backrest. It is available with a matt, transparent finish in the colors black, gray and natural.

PRODUCT
Programm 3000 Njord
Sitzmöbel
Seating

DESIGN
Antonio Scaffidi & Mads K. Johansen
Copenhagen, Denmark

MANUFACTURER
Kusch+Co. GmbH & Co. KG
Hallenberg, Germany

Ein Sessel, schon auf den ersten Blick anders als andere. Stark und – trotz seines schlanken Gestells – stämmig steht er da. Sich oben kelchförmig öffnende Beine tragen die Sitzschale, die mit dem Gestell über vier gestanzte Öffnungen und sichtbare Holznägel als Designmerkmal verbunden wird. Die Sitzschale in ihrer weichen, den Körper umschließenden Form lädt zum Platz nehmen förmlich ein. Spätestens jetzt entdeckt man das Besondere. Anders ist auch die Haptik. Weich und warm fühlt sich die Oberfläche an, denn sie besteht durch und durch aus einem Polyesterfilz. Ein sinnliches Material, dem schwarze und weiße Fasern optische Tiefe geben.

You can tell at a glance that this armchair is rather exceptional! Prominent – and in spite of its slender frame – sturdy. The seat shell is nested on an elegant 4-legged chalice-shaped frame, fixed through four punched openings with visible, oval wooden plugs as an outstanding design feature. The seat shell – moulding to the body – invites everyone to snuggle up. The added attraction of Njord is the soft hand of the material surface, warm to the touch, entirely made of polyester felt, offering a sensual experience. The intermingling black and white fibers add a feeling of extra depth to the texture.

PRODUCT
ARTPOP
Material für feste Oberflächen
Solid surface

DESIGN
LG Hausys, Ltd.
Kyuhong Lee, Hansung Choi, Dongwoo Shin,
Doohawn Lee
Seoul, South Korea

MANUFACTURER
LG Hausys Design Center
Seoul, South Korea

ARTPOP bietet Verwendern einzigartige Möglichkeiten, Designs zu individualisieren. Es ist das erste Material dieser Art im Markt für feste Oberflächen. Verwender können damit ihre Designidentität unterstreichen, aber vor allem bietet es eine Reihe von Designvariationen. Differenzierte Designs und Farbpaletten für mächtige Werbeeffekte oder spezialisierte Designs sind möglich. Die patentierte Herstellungsmethode der Chips ermöglicht strukturierte Muster wie auch zufällige Arrangements. Aufgrund der unvergleichlichen Technologie können Designer ihre Entwürfe vollständig individualisieren, ohne Größe oder Design der Chips begrenzen zu müssen.

ARTPOP is a unique material that allows users to customize designs, the first of its kind in the solid surface market. With ARTPOP, users can emphasize their design identity. First and foremost, it gives users a wider range of design opportunities. It also offers differentiated designs and colors with a range of patterns, producing a powerful advertising effect or specialized designs. Its patented chip manufacturing method enables the production of both organized patterns as well as random arrangements. Due to its unparalleled technology, designers are able to fully customize their designs without having to restrict the size or design of the chips.

PRODUCT
Breathing Wall Tile
Funktionelle Wandfliese
Functional wall tile

DESIGN
LG Hausys, Ltd.
JeeEun Kim, KyungHee Kim, Jihye Choi
Seoul, South Korea

MANUFACTURER
LG Hausys Design Center
Seoul, South Korea

Breathing Wall Tile ist eine funktionelle Fliese aus natürlicher Erde und ist patentiert als gesundes Wanddekorationsmaterial. Anders als die ehemaligen Glasurfliesen sind zahlreiche feine Poren vorhanden, um dadurch die Aufnahme von Formaldehyd, Umwelthormonen und schädlichen Materialen zu reduzieren und somit auch das Sick-Building-Syndrom zu vermeiden. Und da sich durch die feinen Poren der Feuchtigkeitshaushalt selbst reguliert, entsteht ein konstantes Feuchtigkeitsniveau. Dadurch werden Schimmel und Atemwegserkrankungen vermieden. „Atmende Fliesen" tragen so zu einem angenehmen Leben bei.

Breathing Wall Tile is a functional tile made of natural soil harmless to the human body and was patented as a healthy wall decoration material (or finishing material). Differently from existing glaze-finished tiles, it has numerous fine pores for absorption of formaldehyde and environmental hormones, etc. and reduces harmful substances that are created by building materials adhesives in new houses. Also, it absorbs or emits moisture into or out of fine pores to meet the relatively humidity in order to maintain the humidity at a constant level and the Breathing tile may provide fresh living environment always against mold or respiratory diseases.

Sprinkle water on the tile

2 minutes later

PRODUCT
BOW
Kerzenhalter, erweiterbar
Candle holder, extendible

DESIGN
ostwalddesign
Hamburg, Germany

MANUFACTURER
PHILIPPI GmbH
Hamburg, Germany

BOW wächst mit jedem Licht
„Menschen sind wie Engel mit einem Flügel – wenn sie
sich umarmen, können sie fliegen", besagt eine alte
Weisheit. BOW greift diesen Gedanken neu auf. Der
Kerzenhalter besteht in seiner Grundform aus zwei sich
vom Tisch erhebenden Bögen, die sich gegenseitig
halten. Das Stecksystem beruht dabei auf unsichtbar
eingearbeiteten Magneten, die genau so stark sind,
den nächsten Bogen sicher zu halten und zugleich ein
Öffnen von Hand zu ermöglichen. Im Kreise von Familie
oder Freunden brennt so für jeden ein Licht – BOW ist
Bogen um Bogen erweiterbar. Und bei Nichtgebrauch
lässt er sich flach verstauen.

BOW grows with every new candle
"People are like angels with one wing, when they hold
each other tight they can fly." BOW candleholder reinter-
prets this old proverb. Its basic design consists of two
connected bows that appear to rise from the table. The
plug system, based on equally strong invisible magnets,
ensures a secure connection to the next bow and an easy
opening by hand. Expanded bow by bow; every member
of a family and every guest at the table has their own
personal candlelight. And, BOW can be stored away with
minimum space.

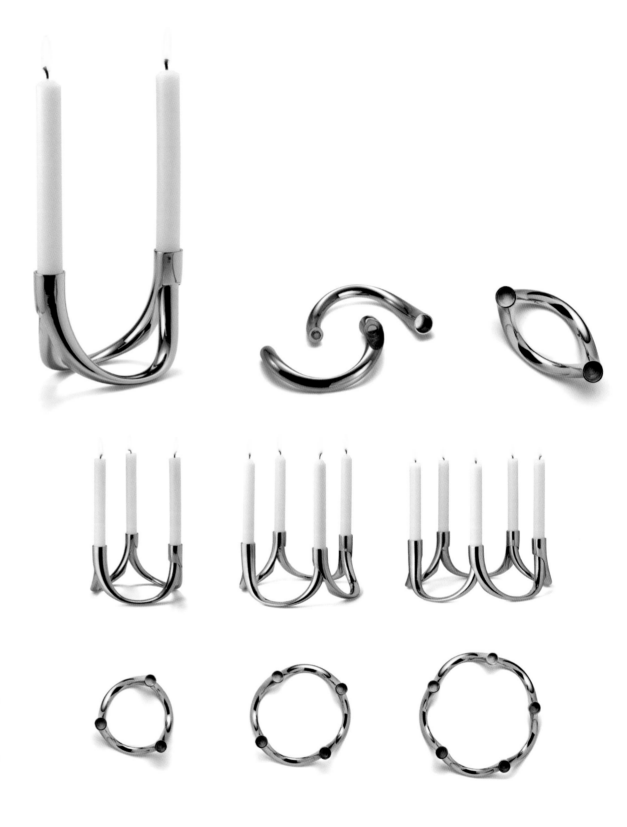

PRODUCT
ICZERO1
Stuhl
Chair

DESIGN
Indio da Costa AUDT
Guto Indio da Costa, André Lobo, Felipe Rangel
Rio de Janeiro, Brazil

MANUFACTURER
PNAPLES
Duque de Caxias - RJ, Brazil

Eine bequem umarmende Rückenlehne, leichte, schlanke und flüssige Formübergänge, eine innovative steife Materialkombination aus flexiblem Polymer und Langfasern. Ein zeitloser und langlebiger Stuhl, der zu 100 % recycelbar ist.

A floating curved surface that comfortably embraces a light, slim and fluid shape, an innovative combination of polymer flexibility and long fibers rigidity. A timeless and long lasting chair, 100 % recyclable.

PRODUCT

AIRE
Senkrechtmarkise
Drop awning

DESIGN

Studio Mario Mazzer
Mario Mazzer (Architect)
Conegliano, Italy

MANUFACTURER

SHADELAB S. R. L.
Motta di Livenza, Italy

AIRE ist eine motorisierte quadratische Senkrechtmarkise, die sich mit der modernsten Technik und Design problemlos in jeden zeitgenössischen Kontext fügt. Die Herausforderung des Produktes bestand darin, eine Beschattungsanlage mit herausragender Leistung und heutiger Ästhetik herzustellen, um dem jetzigen Gebäudetrend gerecht zu werden. AIRE ist aus Aluminium und Edelstahl gefertigt und zu 100% recycelbar; erhältlich in sechs Varianten und zehn Farben. Sie wurde vom TÜV Rheinland nach der EN 13561 geprüft und in allen EU-Mitgliedsstaaten patentiert. Die maximalen Ausmaße sind: Breite von 5 m und Höhe von 4,8 m, je nach Stoffwahl.

AIRE is a square shaped motorized drop awning that perfectly fits in contemporary architecture with its marked design and cutting edge technology, suited for climate control. The challenge underneath this product was the creation of a shading system with outstanding performance and fashionable modern-day esthetic to meet the current building trends. AIRE is made of extruded aluminum and stainless steel, being 100 % recyclable. It is available in six different variants and ten colors. Tested by TÜV Rheinland according to EN 13561. Patented design in all EU States. Maximum sizes: up to 5 m width and 4,8 m height according to the fabric used.

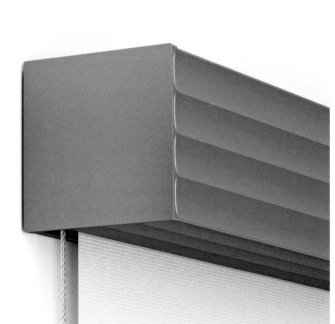

PRODUCT
Ringo
Stuhl zum Lernen
Study chair

DESIGN
SIDIZ Inc.
Seoul, South Korea

MANUFACTURER
SIDIZ Inc.
Seoul, South Korea

Sobald sie mit der Schule anfangen, lernen die meisten Kinder im Klassenzimmer in sitzender Position an einem Tisch. Man sieht leicht, dass ihre Haltung oft schlecht ist. Wenn die Rückenlehne ausreichend stützt, wird die Haltung korrigiert. Daher ist ein Hauptmerkmal des Stuhls Ringo seine verstellbare Rückenlehne. Durch einfache Bewegungen der Armlehnen können Kinder die Höhe der Rückenlehne, die Sitztiefe und die Höhe der Armlehnen anpassen. Darüber hinaus hat der Stuhl Ringo Rollen mit feststehenden Zylindern und Wegrollsperre sowie eine Fußstütze für mehr Konzentration. Seine Form schafft eine angenehme Lernatmosphäre.

After starting school, most children study in the classroom sitting at their desks. It's easy to recognize that most children have poor posture. Ensuring that the backrest provides proper support to children's backs allows posture to be corrected. This is why one of the main features of the Ringo chair is an adjustable backrest. Simply by moving the chair's armrests, children can adjust backrest height, seat depth and armrest height. What's more, the Ringo chair also has fixed-cylinder, sit-brake casters and a footrest for extra concentration. The shape of the Ringo chair creates a friendly studying atmosphere.

PRODUCT
Mirah
Sessel
Armchair

DESIGN
JaderAlmeida design & arquitetura
Princesa, Brazil

MANUFACTURER
Sollosbrasil
Princesa, Brazil

Aus jedem seitlichen Winkel und aus jedem Blickwinkel sind Details des Produktes zu sehen. Dieser Ansatz zu Detailreichtum und anspruchsvolles Design verleihen eine zeitlose Identität des Produkts. Im Gegenzug ermöglicht Massivholz eine Vielzahl von Farben, sodass die Zusammenstellung mit verschiedenen Umgebungen erlaubt ist. Die Leichtigkeit und Einfachheit des Designs, mit präziser Ausführung kombiniert, bilden ein Rezept für ein erfolgreiches Produkt.

At each angle side or the point of view, it can be seen details of the product. This approach to the richness of detail and sophisticated design gives a timeless identity of the product. In turn, solid wood allows a variety of colors, allowing the composition to different environments. The lightness and simplicity of design combined with precise execution form a recipe for a successful product solved, friendly and current.

PRODUCT
Milla
Stuhl
Chair

DESIGN
JaderAlmeida design & arquitetura
Princesa, Brazil

MANUFACTURER
Sollosbrasil
Princesa, Brazil

Der Milla-Stuhl wurde aus einem Konzept der Diversität entwickelt. Multiplikation der einzelnen Teile ergibt kein erschöpfendes Abbild der Umgebung. Die Kreuzungen, Einmündungen, Armaturen zusammen mit den abgerundeten Kanten bilden eine freundliche visuelle Ergänzung, die den Komfort und die Ergonomie des Produktes vervollständigen. Strukturiertes Hartholz mittlerer Dichte und gepolsterte Sitzfläche und Rückenlehne, die Liebe zum Detail, präzise Ausführung und zeitloses Design, verleihen dem Stück markante Identität.

The Milla chair was designed from a concept of diversity within a proposed multiplication, where the number of parts makes the environment not exhaustive. The intersections, junctions, fittings together with the edges rounded off a visual complement friendly, which is complete with the comfort and ergonomics of the product. Structured medium density hardwood and upholstered seat and backrest. Attention to detail, precise execution and timeless design, gives the striking identity of the piece.

PRODUCT

IKIO
Garderobe
Coat rack

DESIGN

fries & zumbühl
Winterthur, Switzerland

MANUFACTURER

Studio Domo Inc.
Taipei, Taiwan

Im Gegensatz zu gewöhnlichen Garderoben, bei denen der Aufhänger nur ein Haken ist, hat der Designer Bäume und Äste aus der Natur nachgebildet. Das Aluminium- rohr wird geschnitten und nach außen in verschiedene Richtungen gebogen, um so das natürliche Wachstum eines Baumes zu symbolisieren. Die einzigartige Hand- werkskunst und das ansprechende Design der IKIO- Garderobe enthält einen modernen, minimalistischen Ansatz, welcher gleichzeitig die Verbindung zur Natur herstellt. Mit IKIO ist das Aufhängen eines Mantels, Schals oder einer Tasche sehr intuitiv.

Unlike ordinary coat racks where the hanger is an addi- tional part, the designers adopted imagery of trees and branches from nature. The aluminum pipe is cut and bent outwards at different directions and angles which symbolize the natural growth of a tree. Hanging a coat, scarf or bag is intuitive with IKIO which makes it very suitable for the bedroom, office, or entrance. The unique craftsmanship and design of IKIO coat rack has a modern minimalist approach, but at the same time connect us with nature.

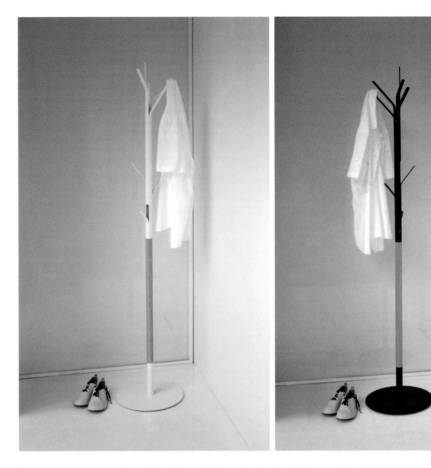

KITCHEN / HOUSEHOLD

ANGELA CARVALHO
DONGHOON CHANG
SERTAC ERSAYIN
CHRISTOPHE DE LA FONTAINE
HENRIK HOLBÆK
PROF. KILIAN STAUSS

PRODUCT
Compact Dishwasher
Geschirrspüler-Produktreihe
Dishwashers product range

DESIGN
Electrolux Group Design EMEA
Stockholm, Sweden

MANUFACTURER
Electrolux Major Appliances EMEA
Stockholm, Sweden

Die Geschirrspüler der Electrolux-Inspiration-Range-Compact bieten ein erstklassiges, unverwechselbares, modernes Aussehen. Ihre klaren architektonischen Linien und Farben (glänzend weiß, schwarz oder rot), das einzigartige Material und der typische Griff verleihen ihnen ein charakteristisches Aussehen, das in jede erstklassige Küche passt. Die intuitive LED-Bedienoberfläche ist schön versteckt und dennoch einfach zu bedienen. Ihr kompaktes Design lässt dennoch Raum für sechs vollständige Einstellungen mit intelligentem automatischem Programm, das effiziente Einstellungen mit nur einem Tastendruck ermöglicht.

The Inspiration Range's Compact Dishwasher from Electrolux has a premium, distinctive and modern look. Its clean architectural lines and colors (glossy white, black or red), unique material and characteristic handle give it an iconic look that fits in any premium kitchen. The intuitive LED user interface is neatly hidden, but easy to use and adapts to your needs for quick and easy washing. Its compact design still has room for six full settings with an intelligent auto program that gives you access to efficient settings with the touch of a button.

product
design award

2013 GOLD

„Das ist ein kompaktes Produkt für Singles und kleine Wohnungen. In dieser Kategorie ist dieses Produkt eine äußerst gelungene Lösung, seine Designsprache kommuniziert seine qualitätvolle Verarbeitung und darüber hinaus ist es in einer ansprechenden Farbstellung gestaltet.

"This is a compact product for those living alone and for small apartments. It is an exceptionally successful solution in this category. Its design language transmits quality workmanship and on top of that the color combination is very appealing."

JURYSTATEMENT

PRODUCT
PWT 6089
Gewerbliche Wasch-Trocken-Säule
Commercial washer-dryer stack

DESIGN
Miele & Cie. KG
Gütersloh, Germany

MANUFACTURER
Miele & Cie. KG
Gütersloh, Germany

Wäschereibetreiber möchten platzsparende Lösungen.
Sie möchten eine Steuerung, die ohne langes Einarbei-
ten von wechselnder Belegschaft fehlerfrei bedient
werden kann. Für die unterschiedlichsten Wäscheposten.
Ergonomisch für das Bedienpersonal. Sie möchten die
Wäsche nach dem Waschen direkt trocknen. Ohne lan-
ge Wege. Ressourcensparend, mit dem bestmöglichen
Wasch- und Trockenergebnis für sich und ihre Kunden.
Sie möchten die höchste Wirtschaftlichkeit, die beste
Langlebigkeit. Auch optisch. Sie bekommen eine
Waschtrockensäule für ihre Ansprüche. Sie bekommen
Miele Professional.

*Laundry operators are always on the lookout for space-
saving solutions. They require a set of controls which can
be used without further study by different members of
staff in a fluctuating workforce. And a machine able to
cope with various laundry loads, ergonomic to operate.
They want to dry laundry immediately after washing
without having to walk great distances. Resource-saving,
achieving the best possible washing and drying results.
Their machine should be highly economical and long-
lasting. And it should look the part, too. So they buy a
washer-dryer stack to meet their every need. But what
they are really getting is Miele Professional.*

product
design award

2013 GOLD

„Die Qualität des Designs ist extrem hoch – allein die Tatsache, dass dieses Produkt nicht nur von vorn, sondern auch von der Seite und von hinten gut aussieht und man darauf bewusst geachtet hat, spricht für sich. Mit einfachen formalen Lösungen hat man hier auf schlichte Weise eine ganze Reihe von Problemen ästhetisch überzeugend gelöst."

"The design is of the highest quality – alone the fact that this product looks good not just from the front, but also from the side and from behind, and the fact that this was a conscious design decision, speaks for itself. Simple solutions have been found to provide a sleek response to a whole range of problems in a way that is esthetically pleasing."

JURYSTATEMENT

PRODUCT

Concept Kitchen

Mobile Küche

Mobile kitchen

DESIGN

Kilian Schindler Produktdesign

Karlsruhe, Germany

MANUFACTURER

Naber GmbH

Nordhorn, Germany

Das System der Mobilküche basiert derzeit auf vier Modulen: Arbeitsfläche mit integrierter Kochfläche, Spülzentrum, Butcher-Block, Raumteiler mit Einbauherd. Die aus Stahl gefertigten Grundelemente sind zerlegbar und verfügen über Rasterbohrungen für die flexible Anordnung von Konstruktions- und Regalböden. Ein einfaches Steckprinzip ermöglicht den unkomplizierten Auf- und Abbau der Grundelemente ohne Werkzeugeinsatz. Die Systemküche lässt sich flexibel an das Leben des Benutzers anpassen.

The mobile kitchen system is currently based on four modules: work surface with integrated hob, sink center, butcher block, partition tower with built-in oven. The stainless steel base elements can be disassembled and have grid holes for the flexible positioning of structural panels and shelves. A simple plug-in principle allows easy assembly and disassembly of the basic elements without the use of tools. The kitchen system can be flexibly adapted to the user's lifestyle.

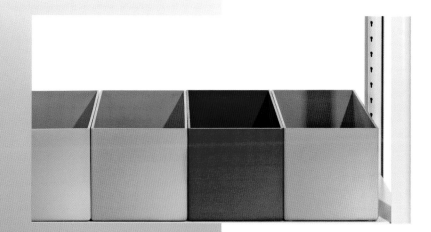

„Küche einmal anders. Nicht unbeweglich, schwer und fixiert, sondern ein low-tech-Vorschlag, wie Küche anders interpretiert werden kann: Als leichtes Modul, das sich flexibel einpasst. Es hat eine freundliche Designsprache, ist nicht so teuer und daher für jüngere Leute geeignet, für einen Lifestyle, der weniger auf Repräsentatives, sondern auf Flexibilität und Easyness setzt. Auch das Farbkonzept ist stimmig und überzeugend."

"A different type of kitchen. Not the usual rigid, heavy, fixed model, but instead a low-tech suggestion of how kitchens could be interpreted: as a lightweight module that can be flexibly adapted to suit. The kitchen is based on a friendly design language and is inexpensive and so suited to young people and to a lifestyle that is happy to forego prestige in favor of flexibility and ease. Even the color concept is consistent and strong."

JURYSTATEMENT

PRODUCT

OSORO
Offenes Geschirrsystems
Open tableware system

DESIGN

MTDO Inc.
Product Design and Concept Build
Tokyo, Japan
Wellness Arena Corporation
Product Concept and Promotion Supervise
Tokyo, Japan

MANUFACTURER

Narumi Corporation Head Office
Nagoya, Aichi, Japan
Narumi Corporation Tokyo Office
Tokyo, Japan

Da sich unser Blick auf das Leben mit der Zeit verändert, kann Geschirr eine Antwort auf viele unserer Probleme sein. Vom Abendessen bis zum Kochen, Kühlen, Einfrieren und Lagern bietet OSORO einige neue Ideen. Narumi, der 1946 gegründete, japanische Hersteller von Geschirr aus feinem Knochenporzellan, könnte Ihren Lifestyle beim Essen revolutionieren. Erleben Sie die Wunder des offenen Geschirrsystems von OSORO. Dieses Geschirr erfüllt Ihre täglichen Wünsche mit einer Vielzahl von Variationen und Kombinationen. So kompakt wie möglich gestaltet machen die Einzelteile das Leben schöner. Genießen und gestalten Sie Ihren eigenen Tag mit OSORO.

As our views on life change with the times, tableware may well be the answer to many of our problems. From the dinner table to the process of cooking, refrigerating, freezing and even storing, OSORO has come up with some new ideas. Founded in 1946 and known in Japan as a manufacturer of fine bone china tableware, Narumi may revolutionize your food lifestyle. Experience the wonders of OSORO's open tableware system. The tableware may fulfill your daily desires with a multitude of variations and combinations. As compact as possible, the tools can make your life happier. Feel free to enjoy and design your own day with OSORO.

product
design award

2013 GOLD

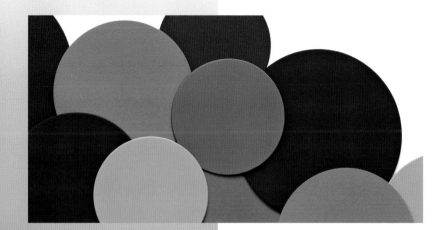

„Dieses Produkt hat eine sehr schöne Funktionalität, es bietet ein Spiel aus Formen und Farben. Einzelne Behälterformen und Größen aus Porzellan bekommen einen Deckel mit farbigem Silikonring, der das Prinzip des „Tellerauflegens" aufnimmt – wie einen Teller deckt man die einzelnen Behälter ab – so lassen sie sich stapeln und Reste können einfach abgedeckt und aufbewahrt werden. Das Ganze ist sehr funktional, ganz einfach und sieht auf dem Tisch auch noch gut aus."

"This product is highly functional and also plays beautifully with shapes and colors. Individual container shapes and sizes in porcelain are given a lid with a colorful silicone ring that takes on the role of the "plate as cover" – as though a plate were laid on top, the individual containers are covered, enabling them to be stacked and leftovers to be covered and stored simply. The whole system is highly functional, very simple, and still looks good as tableware."

JURYSTATEMENT

kitchen / household

PRODUCT

Compact 4 All Series
Frühstücks-Set
Breakfast set

DESIGN

Princess Household Appliances
Jan des Bouvrie
Breda, Netherlands

MANUFACTURER

Princess Household Appliances
Breda, Netherlands

Compact 4 All ist eine Serie von vier kompakten Haushaltsgeräten: einem Toaster, einer Saftpresse, einer Kaffeemaschine und einem Wasserkocher. Die Geräte können separat platziert werden, gestapelt werden oder individuell zusammen einen „Frühstückswürfel" bilden. Zudem verfügt der Entsafter über drei Steckdosen, sodass das gesamte Set dort angeschlossen werden kann.

Compact 4 All is a series of four compact household appliances, specifically, a toaster, a juicer, a coffee machine and a kettle. Each appliance can be placed separately, in a line next to each other, on top of each other or 2 by 2 (together the cubes will form a "breakfast cube"). The juicer has three power sockets on its back where the other three appliances can be plugged into.

product
design award

2013 GOLD

„Eine richtig gute Idee! Das System besteht aus lauter Kuben im gleichen Maß, die modular sind und nach Belieben geschichtet oder gestapelt werden können – eben so angeordnet, wie der User es mag oder braucht. Eine einzige Designsprache für viele Funktionen! Noch dazu ist das System nicht besonders teuer und die einzelnen Kuben damit sehr gute Einstiegsmodelle."

"A really great idea! The system is made up of four sleek cubes, each of the same size, that are modular and can be piled or stacked as desired – organized exactly the way the user wants or needs them. One design language for a spectrum of functions! On top of that the system is not very expensive, making the individual cubes great entry-level modules."

JURYSTATEMENT

PRODUCT
WT727QPNDMW
Waschmaschine
Washing machine

DESIGN
SAMSUNG Electronics Co., Ltd.
Mitsuhiro Shigeri, Atsuhiko Yoneda, Hyunjoo Sim,
Jaewoo Lee, Armada Choi, Neha Yadav
Seoul, South Korea

MANUFACTURER
SAMSUNG Electronics Co., Ltd.
Suwon-si, Gyeonggi-do, South Korea

Diese Zwei-Trommel-Waschmaschine wurde speziell
dafür entwickelt, örtliche Anwendungsmuster nachzu-
ahmen, die sorgfältig beobachtet werden. Das „EZ
Wash Tray" ermöglicht dem Benutzer, die Wäsche vor-
zuwaschen. Dabei verhindert die Form des oberen Teils,
dass Schmutzwasser nach unten fließt. Diese Faktoren
sind Bestandteil eines besonderen Konzepts, das die
Waschmaschine als Arbeitstisch für das Wäschewaschen
auffasst. Die Reihenanordnung erhöht die Leistungsstärke der Waschmaschine. Die abgerundeten Ecken
des PP-Materials im Gehäuse verhindern eine Verformung.
Ein umweltgerechtes Design, das ein Bekenntnis zur
Kostenverringerung darstellt.

*This twin tub washing machine is specially designed to
reflect local usage patterns that are monitored thoroughly.
The „EZ Wash Tray" allows the user to pre-wash the laundry, while shape of the upper part prevents dirty water
from flowing down. These factors are a part of a distinctive design that interprets the washing machine as a
worktable for the clothes washing process. The beaded
form increases the washing machine's strength. The
corners of the PP material in the main body have been
rounded to prevent deformation. This is an eco-friendly
design that is a testament to cost innovation.*

„Eine spezifisch kulturelle Waschmaschine für die Gewohnheiten und kleinen Räume in Japan überrascht zunächst – und spricht doch eine Designsprache, die in ihrer optischen Schlichtheit und ihrem logistischen Minimalismus besticht. Denn diese Maschine dient zugleich als Wasch-tisch, auf dem Wäsche vorgereinigt werden kann. Praktisch, elegant und technologisch hervor-ragend umgesetzt!"

"This culturally-specific washing machine designed for the customs and small spaces in Japan is surprising at first: its sleek appearance and logistical minimalism create a truly captivating design language. However, it is not just a washing machine: this product also serves as a washstand for pre-cleaning the laundry. Practicality and elegance."

JURYSTATEMENT

PRODUCT

TA-FVX610, TA-FV410

Kabelloses Bügeleisen

Cordless iron

DESIGN

Toshiba Corporation

Yukie Kuramoto

Tokyo, Japan

MANUFACTURER

Toshiba Home Appliances Corporation

Tokyo, Japan

Ein kompaktes, kabelloses Bügeleisen, mit dem sowohl breite als auch schmale Teile von Kleidungsstücken gebügelt werden können. Es besitzt eine räumliche Punktdruck-Bügelsohle, die durch eine leicht nach oben gebogene Hinterkante charakterisiert ist. Die Trapezform auf der Rückseite bietet eine Führung zum Bügeln von Manschetten und Bundfalten, um die Benutzung gegenüber herkömmlichen Bügeleisen zu erleichtern. Es kann Rüschen und Krausen bügeln, ohne sie zu zerdrücken. Die breite Fläche an der Vorderseite verhindert Faltenbildung und eignet sich perfekt für breite Stoffbereiche, während das offene Griffdesign Drehungen erleichtert.

A compact cordless iron for ironing both wide and narrow areas of clothing. It features a Point Press 3D ironing surface characterized by a slightly up-tilted back end. The trapezoid shape at the back provides a guide for ironing cuffs and pleats to make it easier to use than conventional irons. It can iron ruffles and gathers without crushing them. The wide area at the front prevents creasing and is perfect for wide areas of material, and the open-handle design makes it easy to rotate. The water tank is larger than usual and is easily opened and closed even if you have long fingernails, and the compact design takes ease-of-use into account.

product
design award

2013 GOLD

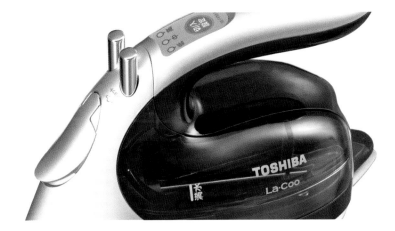

„Das kleine und handliche Bügeleisen kommt zunächst einmal in einer sehr ansprechenden Umverpackung daher, einer Box, die die Form des Produkts auf charmante und handliche Weise aufnimmt. Das Bügeleisen ist klein und handlich, ist einfach zu benutzen und verfügt dabei über einen sehr großen Wassertank – einfach ein ansprechendes, kleines Objekt, bei dem alles stimmt."

"For a start, this petite, easy-to-handle iron comes in very attractive outer packaging: a box that reflects the shape of the product and is both charming and manageable. The iron itself is small and easily maneuvered, simple to use and even has a very large water tank. This is quite simply an attractive little object that gets everything right."

JURYSTATEMENT

PRODUCT

X7 integrate stove
Integrierender Herd
Integrate stove

DESIGN

Zhejiang Marssenger Kitchenware Co., Ltd.
Zhang Xiangcheng
Haining, Zhejiang Province, China

MANUFACTURER

Zhejiang Marssenger Kitchenware Co., Ltd.
Haining, Zhejiang Province, China

Das Produkt sammelt die Funktionen von Dunstabzugshaube, Gasherd, Desinfektions-Schrank und Spind in
einem, um die Bedürfnisse der chinesischen Verbraucher zu erfüllen. Die traditionelle Haube kann den
Dunst absaugen, den das Kochen im chinesischen Stil
erzeugt – und das mit gutem Design. Wir verwenden
eine Teflon-Beschichtung und Anti-Fingerprint-Be-
schichtung aus rostfreiem Stahl, um das Produkt leichter zu reinigen und um den modularen Aufbau im Hinblick auf routinemäßige Wartung und Installation zu
erleichtern.

*This product integrates the functions of range hood, gas
stove, disinfecting cabinet and lockers, catering fully to
the needs of Chinese consumers. What's more, this product provides Chinese users a clean kitchen where traditional hood fails by applying an original design to suck
all the smoke generated by Chinese-style cooking. Besides,
the creative use of Teflon coating and anti-fingerprint
blasting stainless steel makes the product easier to clean;
the modular design facilitates routine maintenance and
installation to maintenance.*

product
design award

2013 GOLD

„Dieses frei stehende Küchenelement kommt in Chinas Straßenküchen zum Einsatz – es ist simpel und schön. Alle Anforderungen wurden sehr gut gelöst. Das einfache, saubere Design sorgt dafür, dass Abzugshaube, Platz für Töpfe und Utensilien und Kochstelle sinnvoll Platz finden, alles bildet eine stimmige Einheit, die gut zu reinigen ist. Dies ist kein supertechnologisches Produkt, aber das einfache, gut überlegte Design macht den Unterschied zu Produkten diesen Segments."

"This free-standing kitchen unit is used in the street kitchens of China. It is simple and looks good, meeting the user's needs very well. The simple, clean design makes sure that there is convenient space provided for the extractor hood, saucepans and utensils as well as the hot plate, all coming together in a coherent unit that is easy to clean. This is not a fantastically high-tech product, but the simple, well-thought-through design makes this unit stand out from other products in this segment."

JURYSTATEMENT

PRODUCT
Water Dispenser
Wasserspender
In-line water dispenser

DESIGN
Speck Design, Ltd.
Gabriel Collins, Pokeys Tong, Jojo Zhu, Min Chi
Shanghai, China

MANUFACTURER
3M China Limited
Shanghai, China

Dieser Wasserspender mit 3M-Filteranlagen bietet dem Anwender Wasser in Umgebungstemperatur sowie kaltes und warmes Wasser, filtriert. Das Gehäuse besitzt eine elegante gebogene Form, um eine abgewinkelte und minimalistische Benutzeroberfläche zur komfortablen Steuerung und Ansicht zu erstellen. Der Wasserspender kann auf einem Tisch oder an einer Wand montiert werden. Die Schnittstelle besteht aus einem großen Display und berührungsempfindlichen Bedienelementen. Die große Auffangschale ermöglicht eine Vielzahl von Becher-Größen. Der Spender enthält auch eine Uhr sowie Energieeinsparungs- und Kindersicherungs-Funktionen.

This in-line water dispenser (HWS-CT-HC / HWS-CT-H), connected to 3M filtration systems, provides the user with ambient, cold and hot filtered water. The housing has a sleek curved body to create an angled and minimalistic user interface for convenient control and view. The water dispenser can be placed on a tabletop or mounted on a wall to optimize the use of space. The interface consists of a large display and touch sensitive controls to enhance the ease of use. Its large drip tray enables dispensing into a large variety of cup sizes. This dispenser also contains a clock, energy saving and child safety lock features.

PRODUCT
Refrigerator
Kühlschrank
Refrigerator

DESIGN
Arçelik A.Ş.
Arcelik Industrial Design Team
Istanbul, Turkey

MANUFACTURER
Arçelik A.Ş.
Istanbul, Turkey

Das Design der neuen Domestic-Appliances-Serie von Grundig wurde darauf ausgerichtet, als starkes, zuverlässiges und vertrauenswürdiges – auf dem deutschen Markt unverwechselbares – Produkt wahrgenommen zu werden. Das Designkonzept von Grundig-Domestic-Appliances mit seiner klavierartigen Benutzerschnittstelle wurde inspiriert von einer Symphonie. Die weißen und klaren Kommunikationselemente im Display erzeugen eine großartige Harmonie. Der Grundig-Kühlschrank ist ein 60 cm hohes vollständig frostfreies Kombiprodukt. Der Grundig-Kühlschrank entspricht der Klasse A+++ und verbraucht 60 % weniger Energie als andere Produkte der A-Klasse.

The new Grundig Domestic Appliances Series is designed to be perceived as strong, reliable and a trusted product of distinction in the German Market. Grundig Domestic Appliances' Design style, providing a piano like user interface that generates great harmony with white and clear communication elements in the display is created by the inspiration of a Symphony. The Grundig Refrigerator is a 60 cm full no-frost combi product. The Grundig Refrigerator is A+++ class, which provides the user with 60 % less energy consumption than other class A products.

PRODUCT
In-Love Series WM
Waschmaschinen
Washing machine

DESIGN
Arçelik A.Ş.
Savas Onur Eroglu, Ozgur Mutlu Oz
Istanbul, Turkey

MANUFACTURER
Arçelik A.Ş.
Istanbul, Turkey

Arçelik -Waschmaschinen der In-Love-Serie, die mit hochmodernen Technologien ausgestattet sind und durch spektakuläres Design und technologische Überlegenheit bestechen, machen die Wäschepflege zu einer wahren Freude – in farbenfroher, modischer Optik, mit einfacher Handhabung, Automatikprogramm und mehreren Sensoren. Die In-Love-Serie bietet jungen Verbrauchern, die Abwechslung mögen und sich durch farbige Produkte abheben möchten, innovatives Design. Die Farben werden unter Berücksichtigung neu aufkommender Trends in verschiedenen Medien weltweit ausgewählt. Die Serie weckt die Energie fröhlicher Farbkombinationen – für ein jugendliches Gefühl.

Arçelik's In-Love Series washing machine, incorporating the state-of-the-art technologies and coming into prominence with its spectacular design and technological superiority turns doing the laundry into a joy with its colorful trendy appearance, ease of use, automatic program and multi-sensors. Arçelik In-Love Series provides innovation for young consumers who want to get changed and become different with its colorful products. The colors are selected considering newly emerging trends in different media all around the world. In-Love series, brought back the energy of happy color combinations to make consumers feel younger.

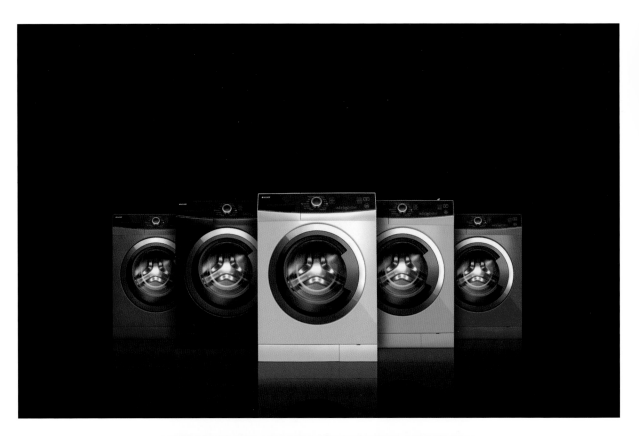

PRODUCT
Arzum Fırrın
Toaster

DESIGN
Atıl Kızılbayır
Bakırköy / Istanbul, Turkey

MANUFACTURER
Arzum Elektrikli Ev Aletleri San. ve Tic. A.Ş
Istanbul, Turkey

Der Fırrın-Toaster ist die neue Innovation von Arzum und revolutioniert das Toasten. Als Alternative zu Standardtoastern bietet seine einzigartige Form und simple Bedienung Verbrauchern weltweit „Einfachheit". Nie wieder Krümel im Toaster oder verbrannte Finger beim Herausnehmen des Toasts - dank der patentierten Technologie mit Schiebetablett. Um es einfach zu reinigen oder den Toast zu servieren kann das Schiebetablett vollständig herausgenommen werden. Das verstellbare Tablett ermöglicht das Toasten verschiedener Brotsorten und -größen wie Toast, Scheiben, Croissants, Bagels und vieler weiterer.

The Fırrın toaster is Arzum's new innovation that revolutionizes toasting. As an alternative to standard toasters, Fırrın's unique form and ease-of-use offers "simplicity" to consumers around the world.
Thanks to its patented sliding-tray technology, there are no more crumbs in your toaster and no more burning your fingers when taking out toasted bread. You can serve your toast and easily clean the tray by removing it completely. The adjustable tray allows you to toast breads of different sizes and types, including toast, sliced loafs, croissants, bagels and many more.

PRODUCT
SVART Presisjon
Kaffeemaschine
Coffee maker

DESIGN
Designit
Copenhagen NV, Denmark

MANUFACTURER
AS Wilfa
Hagan, Norway

Die Wilfa SVART Presisjon-Kaffeemaschine kontrolliert die entscheidenden Schritte der Kaffeezubereitung. Führende Barista-Meister und Industriedesigner gestalteten gemeinsam eine Maschine, die immer erstklassigen Kaffee zubereitet. Maßgebend für das Design sind der abnehmbare Tank zur Gewährleistung von frischem Wasser, das patentierte Heizsystem zur optimalen Brühtemperatur und die einzigartige Pumpe zur Dosierung der richtigen Menge Wasser zum richtigen Zeitpunkt. Portionierung und Stärke des Kaffees lassen sich über die kontrollierbaren Öffnungen regeln. Dadurch ist vom ersten bis zum letzten Tropfen perfekt gekochter Kaffee garantiert.

The Wilfa SVART Presisjon automatic coffee machine is precisely calibrated to control essential components of coffee preparation. Leading barista champions and industrial designers paired up to deliver a stunning machine that makes great coffee every time. The cornerstones of the design are a detachable tank that ensures fresh water, a patented heating system that delivers optimal water temperature and a unique pump that allots the right amount of water, at the right time. The flow control aperture lets the user regulate the amount and strength of the coffee. The system guarantees perfectly brewed coffee from the first to the last drop.

PRODUCT
WMF LINEO
Frühstücks-Set
Breakfast set

DESIGN
TEAGUE
TEAGUE Design Team
Seattle, WA, United States of America

MANUFACTURER
Auerhahn Bestecke GmbH
Altensteig, Germany

Die LINEO-Frühstücksserie, setzt durch die Kombination aus fortschrittlicher Technologie und Fertigungsqualität, Innovation und klassischem Design, einen neuen Standard im Bereich Küchen Elektro-Kleingeräte. Die Recherche der Markenwerte führte zum zeitlosen Design welches WMF's Bekenntnis zur Verbindung von Modernität und Tradition widerspiegelt. Das Design verkörpert Hochwertigkeit, Professionalität, Bedienkomfort und Performance durch einfachste Anwenderschnittstellen und einheitlichen, ergonomischen Griffen. Zylindrische Grundformen, klare Linien, beste Herstellungsqualität, gebürstetes Edelstahl und Cromargan machen LINEO einzigartig.

The LINEO breakfast set, including filter coffee machine, kettle and long slot toaster, brings innovation and classic design to the kitchen combining advanced technologies with superior craftsmanship to set a new standard in small kitchen appliances. In depth research led to the timeless design that embodies WMF's brand commitment to merge modern with traditional. The set is designed for value, performance, and ease of use with a simple and intuitive user interface and uniform ergonomic handle. LINEO is precisely manufactured and one-of-a-kind with cylindrical shapes, clean lines and high-end materials including stainless steel and Cromargan.

PRODUCT

QBK-101
Heimbatteriebank
Home battery bank

DESIGN

Qisda Creative Design Center
Qisda Corporation
Taipei, Taiwan

MANUFACTURER

AUO Corporation
Taoyuan, Taiwan

QBK-101 ist eine Solar-Akkubank mit einer Kapazität von sechs Kilowattstunden. Stellen Sie über den Touch-Screen Solarenergie für die Energieversorgung am Tag ein und kaufen Sie gespeicherte Energie zu Nebenzeiten-preisen hinzu. Während einer Naturkatastrophe oder Stromausfall kann die gespeicherte Energie im Notfall genutzt werden. Das Gerät ist aus Metall und Plastik gefertigt und besitzt eine robuste, haltbare Struktur. Räder unten und Griffe an den Seiten machen das Gerät leicht bewegbar. Der schräg (45 Grad) angeordnete Touch-Screen ist ergonomisch konzipiert und bietet einen idealen Ansichtwinkel.

QBK-101 is a solar energy battery bank, up to 6 kwh capacity. Use the touch screen on top to set solar power as the day energy supply, purchase reserve energy at off-peak prices into QBK-101. During a natural disaster or power outage, the preserved energy can be used for basic power supply in cases of emergency. Made of metal combined with plastic, it has a solid body structure and not easily damaged. The bottom wheels and handles on both sides of the battery make it practical to mobilize the battery. The touch screen is slanted at 45 degrees, ergonomically designed for an optimal view angle.

PRODUCT

SIZZLE
Innovativer Kochtopf
Innovative cookware

DESIGN

SYNTHESIS Design Partner
Pieter Kuschel e. K.
Breckerfeld, Germany

MANUFACTURER

B/R/K Vertriebs-GmbH
Wuppertal, Germany

SIZZLE – das innovative Kochsystem. SIZZLE vereint die Vorteile der drei wesentlichen Garmethoden: Standard-kochen mit Auflagedeckel, Schnellkochen unter Druck, Garen im Dampfgarer. 1. Zeit- und energiesparendes Kochen (bis zu 40 % schneller als Standardkochen), 2. fettarmes, gesünderes und schmackhafteres Kochen durch Dampfgaren (Temperatur bis zu 102 °C mit Nieder-druck im Inneren des Topfes), 3. aktives Kochen (jeder-zeitiges Öffnen und Schließen des luftdicht verschlos-senen Topfes zum Nachfüllen, Würzen, Umrühren und Abschmecken…), 4. intuitive und kinderleichte Hand-habung durch Einhandmechanismus.

SIZZLE – the innovative cooking system. SIZZLE combines the advantages of all three commonly-used cooking methods: standard cooking with a covered pot, fast cooking (pressure-cooking), simmering in a steamer. 1. Saves time and electricity when cooking (up to 40 % quicker than standard cooking), 2. low-fat, healthier and above all tastier cooking by steaming (up to a tempera-ture of 102 °C with low pressure inside the cooker), 3. active cooking (opening and closing the lid which is closed airtight to top up, season, stir and sample the taste etc.), 4. intuitive handling which is child's play, using a single-handed mechanism.

PRODUCT
GreenFan2
Energiesparender Ventilator
Electric fan

DESIGN
BALMUDA Inc.
Tokyo, Japan

MANUFACTURER
BALMUDA Inc.
Tokyo, Japan

Der Ventilator GreenFan2 produziert eine sanfte Brise, ist besonders leise und wirkt effektiv auf größere Distanz. Durch die einzigartige Doppelflügelkonstruktion stellt er einen äußeren und inneren Luftstrom her und verhindert so unregelmäßige Luftwirbel. Durch diese spezielle Technik entsteht eine angenehme naturähnliche Brise. Mit einer Reichweite von bis zu 10 m hebt sich der GreenFan2 stark von herkömmlichen Ventilatoren ab. Durch den bürstenlosen Motor verbraucht er basierend auf jap. Messungen 3 W / max. 17 W, d. h. nur 1/10 im Vergleich zu herkömmlichen Modellen und ist mit 13 dB auf niedrigster Stufe so leise wie kein anderer Ventilator.

The electric-fan GreenFan2 produces a soft breeze, is quiet and efficient even on a long distance with low power consumption. Our unique double-blade-construction generates an outer and inner airflow, which enables the GreenFan2 to prevent irregular air turbulences like a tornado from directory hitting to the body. Due to this special technology, it provides a comfortable and natural breeze. Furthermore, the airflow has a reach up to 10m.Thanks to the brushless motor, the low power consumption (3 W - max. 17 W measured in Japan) marks only one-tenth compared to conventional products. It is innovatively silent with only 13dB at Min. mode.

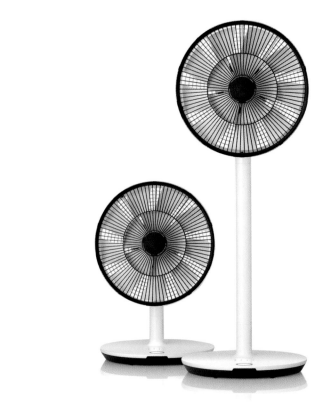

PRODUCT
GreenFan mini
Energiesparender Ventilator
Electric fan

DESIGN
BALMUDA Inc.
Tokyo, Japan

MANUFACTURER
BALMUDA Inc.
Tokyo, Japan

Der GreenFan mini ist ein innovativer, kompakter und tragbarer Ventilator, der dank unserer GreenFan-Technologie eine natürliche, angenehme Luftbewegung erzeugt. Kombiniert mit unserem mobilen Akku erhält man einen kabellosen Ventilator. Die GreenFan-Technologie konzentriert die verschiedenen Luftströmungen durch die in zwei Ebenen liegenden Flügel auf einen Punkt und eliminiert dadurch Verwirbelungen. Der sich dahinter ausbreitende Luftstrom wirkt wie ein natürlicher Windhauch. Der GreenFan mini verbraucht in der kleinsten Stufe nur zwei Watt, was etwa einem Zehntel herkömmlicher Geräte entspricht, und besticht auch durch leisen Betrieb.

The GreenFan mini is an innovative, compact and portable fan, which produces a natural, pleasant breeze by our exclusive GreenFan Technology. When we use with our original mobile battery, it becomes a cordless fan. Our GreenFan Technology concentrates the different airflows at a single point by a dual-layer blade, and the airflows meet to eliminate swirling. Then the air is diffused as if across a flat surface, becoming airflow found in nature. GreenFan mini consumes just 2W at its lowest setting, which is one-tenth of conventional ones. And also GreenFan mini achieves its incredible quietness.

PRODUCT
BLANCOATTIKA
Küchenspüle
Kitchen sink

DESIGN
BLANCO GmbH & Co. KG
Oberderdingen, Germany

MANUFACTURER
BLANCO GmbH & Co. KG
Oberderdingen, Germany

Authentische Materialästhetik und ausgeprägte Manu-
faktur-Merkmale kennzeichnen das Aufsatzbecken
BLANCOATTIKA. Die außergewöhnliche Randgestal-
tung mit der massiven, gleichzeitig filigranen Anmutung und den fein geformten Eckradien ist formales
und funktionales Leitmotiv und grenzt die Aktivzone
des Nassarbeitsbereichs sauber ab. Durch das Zusammenspiel von absenkbarer Armatur und verschiebbarem
Arbeitsbrett aus hochwertigem Esche-Compound lässt
sich das Becken geschickt abdecken. Alle Systemkomponenten folgen konsequent der minimalistisch ausba-
lancierten Formensprache und verleihen der Spüle ihre
ausdrucksstarke Schönheit.

Authentic material esthetics and striking product fea-
tures characterize the BLANCOATTIKA
top-mounted bowl. The exceptional rim design with the
solid yet filigree appeal and delicately shaped corner radii
is the formal and functional leitmotif, and cleanly delin-
eates the active zone of the wet working area. The inter-
play between the retractable mixer tap and movable
chopping board made of a high quality ash compound
allows the bowl to be neatly covered. The system compo-
nents all consistently follow the minimalistically balanced
design language, and give the sink its highly expressive
beauty.

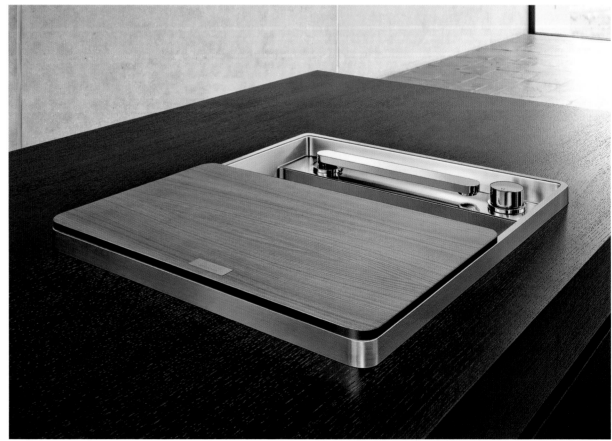

PRODUCT
ACQUA COOL
Kühlkaraffe
Cool carafe

DESIGN
Flöz Industrie Design
Essen, Germany

MANUFACTURER
blomus GmbH
Sundern, Germany

Im Sommer quillt der Kühlschrank schnell über mit kalt gestellten Flaschen. Da hilft die neue ACQUA COOL-Karaffe. Mit der so einfachen wie genialen Lösung werden Getränke hygienisch, unkompliziert und elegant gekühlt und kalt gehalten. Die Kühlstäbe werden vorab im Gefrierfach gefrostet (Material = Kunststoff), sie können also nicht platzen. Kühlflüssigkeit ist Wasser. Ist das Getränk in die Karaffe gefüllt, wird der Kühlstab eingesetzt. Die Führung ist dabei so gestaltet, dass der Stab nicht an das Karaffenglas stoßen kann. Die Karaffe kann mit und ohne Kühlstab genutzt werden. Dank der großen Einfüllöffnung stets leichtes Befüllen und Reinigen.

In summer, the fridge is often filled to the brim with bottles that need cooling. This is when the new ACQUA COOL carafe from blomus comes in a particularly handy format. Both stylish and intelligent, the carafe is a hygienic, convenient and elegant solution for cooling drinks and keeping them chilled. The cooling elements, which are also available individually, are first frozen in the freezer. They are made from plastic, which means that they cannot burst. Water is used as a coolant. Once the drink has been filled into the carafe, the cooling element is inserted. The element is guided in such a way that it cannot knock onto the glass bottom.

PRODUCT

Böker SAGA Santoku Stonewash

Kochmesser

Kitchen knife

DESIGN

Böker Messer-Manufaktur

Jesper Voxnæs

Solingen, Germany

MANUFACTURER

Böker Messer-Manufaktur

Solingen, Germany

Das innovative SAGA Santoku richtet sich mit seinem außergewöhnlichen skandinavischen Design an den kochbegeisterten Mann. Es wird in der Manufaktur in 50 Arbeitsschritten komplett von Hand gefertigt. Als Klingenstahl wird für den durchgehenden Erl hochwertiger 440C verwendet, ein Stahl, der sich im Jagd- und Outdoor-Bereich bewährt hat. Erstmalig wird ein Stonewash-Klingenfinish angeboten, das den Messern höchste Gleiteigenschaften verleiht und sie unempfindlich gegenüber Kratzern macht. Der ergonomische Griff besteht aus dem rutschfesten, glasfaserverstärkten Kunststoff G10. Einen Akzent setzen die roten Fiberunterlagen und die Hohlnieten.

The innovative SAGA Santoku with its extraordinary scandinavian design addresses the male cooking enthusiasts. It is manufactured in the knife-manufactory, Solingen in 50 worksteps completely by hand. For the full tang construction the high quality blade steel 440C is used. This reliable steel is very successful in the hunting and outdoor market. For the first time we offer a "stonewash" blade finish. It upgrades the existing cutting performance, as well as providing extreme resistance against scratches. The ergonomic handles are made of anti-slip and indestructible G-10. A design accent are the red fiber and the large hollow rivets.

PRODUCT

T4ONE Tableware
Tee-Karussell
Tea carousel

DESIGN

Flip Ziedes Des Plantes
Amsterdam, Netherlands

MANUFACTURER

Brabantia International B. V.
Valkenswaard, Netherlands

Dieses ansprechende Tee-Karussell ist ein unbedingtes Muss für jeden Teeliebhaber. Ein Design mit einer Vielzahl von versteckten Neuheiten und Gegensätzen in Materialien. Genießen Sie den Moment des Teetrinkens. Bewahren Sie die Teebeutel oder Teeblätter in fünf Fächern auf, die entnommen werden können und daher einfach zu reinigen sind. Das Design des integrierten Griffes ermöglicht das Heben und Tragen der Teebox mit einer Hand. Haben Sie ein Auge für das Unsichtbare durch Öffnung des Soft-Touch-Deckels und legen ihn unter das Karussell. Durch den integrierten Drehmechanismus haben Sie direkten Zugriff auf die verschiedenen Geschmackserlebnisse!

A must-have for tea-lovers is this high appealing tea carousel. A cheeky design with a lot of hidden novelties and opposites attract in used materials. Stands-out and perfectly suitable for daily use. Truly enjoy your tea-drinking moment. Store your tea bags as well as tea leaves separately together in five compartments which can be taken out and therefore easily cleaned. The sophisticated design of the integrated handle assure to lift and carry the tea box in one hand. Have an eye for the unseen by opening the soft-touch lid, place it underneath and caused by an integrated rotation-mechanism – swing it – picking a new taste delights!

PRODUCT
Siemens KM40FS20TI
Multidoor-Kühlschrank
Multidoor refrigerator

DESIGN
Siemens Electrogeräte GmbH
Christoph Becke, Max Eicher, Tim Richter, Zhang Wei
München, Germany

MANUFACTURER
BSH Home Appliances (China) Co., Ltd.
Nanjing, China

Dies ist ein neuartiges 4-Temperatur- und Klimazonen-
Kältegerät für den asiatischen Markt. Hochwertige
Glastürfronten und Metall-Stangengriffe kombiniert
mit integrierten Schubladengriffen stehen für ein
eigenständiges, zeitloses Design. Im Innenraum sorgen
Schalen mit Vollauszügen, flexibel höhenverstellbare
Türabsteller und Glasplatten für perfekte Platzorgani-
sation. Im 0°-Temperaturbereich können Fisch, Fleisch
und Gemüse perfekt frisch gehalten werden. Alle Aus-
stattungsteile sind an Griffen und belasteten Bereichen
mit robusten Material-Applikationen verstärkt, das Design ist funktional, formal reduziert und langlebig.

This is an innovative refrigerator model with four tem-
perature zones for the Asian market. Its high-quality
glass panel doors and tubular metal handles combined
with integrated drawer handles stand for a unique yet
timeless design. Fully telescopic drawers, adjustable
door bins and glass shelves make organizing the interior
a snap. The zero-degree zone (32°F) is perfect for keep-
ing fish, meat and vegetables fresh. All interior parts fea-
ture robust reinforcements on handles and in high-wear-
ing areas. The design is functional, clean and timeless.

PRODUCT

Bosch KMF40S50TI
Multidoor-Kühlschrank
Multidoor refrigerator

DESIGN

Robert Bosch Hausgeräte GmbH
Ralph Staud, Thomas Tischer, Tim Richter,
Yao Xingen
München, Germany
Eisele Kuberg Design
Neu-Ulm, Germany

MANUFACTURER

BSH Home Appliances (China) Co., Ltd.
Nanjing, China

Der neue Multidoor-Kühlschrank von Bosch setzt Maßstäbe bei Design und Technik. Durch die Doppeltüre wird das Kühlgut ergonomisch ideal und großzügig auf Augenhöhe präsentiert. Das Touch-Control-Display hinter Glas ermöglicht leichte Bedienung. Das innovative flexible Storage-System im Innenraum ist ideal zum Aufbewahren feiner Speisen. Das Außendesign zeichnet sich durch den konsequenten Einsatz von Echtmaterialien aus. So sind Türe und Schubladen aus ColorGlass und die Griffe komplett aus gebürstetem Metall. Die edlen Materialien machen den Kühlschrank zum Kühlmöbel, das sich ideal in die offene Küche und Wohnwelt integriert.

Bosch's new Multidoor refrigerator is a benchmark in design and technology. Through its double-door, food is presented in an ergonomic and generous way at eye level. The Touch control display behind glass enables easy control. Part of the interior design is the innovative flexible storage system which is ideal to store delicate dishes. The exterior design is defined by a consistent use of real materials. Door and drawer front panels are made of ColorGlass and the handles are made of brushed metal. These classy materials transform the refrigerator into a cooling-furniture which matches the architecture of an open kitchen perfectly.

PRODUCT

YOU
Salz- und Pfeffermühle
Salt and pepper mill

DESIGN

Carsten Gollnick Design
Berlin, Germany

MANUFACTURER

CARL MERTENS Besteckfarbrik GmbH
Solingen, Germany

Die neue Mühlenserie von CARL MERTENS überzeugt
mit einem ungewöhnlichen Materialdialog aus Edelstahl, Textil und Leder: Salz bzw. Pfeffer befinden sich
in einem Stoffsäckchen, das als separates Element ober-
halb des Mahlwerks angeordnet ist. Beim Würzen kann
man durch den Stoff die Struktur von Salzkristallen und
Pfefferkörnern fühlen. So wird das Mahlen zu einem
sinnlichen Erlebnis. Charmantes Detail: Zum Verschließen wird der Stoff über einen Lederriemen gerollt und
mit einem hübschem Chicago-Knopf geschlossen.

*The new grinder by CARL MERTENS impresses with the
unusual material dialogue of stainless steel, textile and
leather: salt and / or pepper are stored in a little fabric
sack located above the grinder as a separate element.
While seasoning, one is able to feel the structure of the
salt crystals and pepper corns through the fabric. Grinding becomes a sensuous experience. Charming detail: to
close the little sack the fabric is rolled over a leather
thong and secured with a pretty Chicago button.*

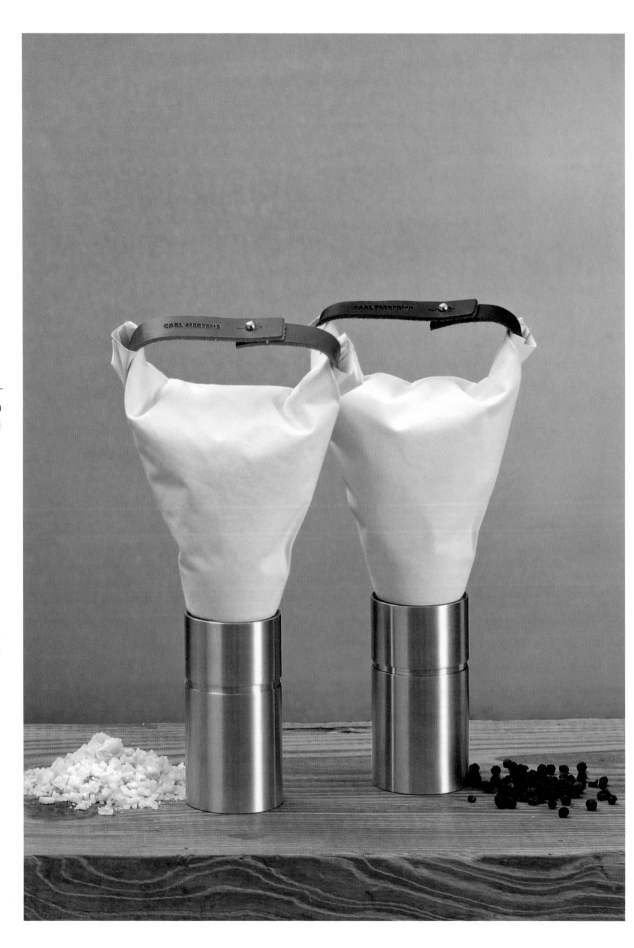

PRODUCT
Seasons
Küchenausstattung
Kitchen and serving ware

DESIGN
nownao Inc.
Nao Tamura
New York, NY, United States of America

MANUFACTURER
COVO S. R. L.
Roma, Italy

Die Serie Seasons interpretiert funktionsbetonte Küchenausstattung neu, inspiriert von Natur und Technologie. Sie wirkt wie durch die Linse der japanischen Kultur wahrgenommen. Jede Servierschale ist so flexibel wie ein echtes Blatt und erfüllt vielseitige Zwecke. Dank der Vorzüge des Silikonmaterials lassen sich die Produkte zum Verstauen platzsparend zusammenrollen, sind perfekt für den Gebrauch in Backöfen und Mikrowellen geeignet und vertragen sogar die häufige Reinigung im Geschirrspüler. Jedes Blatt hat seine eigene Form. Aufgerollt sind die Servierschalen stapelbar und wirken dann wie eine kunstvolle Skulptur.

Seasons is an interpretation of functional kitchen and serving ware, inspired by nature and technology, as seen through the cultural lens of Japan. Like a real leaf, each serving dish is flexible and multi-purpose. Thanks to the benefits of silicone, they roll up for storage for perfect use in ovens and microwaves, and are able to withstand repeated dishwasher cleaning. Each leaf has its own shape. The pieces are stackable when open, creating a sculptural display of serving ware.

PRODUCT
The Giving Tree
Luftfilter und - wäscher
Humidifier and air purifier

DESIGN
Coway
Hun-jung Choi, Sung-wook Jung
Seoul, South Korea

MANUFACTURER
Coway
Seoul, South Korea

Dieser Luftfilter gibt im Wohnzimmer oder im Büro ultrafeine 0,1-nm-Partikel ab, die die Ausbreitung von Mikroben hemmen und Desinfektionsmittel überflüssig machen. Das bojenähnlich gebaute Gerät führt im oberen Bereich keinen Strom, sodass Sie das Wasser direkt in das Gitter oben am Gerät füllen können. Das Design ist an das Kinderbuch „The Giving Tree" angelehnt. Das Gerät gibt antimikrobielle Stoffe und Phytonzide über das integrierte Terpen-Modul ab und weckt im Benutzer durch die Zugabe von Aromen das Gefühl, mitten im Wald zu stehen. Das Gerät besteht zudem aus recycelbaren ABS-Kunststoffen.

Installed in living rooms or offices to purify indoor air and control humidity, this humidifier disperses ultrafine 0.1 nm particles, which inhibit growth of microbes and remove the need for humidifier disinfectants. The top water-feeding system, fitted with a no-power, buoy-type indicator bar, allows you to pour water directly into the top grill. Taking the motif from "The Giving Tree", a children's book, the system emits antimicrobials and phytoncides from the inner terpene module, creating a "bathing in the woods" environment with aromatherapy effects. It is also made of recyclable ABS.

PRODUCT
ZEUS(APD-1212BH10)
Luftreiniger und Luftentfeuchter
Air purifier and dehumidifier

DESIGN
Coway
Hun-jung Choi, Jong-keon Jeon
Seoul, South Korea

MANUFACTURER
Coway
Seoul, South Korea

Dieser Luftentfeuchter /-wäscher reinigt die Raumluft mithilfe seiner modernen 5-Stufenfilter und sorgt dank leistungsstarker Kühlkondensation/Entfeuchtungsfunktion für frische Luft. Normalerweise werden die Griffe an vergleichbaren Geräten verborgen oder minimal ausgeführt, um die Aufmerksamkeit auf das Design zu lenken. Zur Betonung der Mobilität wurden in diesem Fall die Griffe für ein stimmiges Äußeres in den Vordergrund gerückt. Die Bedienelemente und die Anzeigen für Filterwechsel, Wassertank usw. befinden sich auf der rechten Seite und unterstreichen das schlichte und benutzerfreundliche Design.

Zeus is a dehumidifier / air purifier that cleans indoor air by getting rid of pollutants with its state-of-the-art, five-step filters. It provides fresh air with its strong, cooling condensation/dehumidifying function. Usually, there is a tendency to hide or minimize the handles on existing products, since the handles take away from the design. However, to emphasize mobility, this product features its handles, harmonizing its appearance. With its function-related elements, such as controls, filter replacement, water tank, etc. concentrated on the top right side, the product design is simple and easy to use.

PRODUCT
Aroma Genie-Casa
Aroma-Diffusor
Aroma diffusor

DESIGN
TOAST Living
Yungshiun Lin, Cheng-Yuan Hsieh
Taipei, Taiwan

MANUFACTURER
Day & Day Trading Corp.
Taipei, Taiwan

Geh nach einem anstrengenden Arbeitstag einfach nach Hause und aktiviere deinen Lieblingsduft. Lass dich von ihm in einen brandneuen Tag entführen. Mit 2,5 Millionen Ultraschallvibrationen pro Sekunde gibt dieser Aromatherapie-Dispenser erfrischende ätherische Öle an die Luft ab. Der Duftvernebler Aroma Genie-Casa mit seiner Schwarzfels-Porzellanhülle wurde vom TOAST-Design-Team aus Taiwan entwickelt. Das Designkonzept leitet sich von der lebendigen Philosophie von Reinheit, Achtsamkeit und Erkenntnis ab. Das Gerät kreiert einen modernen Duft für das Leben in der Stadt und bringt dabei das Gefühl von „Zuhause" zurück.

After a busy work day, go home and light your favorite fragrance. Let the scent welcome you to a brand new day. At 2.5 million ultrasound vibrations per second, this aroma machine releases the refreshing essential oil into the air. The Aroma Genie-Casa with the black-rock porcelain shell was developed by Taiwan's TOAST design team. The design concept is from the living philosophy of purity, consideration and perception. The Casa creates a modern scent for life in the city and aims for the memorable fragrance of "home."

PRODUCT
TURMIX Linie
Küchengeräte-Linie
Line of kitchen appliances

DESIGN
2nd West
Michael Thurnherr, Manuel Gamper
Rapperswil, Switzerland

MANUFACTURER
DKB Household Switzerland AG
Zürich, Switzerland

TURMIX ist seit 70 Jahren der Schweizer Inbegriff für hochwertige Haushaltsgeräte. Die Arbeit in der Küche und das Zubereiten von Speisen zu vereinfachen, steht dabei im Fokus. Diese Tradition nimmt TURMIX wieder auf – Haushaltsgeräte zu entwickeln für die, die mit Hingabe kochen. Der Stand-, Stab- und Handmixer wie auch Entsafter wurden auf Langlebigkeit, Effizienz in ihrer primären Funktion sowie Einfachheit in der Handhabung und Reinigung getrimmt. Die Motoren sind kraftvoll, leise und vibrationsarm. Form und Materialien sind ergonomisch, schmeicheln der Hand und lassen bereits das Kochen zu einem ästhetischen Augenschmaus werden.

TURMIX has epitomized top-quality Swiss household appliances for 70 years. The focus is on simplifying kitchen tasks, enabling users to prepare wonderful dishes with minimum effort. TURMIX is maintaining the tradition of developing household appliances for those who cook with passion. The blender, stick mixer, hand mixer and juicer have been designed with three main aims: durability, efficiency in terms of their primary functions and simplicity of use and cleaning. The motors are powerful yet quiet and produce only a minimum of vibration. The design and materials are ergonomic and turn the cooking experience into a real feast for the eyes.

kitchen / household

PRODUCT
Garject
Knoblauchpresse
Garlic press

DESIGN
Dreamfarm
Philip Howieson, Alex Gransbury
Brisbane, Australia

MANUFACTURER
Dreamfarm
Brisbane, Australia

Garject ist das einzige Knoblauch-Utensil, das unge-schälte Knoblauchzehen presst, Knoblauchreste beim Öffnen automatisch ablöst und die Schale anschließend auf Knopfdruck entfernt. Diese einzigartige Entwick-lung reinigt sich mühelos selbstständig, ohne dass der Benutzer überhaupt mit dem gepressten Knoblauch oder der Schale in Berührung kommt. Es wird kein Messer oder anderes Werkzeug zum Entfernen des Knoblauchs benötigt, und der „Peel Eject"-Knopf gibt dem Anwen-der völlige Kontrolle. Garject hat einen robusten, leicht industriellen Look, der die gewünschten Stärke in einem solchen kompromisslosen Küchenwerkzeug vermittelt.

Garject is the only garlic tool that presses unpeeled garlic cloves, automatically scrapes itself clean and then ejects the garlic peel into the bin. The unique design seamlessly cleans itself without the user ever needing to touch pressed garlic or the peel. The user doesn't need a knife or other tool to scrape it clean, and the peel eject button gives the user complete control with a playful sense of accomplishment. The garlic press remains a hardcore kitchen tool, so it is apt that the styling of Garject uses strong angular forms. The rugged, slightly industrial look conveys the strength of such an uncompromising kitchen tool.

PRODUCT
Dyson Hot AM04
Heizlüfter
Fan heater

DESIGN
Dyson Ltd.
James Dyson,
Dyson Research, Design and Development Team
Malmesbury, Wiltshire, United Kingdom

MANUFACTURER
Dyson GmbH
Köln, Germany

Der Dyson Hot-Heizlüfter heizt mit großer Reichweite
für schnelle Raumerwärmung und kann von 1 bis 37 °C
eingestellt werden. Sobald die eingestellte Temperatur
erreicht ist, schaltet sich das Gerät aus. Unter Anwendung der patentierten Air Multiplier™-Technologie wird
Luft durch ein schraubenförmiges Antriebsrad einge-
saugt und durch eine 2,5 mm breite Öffnung innerhalb
des Luftrings beschleunigt. Auf diese Weise wird ein
Luftstrahl erzeugt, der über eine tragflächenförmige
Rampe fließt und so seine Richtung kanalisiert. Die um-
liegende Luft wird mit in den Luftstrom gesaugt und
um das sechsfache verstärkt.

*The Dyson Hot™ fan heater heats with long range for
fast room heating. It can be set between 1 and 37 °C to
heat a room. When it hits the desired temperature, it
monitors the room temperature by measuring surrounding air. If a drop is detected, the heater turns back on to
maintain the set temperature. Using patented Air Multi-
plier™ technology, air is drawn in through a mixed flow
impeller. It is then accelerated through a 2.5 mm aperture set within the loop amplifier. This creates a jet of hot
air which passes over an airfoil-shaped ramp channeling
its direction. Surrounding air is drawn into the airflow,
amplifying it six times.*

PRODUCT

original green cup
Becher
Cup

DESIGN

ecojun company
Seoul, South Korea

MANUFACTURER

ecojun company
Seoul, South Korea

Das Design des nachhaltigen Produkts ähnelt Papierbechern. Eine Becherspalte verhindert, dass die Teebeutel in den Becher rutschen. Der qualifizierte 100 % biologisch abbaubare Werkstoff auf Basis von Mais enthält keine schädliche Umwelthormone. Nach Entsorgung löst er sich durch Mikroorganismen auf und stößt keine schädlichen Gase bei der Verbrennung aus. Nur RoHS-zertifizierte Farbstoffe sind verwendet und der ganze Prozess ist auf Umweltschutz ausgerichtet. Die Verpackung aus 100 %-Recyclingpapier wird im Hinblick auf die Abfallverminderung mit verschiedenen Produkten (z. B. Untersetzer, Getränkehalter) kombiniert.

Original green cup is an ecofriendly product designed similar to cups commonly used in coffee shops. Also "V" shaped crack on the top helps to keep your teabag from falling into your cup. Original green cup is made of 100 % biodegradable corn starch plastic(certificated in Korea), so environmental hormones do not come out with the hot water. It decomposes when it is buried also emits no harmful gases when it is incinerated. We use RoHS ink from Germany to print, so we have considered all of processes (life circle assessment-LCA). Packaging is made of 100 % recycled paper and combined various ideas (a cup saucer/holder) to reduce waste.

original green cup

4R Manual
Original Green Cup

'original green cup' is the eco-friendly and LCA-conducted product by green design

Reduce
made of biodegradable corn starch

Redesign
designed for user convenience

Reuse
the sleeve made of coffee burlap sack

Recycle · Reuse
the cup holder made of 100% recycled paper packaging

PRODUCT
Ultramix / PRO
Stabmixer
Stick mixer

DESIGN
Electrolux AB
Electrolux Group Design
Stockholm, Sweden

MANUFACTURER
Electrolux AB
Stockholm, Sweden

Electrolux hat eine starke Tradition und Erfahrung in Produkten für die professionelle Küche. Der Ultramix / Pro-Stickmixer bringt professionelle und leistungsstarke Funktionen. Der einzigartige Fuß wurde von unserer professionellen Linie inspiriert. Das Messer und die Glockenform erzeugen einen Vortex-Effekt, der die Nahrung in die Messer saugt und so für ein sehr feines Ergebnis sorgt. Die offene Glocke verhindert das Nahrung stecken bleibt, während die Anti-Splash-Form Ihre Küche sauber hält. Das gesamte Design ist eine einfache, aber elegante Kombination von Profi- und Konsumer Performance.

"Inspired by our professional chefs. Designed for You."
Electrolux has a strong tradition and experience in products for the professional kitchen. The Ultramix / Pro stickmixer brings professional and high performance features to your home. The unique foot was inspired by our professional line. The knife and the bell shape creates a vortex effect, which sucks the food into the blades and thus provides a very fine result. The open bell prevents food getting stuck, while the anti-splash-form keeps your kitchen clean. The overall design is simple yet elegant. Special emphasis was placed on the ergonomically designed handle and slim design.

PRODUCT

Zanussi New Quadro
Kompakt-Produktreihe
Compact product range

DESIGN

Electrolux Group Design EMEA
Stockholm, Sweden

MANUFACTURER

Electrolux Major Appliances EMEA
Stockholm, Sweden

Einfache und einfach zu bedienende Geräte, angelehnt
an die erfolgreiche Zanussi-„Quadro"- Kompaktback-
ofenreihe mit dem unverwechselbaren vertikalen kurzen
Griff finden Sie jetzt in einer klaren architektonischen
Küchenumgebung. Einzigartige Designelemente: Griff
in unverwechselbarer Bogenform, bernsteinfarbene
LEDs und schwarzes getöntes Glas mit Punktmuster.
Der Grundgedanke: ein müheloses Leben zu Hause mit
einfach zu handhabenden Bedienblenden, großen Knöpfen und Touch-Controls, unentbehrlichen Programmen
und unverwechselbaren Symbolen in einem klaren architektonischen Rahmen.

*Taking inspiration from the successful Zanussi "Quadro"
compact oven family, a range of simple and easy-to-use
appliances has been created that builds on the distinctive vertical alignment of the short handle and recreates
the same impact within the clean and architectural
kitchen environment. Unique design elements for the
compact ovens include a distinctive arched handle
shape, amber LEDs and black tinted glass with a dotted
pattern. The range is built based on the concept of effortless home life, with easy-to-use control panels, large
knobs and touch controls, essential programs and distinctive graphics in a clear and architectural frame.*

PRODUCT
Electrolux 2D oven
Backöfen-Produktreihe
Ovens product range

DESIGN
Electrolux Group Design EMEA
Stockholm, Sweden

MANUFACTURER
Electrolux Major Appliances EMEA
Stockholm, Sweden

Die neuen Backöfen Electrolux 2D der „Inspiration Range" besitzen klare, architektonische Linien und sind insgesamt schlicht. Das Design der Bedienblenden ist modern – Edelstahl hinter Glas. Daher sind sie leicht zu reinigen. Verschiedene Bedienelemente stehen zur Auswahl – Sensortasten, Drehknöpfe, Tasten – um den Bedarf unterschiedlicher Anwender abzudecken, damit sie aus 90 voreingestellten Garprogrammen wählen können. Weitere Designelemente, wie das größte Backblech auf dem Markt, flexible Teleskopschienen und der gedämpfte Schließmechanismus der Tür ergänzen diese Premiumreihe.

The new Electrolux 2D ovens from "The Inspiration Range" have clean, architectural lines and an overall simplicity. The control panels are designed to be modern and easy to clean, with glass behind stainless steel. Different controls are available – from touch keys to rotaries and buttons – to meet the needs of different users and let them choose from among 90 preset cooking programs. Other design elements such as the largest baking tray on the market, flexible telescopic runners and a soft-closing door system contribute to create this premium range.

kitchen / household

PRODUCT
Electrolux 3D oven
Backöfen-Produktreihe
Ovens product range

DESIGN
Electrolux Group Design EMEA
Stockholm, Sweden

MANUFACTURER
Electrolux Major Appliances EMEA
Stockholm, Sweden

Das Design der neuen Backöfen Electrolux 3D der „Inspiration Range" ist exklusiv: Bedienblende unter Glas auf Edelstahl, um die Reinheit der Materialien hervorzuheben. Weiße LED-Symbole sind in der gesamten Produktreihe vorhanden und verschiedene Bedienelemente, wie Sensortasten, Drehknöpfe und Tasten decken den Bedarf unterschiedlicher Anwender ab. Die Vielfalt der Funktionen wird mit Grafiken auf der Tür abgebildet und weitere Designelemente, wie das größte Backblech auf dem Markt, flexible Teleskopschienen und der gedämpfte Schließmechanismus der Tür ergänzen diese Premiumreihe.

The new Electrolux 3D ovens from "The Inspiration Range" feature an exclusive design with the control panel glass overlaid on stainless steel to highlight the pureness of the materials. White LED icons are present throughout the entire range and different controls are available – from touch keys to rotaries and buttons – to meet the needs of different users. The large capacity is shown with graphic patterns on the door, and other design elements such as the largest baking tray on the market, flexible telescopic runners and a soft-closing door system contribute to create this premium range.

PRODUCT
Electrolux FreshPlus
Kühlschrank-Produktreihe
Fridge product range

DESIGN
Electrolux Group Design EMEA
Stockholm, Sweden

MANUFACTURER
Electrolux Major Appliances EMEA
Stockholm, Sweden

Diese Designlinie der „Inspiration Range" zeichnet sich durch ein elektronisches Sensordisplay auf der Tür und weiße LED oder Bedienelemente oben hinter der Tür aus. Das Premiumdesign im Inneren ist klar und bietet Platz für die Lagerung unterschiedlicher Lebensmittel in verschiedenen Staufächern und -räumen. Die von Kühlschränken in Restaurantküchen abgeleitete Twin-Tech-Kühltechnik, bei der zwei getrennte Kühlkreisläufe für die Kühl-Gefrierkombination verwendet werden, liefert im Kühlschrank das optimale Klima für länger anhaltende Frische und verhindert die Vereisung im Gefrierschrank.

This design line from "The Inspiration Range" features an electronic touch display on the door with white LEDs or top controls behind the door. The interior has a pure and premium design that offers room to store all types of groceries with different compartments and spaces. The TwinTech cooling technology, inspired by refrigerators found in restaurant kitchens, uses two cooling systems for the fridge and freezer unit to provide the optimal climate inside the fridge for longer lasting freshness and prevent any build up of frost in the freezer.

PRODUCT
Electrolux Compact
Kompakt-Produktreihe
Compact product range

DESIGN
Electrolux Group Design EMEA
Stockholm, Sweden

MANUFACTURER
Electrolux Major Appliances EMEA
Stockholm, Sweden

Die Produktreihe-Electrolux-3-D- Compact besteht u. a.
aus Kompaktbacköfen, Kaffeemaschinen und Warm-
halteschubladen. Sie ermöglicht die Kombination der
von Ihnen benötigten Geräte auf modische und wirkungs-
volle Art sowohl in horizontaler als auch in vertikaler
Ausrichtung zu den anderen Electrolux-Kücheneinbau-
geräten der „Inspiration Range". Das Design ist exklusiv:
Bedienblende unter Glas auf Edelstahl mit charakteristi-
schem Erscheinungsbild. Weiße LED-Symbole sind in
der gesamten Produktreihe vorhanden und verschiedene Bedienelemente, wie Sensortasten, Drehknöpfe und
Tasten decken den Bedarf unterschiedlicher Anwender
ab.

*The Electrolux 3D Compact product range consists of
compact ovens, coffee machines, warming drawers and
a number of other exciting products. It lets you combine
the appliances you need in an impressively stylish manner and enables both horizontal and vertical alignments
with the rest of the Electrolux built-in kitchen appliances
from "The Inspiration Range". The design is exclusive,
with the control panel glass overlaid on stainless steel
and featuring iconic flow lines. White LED icons are present throughout the entire range and different controls
are available – from touch keys to rotaries and buttons –
to meet the needs of different users.*

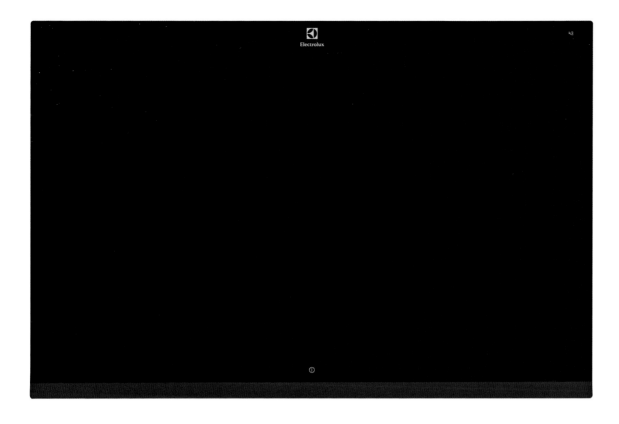

PRODUCT
Electrolux Infinite
Kochmulde
Hob

DESIGN
Electrolux Group Design EMEA
Stockholm, Sweden

MANUFACTURER
Electrolux Major Appliances EMEA
Stockholm, Sweden

InfinitePure™ weist ein randloses flaches Design mit elegantem Aussehen auf. Es ist die erste vollständig von hinten beleuchtete Kochmulde. Wenn die Kochmulde nicht benutzt wird, zeichnet sich ihre Oberfläche durch ein „klares" schwarzes Design aus und ergänzt somit das Küchendesign. Beim Gebrauch visualisiert Licht an Stelle von Druck Kochzonen sowie Bedienelemente. Mit Infinite-Induktionsfeldern passt sich der Kochbereich an die Größe des Kochgeschirrs an und liefert gleichmäßige Ergebnisse unabhängig davon, wo der Topf oder die Pfanne steht. Drehelektronik mit Direktzugriff bietet eine sofortige Wärmeregelung.

The Electrolux InifinitePure™ hob offers a seamlessly flat design with an elegant appearance. It is the first fully backlit hob. When not in use, the hob surface has a 'pure', clean black design that complements the kitchen design. When in use, light visualizes the cooking zones and controls in place of printing. With infinite induction zones the cooking area adapts to the size of the cookware to produce even results wherever you place the pan. Intuitive direct access rotary electronics offer instant heat control at the required power level.

PRODUCT
AEG Window
Abzugshaube
Hood

DESIGN
Electrolux Group Design EMEA
Stockholm, Sweden

MANUFACTURER
Electrolux Major Appliances EMEA
Stockholm, Sweden

Das Design der Abzugshauben AEG Window-Hood aus Edelstahl ist innovativ und minimalistisch und schafft in Ihrer Küche ein elegantes Ambiente. Der Hochgeschwindigkeitsmotor saugt leistungsstark und effizient alle Kochdünste ab. Elektronische Drucktasten ermöglichen genaue Einstellungen. Durch die Halogenleuchten ist der Kochbereich sehr gut sichtbar und sie dienen als angenehme Küchenbeleuchtung.

The AEG Window hood comes with an innovative and minimalistic design in stainless steel for an elegant atmosphere in your kitchen. The powerful high-speed motor delivers high performance and efficiency for cooking vapor extraction. Electronic push buttons enable precise control of the setting levels. Halogen lights provide excellent visibility for all cooking and can be used for soft lighting in the kitchen.

PRODUCT
AEG Movida
Abzugshauben-Produktreihe
Hood product range

DESIGN
Electrolux Group Design EMEA
Stockholm, Sweden

MANUFACTURER
Electrolux Major Appliances EMEA
Stockholm, Sweden

Die AEG Movida-Hood-Abzugshaube besticht durch ihr Design aus schwarzem Glas und Edelstahl, welches das modische Aussehen der 80 cm breiten Abzugshaube in der Küche betont. Ihr anspruchsvolles erstklassiges Design enthält erweiterte Funktionen zur Erfüllung hoher Leistungsstandards. Der Hochgeschwindigkeitsmotor saugt leistungsstark und effizient alle Kochdünste ab. Die vordere Abdeckung kann für einfaches Zugreifen auf den Fettfilter geöffnet werden.

The AEG Movida hood features an eye-catching design with black glass and stainless steel profiles that underscore the 80 cm-wide hood for a stylish look in the kitchen. Its sophisticated and premium design incorporates advanced features to meet high efficiency standards. The powerful motor delivers high performance and efficiency for cooking vapor extraction. The front panel opens for easy access to the grease filter.

PRODUCT
Kitchen Line
Kühlschrank-Produktreihe
Fridge product range

DESIGN
Electrolux Group Design EMEA
Stockholm, Sweden

MANUFACTURER
Electrolux Major Appliances EMEA
Stockholm, Sweden

Das Lebensmittelzentrum der Electrolux-Küchenlinie bietet ein fantastisches professionelles Design, in das sich Küchenmöbel und andere Geräte der Inspiration Range perfekt einfügen und integrieren. Das Äußere zeichnet sich durch eine klare Edelstahlfront und einen architektonischen Griff aus. Das Premiumdesign im Inneren ist klar und bietet Platz für die Lagerung unterschiedlichster Lebensmittel in verschiedenen Staufächern und -räumen. Die von Kühlschränken in Restaurantküchen abgeleitete TwinTech-Kühltechnik liefert das optimale Klima für länger anhaltende Frische und verhindert die Vereisung im Gefrierschrank.

The Electrolux Kitchen Line food centre offers stunning professional design with perfect alignment and integration for the kitchen furnishings and other appliances from "The Inspiration Range". The exteriors feature a pure, distinctive stainless steel front and an architectural handle. The interiors have a pure and premium design that offers room to store all types of groceries with different compartments and spaces. The TwinTech cooling technology, inspired by refrigerators found in restaurant kitchens, provides the optimal climate for longer lasting freshness and prevents any build up of frost in the freezer.

PRODUCT
Zanussi Casual
Abzugshaube
Hood

DESIGN
Electrolux Group Design EMEA
Stockholm, Sweden

MANUFACTURER
Electrolux Major Appliances EMEA
Stockholm, Sweden

Die Abzugshaube der Reihe Zanussi Casual-Hood ist glatt, modern und dekorativ; sie ergänzt Ihre Küche und hält sie immer frisch. Jetzt können Sie endlich die perfekte Abzugsstufe für ihre Kochbedürfnisse einstellen. Ganz gleich, ob Sie nur die Luft reinigen oder Höchstleistung wollen: Sie können aus drei Leistungsstufen und einer zusätzlichen „intensiven" Einstellung für maximalen Abzug wählen. Bedienelemente auf der Vorderseite mit Drucktasten erleichtern zusätzlich die Einstellung der richtigen Stufe.

The Zanussi Casual hood is a sleek and modern decorative hood that complements and keeps your kitchen fresh at all times. Now you can finally set the perfect extraction speed for your cooking needs. Whether you need full power or just want to refresh the air, you have three speed levels to choose from plus an "intensive" setting for maximum extraction. Front controls enhanced with push buttons make it even easier to set the right speed level.

PRODUCT
SteamSystem
Waschmaschinen-Produktreihe
Washing machine product range

DESIGN
Electrolux Group Design EMEA
Stockholm, Sweden

MANUFACTURER
Electrolux Major Appliances EMEA
Stockholm, Sweden

Professionelle Wäschereien frischen Wäsche auf und
glätten sie mit Dampf; Haushaltswaschmaschinen der
„Inspiration Range" sollen dem Nutzer die gleichen
Funktionen mit nur einem Tastendruck zur Verfügung
stellen. Verschiedene Bedienelemente decken den Bedarf unterschiedlicher Anwender ab; die Programme
werden direkt mittels Tastendruck oder verchromtem
transparentem Knopf mit hochwertiger Abdeckkappe
gewählt. Exklusives Design mit glatten Linien, klare
transparente Bedienblende in silber oder weiß, weiße
oder bernsteinfarbene Symbole und Sensortasten.

*Professional laundries freshen and dewrinkle clothes
with steam, and these domestic washing machines from
Electrolux – The Inspiration Range – have been designed
to give the user the same capabilities with the touch of a
button. Different controls are available to meet the
needs of different users, so programs can be selected
with direct touch access or through a chromed transparent knob with a premium brushed cap. They feature an
exclusive design with clean lines, a pure transparent in-
lay in silver or in white protruding on top of the control
panel, white or amber LED icons and touch buttons
throughout the entire range.*

PRODUCT
AEG Slim Backstein
Abzugshauben-Produktreihe
Hood product range

DESIGN
Electrolux Group Design EMEA
Stockholm, Sweden

MANUFACTURER
Electrolux Major Appliances EMEA
Stockholm, Sweden

Die Abzugshauben der Produktreihe AEG Slim Back-
stein-Hood bieten ein elegantes erstklassiges Design in
verschiedenen Abmessungen mit erweiterten Funktionen zur Erfüllung hoher Leistungsstandards. Die Touch-
Controls aus Glas ermöglichen genaue Einstellungen.
Der Hochgeschwindigkeitsmotor saugt leistungsstark
und effizient alle Kochdünste ab. Durch die Halogenleuchten ist der Kochbereich sehr gut sichtbar und sie
dienen als angenehme Küchenbeleuchtung.

*The AEG Slim Backstein hood product range comes
with an elegant high-end design in different dimensions combined with advanced features to meet high
efficiency standards. The glass touch controls enable
precise setting levels. The powerful motor delivers high
performance and efficiency for cooking vapor extraction. Halogen lights provide excellent visibility for all
cooking and can be used for soft lighting in the kitchen.*

PRODUCT
Zanussi Ultra Flat
Gaskochmulde
Gas hob

DESIGN
Electrolux Group Design EMEA
Stockholm, Sweden

MANUFACTURER
Electrolux Major Appliances EMEA
Stockholm, Sweden

Die neue 75-cm-Gaskochmulde von Zanussi aus Edelstahl bietet eine größere Kochfläche für das Aufstellen aller Töpfe und Pfannen. Der Wok-Brenner ist bequem auf der linken Seite platziert, um flexibler zu sein, wenn man mehr kochen oder größeres Geschirr verwenden möchte. Das moderne ultraflache Design macht die Reinigung wirklich einfach, und die Selbstentzündung eignet sich hervorragend für die Bedienung mit einer Hand. Das Design der Topfträger ist charakteristisch, es fügt sich in die meisten Küchen ein; das Design der Knöpfe ist ergonomisch ausgerichtet.

The new Zanussi 75 cm stainless steel gas hob offers a wider cooking space to accommodate all pots and pans. The wok burner is conveniently placed on the left-hand side for greater flexibility to cook more or use bigger dishes. The modern ultra flat design makes cleaning very simple, and the auto-ignition is great for one-handed operation. Pan supports have an iconic design that fits in most kitchens, and knobs are designed for the best ergonomy.

PRODUCT
RealLife Dishwasher
Geschirrspüler-Produktreihe
Dishwashers product range

DESIGN
Electrolux Group Design EMEA
Stockholm, Sweden

MANUFACTURER
Electrolux Major Appliances EMEA
Stockholm, Sweden

Die halbintegrierten Geschirrspüler der Electrolux-Inspiration-Range-RealLife bieten ein erstklassiges, unverwechselbares, modernes Aussehen. Ihr Design mit integrierter sichtbarer Bedienblende ist exklusiv. Der typische invertierte Griff fügt sich harmonisch in jede erstklassige Küche ein und eine intuitive Bedienoberfläche mit weißen oder bernsteinfarbenen LEDs bietet ultimative Flexibilität zur Abdeckung der Bedürfnisse jedes Haushalts. Der XXL Bottich und der einzigartige Sprüharm sind mit einem intelligenten „AutoFlex"-Programm kombiniert, das leistungsfähige Einstellungen mit nur einem Tastendruck zulässt.

The Inspiration Range's RealLife Semi-integrated Dishwashers from Electrolux have a premium, distinctive and modern look. They feature an exclusive design with an integrated, visible control panel. The characteristic inverted handle blends smoothly into any premium kitchen and intuitive user interfaces with white or amber LEDs give you ultimate flexibility to meet the needs of any home. The XXL tub and the unique spray arm are combined with an intelligent "AutoFlex" program that gives you access to efficient settings with the touch of a button.

PRODUCT
Electrolux Pearl
Abzugshauben-Produktreihe
Hood product range

DESIGN
Electrolux Group Design EMEA
Stockholm, Sweden

MANUFACTURER
Electrolux Major Appliances EMEA
Stockholm, Sweden

Das Design der Abzugshauben Electrolux Pearl-Hood
basiert auf einem charakteristischen Erscheinungsbild,
das auf die gesamte „Inspiration Range" abgestimmt
ist. Die Bedienblende aus Glas auf Edelstahl unterstreicht
die klaren Materialien. Einfaches Berühren der Bedienelemente aus Glas erlaubt eine stufenlose Einstellung
der gewünschten Absaug- und Beleuchtungsintensität.
Die Sensortechnologie bietet mehr Freiraum für Kreati-
vität in der Küche, während sich die Abzugshaube um
die Kochdünste kümmert. Diese Produktreihe ist zusätzlich mit Perimeterabsaugung ausgestattet, damit
Gerüche und Rauch optimal entfernt werden.

*The Electrolux Pearl Hood range is designed with iconic
flow lines to complement "The Inspiration Range". The
control panel is glass overlaid on stainless steel and highlights the pureness of the materials. Pure touch on glass
controls enable smooth setting of the desired absorption
speed level and light illumination. Sensor technology offers increased freedom to be creative in the kitchen,
while the cooker hood takes care of cooking fumes. This
product range also features Perimeter Aspiration for perfect removal of odors and smoke.*

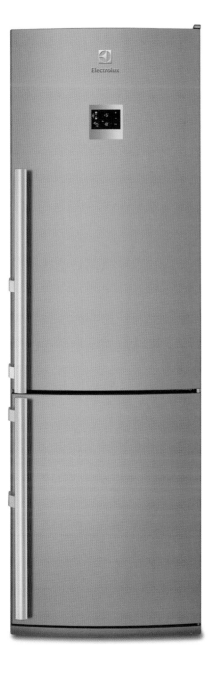

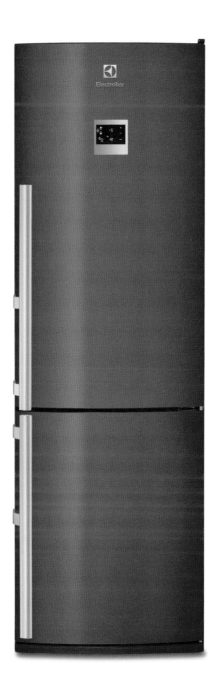

PRODUCT
Colour Line
Kühlschrank-Produktreihe
Fridge product range

DESIGN
Electrolux Group Design EMEA
Stockholm, Sweden

MANUFACTURER
Electrolux Major Appliances EMEA
Stockholm, Sweden

Diese Designlinie der „Inspiration Range" zeichnet sich durch zeitgemäßes Design und herausragendes Aussehen, fantastische Leistung und fachgerechte Technologie aus, die Lebensmittel länger frisch hält. Sie ist in vier verschiedenen Farben lieferbar: schwarzer Edelstahl, rot, braun oder grün mit elektronischem Sensordisplay auf silbernem Feld auf der Tür und weißen LED. Das Premiumdesign im Inneren ist klar und bietet Platz für die Lagerung unterschiedlicher Lebensmittel in verschiedenen Staufächern und -räumen.

This design line from Electrolux – The Inspiration Range – features contemporary design and outstanding looks together with stunning performance and professional technology that keeps food fresher for longer. It comes in four distinct colors: black stainless steel, red, brown or green, with electronic touch display on a silver panel on the door with white LEDs. The interior has a pure and premium design that offers room to store all types of groceries with different compartments and spaces.

PRODUCT
Zanussi Curva
Abzugshauben Produktreihe
Hood product range

DESIGN
Electrolux Group Design EMEA
Stockholm, Sweden

MANUFACTURER
Electrolux Major Appliances EMEA
Stockholm, Sweden

Die neue Abzugshauben-Reihe Zanussi Curva besteht
aus Abzugshauben mit geschwungenem Glas, die ins
Auge springen und sich hervorragend in moderne
wohnliche Küchen einfügen. Schlichtheit ist eine ihrer
großen Stärken; die maximale Leistungsstufe wird
durch einmaliges Berühren eingestellt, um Kochdünste
und Rauch rasch zu entfernen, und die Absaugstärken
werden mit den Druckknöpfen gewählt. Besondere
Sorgfalt wurde auf das Design der Beleuchtung verwendet, von angenehmer Raumbeleuchtung bis zu heller Beleuchtung des Kochbereichs dank Halogenbeleuchtung.

The new Zanussi Curva hood range is an eye-catching
collection of hoods with curved glass that blends beauti-
fully with modern, convivial kitchen styles. Simplicity is
one of its main strengths; speed is set with one touch to
quickly whisk away cooking smells and smoke, and aspi-
ration speed levels are selected with the push buttons.
Special care has been taken in the design to focus on the
lighting, from comfortable ambient lighting to bright il-
lumination of the cooking area thanks to halogen lights.

PRODUCT
Zanussi New Quadro
Backöfen-Produktreihe
Ovens product range

DESIGN
Electrolux Group Design EMEA
Stockholm, Sweden

MANUFACTURER
Electrolux Major Appliances EMEA
Stockholm, Sweden

Einfache und einfach zu bedienende Geräte, angelehnt an die erfolgreiche Zanussi-„Quadro" -Backofenfamilie mit dem unverwechselbaren vertikalen kurzen Griff finden Sie jetzt in einer klaren architektonischen Küchenumgebung. Einzigartige Designelemente: Griff in unverwechselbarer Bogenform, bernsteinfarbene LEDs und schwarzes getöntes Glas mit Punktmuster. Der Grundgedanke: ein müheloses Leben zu Hause mit einfach zu handhabenden Bedienblenden, großen Knöpfen und Touch-Controls, unentbehrlichen Programmen und unverwechselbaren Symbolen in einem klaren architektonischen Rahmen.

Taking inspiration from the successful Zanussi "Quadro" oven family, a range of simple and easy-to-use appliances has been created that builds on the distinctive vertical alignment of the short handle and recreates the same impact within the clean and architectural kitchen environment. Unique design elements for the ovens include a distinctive arched handle shape, amber LEDs and black tinted glass with a dotted pattern. The range is built based on the concept of effortless home life, with easy-to-use control panels, large knobs and touch controls, essential programs and distinctive graphics in a clear and architectural frame.

PRODUCT
Zanussi Induction
Kochfelder-Produktreihe
Hob product range

DESIGN
Electrolux Group Design EMEA
Stockholm, Sweden

MANUFACTURER
Electrolux Major Appliances EMEA
Stockholm, Sweden

Angelehnt an die erfolgreiche Zanussi- „Quadro"-
Backofenfamilie wurde eine neue Glaskeramik-Reihe
geschaffen, bei der das Design die Botschaft des Marken-
werts eines einfachen und einfach zu benutzenden Geräts bestätigt und informative Symbole den Benutzer
leiten, um ein einfaches und selbsterklärendes Kocher-
lebnis zu genießen. Dies ist Teil der Markenbotschaft:
weg von einem Industrieprodukt und hin zu einem
Küchenpartner mit einer klaren, unverwechselbaren
Persönlichkeit.

Taking inspiration from the successful Zanussi "Quadro"
oven family, a new vetroceramic range has been created
in which the design reaffirms the brand value message
of a simple and easy-to-use appliance, and where the in-
formation graphics guide users so they can enjoy a sim-
ple and self-explanatory cooking experience. This is part
of the brand message, moving away from an appliance
as an industrial product and becoming a kitchen partner
with a distinctive and clear personality.

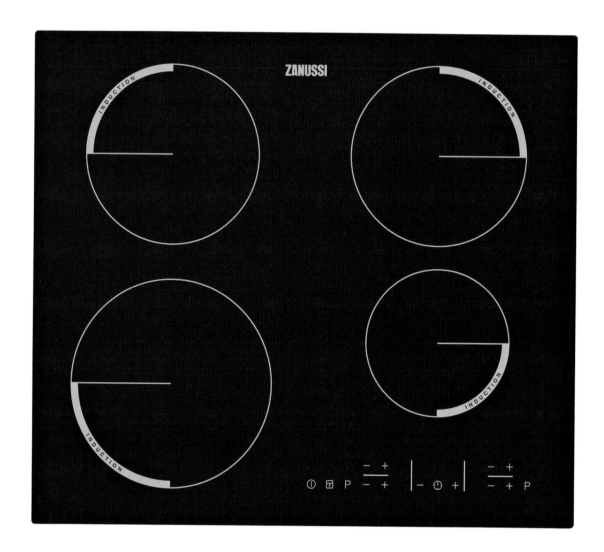

PRODUCT
Electrolux Wing
Abzugshauben-Produktreihe
Hood product range

DESIGN
Electrolux Group Design EMEA
Stockholm, Sweden

MANUFACTURER
Electrolux Major Appliances EMEA
Stockholm, Sweden

Abzugshauben der Produktreihe Electrolux Wing-Hood verfügen über eine einzigartige Materialkombination aus Glas und Edelstahl; das charakteristische Erscheinungsbild ist auf die anderen Produkte der Inspiration Range abgestimmt und gewährleistet ein optimales Äußeres in jeder Küche. Die digitalen Schieberelemente mit reinweißen LEDs ermöglichen eine stufenlose Einstellung der gewünschten Absaug- und Beleuchtungsintensität auf Grund der Möglichkeit, Stärke und Licht anzupassen. Funktionen wie die Inverter-Technologie, dimmbare LED-Beleuchtung und Perimeterabsaugung wurden entwickelt, um die Erstklassigkeit der Produktreihe zu steigern.

The Electrolux Wing Hood product range comes with a unique material combination of glass and stainless steel and features iconic flow lines to complement the other products in The Inspiration Range and create a perfect appearance in every kitchen. The digital slider controls with pure white LEDs enable smooth setting of the desired absorption speed level and light illumination thanks to the possibility to modulate speeds and light. Features such as Inverter Technology, dimmable LED lighting and Perimeter Aspiration were designed to enhance the premium quality of the product range.

PRODUCT

Sweet

Haube

Kitchen hood

DESIGN

Fabrizio Crisà

Elica Design Center

Fabriano, Italy

MANUFACTURER

Elica

Fabriano, Italy

Sweet ist die Neuinterpretation des klassischen Kaminabzugs. Die Verwendung des technischen Polymers ermöglicht das Design weicher Linien, die die Form veredeln und diesem wohl bekannten Objekt das harmonische Äußere verleihen, sodass es zu jeder Kücheneinrichtung passt. Eine schmale Linie aus glänzendem Edelstahl kennzeichnet die Abzugshaube und hebt die gewundene, harmonische Linie hervor. Das elegante perimetrische Absaugsystem ermöglicht einen schnelleren und effizienteren Dunstabzug. Die frontal angebrachten wirkungsvollen Leuchtschalter regulieren den Dunstabzug und die Beleuchtung.

Sweet is the reinterpretation of the classic icon of the chimney hood. The technopolymer construction creates smooth lines that soften the forms and create harmony in an object that will stand the test of time and can now be adapted to any kitchen environment. A thin, polished steel line helps the hood stand out, enhancing the curved, harmonious forms. The elegant perimeter extraction system makes it possible to increase the speed with which cooking fumes are captured, improving effectiveness. The illuminated capacitive commands, positioned at the front, adjust the extraction and lighting features.

PRODUCT
Tiffany
Haube
Kitchen hood

DESIGN
Fabrizio Crisà
Elica Design Center
Fabriano, Italy

MANUFACTURER
Elica
Fabriano, Italy

Die Komposition besticht durch ihre Schlichtheit: Ein einziges elegantes Element, der elegante Front-Paneel mit seinen abgerundeten Ecken, der das leistungsstarke Herz der Technologie verbirgt. Der Paneel verfügt über ein neues System mit einem Zwischenraum, der die Luft rund um den gesamten Perimeter ansaugt. In dem flachen Paneel verbirgt sich ein erstaunliches Absaugsystem, das sich über eine Länge von 3 Metern erstreckt und an allen Punkten Rauch und Kochdünste einfängt. Tiffany, aus weißem oder schwarzem Glas oder aus Silestone besitzt ein revolutionäres Infrarot-Steuersystem.

An object with a simple composition: a single element, the elegant front panel with rounded corners that conceals a high performance technological core. The panel is a new system with a cavity that captures the air conveyed from the entire perimeter. A surprising extraction system that develops in the thickness of the panel and extends for a length of 3 meters, capturing cooking fumes and vapors from any point. Tiffany, made using white glass, black glass or Silestone, has a revolutionary infrared control interface.

PRODUCT
Pump vacuum jug
Pump-Isolierkanne
Pump vacuum jug

DESIGN
Tools Design
Copenhagen, Denmark

MANUFACTURER
Eva Solo A/S
Maaloev, Denmark

Die Pump-Isolierkanne von Eva Solo ist wie geschaffen für das Picknick, für Freizeitaktivitäten oder Besprechungen, bei denen viele etwas Warmes oder Kaltes trinken möchten. Die Pump-Isolierkanne hat einen praktischen Griff und ist daher leicht mitzunehmen. Die Kanne kann auf ihrem Fuß 360 Grad gedreht werden, so dass sich alle am Tisch mit Kaffee bedienen können, ohne die Kanne herumreichen oder anheben zu müssen. Der Pumpmechanismus garantiert mindestens 30.000 Pumpbewegungen. Hergestellt aus Kunststoff mit Glaseinsatz. Fasst 1,8 Liter.

The Pump vacuum jug from Eva Solo is ideal for picnics, leisure activities or meetings where participants need a hot or cold drink. With its practical handle, the pump vacuum jug is easy to carry around. The jug can rotate 360° on its base, enabling everyone around the table to serve themselves coffee without having to move or lift the flask. The pump system is guaranteed for min. 30,000 pumps. The outer jug is made of plastic with an inner glass flask. Volume 1.8 liters.

PRODUCT
Pebel
Küchenspüle, Familie
Kitchen sink, range

DESIGN
Franke
Product Line Color
Falkirk, United Kingdom
Cramasie Ltd.
Simon Salter
Edinburgh, United Kingdom

MANUFACTURER
Franke
Product Line Color
Falkirk, United Kingdom

Franke hat das Pebel-Sortiment von Granit-Spülbecken geschaffen, um die neuesten Trends in der Küche zu erobern. Jüngst war ein Küchendesign inklusive des Spülbeckens elementar, aber die neuesten Trends zeigen die Wiedereinführung moderner Kurven. Das Pebel-Design beinhaltet die eleganten Details der einfachen Formen, wie z. B. die Beckenkanten, kombiniert diese aber mit einem insgesamt weicheren Aussehen. Dieses Design wird zusätzlich durch die subtile Abtropffläche verbessert, welche die Eigenschaften des geformten Materials nutzt, was mit Stahl nicht möglich wäre. Die Verfügbarkeit diverser Farben ergänzt zudem die Attraktivität des Sortiments.

Franke has created the Pebel range of granite kitchen sinks to capture the latest design trends in the kitchen. Recently, kitchen design, including sinks has been minimalist but latest trends are reintroducing curves that are modern rather than retro. The Pebel design includes the sharp details of minimalism on features such as the bowl edges but combines them with an overall softer feel and appearance. This design is further enhanced by the subtle draining board which uses the properties of the moulded material to achieve a feature not possible in pressed steel. Availability of different colors adds to the desirability of the range.

PRODUCT
BOP/BSP/BMP/CMP/WSP
Backofen-Serie 200
Ovens 200 series

DESIGN
Marken-Design Gaggenau
Sven Baacke, Janina Fey, Sören Strayle,
Gerd Wilsdorf
München, Germany

MANUFACTURER
Gaggenau Hausgeräte GmbH
München, Germany

Die neue Backofen-Serie 200 zeichnet sich durch ihre
graphisch reduzierte, gradlinige Formensprache der
durchgehenden Vollglasfronten aus. Diese fügen sich
als schwebende Flächen in den Farbtönen Anthrazit,
Metallic oder Silber perfekt in jedes Interieur ein. Die
sichtbaren Kanten der Lüfterleisten setzen dabei einen
Akzent, der die Linearität betont. Die Geräte der Serie
können sowohl neben- als auch übereinander kombiniert werden. Das Bedienmodul mit TFT-Touch-Display
und Edelstahl-Drehknebeln ist übersichtlich und intuitiv
in der Handhabung. Inhaltlich greift es das Konzept der
Serie auf und zeichnet sich durch bewussten Farbein-
satz aus.

*The new ovens 200 series is characterized by the mini-
malist linear design language of its smooth all-glass
fronts, which blend seamlessly into any setting as weight-
less elements in Anthracite, Metallic or Silver. The visible
edges of the ventilation strips subtly accentuate the lin-
earity. The appliances in the series can be combined
both in a side-by-side or stacked arrangement. The control module with TFT touch display and stainless steel rotary controls is clearly designed and operated intuitively.
Reflecting the series concept, the intentional use of color
lends it a distinctive character.*

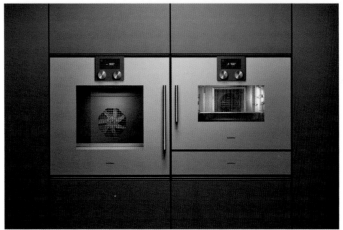

PRODUCT
GROHE Blue
Wasser-Filter-System
Waterfiltration system

DESIGN
Grohe AG
Düsseldorf, Germany

MANUFACTURER
Grohe AG
Düsseldorf, Germany

Eine intelligente Alternative zu in Flaschen abgefülltem Mineralwasser. Das System liefert jederzeit frisch gefiltertes und gekühltes Tafelwasser, ganz nach Wunsch sprudelnd, medium oder still. Die reduzierte Formsprache basiert auf sorgfältig proportionierten Zylindern und einem schnörkellosen Hebel, der rechtwinklig am Armaturenkörper ansetzt. Eindeutige Symbole kennzeichnen die Kohlensäurestufen, und die ProGrip-Veredelung der Hebelspitze führt die Hand des Bedieners intuitiv zur ergonomisch vorteilhaftesten Griffposition. Jederzeit wohlschmeckendes Wasser – komfortabel, umweltfreundlich, wirtschaftlich und auch optisch eine Bereicherung für jede Küche.

Providing a viable alternative to bottled water; this modern compact device dispenses still, medium and fully carbonated chilled and filtered water. The balanced yet reduced form is the result of carefully proportioned cylinders, with a simple lever placed perpendicular to the main body. The lever offers three choices clearly indicated by intuitive icons. The full metal lever is further enhanced with ProGrip on the tip, a machined texture which guides the user intuitively to the point of interaction and ensures a good grip on the lever. Convenient, ecological, economical, tastes great and will enhance the kitchen interior.

PRODUCT
Appliance Link
Einbaugeräte-Produktserie
Built-in appliance series

DESIGN
Guangdong Midea Microwave and Electrical
Appliances Manufacturing Co., Ltd.
Guang Dong, China

MANUFACTURER
Guangdong Midea Microwave and Electrical
Appliances Manufacturing Co., Ltd.
Guang Dong, China

Die Produktserie besteht aus einer eingebauten Mikro-
wellen-Ofen-Kombination und einer Side-by-Side-Kühl-
Gefrierkombination. Das markante Design der Geräte
ist klar und gradlinig. Hauptmerkmale sind kompaktes
und gehärtetes Flachglas in Schwarz sowie der verdeckte
Metallgriff. Das faszinierende LED-Display ist vom
nächtlichen Sternenhimmel inspiriert. Das ausgeklügelte Design des Metallgriffs bietet hohen Griffkomfort. Die
hochqualitative Produktserie in ihrem minimalistischen
Design zeichnet sich durch ein professionelles Erscheinungsbild aus, welches perfekt in moderne Wohnwelten
passt.

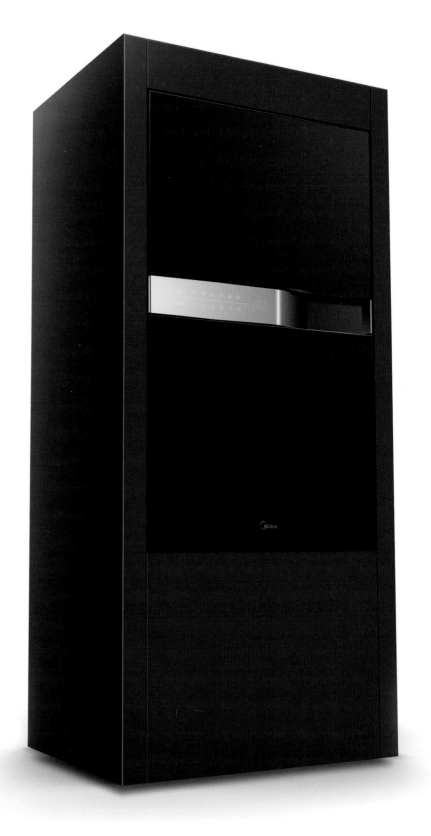

The product series consists of a built-in microwave / oven combination and a built-in side-by-side refrigerator. The appliances' distinctive designs are simple and straight-forward. Compact, flat black tempered glass and the hidden metal handle are key features. The LED display is inspired by the stars at night, offering users a fascinating operational experience. The hidden metal handle's detailed design emphasizes grip comfort. At the same time, with their minimal design and quality, the products present a professional appearance that is ideally suited to the modern home environment.

kitchen / household

PRODUCT
WMF 8000S
Gastronomie-Kaffeevollautomat
Professional coffee machine

DESIGN
Metz & Kindler Produktdesign
Guido Metz, Michael Kindler
Darmstadt, Germany
WMF AG
Peter Bockwoldt (Designmanagement)
Geislingen, Germany

MANUFACTURER
WMF AG
Geislingen, Germany

New Generation – die neue Technologieplattform des
Premium-Kaffeevollautomaten WMF 8000S: Alle zentralen Maschinenkomponenten inklusive der Maschinen-
architektur wurden neu entwickelt. Die MMI für die
Steuerung und Wartung der WMF 8000S setzt Maßstäbe in dieser Kategorie. Diese Klarheit wurde in der
Gestaltung fortgesetzt: Ein gekonntes Wechselspiel
zwischen bewusst polierten wie gebürsteten Edelstahl-
flächen, diversen Kunststoffen, Lichtdesign sowie ein
gläsernes Acht-Zoll-Touch-Display, vereinen Form und
Funktion. Revolutionäre Zugänglichkeit und Pflegekon-
zepte, in Kombination mit ihrer kompakten Bauweise,
runden die Spezialitätenmaschine ab.

*New Generation – that's the call for the new technical se-
ries featuring the premium-coffee-machine WMF 8000S:
All integral components, including the machine architecture, have been re-designed. The MMI for navigating and
maintenance redefines the state of the art in its class. This
clean style is conveyed throughout the product: a distinguished mix of polished and brushed stainless steel, various plastics, night design as well as an eight inch glass
touch display, unite form and function. The revolutionized
accessibility and hygiene concepts, in combination with its
compact dimensions, round up this specialized machine.*

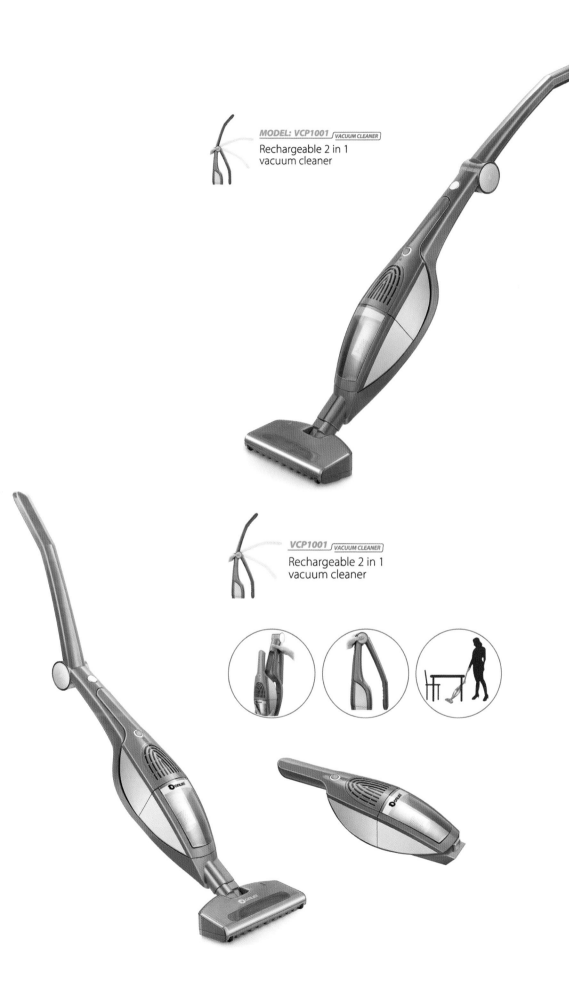

MODEL: VCP1001 [VACUUM CLEANER]
Rechargeable 2 in 1
vacuum cleaner

VCP1001 [VACUUM CLEANER]
Rechargeable 2 in 1
vacuum cleaner

PRODUCT
Vacuum cleaner
Haushaltsgeräte
Home appliances

DESIGN
Donlim® Innovation Design Center
Chen Longhui (Design Director),
Yu Haixiu (Design Manager),
Hua Mingying (Senior Designer)
Foshan, China

MANUFACTURER
Guangdong Xinbao Electrical Appliances Holdings Co., Ltd.
FoShan City, GuangDong Province, China

Der Donlim® VCP1001 ist ein aufladbarer Akku- und
Handstaubsauger in einem kompakten, geschwungenen
Design. Benutzer waren begeistert, wie praktisch und
günstig das Produkt ist. Wenn der Benutzer diesen neuartigen Staubsauger zum Reinigen des Bodens unter
Möbelstücken verwendet, muss er sich nicht bücken
oder in die Hocke gehen. Ein einfaches Drücken der
Taste neigt den Griff um 135°. Damit kann der darunter-
liegende Boden bequem gereinigt werden. Einfach die
Taste noch einmal drücken und der Griff klappt um
180° zusammen und verringert so den für die Aufbewahrung benötigten Platz um die Hälfte. Das spart
Stauraum und senkt Transportkosten.

*The Donlim® VCP1001 is a rechargeable stick and hand-
held vacuum cleaner with a compact and curved design
element. Users were satisfied with how convenient and
affordable the product is. When using this innovative
vacuum cleaner to clean the floor underneath furniture,
the user does not need to squat down or bend. Simply
pressing the button tilts the handle by 135° so the floor
underneath can be cleaned easily. Simply press the button again to fold up the handle by 180° and the storing
space needed will be reduced by half. This saves storage
space and cuts the cost of transportation.*

kitchen / household

PRODUCT

mini washer
Waschmaschine
Washer

DESIGN

Haier Innovation Design Center
Liu Wei, Kong Zhi, Jiang Chunhui, Zheng Yuntai
Qingdao, China

MANUFACTURER

Haier Group
Qingdao, China

Diese Mini-Waschmaschine ist speziell für Unterwäsche und Kleidung von Säuglingen und Kleinkindern entwickelt. Das sanfte Bogen-Design macht das Produkt noch benutzerfreundlicher. Decke und Chassis sind eine Kombination aus quadratischer und runder Gestalt. Sinnreich wird der Öffnungsgriff darin integriert. Durch transparentes Acryl und Beschichtungsmaterial wird das Besondere des Produkts hervorgehoben. Die Mini-Waschmaschine löst das Problem von Ordnung und Sorge um Kleidung verschiedener Arten und verschiedener Größen. Energie- und wassersparend, bequem und praktisch funktionierend. Mit Desinfektionsfunktion.

This mini washer is specially designed for washing underware and clothes of infants and children. It is more approachable owing to its mellow curve-type body. The upper cover and supporting base are designed with the shape combining square and round model and the uncovering handle is ingeniously integrated thereof, which makes users feel the upper cover is suspending. Mini washer solves the problems of washing clothes in different types and sizes, which is power-saving, water-saving and time-saving as well as convenient and practical. Meanwhile, the washer has the function of sterilization.

PRODUCT
cloud power washer
Waschmaschine
Washer

DESIGN
Haier Innovation Design Center
Jiang Chunhui, Kong Zhi
Qingdao, China

MANUFACTURER
Haier Group
Qingdao, China

Die Gesamtkonzeption des Produktes ist stereoskopisch und eine Kombination von Emotionale und Rationalismus. Das super einfache Design der integrierten Glasdecke spiegelt das Gefühl vom High-End des Produktes und den Sinn für die Qualität des Materials wider. Die geführte explizite-implizite Manipulationsschnittstelle ist benutzerfreundlicher und verkörpert Wissenschaft und Technologie. Bei der Technologie ist intelligente Manipulation eingesetzt, Reinigungs-und Desinfektionsmittel werden automatisch zugesetzt.

The simple integrated glass cover designed embodies the grade and high quality of both product and material; the leading type fully explicit/implicit interface makes the washer more humanized and scientific. Full-intelligent control technique is adopted, which makes the washer to put detergent and disinfectant automatically, thus removing users' trouble in putting detergent and disinfectant repeatedly and incapability of grasping the accurate quantity every time, so it is more healthy and environmental and enables users to finish heavy laundry easily.

PRODUCT

T800 range hood
Dunstabzugshaube
Chimney hood

DESIGN

Haier Innovation Design Center
Yan Yurui, Wang Junpeng, Feng Zhiqun,
Sun Wen, Jiang Yali
Qingdao, China

MANUFACTURER

Haier Group
Qingdao, China

Das Design des Produkts betont das Design-Konzept
von „Reinheit und Sauberkeit". Die T800-Serie verwendet Glas und Edelstahl. Öltropfen sammeln sich nicht
und die Reinigung ist leicht. Der Körper der Anlage ist
nahtlos geschweißt, damit sich kein Öl sammeln kann.
Das Aussehen der Haube ist prägnant. Der Einbau-Filter
ist prägnant und innovativ. Die tiefe Rauchkammer und
der Inverter-Motor saugen effektiv Ruß ab und machen
den Innenraum frei von Verschmutzung. Mittels Touch-
Tasten kann man die Anlage mit nur einer leichten Berührung steuern. Das vermeidet den lästigen Rauch.
Künstlerisches Zusammenwirken von Glas und Edelstahl
macht das Produkt professionell und modern.

*Adhering to the design concept of "purification and
cleanness", T800 series range hood is made of glass and
stainless steel. Oil drops on the range hood is uneasy to
accumulate and the cleaning is easy. The main tank of
the range hood is made through solder less joint technique, which avoids oil leakage, and the appearance is
simpler. With the innovative concave filtering net, deeper
smoke chamber and frequency conversion motor. The
range hood can be operated only through touching ex-
plicit / implicit key, to solve trouble from oil smoke. The
proportional division of glass and stainless steel parts in
an artistic, professional and fashionable style.*

PRODUCT

V60 DripScale / Station
Zubehör für Kaffeezubereitung
Coffee making tools

DESIGN

HARIO Co., Ltd.
Hario International Department (Producer),
Ryohei Uno (Director), Shiro Watabe,
Shinsaku Fukutaka (Designers)
Tokyo, Japan

MANUFACTURER

HARIO Co., Ltd.
Tokyo, Japan

Die V60-Kaffeewaage / Kaffeestation ist eine ganz neue Kaffeemaschine, die so ausgelegt ist, dass man während der Kaffeezubereitung die Zeit vom Timer und das Gewicht der Waage gleichzeitig und sehr gut sichtbar ablesen kann, womit sie auch den Bedürfnissen professioneller und anspruchsvoller Anwender wie Baristas entgegen kommt. Dieses Produkt bietet die Möglichkeit, neue originelle Rezepte zu erstellen oder die Rezepte mit anderen Baristi zu teilen. Dieses innovative Produkt setzt einen neuen Standard für „OMOTENASHI = GAST-FREUNDLICHKEIT" und für von Hand zubereiteten Filterkaffee.

V60 DripScale / Station is designed for the professional Baristas. This tool enables the baristas who are fastidious when it comes to brewing coffee, to be able to see the timer and the scale together on the same screen while in the brewing process. By using this tool it will enable the user to create new original recipes, and share the recipes with other baristas. This innovative product sets a new standard for "OMOTENASHI=HOSPITALITY" of hand drip coffee.

PRODUCT
TAVIS PLUS
Brotkasten
Bread box

DESIGN
Hightrend Merchandise Corp.
Chun-Yi Chang, Shih-Wei Yang
Taipei, Taiwan

MANUFACTURER
Hightrend Merchandise Corp.
Taipei, Taiwan

Genießen Sie frisches Brot und starten Sie in einen wundervollen Tag! TAVIS PLUS. Der eingelegte Brotbeutel ist aus 100 % hochwertiger Baumwolle hergestellt und kann in 40 °C warmem Wasser gewaschen werden. Er ist leicht herausnehmbar und leicht wieder einzusetzen. Der funktionale Deckel aus Naturholz ist nicht nur eine Abdeckung, sondern die Rückseite kann als Schneidebrett genutzt werden. Im Inneren des Deckels kann durch einen Magneten das exklusive Brotmesser perfekt verstaut werden. Der TAVIS-Brotkasten bietet eine stilvolle Lagerung von Backwaren. Die bunten Farben zaubern eine fröhliche und lebendige Atmosphäre auf Ihren Tisch.

Enjoy fresh bread to start the wonderful day! TAVIS PLUS. The bread bag is made from 100 % high quality cotton which can be washed by warm water. Also, it is easy folding and storing suitable for any shape of bread. Moreover, it is easy to carry. The functional natural wood cover is not only a cover. Its back side can be used as a cutting board. Inside the cover with the magnetic the exclusive bread knife can be stored perfectly. TAVIS bread box offers stylish storage of baked goods. The colorful vision is creating a joyful and lively atmosphere on your table.

PRODUCT
Hitachi CV-SU Series
Staubsauger
Vacuum cleaner

DESIGN
Hitachi, Ltd.
Design Division
Toru Ebihara, Takashi Owada
Tokyo, Japan

MANUFACTURER
Hitachi Appliances, Inc.
Tokyo, Japan

Das neue expressive und kompakte Design des Hitachi-Cyclone-Staubsaugers reflektiert die Leistung und die hohe Saugkraft des Gerätes. Der einzigartige flexible Reinigungskopf der Modelle CV-SU21V, 22V und 23V erfasst den Staub selbst in den engsten Zwischenräumen. Über ein integriertes Display und eine Infrarot-Fernbedienung am Handgriff lässt sich das Gerät einfach mit einer Hand steuern. Der Staubbehälter wurde so konzipiert, dass ein direkter Staubkontakt vermieden werden kann und ermöglicht eine einfache hygienische Staubentsorgung.

A compact cyclone type vacuum cleaner with high suction power. It has an infra-red wireless remote control system which makes it possible to adjust the power setting via the hand grip. With the remarkable multi-angle cleaning head, the models CV-SU23V, 22V and 21V can fit into narrow gaps between furniture for dust collection. Its hygiene-conscious, easy to clean dust storage case means that users can avoid direct contact with the dust during disposal. The machine body style emphasizes its high power and the large indicator can display high quality images and graphics on the hand grip control area, making the interface more intuitive.

PRODUCT
cuppo
Wandtasche
Wall pocket

DESIGN
ideaco&associates
Hideaki Yagi
Osaka, Japan

MANUFACTURER
ideaco&associates
Osaka, Japan

Mit cuppo bekommt man eine praktische Möglichkeit zum Verstauen kleiner Dinge. Der Behälter lässt sich auf allen magnetischen Flächen anbringen, wie etwa an Kühlschränken oder Metalltüren. Man kann man eine Menge Zeit und Energie sparen, indem man cuppo zum Aufbewahren von oft schwer auffindbarem Kleinkram wie Schlüsseln verwendet. Eine ganze Wand voller cuppos wirkt wie eine Kletterwand. Die cuppo-Klein-aufbewahrung lässt sich mit dem beigefügten Metall-blech leicht überall anschrauben.

cuppo is a useful place to store small items that attaches to all surfaces compatible with regular magnets, such as refrigerators or metal doors. You can save time and energy by using it to store small items that are usually hard to find, such as keys. A wall covered in cuppos looks like a climbing wall. With extra screws, cuppo can be easily fitted to any wall with an attached metal board.

PRODUCT

iRobot Roomba ® 780
Roboter-Staubsauger
Robotic vacuum

DESIGN

iRobot
Bedford, MA, United States of America

MANUFACTURER

iRobot
Bedford, MA, United States of America

Der iRobot Roomba ® 780 Staubsauger-Roboter nimmt
erstaunliche Mengen an Schmutz, sodass Sie mehr Zeit
damit verbringen zu tun, was Sie tun möchten und weniger Zeit mit der Reinigung von Böden. Mit einem
Knopfdruck entfernt Roomba ® Schmutz und Ablage-
rungen aus Teppichen und harten Oberflächen. Seine
iAdapt Responsive Cleaning Technology ™ saugt jeden
Teil Ihres Zimmers mehrfach. Er gelangt in Bereiche, die
Sie nicht erreichen können, auch unter Möbelstücke –
das bedeutet Staubsaugen, bis der Auftrag abgeschlos-
sen ist.

*The iRobot Roomba® 780 vacuum cleaning robot picks
up amazing amounts of dirt so you can spend more time
doing what you want to do and less time cleaning floors.
With the touch of a button, Roomba® removes dirt and
debris from carpets and hard surfaces. Its iAdapt™ Responsive Cleaning Technology ensures Roomba® vacu-
ums every part of your room multiple times. It gets into
areas you can't easily reach, including under and around
furniture, vacuuming until the job is complete.*

PRODUCT
MaxiTHAW
Auftauhilfe
Defrost aid

DESIGN
ISHUJA Inc.
Taipei, Taiwan

MANUFACTURER
ISHUJA Inc.
Taipei, Taiwan

Verkürzen Sie die Auftauzeiten von Gefriergut mit MaxiTHAW! Das aus stranggepresstem Aluminium gefertigte MaxiTHAW funktioniert dank des optimierten internen Lamellen-Designs ganz ohne elektrischen Strom und garantiert herausragende Wärmeleitfähigkeit. Aufgrund der einzigartigen Bauweise – Aluminiumstäbe, die durch lebensmittelverträgliches Silikon verbunden sind – ummantelt MaxiTHAW das Gefriergut flexibel und maximiert die Kontaktfläche des Gefrierguts für eine schnelle und gleichmäßige Wärmeübertragung. Nach dem Gebrauch wickeln Sie MaxiTHAW für eine platzsparende Lagerung oder den komfortablen Transport einfach auf.

Minimize thawing time of frozen food with MaxiTHAW! This non-powered thawing aid is done in aluminum, extruded with optimized internal-fins design, for superior thermal-transfer performance. Most uniquely, its flexible form factor – bars interconnected by food-grade silicon – enables it to "wrap" around its frozen subject, maximizing the contact surface area for swift & even heat transfer. MaxiTHAW covers all shapes literally, speed-thaws steak, seafood, meatloaf... equally impressively. And once the task is done, simply roll it up for easy storage and transportation.

PRODUCT
Sino
Messer und Schneidebrett
Knives and chopping board

DESIGN
Office for Product Design
Hong Kong

MANUFACTURER
JIA Inc. Limited
Kowloon Bay, Hong Kong

Sino ist ein kompaktes, im chinesischen Stil gehaltenes Allzweckmesser-Set. Chefkoch- und Schälmesser besitzen fortschrittliche Keramikklingen, welche alles schneiden und schälen ohne jemals nachgeschliffen werden zu müssen. Das Hackbeil hingegen besitzt eine stabile Edelstahlklinge, schwer genug zum Hacken und scharf genug für feines Schneiden. Die vorteilhafte Kombination verschiedener Materialien ist auch im passenden Küchenbrett zu sehen. Es besteht aus laminiertem Bambusholz mit einer Fläche aus Holzstreifen zum Schneiden und auf der anderen Seite aus widerstandsfähigen Holzblöcken zum Hacken.

Sino is a compact set of knives with Chinese character designed to address most cooking needs. The chef's knife and paring knife, both with advanced ceramic blades which are suited for cutting and slicing without the need for re-sharpening. In contrast, the Chinese cleaver has a durable stainless steel blade which combines the weight required for chopping with the sharpness necessary for delicate cutting. The consideration of materiality is reflected in the matching chopping board. Machined from laminated bamboo, it has an edge grain cutting side and an opposing end grain chopping surface which can withstand the impact of the cleaver.

PRODUCT
Persona
Teetassen-Set
Teacup set

DESIGN
Office for Product Design
Hong Kong

MANUFACTURER
JIA Inc. Limited
Kowloon Bay, Hong Kong

Ein Set aus Teetassen. Auf den ersten Blick sehen die Tassen gleich aus, doch bald sind Unterschiede sichtbar. Die Grundsilhouette ist eine zeitgenössische Neuinterpretation der traditionellen Teetasse mit Deckel. Bei näherer Betrachtung erkennt man unterschiedliche Strukturen, die eher fühl- als sichtbar erscheinen. Die wahre Qualität dieser Tassen ist erst erkennbar, wenn man sie anfasst oder gegen das Licht hält und die Muster durch die Transparenz des zarten Porzellans hervortreten.

A family of simple teacups which initially seems identical but soon show their own subtle personality. The basic silhouette of Persona's is a contemporary reinterpretation of the traditional Chinese tea cup with lid. Closer inspection reveals a series of individual texture like patterns which are almost more tactile than visual. The true quality of these cups is only fully appreciated once held in the hand or up against the light, when the translucency of the delicate porcelain accentuates the patterns.

PRODUCT
Xtend
Lichtregal
Illuminated shelf

DESIGN
LEICHT Küchen AG
Waldstetten, Germany

MANUFACTURER
LEICHT Küchen AG
Waldstetten, Germany

Xtend ist ein filigran konturiertes Lichtregal. Auf der Arbeitsplatte dient es der offenen Gestaltung des Arbeitsraumes und ist dank seiner lichten Erscheinung ein raumprägender Blickfang. Als frei stehender Raumteiler sorgt es durch seine Brillanz für klar gegliederte Strukturen im Übergang von Küche zu Wohnraum. Das Design von Xtend vereint technischen Fortschritt mit der Wohnlichkeit unserer Möbeloberflächen. Die tragenden Elemente aus Aluminium bewirken eine schlanke und steife Konstruktion und nehmen die gesamte Lichttechnik auf. In der Bodenvorderkante integrierte LEDs mit einem CRI ≥ 95 garantieren eine natürliche Ausleuchtung.

Xtend is a daintily shaped illuminated shelving system. Situated on the worktop, it contributes to the open design of the room and, thanks to its lightweight structure, is a central eye-catcher. As a free-standing room divider, its brilliance gives a clear structure to the transition from kitchen to living room. Xtend's design combines technical progress with the homeliness of our furnishing surfaces. The supporting aluminum elements result in a slim-line, rigid structure and accommodate all the lighting technology. LEDs with a CRI ≥ 95, integrated in the bottom front edge, guarantee natural lighting.

PRODUCT

Q-Box
Innenausstattungssystem
Interior system

DESIGN

LEICHT Küchen AG
Waldstetten, Germany

MANUFACTURER

LEICHT Küchen AG
Waldstetten, Germany

Q-Box / Q-Vario ist ein durchdachtes Organisations-
system für Schubkästen und Auszüge, schlicht in der
Anmutung, flexibel in der Praxis. Der Q-Box-Besteckein-
satz aus Eiche ist mit formschlüssigen, hartelastischen
Schalen ausgestattet, die dämpfend und rutschhem-
mend wirken. Elegant stellt sich der erhöhte, bündige
Materialübergang von Schale zu Trennsteg dar. Funk-
tionselemente wie Messerblock und Folienspender
werden optional eingelegt. Das Angebot umfasst auch
aromadichte Porzellandosen. Für die Q-Vario-Zugaus-
stattung kommen Lochrasterplatten zum Einsatz, die
durch diverse Funktionen erweitert oder mit Anti-
rutsch-Linsen ausgekleidet werden.

*Q-Box / Q-Vario is a well-thought-out, slim-line, flexible
organization system for drawers and pullouts. The Q-Box
oak cutlery tray features consistently shaped, hard-elas-
tic inserts which have a cushioning and slip-resistant effect. Even the raised, flush material transition from insert
to separating strip is elegant. Functional elements such
as knife blocks and foil or film holders are optional extras. The range also includes flavor-retaining porcelain
containers. Perforated wooden bases are used for the
Q-Vario pullouts enabling a whole range of additional
functions. Anti-slip pads can be attached to the individual perforations as required.*

PRODUCT

Air washer
Entfeuchter und Luftfilter
Humidifier and purifier

DESIGN

LG Electronics, Inc.
Corporate Design Center
Bohyun Nam, Hyoungwon Roh, Jungkyu Son
Seoul, South Korea

MANUFACTURER

LG Electronics, Inc.
Corporate Design Center
Seoul, South Korea

Als 3-in-1-Luftreiniger mit Entfeuchter und antibakterieller Luftfilter-Funktion gibt dieses Gerät Nano-Plasma-Ionen (NPI) ab und kann immer verwendet werden. Ein Zyklus liefert Wasser und reinigt das interne Verdampfermodul und ist hygienisch einfach zu verwalten. Die verborgene Teilungsstruktur ist stabil und sauber mit schöner Veredelung, die sehr gut zu verschiedenen Inneneinrichtungen passt. Das sprühfreie Verfahren ist umweltfreundlich und sicher, außerdem werden Recyclingkosten beim Entsorgen geringer. Die natürliche Entfeuchterscheibe kann durch Waschen sicher und wiederholt verwendet werden, was keine Zusatzkosten verursacht.

As the 3-in-1 Air Washer with natural humidifier and anti-bacterial air filter function, this emits Nano Plasma Ion (NPI) and can be used in all seasons. One operation supplies water and cleans the internal evaporator module and is easy to manage from hygiene perspective. Hidden parting structure is firm and clean with good finishing and matches well with various interior environment. Non-spray processing is environment friendly and safer, it also reduces recycling cost for disposal. Natural evaporation type humidifier disk can be used safely and permanently by washing, without extra cost.

231

PRODUCT
Styler
Bekleidungsmanagement
Total clothing care device

DESIGN
LG Electronics, Inc.
Corporate Design Center
Kihyuk Kim, Junghoi Choi, Eunyoung Jee
Seoul, South Korea

MANUFACTURER
LG Electronics, Inc.
Corporate Design Center
Seoul, South Korea

Dieser Bekleidungsmanager gehört zur neuen Konzeptreihe, die für neue Werte im Bekleidungsmanagement sorgt. Er hat eine Funktion, die Kleidung durch bloßes Aufhängen auffrischt, z. B. schwierige Textilien wie Anzüge und Bettzeug. Das angenehm bewegliche Gerät in Kleiderlänge entfernt Knitterfalten und bewahrt die Form der Kleidungsstücke. Zusätzlich gibt es ein exklusives Zubehör-Regal. Das flache und eckige Design für frei stehende oder eingebaute Konzepte verbindet sich mit verschiedenen Innenräumen wie dem Ankleidezimmer, dem Schlafzimmer und der Wäschekammer usw. Das Sicherheitsglas erschafft ein Highend-Muster und Spiegel-Gefühl.

This clothing manager is a product of new concept that provides new value in apparel management. This has a function to refresh the clothes just by hanging any hard to wash clothes such as suit and bedding. The convenient to use movable shelf which is based on the length of clothes is able to remove any wrinkle while maintaining the shape of clothes. In addition, there is an exclusive accessory shelf. The flat and square design for free standing or built in concepts blends with various interiors such as dress room, bed room and laundry room etc. Also safe tempered glass gives high end pattern and mirror feeling.

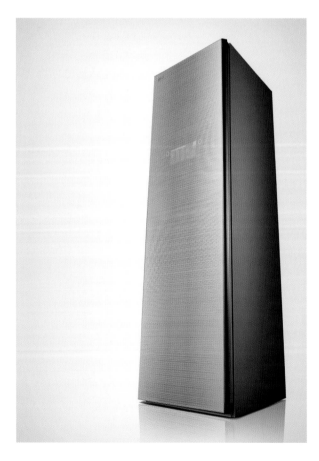

PRODUCT
Robot Vacuum Cleaner
Staubsaugerroboter
Robotic vacuum cleaner

DESIGN
LG Electronics, Inc.
Corporate Design Center
Hyunseon Shin, Yonggyun Ghim, Seonil Yu,
Kiwan Nahm
Seoul, South Korea

MANUFACTURER
LG Electronics, Inc.
Corporate Design Center
Seoul, South Korea

Der neue quadratische Staubsaugerroboter unterscheidet sich durch andere als die herkömmlichen Formen und durch die verbesserte Reinigungsleistung in Ecken. Mit minimalistischem Design und nahtloser Form mit digitalem statt mechanischem Stoßdämpfer bietet er ein solides Bild. Die verschiebbare Mopp-Halterung ermöglicht den Mopp-Austausch, ohne den Reiniger zu drehen, der Zugriff auf den Staubbeutel von oben und der größere, neu platzierte An- / Ausschalter erhöhen die Nutzerfreundlichkeit. Speziell beim Modell mit Spracherkennung kann der Reiniger zur Position des Nutzers gerufen werden, was das Heben und Bewegen des Roboter-Reinigers erübrigt.

New soft-square shaped robot cleaner deviates from the existing round shape and improves the cleaning performance for corners. With minimal design and seamless shape with digital bumper applied rather than the mechanical, it provides a durable image. Slide type mop board that enables replacement of mop without flipping the cleaner, accessing dust bin from top and larger relocated Start / Stop button increases the user convenience. Especially for the voice recognition model, the cleaner can be called to the current location of user along with the basic operation, removing the inconvenience of having to lift and move the robot cleaner.

233

PRODUCT
Signature 4D
Kühlschrank mit französischer Tür
French door refrigerator

DESIGN
LG Electronics, Inc.
Corporate Design Center
Jungyeon Hwang, Woonkyu Seo, Deasung Lee,
Boram Lee
Seoul, South Korea

MANUFACTURER
LG Electronics, Inc.
Corporate Design Center
Seoul, South Korea

Der Kühlschrank mit französischer Tür wurde zur effektiven Lebensmittel-Verwaltung entworfen. Das Tür-in-Tür-System (LGs Lagermethode erlaubt einfachen Zugriff auf Tastendruck, ohne den Kühlschrank öffnen zu müssen) wurde zur innovativen Nutzbarkeit beim Verwalten häufiger Gerichte (Kindergerichte, Käse, Wein, Getränke usw.) eingesetzt. Die neue Blast-Chiller-Funktion kühlt Getränke wie Bier und Cola in vier Minuten. Das Gefrierfach ist in einen oberen Bereich für häufige Gerichte und einen unteren Bereich für große, schwere Gerichte aufgeteilt, um Effizienz zu ermöglichen. Die Öffnungstechnologie vereinfacht das Öffnen der Schublade.

French door refrigerator is designed to manage the food efficiently. "Door in Door" (LG's unique storage method gives easy access by pressing a button without opening the refrigerator) is applied for innovative usability to manage frequently used food (children's snack, cheese, wine, beverage etc.) Also new "Blast Chiller" functions cools beverages such as beer and cola in four minutes. The bottom freezer drawer is divided into top for frequently used food and bottom for large and heavy food for maximum efficiency. The easy to open technology makes it easier to open the drawer.

PRODUCT
Standing Rice Scoop
Reislöffel
Rice scoop

DESIGN
Marna Inc.
Tokyo, Japan

MANUFACTURER
Marna Inc.
Tokyo, Japan

Aufgrund seiner speziellen Beschichtung haftet gekochter Reis nicht mehr so stark an diesem neuen Reislöffel und dank seiner besonderen Form kann er selbstständig stehen. Man muss ihn daher nicht am Gehäuse des Reiskochers einhängen oder auf der Löffelseite ablegen. Dies ist nicht nur hygienischer, sondern er ist bei Bedarf auch sofort wieder einsatzfähig. Vorbild für dieses Produkt ist das Katana, das japanische Schwert. Die Löffelmulde wurde möglichst dünn gestaltet, um beim späteren Auflockern des gekochten Reises ein Zerdrücken der Reiskörner zu vermeiden. Durch die ergonomische Formgebung liegt er beim Gebrauch angenehm in der Hand.

A rice scoop remains a classic Japanese utensil owing to its timeless design and functionality, yet we've managed to improve it even further! With most other scoops, one usually faces the pesky problem of knowing where to place the rice scoop after use. Standing rice scoop stands upright, keeping the table and kitchen counters clean and providing easy access. The scoop's embossed surface is ideal for preventing sticking, while its ultra-thin edge-inspired by the Japanese Katana-prevents the smashing of rice during mixture. Additionally, the handle's sleek, simple design provides for a smooth, comfortable grip.

PRODUCT
Foldable Travel Cup
Silikon-Tasse
Silicone cup

DESIGN
Marna Inc.
Tokyo, Japan

MANUFACTURER
Marna Inc.
Tokyo, Japan

Eine flach zusammenfaltbare Tasse aus Silikon. Wenn man diese Tasse zusammenfaltet, ist sie lediglich 16 mm dick. Man kann sie in die Hosentasche stecken oder in der Handtasche verstauen und so einfach mitnehmen. Zieht man an dem Griff, wird daraus sofort eine Tasse. Wenn man außer Haus unterwegs ist, benötigt man bisweilen eine Tasse: beim Mundspülen, Zähneputzen oder wenn man Medikamente einnehmen muss. Die Tatsache, dass der Griff am Boden angebracht ist, verleiht der Tasse eine hohe Stabilität und garantiert gleichzeitig eine hygienische Benutzung, da sich die Tasse auffalten lasst, ohne mit dem Finger hineingreifen zu müssen.

Foldable Travel Cup is a portable, collapsible silicone cup. Simply expand by pulling out the tab on the bottom of cup or compress by pressing down from the top. Approximately 16 mm when flattened, it can be easily fitted in a pocket or purse, making it ideal for taking medication and traveling. The pull tab constructed on the bottom of the cup not only provides a sturdy structure but also proves suitably hygienic since fingertips doesn't need to run across the rim or inside of the cup while folding and unfolding. It's a fantastic alternative to disposable cups!

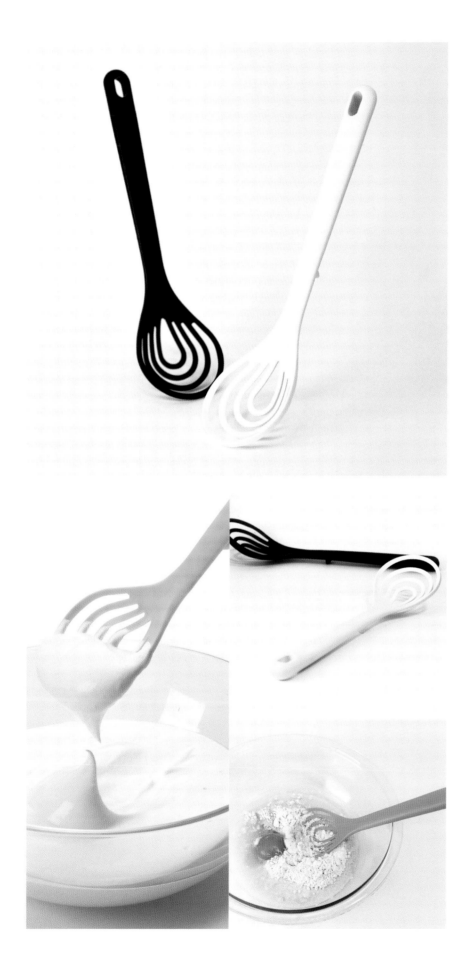

PRODUCT
Spoon Whisk
Schneebesen
Whisk

DESIGN
Marna Inc.
Tokyo, Japan

MANUFACTURER
Marna Inc.
Tokyo, Japan

Hierbei handelt es sich um einen völlig neu gestalteten Schneebesen. Aufgrund seiner einem Löffel angenäherten Form gibt es im Gegensatz zu konventionellen Modellen keine sich überschneidenden Draht- oder Kunststoffschlaufen. Hierdurch wird ein Anhaften von Lebensmitteln vermieden und die Reinigung vereinfacht. Die Löffelmulde besteht aus mehreren, versetzt angeordneten Lamellen. Diese sind in der Lage, das nötige Luftvolumen "anzusaugen" und z. B. Sahne ebenso wie ein herkömmlicher Schneebesen aufzuschlagen. Anschließend kann er auch zum Schöpfen bzw. Portionieren verwendet werden, so dass kein zusätzliches Küchenutensil benötigt wird.

Spoon Whisk combines the features of whisk and spoon for optimal results. Its flexible, spoon-like whisk head provides max aeration with its innovative triangular-edge wire and helps in scooping the mixture after the beating. The wires are uniquely constructed so they don't cross and their surface is flat. This design reduces the amount of clogging in the wires for an easier clean-up.

PRODUCT

Standing Peeler

Schäler

Peeler

DESIGN

Marna Inc.

Tokyo, Japan

MANUFACTURER

Marna Inc.

Tokyo, Japan

Der aufrecht stehende Schäler kann wie ein Messer verwendet werden und sorgt für eine zusätzliche Zeitersparnis beim Kochen. Die Kunststoff-Schneide ist geeignet, die dünne Haut von Wurzelgemüse abzuschaben, und die Vertiefung an der Spitze entfernt Triebe durch Anwendung des Hebel-Prinzips. Durch sein ansprechendes, stehendes Design lässt er sich während des Kochens einfach platzieren. Seine durchgängig dreieckige Form liegt angenehm in die Hand und erlaubt einen festen Griff.

Standing peeler stands upright to offer instant access and takes up little room while cooking. The features include: a vertical blade allowing for great control when peeling all fruits and vegetables; a triangular handle for a secure grip, a top tip potato eye remover; a plastic blade on the opposite end of the stainless steel blade to scrape off thick skins.

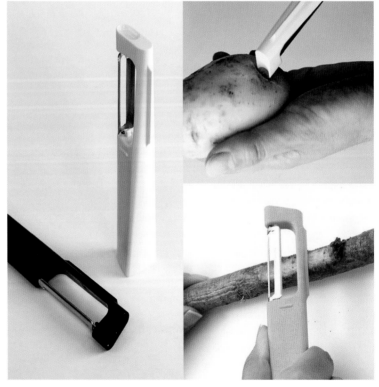

PRODUCT

KM 6395 FlexTouch
Vollflächen-Induktionskochfeld
Full-surface induction hob

DESIGN

Miele & Cie. KG
Gütersloh, Germany

MANUFACTURER

Miele & Cie. KG
Gütersloh, Germany

Maximale Flexibilität: Die gesamte Oberfläche des In-
duktionskochfeldes steht zum Kochen zur Verfügung.
Bis zu fünf Töpfe werden im Multi-Modus an jeder beliebigen Position, ohne vordefinierte Kochzonen, automatisch erkannt. Bedient wird über ein großzügiges
Touch-Display. Die genaue Position der Töpfe wird 1:1
abgebildet. Wahlweise kann das Kochfeld als einzelne
Riesenkochzone (Solo-Modus) oder dreigeteilte Kochfläche (Trio-Modus) verwendet werden. Drei Kochfel-
der in einem! Die elegante Glaskeramikbedruckung
unterstreicht die Vollflächigkeit in besonderer Weise.
Das Design ist konsequent auf die Miele Einbaugeräte
abgestimmt.

*Max. flexibility: the entire area of the induction hob is
available for cooking. Up to 5 pots and pans can be freely located on the ceramic screen in Multi-Mode, without
having to observe pre-defined zones, and are automatically detected. The unit is operated via a spacious touch
display. The precise position of pots and pans is recorded. Alternatively, the hob unit can be used as one large
single zone (Solo mode) or as a three-zone unit (Trio
mode). Three hob units in one! The elegant glass ceramic
graphics underline the full-surface cooking feature in a
very special way. The design is in line with that of all other Miele built-in appliances.*

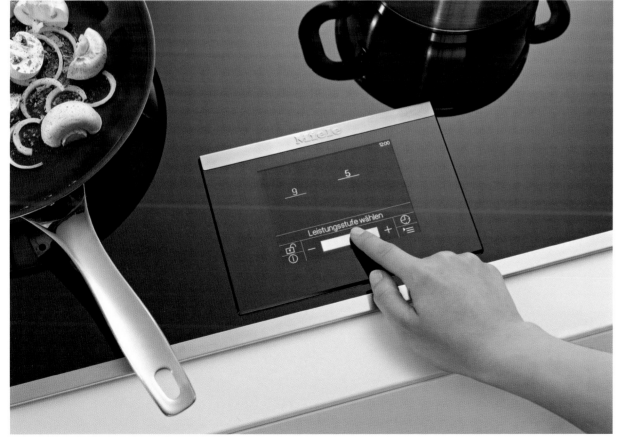

PRODUCT
KWT 6832 SGS
3-Zonen-Weintemperierer
Freestanding wine conditioner

DESIGN
Miele & Cie. KG
Gütersloh, Germany

MANUFACTURER
Miele & Cie. KG
Gütersloh, Germany

Der vibrationsarme Miele-Weintemperierer verfügt über drei individuell regelbare, LED-beleuchtete Temperatur-zonen. Das Gerät fasst bis zu 178 Flaschen, welche auf zehn neuartigen Buchenholzrosten mit abnehmbaren Notizleisten ruhen, die sich auf individuelle, unterschied-liche Flaschendurchmesser einstellen lassen. In der ver-schließbaren Schatulle bringt man alle wichtigen Utensi-lien unter, welche in der Box für stehende Flaschen ihren Platz findet. Ein Weinglashalter für temperierte Gläser, Dekantierroste sowie Flaschenpräsenter komplettieren die Ausstattung.

Miele's low-vibration wine conditioning unit features three temperature zones with separate temperature con-trols and LED lighting. This appliance offers space for up to 178 bottles on 10 beechwood racks with removable strips for notes. The racks can be adjusted to suit different bot-tle sizes. All important utensils can be stored in a lockable casket which can be placed in the box for storing opened bottles in an upright position. Decanting racks, bottle pre-senters and a wine glass holder for chilling glasses com-plete the line-up of features.

PRODUCT

Arbor 2-Way
Küchenarmatur zur Wasserfilterung
Water filtering kitchen faucet

DESIGN

Moen (Shanghai) Kitchen & Bath Products Co., Ltd.
Aniwat Rerkrai
Shanghai, China

MANUFACTURER

Moen (Shanghai) Kitchen & Bath Products Co., Ltd.
Shanghai, China

Moen-Arbor 2-Way Küchenarmatur liefert kaltes gefiltertes Trinkwasser on-Demand und Leitungswasser innerhalb eines Wasserhahns. Verschiedene Drücker sorgen dafür, dass gefiltertes Wasser sich nicht mit Leitungswasser mischt. Ein getrennter Drücker zur Filtration mit Zulaufschlauch für kaltes gefiltertes Wasser ist getrennt vom Leitungswasser-Auslauf. Durch das Double-Layer-Verfahren ohne Blei- oder Messing-Auslauf ist die Gesundheit der Benutzer geschützt. Ein eleganter und moderner Stil mit ergonomischem Design-Griff kombiniert den Vorteil der Ein-Hebel-Küchenarmatur mit der Verfügbarkeit für alle Filtersysteme.

Moen Arbor 2-Way kitchen faucet provides cold filtered drinking water on demand and tap water within one faucet with separated lever handle, filtration inlet hose for cold filtered water and separated filtration outlet with different angle and depth from tap water outlet ensures that filtered water will never mix with tap water. Double layer and no lead brass spout for all user's health benefit. Elegant modern style and ergonomic design handle combine the benefit of single-lever kitchen faucet with availability for any filtering systems. Arbor 2-Way kitchen faucet provides convenience, environment awareness and proves user's healthy lives.

PRODUCT

ZQB235-RA
Dampfherd
Steam oven

DESIGN

Ningbo Oulin Kitchen Utensils Co., Ltd.
Chen Hao, Guo Lingli, Sun Sheng
Ningbo, China

MANUFACTURER

Ningbo Oulin Kitchen Utensils Co., Ltd.
Ningbo, China

Intelligent gesteuerte Wasserdampf-Heizanlage. Dreifach-Schutz durch Feststellverriegelung, Schließmechanismus der Tür und Überhitzungsschutz, original LCD-Monitor-Steuerungssystem, Aluminiumgriff in benutzerfreundlichem Design. Der dynamische LCD-Monitor ist besonders übersichtlich, wodurch der Betriebszustand augenfällig ist. Voreinstellung von Temperatur und Kochzeit möglich, bewirkt Nährstofferhaltung und Geschmacksverbesserung der Lebensmittel.

Intelligent controlled and water vapor loop heating system; triple protection with brake lock, door switch and overheating; original LCD display control system; aluminum alloy handle as humanizing design; dynamic LCD display screen for clear working condition; preset temperature display for customer to preset the temperature and cooking time; keep nutrition and furthest improve the taste and preserve the most nutrition constituent. Succinct line design, aluminum alloy handle matching black toughened glass to reach terse workmanship and strong workability.

PRODUCT
F-GMHK10
Luftbefeuchter und Nano-e-Erzeuger
Humidifier and nano-e generator

DESIGN
Panasonic Corporation
Design Company
Ryota Uchida
Tokyo, Japan

MANUFACTURER
Panasonic Corporation
Osaka, Japan

Die „Nano-e"-Ionisationstechnologie ermöglicht eine Befeuchtung und Minderung der Ansteckungsgefahr durch Viren sowie der Ausbreitung von Schimmel und Allergenen in der Luft. Die Wasserminiaturisierungs-technik ermöglicht eine kraftvolle Geruchsbeseitigung aus Kleidung und Luft (5 - 20 nm kleine Wassermoleküle dringen tief in die Fasern ein und beseitigen Geruchs-ursachen). Winzige Wassermoleküle durchdringen und befeuchten die Haut. Schlichtes und pures Design ver-birgt die Einlassöffnung gekonnt. Die drehbare Lüftungs-abdeckung ermöglicht den Wechsel zwischen Gezieltem und weiträumigem Luftausstoß. In zwei Farben erhält-lich.

Using proprietary "Nano-e" ionization technology, pro-vides humidification while suppressing virus infectious-ness, mould proliferation and airborne allergens. Water miniaturization technology delivers powerful deodorization of clothes and air (water molecules 5 - 20 nm in diameter penetrate deep into fibers and break down the cause of smells). Miniature water molecules permeate and mois-turize the skin. Simple and clean design that disguises the inlet port. Revolving louver to switch between concentrated and wide-angle air output. Available in two colors.

PRODUCT
Libell Extendo
Auszugstablar
Pull-out shelf

DESIGN
PROCESS LUZERN
Luzern, Switzerland

MANUFACTURER
peka-metall AG
Mosen, Switzerland

Extendo-Auszugstablare werden aus einem Stück Stahlblech gebogen. Die runde Formsprache nutzt die Stellfläche bis an den äußersten Rand und die Tablare lassen sich dank der offenen Ecken angenehm reinigen. Das schlichte Auszugstablar Extendo vereint sich harmonisch mit Küchenfront, Wohnraum, Garderobe oder Ankleide. Die hohe Steifigkeit des Materials eignet sich insbesondere für Tablarbreiten von 600 bis 1.200 mm. Die magnetischen und antibakteriell beschichteten Antirutschmatten in dezenten Farben bleiben am Tablarboden haften und können zum Reinigen entfernt werden.

Extendo pull-out shelves are formed from a single piece of sheet steel. The rounded shape of the elements ensures that every last inch of storage space is put to good use. Besides, the fact that there are curved corners makes them easy to clean. Extendo, the discreet pull-out shelf, blends in perfectly in kitchens, living rooms, wardrobes and dressing rooms. The material's rigidity makes it especially suitable for use in widths of 600 to 1,200 mm. Discreetly-colored non-slip mats with a magnetic antibacterial coating stick to the bottom of the shelves, but can be removed for cleaning.

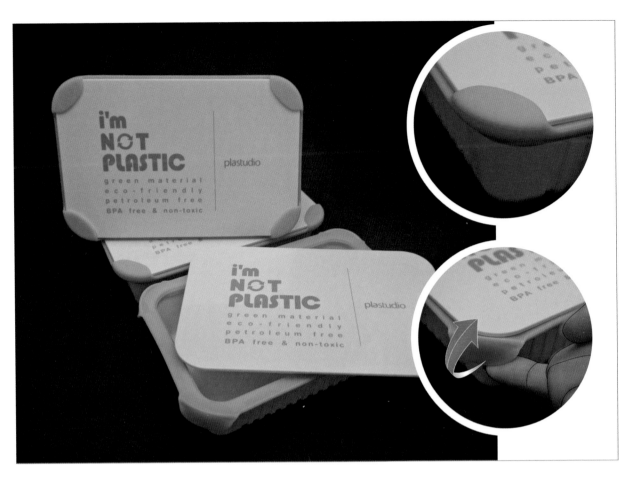

PRODUCT
ECO container
Lebensmittel-Container
Food container

DESIGN
PLA STUDIO
Taipei, Taiwan

MANUFACTURER
PLA STUDIO
Taipei, Taiwan

Dieser ECO-Container wird aus Polymilchsäure (PLA) hergestellt, die aus Maisstärke oder anderer Pflanzenstärke gewonnen wird. Dieses Material verfügt über ähnliche Eigenschaften wie erdölbasierte Kunststoffe, ohne aber deren nachteilige Auswirkungen auf die Umwelt zu haben. Es ist für Anwendungen im Nahrungsmittelbereich zertifiziert worden und kompostierbar. Um den ECO-Container sicher zu verschließen, muss man einfach nur mit Hilfe des Dichtungsrings den Deckel der Verpackung versiegeln.

This ECO container component is made from PLA (polylactic acid), which is derived from corn starch or other plant-based starch. This material has properties similar to oil-based plastics but without the negative effects. It has been certified for food applications and can be composted. Simply trigger the seal ring to close the container's lid, securely sealing the packging.

PRODUCT
Konvex Class
Schere
Scissors

DESIGN
IWASAKI DESIGN STUDIO
Tokyo, Japan

MANUFACTURER
PLUS Corporation
Tokyo, Japan
PLUS Europe GmbH
Düsseldorf, Germany

Die innovative Konvex-Schere schneidet dreimal schär-
fer als herkömmliche Scheren und setzt somit einen
völlig neuen Leistungsstandard. Dank ihrer nach dem
Bernoulli-Prinzip perfekt geschwungenen Scherenblätter
stehen die Klingen am Schnittpunkt immer im optimalen
Schnittwinkel von 30 Grad. So benötigt man lediglich
ein Drittel des normalen Kraftaufwands. Sogar harte
Materialien wie Pappe oder sehr dünne wie Folien, lassen
sich mit dieser einzigartigen Schere problemlos schneiden.

*The innovative Konvex scissors with its curved blades
work three times sharper than conventional ones. The
angle of the blades is kept at a constant magnitude of
30 degree, which is most efficient to leverage the strength
when cutting. Even strong materials are cut perfectly.
The curved blades firmly hold objects, not only a paper
but also hard materials like cardboard or sheer materials
like vinyl sheet which are difficult to cleanly cut through
with conventional scissors.*

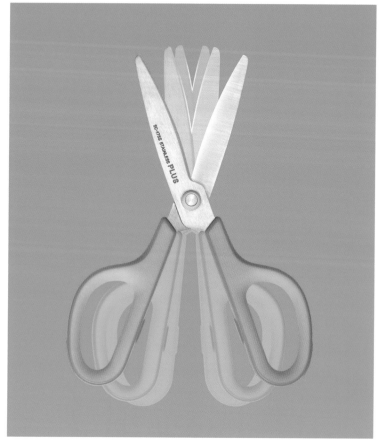

PRODUCT
Dinner 4 All
Individueller Tischgrill
Individual table grill

DESIGN
CQ International
design | develop | deliver
The Hague, Netherlands

MANUFACTURER
Princess Household Appliances
Breda, Netherlands

Dinner 4 All bietet eine neue und einzigartige Weise, um direkt am Tisch seine persönliche Mahlzeit individuell zuzubereiten. Eine neue Möglichkeit für ein festliches Abendessen mit Freunden oder Familie. Kreiere dein eigenes Rezept. Das Set besteht aus vier Keramiktellern, wobei jeder mit einer kleinen eigenen Pfanne ausgestattet ist. Die Pfannen, mit einer Anti-Haftbeschichtung ausgestattet, sind herausnehmbar und spülmaschinenfest.

Cook by yourselves and together at the table. A unique way to have a celebratory dinner. Decide your meal and recipe yourself; no flavors will mix. Dinner 4 All is a new and unique way of dining at the table with each other: enjoy cooking together and by yourself at the same time! This set consists of four earthenware plates, each with its own small griddle: prepare your meal in your own way. The earthenware plate is removable and dishwasher safe. The grill plate has a non-stick coating, making it easy to clean.

PRODUCT
Table Chef Pure
Tischgrill
Table grill

DESIGN
CQ International
design | develop | deliver
The Hague, Netherlands

MANUFACTURER
Princess Household Appliances
Breda, Netherlands

Pure ist eine gewölbte Luxus-Grillplatte, welche Säfte
oder Fette in einer herausnehmbaren Tropfschale auf-
fängt. Die luxuriöse und spülmaschinenfeste Grillplatte
ist mit einer haltbaren keramischen Antihaft-Beschich-
tung ausgestattet. Die Verwendung von Bambus ist
sehr einzigartig bei elektrischen Küchengeräten. Die
Pfanne ist ideal zum Zubereiten von Fleisch, Fisch, Gemüse oder Pfannkuchen. Nützlich in der Küche - Spaß
auf dem Tisch, im Garten oder auf dem Balkon.

Pure is a luxury griddle with a curve that ensures that
juices or fats run off into the removable drip tray. The
griddle is 50 x 25 cm and is luxuriously finished with a
durable bamboo wooden base. Applying bamboo is
very unique within electric kitchen appliances. The prod-
uct has a durable ceramic non-stick coating which pre-
vents burning and is easy to clean with kitchen paper or
in the dishwasher. The griddle is perfect for preparing
meat, fish, vegetables, eggs and pancakes without using
butter, making your meals healthier. Useful in the kitch-
en and fun on the table, garden or balcony.

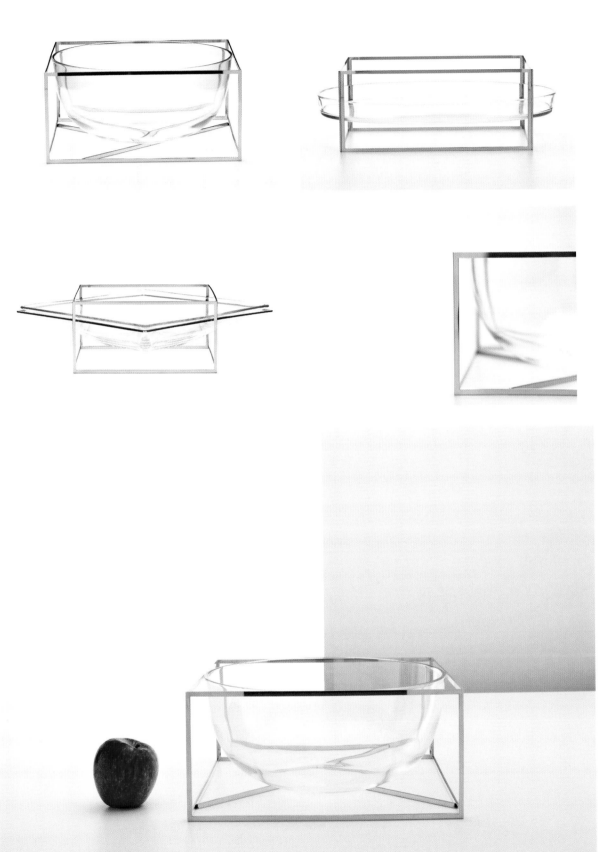

PRODUCT
K Collection
Küchenaccessoires
Kitchen accessories

DESIGN
Guilherme Wentz
Rio Grande do Sul, Brazil

MANUFACTURER
Riva
Caxias do Sul, Brazil

Durch die moderne Architektur inspiriert – der Zusammenschluss zwischen Kurven und Linien, zwischen Konkretem und freien Räumen. Riva schuf eine mutige und selbstbewusste Kollektion. In den Stücken der K Collection haben wir Platz geschaffen für Leichtigkeit und Wölbungen des Glases und die konsumierte Leere aber mit einem objektiven Ziel, dargestellt durch die Härte des Stahls. Schwebende Stücke mit einem abstrakten Kern, eingegrenzt durch die geometrische Ordnung. Die Kreation des Designers Guilherme Wentz simuliert ein Gebäude: Die Stücke wurden aus rostfreiem Stahl 18 / 10 geschaffen, in einem Gebilde das das kristalline Glas ohne Blei umgibt.

Inspired by the modernism architecture – the conversation between curves and lines, between the concrete and free space, Riva created a bold and conscious collection. In those pieces of the K Collection we made room for lightness and buoyancy of the glass and the empty it consumes, but with an objective purpose represented by the stiffness of steel. Pieces with an abstract essence, that float, but limited by a geometric order. The creation of the designer Guilherme Wentz simulates a building: the pieces were constructed in Stainless Steel 18 / 10 in a structure that surrounds the crystalline glass, lead-free composition.

PRODUCT

Fruit Holder Toledo
Früchtekorb
Fruit holder

DESIGN

Rubens Simões
Rio de Janeiro, Brazil

MANUFACTURER

Riva
Caxias do Sul, Brazil

Der Früchtekorb ist ein Vorzeigebeispiel der Vielfältigkeit des rostfreien Stahls 18 / 10 in einem gewagten Projekt, gut strukturiert und trotzdem delikat. Toledo betont das Material in einer Rüstung welche sich über die Gesamtheit ausbreitet, sich aber auf seine zentrale Basis mittels einer harmonischen Bewegung konzentriert. Der Früchtekorb Toledo, vom Designer Rubens Simões – Gründer und kreative Kraft hinter Riva – gezeichnet, wurde von einem kreativen Experiment geboren und wurde zur Übung für neue Kollektionen. Er stützt sich auf eine anpassbare Grundstruktur, welche unzählbare Möglichkeiten bietet.

The Fruit Holder Toledo is the demonstration of the versatility of Stainless Steel 18 / 10 in a bold, well-structured and delicate project. Toledo valorizes the material in an armor that expands into the space, but focused on its central base in a flowing movement. The Fruit Holder Toledo, signed by Rubens Simões – founder and creative behind Riva, emerged from a creative experiment and became a trial for new collections: it is based on an manipulable initial structure, allowing the emergence of numerous forms.

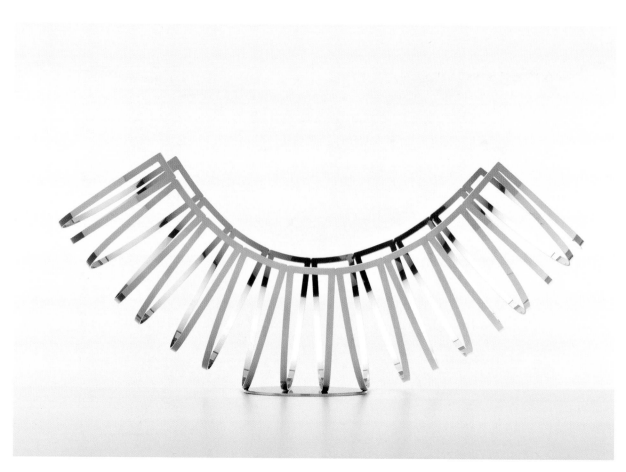

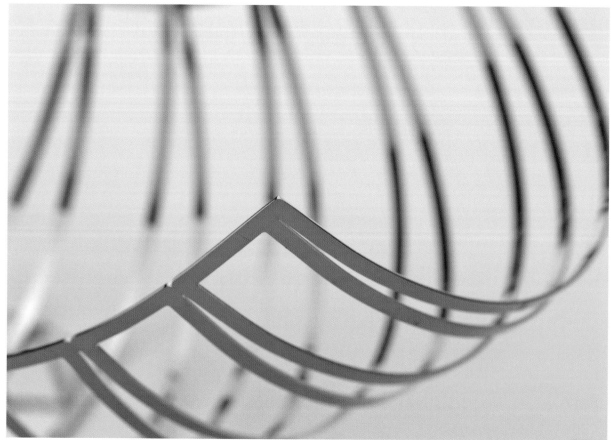

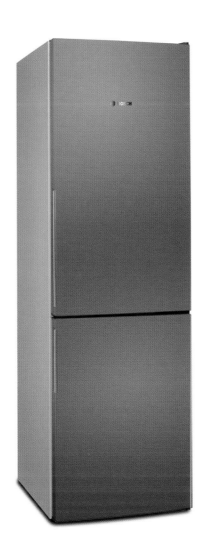

PRODUCT
KGV36VD30S KGV36VE30
Farbiges Kühl-Gefrier-Gerät
Colored fridge-freezer

DESIGN
Robert Bosch Hausgeräte GmbH
Ralph Staud, Thomas Tischer
München, Germany

MANUFACTURER
Robert Bosch Hausgeräte GmbH
München, Germany

Die reduzierte Gestaltung mit integrierten Griffen, in der Kombination mir der neuen, samtartigen Oberflächen-beschichtung integriert sich hervorragend in moderne, wohnliche Küchenumfelder. Dabei ist die in verschiedenen Farben erhältliche matte Struktur der Oberfläche nicht nur schön, sondern vor allem auch besonders pflegeleicht.

The minimalist design with integrated handles and new satin surface finish blend in perfectly into modern open-plan kitchens. Available in a range of colors, the matte surface finish is not only beautiful but also exceptionally easy to clean.

PRODUCT

HBG78B750 Edelstahl
Einbaubackofen, kalte Tür
Built-in oven, cold door

DESIGN

Robert Bosch Hausgeräte GmbH
Robert Sachon, Ulrich Goss, Bernd Kretschmer
München, Germany

MANUFACTURER

Robert Bosch Hausgeräte GmbH
München, Germany

In der Gestaltung des Gerätes wird Qualität und technische Perfektion durch Materialität und präzise gestaltete Designdetails wie die facettierten Türapplikationen, die speziell entwickelten Edelstahl-Touch-Sensoren oder die beleuchteten Vollmetallknebel sinnlich erfahrbar gemacht. Der Temperatur-Sinn soll allerdings aus Sicherheitsaspekten nicht überbeansprucht werden. Trotz 500 °C Innentemperatur im Pyrolyseprozess erreicht die Fronttemperatur dank speziellem Türaufbau mit maximal 30 °C kaum mehr als Raumtemperatur.

The appliance design focuses on a sensuous experience of quality and technical perfection through the medium of materiality and precision-crafted design features like the faceted door applications, stainless steel touch sensors and illuminated solid metal controls. The user's sensation of temperature is however modulated for safety's sake. Despite an interior temperature of 500 °C during the pyrolysis process, at 30 °C the temperature of the oven front is hardly more than the ambient temperature thanks to a special door design.

PRODUCT
Bosch KGF23557TI
Kühlschrank
Refrigerator

DESIGN
Robert Bosch Hausgeräte GmbH
Ralph Staud, Thomas Tischer, Tim Richter,
Yao Xingen
München, Germany

MANUFACTURER
BSH Home Appliances (China) Co., Ltd.
Nanjing, China

Dieser hochglänzende schwarze Kühlschrank spart an allem was unnötig ist, um das saubere und reduzierte Design zu unterstützen. Die an beiden Seiten integrierten Griffleisten definieren die ganze Vorderseite und unterstreichen die Geradlinigkeit des Produkts. Die Profile sind aus extrudiertem Aluminium, das leicht sandgestrahlt und eloxiert ist. Bedienung und Anzeige sitzen hinter der oberen Tür und erlauben die komfortable Einstellung der Temperatur aller Kühl- und Gefrierzonen. Im Innenraum finden sich gut organisierte transparente Schalen und Regalböden die der Aufbewahrung verschiedenster Lebensmittel gerecht werden.

This glossy black refrigerator saves all unnecessary elements to support an extremely clean and pure appearance. The integrated handles on both sides trim the front surface and enhance the products straightness. The profiles are made of real aluminum, finely sand blasted and anodized. The hidden control and display behind the upper door allows to adjust the temperature of each compartment with a maximum comfort. The clear transparent interior parts are well organized and very easy to use to store various kinds of food.

PRODUCT

SMV 69 U 60 EU
Vollintegrierter Geschirrspüler
Fully integrated dishwasher

DESIGN

Robert Bosch Hausgeräte GmbH
Robert Sachon, Thomas Ott
München, Germany

MANUFACTURER

Robert Bosch Hausgeräte GmbH
München, Germany

„Gutes Design ist unsichtbar" – nicht ganz! Der vollinteg-
rierte Spüler projiziert Restzeit und weitere Programmin-
formationen auf jeden Untergrund. Im Inneren überzeugt
er durch innere Werte wie das ebenso atmosphärische
wie funktionale Lichtdesign, flexible Körbe, eine intuitive
Touch-Bedienung und ein Höchstmaß an Ressourcen-
schonung.

*"Good design is invisible" – not quite! The fully integrated
dishwasher projects remaining time and other program
information on any surface. Inside it impresses with qualities like the atmospheric yet practical light design, flexible
baskets, intuitive touch operation and maximum saving
of resources.*

PRODUCT
KDN56SM40N
Topfreezer

DESIGN
Robert Bosch Hausgeräte GmbH
Ralph Staud, Thomas Tischer, Robert Sachon
München, Germany

MANUFACTURER
Robert Bosch Hausgeräte GmbH
München, Germany

Die überbreite Topfreezer-Variante in edler „Edelstahl-hinter-Glas"-Ausführung unterstreicht den Anspruch der Marke Bosch als Trendsetter in Material und Farbe im Hausgerätebereich. Ein neuartiges Klebeverfahren ermöglicht die rahmenlose Schichtung der unterschiedlich glänzenden Materialien und generiert eine einzigartige Tiefenwirkung.

The extra-wide topfreezer model in a select "stainless steel behind glass" design underscores the Bosch brand's claim as a trendsetter in terms of material and color in the home appliances sector. Thanks to an innovative bonding process, materials of various lusters can be layered without the need for a frame to create a unique illusion of depth.

PRODUCT

KDD74AL20N
Kühl-Gefrier-Kombination
Fridge-freezer combination

DESIGN

Robert Bosch Hausgeräte GmbH
Ralph Staud, Thomas Tischer
München, Germany

MANUFACTURER

Robert Bosch Hausgeräte GmbH
München, Germany

Die neue XXL-Kühl-Gefrier-Gerätereihe von Bosch setzt neue Maßstäbe in Design und Technik. Das Außendesign zeichnet sich durch den konsequenten Einsatz von Echt-materialien aus. So ist das Bedienpanel flächenbündig in die Tür eingesetzt und lässt sich bequem ablesen und per speziell entwickelten, wertigen Metall-Touch-Sensoren einfach bedienen. Der Dispenser führt sich ebenfalls flächenbündig in der Tür weiter. Das XXL-Format lässt keine Platzwünsche mehr offen.

The new Bosch XXL fridge-freezer range sets new stan-dards in design and technology. The exterior design is characterized by the consistent use of authentic materi-als. The control panel is integrated flush with the door. It is easy to read and operate with specially designed high quality metal touch sensors. The dispenser is also flush-mounted in the door. All storage space requirements are fully satisfied by the XXL format.

PRODUCT
BGL35Move Serie
Staubsauger
Vacuum cleaner

DESIGN
Robert Bosch Hausgeräte GmbH
Helmut Kaiser, Jörg Schröter
München, Germany

MANUFACTURER
Robert Bosch Hausgeräte GmbH
München, Germany

Der "MoveOn"-Staubsauger überzeugt nicht nur durch innere Werte. Für Mobilität beim Hindernislauf in der Wohnlandschaft sorgen ein 360°-Gelenk und XXL-Räder. Durch die matte, schockabsorbierende Unterschale und eine Stoßleiste ist das Gerät für den Alltag bestens gewappnet. An dem gut zugänglichen Bedienelement sind alle Funktionen direkt anwählbar. Metallapplikationen setzen zusätzliche Akzente. Dank neuer Technologie erzielt der "MoveOn" bis zu 25 % mehr Reinigungsleistung als sein Vorgänger.

The "MoveOn" vacuum cleaner not only impresses with its internal features. The 360-degree ball connection and XXL wheels make it easier to navigate around obstacles in the living area. With its mat shock-absorbing bottom shell and bumper strip, the appliance is well equipped for everyday use. All features can be selected directly via the easily accessible control elements. Metal applications set additional accents. "MoveOn" is up to 25 % more powerful than its predecessor thanks to the latest technology.

PRODUCT

BGS5 Serie
Beutelloser Staubsauger
Bagless vacuum cleaner

DESIGN

Robert Bosch Hausgeräte GmbH
Helmut Kaiser, Daniel Dockner
München, Germany
designkonzentrat
Köln, Germany

MANUFACTURER

Robert Bosch Hausgeräte GmbH
München, Germany

Die Gestaltung der BGS5-Relaxx-Bodenpflege-Serie
kommuniziert deren technologischen Anspruch und
greift die Ästhetik der Bosch-Bagless-Staubsauger auf.
Klar gegliedert reduziert die geschlossene Form in
Verbindung mit schalloptimierten Dämmstoffen, einer
verbesserten Luftführung und dem speziellen Sound-
Reducer-Deckel Geräusche auf ein Minimum. Gleichermaßen leistungsfähig sorgen die innovative Compressor
Technology und das RobustAir System für einwandfreie
Reinigungsergebnisse. Die 360°-Lenkrollen garantieren
ein hohes Maß an Bewegungsfreiheit.

*The design of the BGS5-Relaxx floor care series commu-
nicates its technological claim and follows the look of
the Bosch-Bagless vacuum cleaners. With its noise-opti-
mized sound-damping materials, improved air flow and
the special SoundReducer cover, the clearly structured,
closed shape reduces noise to a minimum, while the innovative CompressorTechnology and the RobustAir system ensure optimum results. The 360-degree wheels
make the vacuum cleaner exceptionally easy to move
around.*

PRODUCT
DWK09M850
Glas-Esse
Glass hood

DESIGN
Robert Bosch Hausgeräte GmbH
Christoph Ortmann, Oliver Kraemer, Robert Sachon
München, Germany

MANUFACTURER
Robert Bosch Hausgeräte GmbH
München, Germany

Durch ihr beruhigtes und innovatives Design fügt sich
die neue „Bosch Glass Cover" harmonisch in jede Küchen-
landschaft ein. Optisch und funktional einzigartig wird
die Esse durch ihre klappbare Blende. Im geschlossenen
Zustand werden die Filter abgedeckt, was der Esse
seine möbelhafte Anmutung verleiht. Ist die Glasblende
geöffnet, dient diese nun als funktionaler und leicht zu
reinigender Spritzschutz, die die Wand hinter der Kochstelle vor Kochspritzern schützt. Die Glass Cover-Dunst-
abzughaube von Bosch harmoniert exzellent mit innovativen Glasoberflächen, wie sie in modernen Küchen
zu sehen sind.

*Thanks to its sleek innovative design the new "Bosch Glass
Cover" blends into any kitchen scenario seamlessly. Its
folding cover lends this canopy hood a unique visual and
practical aspect. When closed, the filters are concealed, so
that the canopy hood looks like a furniture element. Once
opened, the glass cover serves as a practical easy-to-clean
splash guard and protects the wall behind the cooking
area from splashes. Bosch Glass Cover canopy hoods combine perfectly with the innovative glass surfaces featured
in modern fitted kitchens.*

PRODUCT

BSGL50S Serie
Staubsauger
Vacuum cleaner

DESIGN

Robert Bosch Hausgeräte GmbH
Helmut Kaiser, Daniel Dockner
München, Germany
BRANDIS Industrial Design
Nürnberg, Germany

MANUFACTURER

Robert Bosch Hausgeräte GmbH
München, Germany

Die Gestaltung des „Bosch Free´e ProSilence" bringt auf
innovative Weise zum Ausdruck, wie hohe Saugleistung
und Flexibilität bei einem besonders niedrigen Geräusch-
pegel vereinbar sind. Im Fokus steht das ausgefeilte
SilenceSound System, das durch einen vibrationsarmen
Motor und einer Kombination aus flexiblem Fasergewebe
und Akustikschäumen den Lärm reduziert. Ein farblich
abgesetzter Schalldämpfer im Ausblasbereich kommuniziert die Funktionalität nach Außen und sorgt für zusätzliche Schallabsorption. Integrierte Stoßleisten schonen
Möbel und Wände. Für Mobilität sorgen Lenkrollen, ein
patentiertes 360° Kugelgelenk und 15 m Aktionsradius.

*The design of the "Bosch Free'e ProSilence" innovatively
expresses how high suction performance and flexibility
can be combined with an exceptionally low noise level.
The model's sophisticated SilenceSound system uses a
low-vibration motor and the combination of flexible fiber
fabric and acoustic foam to reduce the noise level. A contrasting baffle in the exhaust area communicates this
feature and provides additional noise absorption. Integrated bumper guards protect furniture and walls, while
caster wheels, a patented 360° ball joint and a 15 m operating range provide mobility.*

PRODUCT
SMI 69 U 65 EU
Integrierter Geschirrspüler
Integrated dishwasher

DESIGN
Robert Bosch Hausgeräte GmbH
Thomas Ott, Robert Sachon
München, Germany

MANUFACTURER
Robert Bosch Hausgeräte GmbH
München, Germany

Neben einer klar gegliederten, auf das wesentliche redu-
zierten Blende und intuitiver Touch-Bedienung, besticht
dieser Spüler durch seine Anzeige. Das neue hochauflösende Farb-TFT-Display bietet zusätzliche Informationen
zu Programmen sowie Hinweise zur Nutzung und Ver-
brauchsmittelzugabe. Dabei kann der Programmstatus
auch aus größeren Entfernungen abgelesen werden.
Die inneren Werte überzeugen mit flexiblen Körben,
einer Besteckschublade sowie, selbstverständlich für
die Marke Bosch, einem Höchstmaß an Ressourcen-
schonung.

*Aside from its minimalist control panel which focuses on
essentials and intuitive touch controls, this dishwasher's
display catches the attention. The new HD color TFT
display provides additional program info, usage instructions and dosage recommendations. The program status
can also be read from a distance. Impressive interior features include flexible baskets, a cutlery drawer, and as
you'd expect from the Bosch brand, maximum saving of
resources.*

PRODUCT

Siemens HS223300W
Einstiegs-Sterilizer
Entry sterilizer

DESIGN

Siemens Electrogeräte GmbH
Julia Ehrensberger
München, Germany

MANUFACTURER

Siemens Electrogeräte GmbH
München, Germany

Hier ist Siemens ein in seiner Erscheinung anspruchsvoller Einstiegs-Sterilizer gelungen. Die durchlaufenden,
geschlossenen Fronten haben gepulverte Oberflächen.
Diese werden nur durch die schmalen, integrierten
Griffleisten unterbrochen. Dies verleiht dem Gerät ein
edles, pures Aussehen. Die Geometrie der Griffprofile
lässt das Öffnen der Schubladen mit unterschiedlichsten Handhaltungen zu. Die Bedienung erfolgt über
Touch-Tasten und eine 7-Segment-Anzeige (weiße
LEDs), was zum hohen Reinigungskomfort des Gerätes
beiträgt. Wegen seines Desinfizierungsgrades ist der
Sterilizer mit dem chinesischen 2-Sterne-Qualitätsstan-
dard ausgezeichnet.

*With this design, Siemens created a visually sophisticated
entry-sterilizer. The fully continuous front panels have a
powder painted surface. The slim handles are well integrated to support the pure and classy appearance. The
form of the handles allows opening the sterilizer in an
ergonomic way while approaching from different angles. The product is controlled via touch buttons and a
white 7-segment-display which is easy to clean. Due to
its level of disinfection, the sterilizer is rated with 2 stars
according to the Chinese national standard.*

PRODUCT
Avance Collection coffee maker
Drip-Filter-Kaffeemaschine
Drip filter coffee machine

DESIGN
Philips Design
Eindhoven, Netherlands

MANUFACTURER
Royal Philips Electronics
Eindhoven, Netherlands

Mit ihrer eleganten Ausführung und dem 2-in-1-Behälter für Wasser und Kaffee, ist die Philips Avance Collection Kaffeemaschine einfach, sauber und intelligent. Ihr kompaktes Design ermöglicht ein einfaches Verstauen der Drip-Filter-Kaffeemaschine. Der Geräterahmen hält die beiden Gefäße zusammen, die beide nach unten geneigt sind, um den gravitätsbasierten Brühvorgang optisch zu vermitteln. Eine innovative Wasserstandsanzeige zeigt dem Benutzer, wie viele Tassen in den Wassertank gefüllt wurden. Die Kaffeemaschine hält Kaffee 120 Minuten warm und schaltet dann automatisch ab, um Strom zu sparen.

With its stylish architectural profile and two-in-one loader for water and coffee filling, the Philips Avance Collection coffee maker is easy, clean, and smart. Its compact design makes the drip-filter coffee maker simple to store. The frame around the appliance binds the two jugs together, which both slope downwards to visually convey the gravity-based brewing process. An advanced water level indicator tells users how many cups they have filled in the water tank. After keeping coffee warm for 120 minutes, the coffeemaker shuts off automatically to save energy.

PRODUCT

Philips Jamie Oliver HomeCooker range
Küchenmaschine
Kitchen appliance

DESIGN

Philips Design
Eindhoven, Netherlands

MANUFACTURER

Royal Philips Electronics
Eindhoven, Netherlands

Der Philips HomeCooker ist der erste einer neuen Reihe
von Küchengeräten, die gemeinsam mit dem englischen
Koch Jamie Oliver entwickelt wurden. Der HomeCooker
kann Zutaten hacken und raspeln sowie rühren, dämp-
fen und sautieren und dann unbeaufsichtigt weiter-
kochen. Durch die speziell entwickelte AutoStir-Techno-
logie kann der Benutzer anderen Aufgaben nachgehen,
ohne sich Sorgen zu machen, dass etwas während des
Kochens anbrennt. Sein vertrautes und zeitgemäßes
Aussehen und eine intuitive und einfache Benutzeroberfläche machen den HomeCooker zugänglich. Das
System ist flexibel und modular aufgebaut, leicht zu
demontieren und spülmaschinenfest.

*The Philips HomeCooker is the first in a new range of
kitchen appliances co-created with UK chef Jamie Oliver.
The HomeCooker can chop and grate ingredients as well
as stir, steam and sauté, then be left cooking unattend-
ed. Specially-designed AutoStir technology allows users
to get on with other tasks without worrying that the meal
will burn while it is cooking. To make the new product
approachable, the HomeCooker was designed to have a
familiar but contemporary look and feel, and a user-in-
terface that is intuitive and simple. The whole system is
flexible and modular, easy to disassemble and dishwasher
safe.*

PRODUCT
SENSEO® Twist range
System für Kaffeepads
Coffee pod system

DESIGN
Philips Design
Eindhoven, Netherlands

MANUFACTURER
Royal Philips Electronics
Eindhoven, Netherlands

Das freche, moderne Design der neuen SENSEO® trifft auf neue Technik für verbesserte Features und Geschmack. Die SENSEO® Twist brüht zwei Tassen Kaffee in weniger als einer Minute und hat zwei Kaffeestärkeneinstellungen: klein stark oder mild lang. Das clevere Touch-Panel führt den Benutzer durch die verschiedenen Funktionen und speichert eine bevorzugte Kaffee-Einstellung. Der neuartige Auslauf gibt der Twist ihr besonderes Aussehen und ist für jede Tassengröße höhenverstellbar. Eine Vielzahl von Farb- und Akzentkombinationen ermöglicht ein Anpassen der Kaffeemaschine an die Inneneinrichtung. Erhältlich mit eingebautem BRITA® MAXTRA Filter.

The bold, modern design of the new SENSEO® comes together with new technology to deliver improved features and taste. The SENSEO® Twist can make two cups of coffee in less than a minute and has two strength-select functions: short strong or mild long. The smart touch panel intuitively guides users through the different functions, and can memorize a favorite coffee setting. The new-look spout that gives the Twist its characteristic profile retains its height adjustability to fit any cup size. A wide range of color and accent combinations allows people to match their coffee machine with their decor. Available with integrated BRITA® MAXTRA filter.

PRODUCT
Daily Collection
Küchengeräte
Range of kitchen appliances

DESIGN
Philips Design
Eindhoven, Netherlands

MANUFACTURER
Royal Philips Electronics
Eindhoven, Netherlands

Bekannte Formen, klare großzügige Details und dezente Farbtupfer tragen zum archetypischen Aussehen der Philips Daily Collection bei. Diese bezahlbare Produktpalette mit grundlegenden zuverlässigen Funktionen wurde für den alltäglichen Gebrauch entwickelt. Das einfache, funktionelle und freundliche Design ist modern und frisch und bietet ein stilvolles Preis- / Leistungs-Verhältnis und Verlässlichkeit einer vertrauten Marke. Obwohl jedes Produkt auf seine Weise zu bedienen ist, garantieren die weichen Formen und Farbdetails ein einheitliches Erscheinungsbild. Das Sortiment umfasst Wasserkocher, Handmixer, Stabmixer, Küchenmaschine und Toaster.

Familiar forms, clear generous details, and subtle splashes of color help create the archetypical appeal of the Philips Daily Collection range. This affordable range of products is designed for daily use, with basic reliable functionality. The simple, functional, and friendly design is modern and fresh, offering stylish value for money and dependability from a trusted brand. Even though each product has its own way of handling, the soft curves and color details ensure a consistent look and feel. The range includes a kettle, a blender, a hand blender, a food processor and a toaster.

PRODUCT
SENSEO® Sarista range
Bohnentrichter Kaffee-System
Bean-funnel coffee system

DESIGN
Philips Design
Eindhoven, Netherlands

MANUFACTURER
Royal Philips Electronics
Eindhoven, Netherlands

Durch ihr einzigartiges und unverkennbares Design bietet die Philips SENSEO® Sarista köstlichen, hochwertigen Kaffee, gebrüht aus frisch gemahlenen Bohnen. Die Maschinen bieten beispiellose Flexibilität. Kaffeetrinker wählen per Knopfdruck eine Tasse, zwei Tassen oder eine Kanne frisch gemahlenen und gebrühten Kaffee. Eine Auswahl von sechs erstklassigen Bohnensorten kann im Handumdrehen für jede Tasse ausgetauscht werden. Die Bohnentrichter werden beim Abnehmen vom Kaffeeautomaten wieder verschlossen, um das delikate Aroma und den individuellen Geschmack zu bewahren. Die SENSEO® Sarista ist in den Farben Pearl White und Deep Black erhältlich.

With its unique and distinctive design, the Philips SENSEO® Sarista offers delicious, high-quality coffee brewed from freshly ground beans. The machines also offer unprecedented flexibility. Coffee drinkers can choose to freshly grind and brew one cup, two cups, or a full jug of coffee at the touch of a button. There is a choice of six premium bean blends which can be interchanged cup by cup with a simple twist. The bean-funnels are reclosed when they are removed from the coffee maker to preserve their delicate aroma and individual taste profile. The SENSEO® Sarista is available in two colors, Pearl White and Deep Black.

PRODUCT
CompactTouch garment steamer GC400 series
Bedampfer
Garment steamer

DESIGN
Philips Design
Eindhoven, Netherlands

MANUFACTURER
Royal Philips Electronics
Eindhoven, Netherlands

Das Philips CompactTouch bietet eine leichte, tragbare Lösung für den chinesischen Markt, wo Menschen häufig einen Bedampfer zum Auffrischen ihrer Garderobe verwenden. Es wurde entwickelt, um zu vermeiden, dass Staub mit dem Dampfkopf in Kontakt kommt, wenn es nicht in Gebrauch ist. Dafür verfügt das CompactTouch über eine integrierte Box. Alle Kabel können einfach innen um den Dampfkopf geschlungen und dann mit der steckbaren Abdeckung verschlossen werden. Der durchsichtige Behälter enthält bis zu 600 ml Wasser und bietet den Benutzern eine große Dampfautonomie zum Auffrischen der Garderobe.

The Philips CompactTouch offers a lightweight, portable solution for the Chinese market, where people often use a steamer to touch up or refresh their garments. Designed to stop dust coming into contact with the steamer head when not in use, the CompactTouch comes with an integrated box. All cables can easily be looped inside around the steamer head, then locked away using the clip-on cover. The transparent tank can contain 600 ml of water to provide users with great steam autonomy for touching up and refreshing garments.

PRODUCT
PerfectCare Xpress GC5050/55/57/60
Dampfdruckbügeleisen
Pressurized steam iron

DESIGN
Philips Design
Eindhoven, Netherlands

MANUFACTURER
Royal Philips Electronics
Eindhoven, Netherlands

Das PerfectCare Xpress ist das erste Dampfdruckbügeleisen. Dampferzeuger-Technologie verbindet sich mit
der kompakten Form eines direkten Dampfbügeleisens
und bietet dem Verbraucher das Beste aus zwei Welten.
Ein ultra-kompakter Dampfgenerator ist in das Bügeleisen eingebaut, um feuchtigkeitsintensiven Druckdampf
zu erzeugen, und macht es effektiver und schneller als
herkömmliche Dampfbügeleisen. Das Xpress zeichnet
sich aus durch die einzigartige OptimalTemp-Technologie,
die optimale Kombination aus Temperatur und Dampf
für bügelbare Stoffe.

*The PerfectCare Xpress is the first ever pressurized steam
iron. Combining steam generator technology into the
compact form of a direct steam iron gives consumers the
best of both worlds. An ultra-compact steam generator
is built inside the iron to deliver pressurized, moisture
rich steam, making it more effective and faster than
regular steam irons. The Xpress features the unique
OptimalTemp technology, which maintains the perfect
combination of temperature and steam suitable for every ironable fabric.*

PRODUCT
La Rose
Kochgeschirr
Cookware

DESIGN
Samkwang Glass Co., Ltd.
Joohee Kim, Seungwook Park
Seoul, South Korea

MANUFACTURER
Samkwang Glass Co., Ltd.
Seoul, South Korea

La Rose, das sichere und gesunde Kochgeschirr aus
Keramik wird umweltfreundlich hergestellt. Das Designkonzept inspiriert das Auftreten einer blühenden Blume,
eine der schönsten Augenblicke, die uns die Natur bietet. Die Eleganz und Weiblichkeit der Form betont den
ästhetischen Aspekt von Blüten. Durch die asymmetrische Form der Griffe scheint es, als wäre der Topf von
Rosenblättern bedeckt. Die kurvenförmige Linie an der
Seite des Topfes stellt die Überlappung der Rosenblätter
dar und dient zum bequemen Ausgießen von Inhalten.
Der Knauf symbolisiert eine Rosenknospe und vervollständigt das Bild einer Rose.

*La Rose, the safe and healthy ceramic cookware, is made
of natural minerals through an eco-friendly manufacturing process. The design concept of La Rose is fully inspired
by the appearance of blooming flower which is one of the
beautiful aspects in nature. The design of the pot is recog-
nized for its elegance and feminity, hereby it accentuates
aesthetic aspect of flowering. The asymmetric shape of
the handles looks like the pot is covered by the rose pedals. The curved line on the side of the pot embodies the
rose pedals overlapping one another, and it is functional
for pouring out the contents easily. The knob symbolizes
the image of the rose bud.*

PRODUCT
SC96
Staubsauger
Vacuum cleaner

DESIGN
SAMSUNG Electronics Co., Ltd.
Kyungtae Kim, Jungkyung Kwack, Sei-ill Jeon,
Inhee Kim
Seoul, South Korea

MANUFACTURER
SAMSUNG Electronics Co., Ltd.
Seoul, South Korea

Soft feeling Guard

Entsprechend der „Space Tension"-Idee ist das Außendesign kraftvoll und dynamisch. Es spiegelt Grundfunktionen wie Saugfähigkeit und Geräuscharmut wider.
Die „Neo Spiral"-Zyklontechnologie ermöglicht eine
Feinstaubabscheiderate von 99,7 %. Der Soft Guard an
der Vorderseite schützt Einrichtung und Staubsauger.
Dank der Räder und Radlager ist das Staubsaugen für
den Benutzer weniger anstrengend. Außerdem wird
ein Ökopaket mit einem 1.200-W-Motor, einer Silencio
Plus-Bürste und einem HEPA H12-Kohlefilter angeboten. Dank der Reduzierung des Stromverbrauchs (32 %)
und der Kohlenmonoxidemissionen ist der Staubsauger
auch umweltfreundlich.

*We adopted a dynamic, powerful exterior design based
on the „space tension" concept. The exterior reflects basic functions, including strong suction and low noise. The
„neo spiral" cyclone technology features a 99.7 % fine
dust separation rate. The soft guard at the front protects
objects in the home and the vacuum cleaner itself. The
wheels and wheel bearings make vacuum cleaning less
tiring for the user. There is also an ECO package on offer
that includes a 1,200 W motor, Silencio plus brush and
carbon HEPA H12 filter. The vacuum cleaner is also eco-
friendly thanks to reductions in power consumption (32 %)
and carbon monoxide emissions.*

PRODUCT

VC-RM94W
Roboter-Staubsauger
Robot vacuum cleaner

DESIGN

SAMSUNG Electronics Co., Ltd.
Deoksang Yun, Sei-ill Jeon, Jungkyung Kwack,
Changae Lim
Seoul, South Korea

MANUFACTURER

SAMSUNG Electronics Co., Ltd.
Suwon-si, Gyeonggi-do, South Korea

Dieser clevere Staubsauger ist das absolut zeitspar-
endste Reinigungsgerät. Der Benutzer drückt nur die
„Clean"-Taste und kann sich setzen, Zeitung lesen oder
eine Tasse Kaffee genießen, während der VC-RM94W
den Hausstaub beseitigt. Der Staubsauger schafft Tür-
schwellen mit Leichtigkeit und erreicht so jede Ecke des
Hauses. Mit der Automatikfunktion können Benutzer
den Staubsauger so programmieren, dass er saugt,
wenn sie weg sind. Wenn der Staubsauger fertig ist,
kehrt er automatisch zur Aufladestation zurück. Der
Benutzer kann auch sein Handy oder den PC mit der
Onboard-Kamera des VC-RM94W verbinden und die
Reinigung aus der Ferne verfolgen.

*This smart vacuum cleaner is the ultimate time-saving
cleaning device. Simply by pushing the clean button the
user can sit down, read the newspaper or enjoy a cup of
coffee while the VC-RM94W gets on with vacuuming up
all that household dust. The vacuum cleaner clears door-
sills with ease and can therefore clean every corner of
the home. By using the automatic function, users can
program the vacuum cleaner to clean when they are out.
Once it's done, the vacuum cleaner automatically returns
to its charger. The user can also connect their mobile
phone or PC to the VC-RM94W's onboard camera and
monitor the cleaning process remotely.*

PRODUCT

GS36DPI20/KS36WPI30
Kühl-Gefrier-Twin-Center
Fridge-freezer twin center

DESIGN

Siemens Electrogeräte GmbH
Max Eicher, Christoph Becke, Swetlana Gorodezki
München, Germany

MANUFACTURER

Siemens Electrogeräte GmbH
München, Germany

Kühl- und Gefrierschrank werden side-by-side zu einem großvolumigen Vorratszentrum kombiniert. Design Akzente setzt der automatisierte Wasser- bzw. Eisspender. Neben großem Volumen bestechen die Geräte mit sehr hoher Energieeffizienz, blendfreier LED-Beleuchtung und robusten Applikationen an stark beanspruchten Bereichen, wie den Griffen. Besonderen Komfort im Kühlteil bieten die ausziehbaren Schalen und Glasablagen, sowie die hydroFresh-Zone mit speziellem Klima für Obst und Gemüse. Die perfekte Raumaufteilung im Gefrierteil mit hochwertigen, robusten, ausziehbaren Schubladen und extra großem Fach bieten optimalen Zugriff und Lagerung.

Refrigerator and freezer are positioned side-by-side to form a large food storage center. The automatic water and ice dispenser sets design accents. In addition to their large volume, the appliances impress with high energy efficiency, glare-free LED lighting and robust applications in areas subject to heavy wear such as handles. Fully extractable bins and glass shelves as well as the hydroFresh zone with its special cooling climate for fruits and vegetables provide special convenience. The perfect space arrangement in the freezer with its high-quality, sturdy extractable drawers and an extra-large bin provide optimum storage and access.

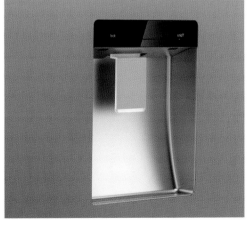

PRODUCT

HF25G5R2
Mikrowelle mit Grill
Microwave with grill

DESIGN

Siemens Electrogeräte GmbH
Frank Rieser
München, Germany

MANUFACTURER

Siemens Electrogeräte GmbH
München, Germany

Teil des Einbaugeräteprogramms in Edelstahl. Neue Interpretation des Zusammenspiels von hochwertigen Materialien nach der Idee, nicht die Menge eines Materials ist entscheidend, sondern es kommt darauf an, wie man gestalterisch damit umgeht. Kombination von glänzenden schwarzen Glasflächen mit Edelstahlapplikationen und Bedienelementen aus Edelstahl. Neu entwickeltes Bedienkonzept mit Direktwahlmodus, sowie weiß / schwarzer Displayanzeige und blauer Tastenquittierung, die den technisch-innovativen Designanspruch unterstützen. Hohe formale Abstimmung der Einzelkomponenten.

Part of the program of built-in stainless-steel appliances. A new interpretation of the interaction of high-quality materials that is based on the idea that not the quantity of materials is critical, but how the design uses them. Combination of shiny black glass areas with stainless-steel accents and control elements. Newly developed operating concept with direct-selection mode, white / black display and blue button confirmation that support the innovative technical design claim. High degree of coordination of individual components.

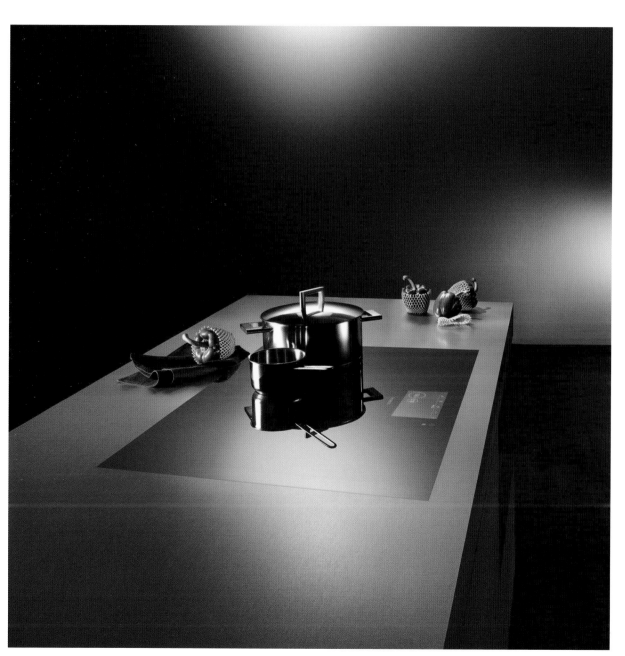

PRODUCT

EH801KU11E/EH875KU11
Flächen-Induktions-Kochstelle
Induction hob

DESIGN

Siemens Electrogeräte GmbH
Designabteilung
Jörn Ludwig
München, Germany
Zinosign
Baldham, Germany

MANUFACTURER

Siemens Electrogeräte GmbH
München, Germany

Die „freeInduction"-Kochmulde von Siemens zeichnet sich dadurch aus, dass das Kochgeschirr unabhängig von Größe und Form frei auf dem gesamten Kochfeld platziert werden kann. Ein Touch-Screen ermöglicht eine einfache und intuitive Bedienung. Während des Kochens kann das Geschirr verschoben und die einge-stellten Informationen mitgenommen werden. Auf der neuen Position kann dann ohne Unterbrechung weiter-gekocht werden. Die dezente Bedruckung verhindert ein Zerkratzen des Kochfeldes. Das Kochfeld kann mit aufgesetzter Keramikglasscheibe und seitlichen Metall-leisten oder flächenbündig in Glas- / Steinarbeitsplat-ten eingebaut werden.

The main feature of the Siemens "freeInduction" cook-top is that cooks can place their pots and pans anywhere on the cooking surface. A touch screen provides simple and intuitive operation. Cooks can push pots and pans around without losing their settings. The cooking process continues uninterrupted. The subtle pattern printed on the cooking surface prevents it from getting scratched. The cooktop can be installed with a ceramic glass disk and side-mounted metal rails or flush in glass or stone countertops.

PRODUCT

LC98KA570
Dunstabzugshaube, Glas
Chimney hood, glass

DESIGN

Siemens Electrogeräte GmbH
Julia Ehrensberger
München, Germany
Digitalform. Industrial Design
München, Germany

MANUFACTURER

Siemens Electrogeräte GmbH
München, Germany

Diese Glas-Schrägesse von Siemens besticht durch ihre filigrane Erscheinung: In eine 6 mm dünne Glasscheibe, am Stück gefertigt, sind bewegliche Filterpaneele eingelassen. Diese lassen sich aus der Fläche herausbewegen und geben somit die Absaugöffnungen frei. Das sehr dünne, dimmbare LED-Lichtband, was an der unteren Kante der Glasscheibe positioniert ist, beleuchtet in voller Breite der Esse das Kochfeld im idealen Winkel. In Verbindung mit der funktionsreichen Touch-Bedienung inkl. der Siemens typischen blauen „lightLine", setzt diese Glas-Schrägesse nicht nur in gestalterischer, sondern auch in innovativer Hinsicht Maßstäbe.

This slanted glass hood from Siemens impresses with its delicate appearance: movable filter panels are inserted into a solid piece of glass that is 6 mm thick. These panels can be pulled out to operate the extraction vents. The very thin, dimmable LED light band along at the lower edge of the glass and illuminates the cooktop from an ideal angle across the whole width of the hood. In combination with the touch controls and the typical Siemens blue "lightLine", the slanted extractor hood model sets new standards both in terms of design and innovation.

PRODUCT
Foldable Dish Rack
Geschirr
Kitchenware

DESIGN
Karim Rashid
New York, NY, United States of America

MANUFACTURER
Silicone Zone International Limited
Kowloon, Hong Kong

Dieser stilvolle und doch funktionelle Geschirrständer, mit einer Silikonmatte als Schale für abtropfendes Wasser, ist ein eleganter Schmuck Ihrer Küche. Mit diesem Ständer können Sie Ihr Geschirr oder Ihre Teller in den Rillen stapeln wie Sie möchten. Zur einfachen Aufbewahrung wurde dieses Produkt entwickelt und geformt, um vollständig zu einem schönen Objekt zu werden.

This functional foldable dish rack has derived from a traditional bamboo rack for dishes. Its reinterpretation is construed to be completely foldable when not in use. There is a non-slip silicone matching mat on which the dish rack safely rests. This mat catches water drips and snaps onto the flattened rack. With this rack, you can pile your dishes or plates into the grooves in any way you like and the small utensil tray can slide and lock automatically when unfolding the dish rack, creating a mono-form that is easy to store. More than a product, it is a unique well though out system.

PRODUCT

Asterion
Deckenhaube
Ceiling-mounted cooker hood

DESIGN

SILVERLINE Küchengeräte und Handel GmbH
Grevenbroich, Germany

MANUFACTURER

SILVERLINE Küchengeräte und Handel GmbH
Grevenbroich, Germany

Die besonders leise und schlichte Vollglas-Deckenhaube Asterion zeichnet sich durch puristisches Design aus und wird dort eingesetzt, wo durchgängig freier Blick erwünscht ist. Sowohl der Außenrahmen als auch die beiden Randabsaugungsplatten sind aus einer Hartglasoberfläche gefertigt, die mit einem schicken Facettenschliff an der Außenkante versehen sind. Die fernbedienbare Asterion ist mit einem innovativen und energiesparenden Motor von EBM-Papst aus Deutschland ausgestattet, die mit nur 39 dB (A) in der zweiten Leistungsstufe nahezu geräuschlos arbeitet und mit bis zu 1.200 cbm / h gutes Klima in die Küche zaubert.

The puristic and straight-line design full-glass ceiling hood Asterion is suitable for continuous and clearly view in the kitchen. Outer frames as well as the both perimetral exhaustion glass plates are made of tempered glass with an impressive facet cut. The remote-controlled Asterion is equipped with an innovative and energy-saving exhauster from EBM-Papst, made in Germany. Thanks to 39 dB (A) in second power level the ceiling hood is working almost noiseless and performs with 1200 cbm / h agreeable kitchen climate.

PRODUCT

VH-B75SN / B75GN / B80SN / B80GJN / B100WJN /
B110WJN
Doppelwannen-Waschmaschinen
Twin-tub washer

DESIGN

Toshiba Corporation
Shoichi Hibi, Hideto Shimizu
Tokyo, Japan

MANUFACTURER

Toshiba Home Appliances Corporation
Tokyo, Japan

Die Doppelwannen-Waschmaschinen sind auf die
Märkte von ASEAN- und Nahost-Ländern abgezielt
und haben ein Fassungsvermögen von 7,5 kg, 8 kg,
9 kg, 10 kg und 11 kg. Die Gehäuse sind aus Kunststoff
gefertigt, um hoher Luftfeuchtigkeit zu widerstehen.
Sie besitzen verbesserte Haltbarkeit und Rostschutz
und sind dennoch preiswert. Der Ag-Waschfilter verbessert die Wascheffizienz und besitzt antibakterielle
Eigenschaften und macht so das Gerät perfekt für die
örtlichen Bedingungen. Das Design ist einfach und elegant, und Form, Farbe und Funktionen strömen ein
Gefühl von Qualität und Hygiene aus.

*These twin-tub washing machines are aimed at the ASEAN
and Middle Eastern markets, and have capacities of 7.5 kg,
8 kg, 9 kg, 10 kg and 11 kg. The housings are made of resin to withstand high humidity, and they have improved
durability and rustproofing, as well as being inexpensive.
They have been designed with Ag washing filters for better washing and antibacterial effects, which makes them
perfect for local conditions. The design is simple and elegant and the shape, color and operational layout give a
sense of quality and hygiene.*

kitchen / household

PRODUCT
TW-Z9500/Z8500
Trommelwaschmaschine
Drum washing machine

DESIGN
Toshiba Corporation
Kana Nishimura
Tokyo, Japan

MANUFACTURER
Toshiba Home Appliances Corporation
Tokyo, Japan

Die hochwertige Trommelwaschmaschine und der Wärme-
pumpentrockner haben eine Kapazität von 9 bzw. 6 kg.
Die von Toshiba entwickelte aktive Aufhängung gewährleistet geräusch- und vibrationsarmen Betrieb und
die schnellste Waschgeschwindigkeit auf dem Markt.
Toshibas eigene PMV (Pulse Motor Valve) gesteuerte
Wärmepumpe ist ebenfalls sanft zu Kleidern und gibt
diesen ein hochwertiges Finish. Drei Sensoren erkennen
automatisch den Zustand der Kleider und wählen den
Waschmodus. Des Weiteren weist die Maschine das
höchste Energiesparpotenzial der Industrie auf.

This is a high-range drum-type washing machine and
heat-pump dryer with a capacity of 9 kg or 6 kg. Active
suspension, developed by Toshiba, ensures low-noise
and low-vibration operation and the industry's fastest
washing speed. Toshiba's own PMV (Pulse Motor Valve)
controlled heat pump is gentle on clothes to give them a
quality finish. Three sensors detect the clothes and auto-
matically select the wash mode, and it also boasts the in-
dustry's top energy-saving capabilities. The design is
simple and elegant and the shape, color and operational
layout have a sense of quality and hygiene that allows it
to match all styles of interior design.

PRODUCT
SIGN 0.6l & 1.2l
Teekanne mit integriertem Wärmer
Teapot with integrated warmer

DESIGN
Delphin Design GbR
Thomas Wagner, Dirk Loff
Berlin, Germany

MANUFACTURER
Trendglas Jena GmbH
Jena, Germany

Die Teekanne SIGN zeichnet sich durch eine kompakte Gestaltung und eine neuartige Kombination von Teekanne und Stövchen aus. Sie besitzt einen großzügigen Edelstahlfilter, der auch losen Teeblättern viel Raum zur Entfaltung bietet. SIGN ist leicht zu handhaben, platzsparend zu lagern und spülmaschinentauglich. Durch ihre klassische Form und die Herstellung aus Borosilikat-Glas sowie Edelstahl in den Größen 0,6 und 1,2 Liter ist sie Zeichen für Solidität und lange Haltbarkeit.

The teapot SIGN features a consolidated design and a novel combination of teapot and warmer. It houses a spacious stainless steel strainer which offers a wide interior so in which the leaves can brew. SIGN is simple to use, space saving and dishwasher safe. Its classic design featuring borosilicate glass is a symbol of solidity and durability.

kitchen / household

PRODUCT
Moonscape
Porzellanserie
Porcelain series

DESIGN
CULTURE FORM GmbH
Berlin, Germany

MANUFACTURER
VEGA Vertrieb von Gastronomiebedarf
Wertingen, Germany

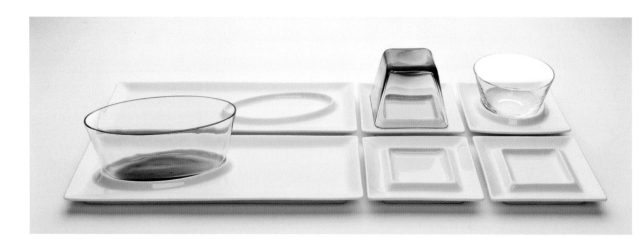

Auf innovative Weise kombiniert die Serie Moonscape
die Verschiedenartigkeit der Materialien Porzellan und
Glas. Der betont grafische Ansatz der einzelnen Teller
addiert sich zu einer erkennbaren Landschaft und bildet die Bühne für vielseitige Möglichkeiten der Speisen-
präsentation. Die farblichen und funktionalen Akzente
erhält die Serie durch ihre ergänzenden und formal aufeinander abgestimmten Highlights aus Glas. Durch die
Multifunktionalität der einzelnen Teile deckt die Serie
die vielfältigen Ansprüche und Bedürfnisse der Gastronomie auf neuartige Weise ab.

*The series Moonscape innovatively combines the diversity
inherent in porcelain and glass. The graphical approach
emphasized in the individual plates amasses in a recognizable landscape and forms a stage for numerous possibilities to present dishes. Color and functional accents are
given to the series through its complementing and compatible glass highlights. Due to the multi-functionality of
each article the series covers the diverse demands and requirements of the gastronomy in an entirely new manner.*

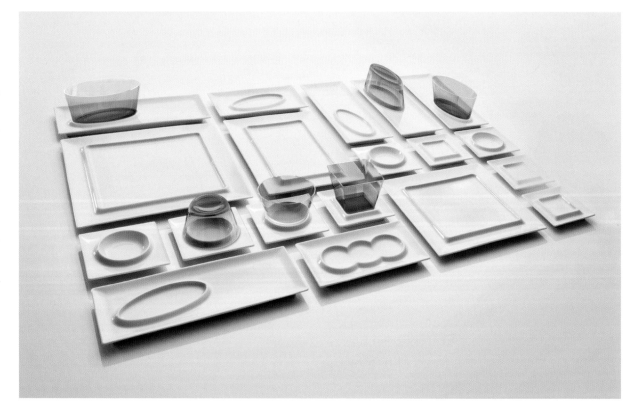

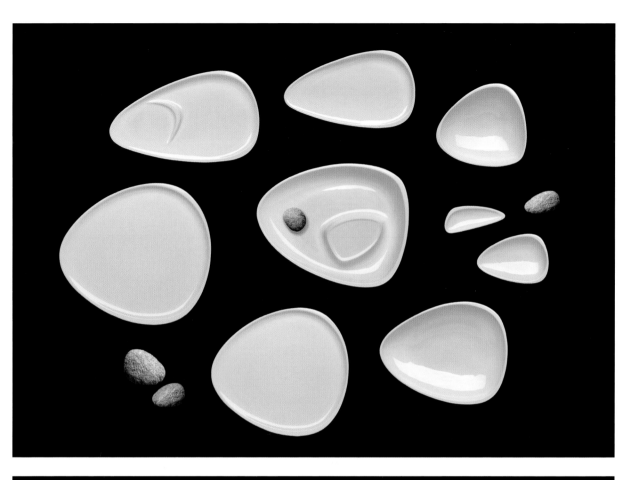

PRODUCT
Islands
Porzellanserie
Porcelain series

DESIGN
CULTURE FORM GmbH
Berlin, Germany

MANUFACTURER
VEGA Vertrieb von Gastronomiebedarf
Wertingen, Germany

Die Assoziationen und Inspirationen eines Strandspaziergangs verleihen dieser organischen Serie ihren unverwechselbaren Charakter. Spannungsvoll kontrastieren weiche Konturen die präzisen Schnitte und Flächen. Die partiell aus den Formen hervortretenden Flächen bilden bei dieser Serie Bühnen für die Präsentation besonderer Speisen. Dabei bilden die weiß und schwarz glasierten Elemente mit ihren variierenden Wandstärken gewachsene Strukturen nach. Die aus tiefen und flachen Tellern bestehende Serie ist stapelbar und im Handling auf die Bedürfnisse der Gastronomie optimiert.

Associations and inspirations taken from a walk on the beach lend this organic series its distinctive character. Smooth contours are intriguingly contrasted with precise cross-sections and surfaces. Shapes partially protruding from the surface form stages to present gourmet creations. Here the white and black glazed elements, with their varying wall thicknesses emulate evolved structures. The handling of this series, consisting of stackable plates and bowls, is optimized to deal with the demands of the gastronomy.

283

PRODUCT
ALINE
Geschirrspüler
Dishwasher

DESIGN
VESTEL
White Goods
VESTEL White Industrial Design Group
Serpil Sedef Yağcı
Manisa, Turkey

MANUFACTURER
Vestel Beyaz Eşya San. ve Tic. A.Ş.
Manisa, Turkey

ALINE ist einer der High-End-Design-Geschirrspüler, die die Reinheit und Qualität im Design dieses erstklassigen Produkts der VESTEL-Geschirrspüler reflektiert. Die neue Geschirrspüler-Kombination mit Glastür bietet Gelegenheit, verschiedene Farben auf dem Glas zu verwenden. Das elegante Erscheinungsbild wird durch das Chrom beschichtete schlanke Profil, das die seitlichen Griffe mit glitzernden Glasflächen trennt, erreicht. Die Übersichtlichkeit dieses Geschirrspülers mit großer Kapazität ist mit der intelligenten Trennung der Kontrollen geschaffen.

ALINE is one of the high-end dishwashers design, reflecting the purity and quality design of this top-notch product of VESTEL dishwashers. New dishwasher combination with glass door gives opportunity to use different colors on the glass. The elegant appearance is reached by the chrome coated slim profile that separates the handle with glittering surface. The intuitiveness of this large capacity dishwasher is created with the smart separation of the controls. While the most used controls like on / off button, program button and remaining time are located on the tilted panel; the rest is integrated hidden on the top of the door.

PRODUCT
K5 - Kochmesser
Großes Kochmesser
Large chef's knife

DESIGN
Windmühlenmesser-Manufactur Robert Herder
GmbH & Co. KG
Solingen, Germany

MANUFACTURER
Windmühlenmesser-Manufactur Robert Herder
GmbH & Co. KG
Solingen, Germany

Hier haben wir für die Klinge die sehr effiziente Form des japanischen Gyouto-Kochmessers zugrunde gelegt, gepaart mit der Balance unseres „K-Griff-Designs". Für klassische Kochmesserarbeit. Stärker als früher spielt ein gutes Griffdesign heute eine wichtige Rolle. Der Griff muss gut ausgewogen in der Hand liegen. Die Attribute sind: sehr gute Balance von Klinge und Griff für ermüdungsfreies Arbeiten; die feine Rundung am Übergang von Klinge zum Griff schützt die Finger; hohe Ergonomie des „K"-Designs dank der ovalen, geschwungenen Form entlastet die Hand; Hölzer wie Pflaume, Walnuss und der griffige POM-Kunststoff bedingen eine angenehme Haptik.

A full-sized chef's knife with a blade based on the highly efficient form of the Japanese Gyouto. This, coupled with the well balanced "K-Series handle design", makes it the ideal knife for all types of cutting classically done with a chef 's knife. Special importance is placed on the handle design: optimum balance and grip during cutting; outstanding balance between blade and handle for effortless cutting; gently rounded where blade and handle meet to protect fingers; excellent comfort thanks to the oval, curved handle design of the K-Series; woods like plum and walnut or high-quality POM synthetics offer a good grip and pleasant feel.

PRODUCT
Push-pull multiconcent
Allzweck-Buchse
All-purposed socket

DESIGN
winners Co., Ltd.
Park Kwang-sue
Kyeonggi-do, South Korea

MANUFACTURER
winners Co., Ltd.
Kyeonggi-do, South Korea

Diese Universalsteckdose kann in die Oberfläche von Arbeitstischen eingebaut werden. Dank des Push-Pull-Systems nimmt sie auf dem Tisch kaum Platz weg. Sie ist einfach zu verwenden und erhebt sich zum Gebrauch extrem leichtgängig aus der Tischplatte. Wird sie nicht benötigt, versinkt sie aus Sicherheitsgründen wieder im Tisch. Ist die Netzsteckdose ausgeschaltet, kann sie die Standby-Leistungsaufnahme blockieren. Sie ist durch ihren zweipoligen Reset-Schalter vor Überspannung geschützt. Dank NET (New Excellent Technology) ist die Steckdose besonders sicher, komfortabel und sogar vollkommen wasserdicht.

This all-purpose socket can be fitted into tables or desks. Thanks to the push-pull system, the power socket doesn't take up precious space on tables or desks. It's simple to use and simply rises up from the table or desk. The motion is super smooth. For safety reasons, the power socket only appears when it is being used. When out of use, it slots back into the table or desk – increasing overall safety. It can block off standby power when it is switched off and prevents overloading thanks to its two-pole reset switch. Thanks to NET (New Excellent Technology), the socket is ultra-safe and convenient and also completely waterproof.

BATHROOM / WELLNESS

TORSTEN FRITZE
ANDREAS HAUG
MARKUS WILD

  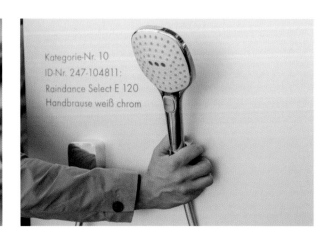

PRODUCT
OpenSpace
Duschabtrennung
Shower enclosure

DESIGN
EOOS Design GmbH
Wien, Austria

MANUFACTURER
Duravit AG
Hornberg, Germany

OpenSpace ist eine Duschabtrennung, die nur da ist, wenn sie gebraucht wird – nämlich beim Duschen. Danach werden beide Türen einfach „weggeklappt". So öffnet OpenSpace nicht nur optisch den Raum, sondern erweitert zudem den Bewegungsradius – ein Vorteil insbesondere für kleine Bäder. Möglich macht diese neue Form der Raumeffizienz ein Rahmen in hochglänzender Chrom-Optik. Darin sind zwei großflächige, selbst arretierende und wahlweise verspiegelte Glastüren eingelassen. Sie verdecken sowohl Armaturen als auch den Brausenschlauch. Zudem kommt die Konstruktion komplett ohne Trägerschiene aus, die in den Raum hineinragt.

A shower enclosure takes up a lot of valuable space in the bathroom. But does it really have to? OpenSpace is only there when needed – during showing. Afterwards, the doors can simply be „folded" against the wall. In addition to creating a more spacious feeling, this enables greater freedom of movement in the bathroom – a particular benefit for small bathrooms. A frame in brilliant chrome look provides this new form of room efficiency. Two large glass doors in option of mirror glass are fitted in the frame. They conceal the tap fittings and shower hose and avoid a rail protruding into the room.

product
design award

2013 GOLD

„Platzprobleme im Bad sind mit OpenSpace clever gelöst. Wenn nicht geduscht wird, kann man die Duschabtrennung verschwinden lassen, indem man ihre Flügel ganz an die Wand klappt. Mit einer bodenbündigen Duschwanne steht das Produkt voll im Trend."

"The OpenSpace is a clever solution to space problems in small bathrooms. When the shower is not in use, the shower screen disappears by folding the doors against the wall. With a flush-fitting floor shower tray, the product is right on trend."

JURYSTATEMENT

PRODUCT
WC Inspire
WC-Kollektion
WC collection

DESIGN
Design 3
Bjoern Vibrans, Wolfgang Wagner
Hamburg, Germany

MANUFACTURER
AM.PM
Berlin, Germany

Das wandhängende WC der Inspire-Kollektion spielt mit dem Kontrast von geometrischer Strenge und dynamischen Gestaltungselementen. Es erzeugt ein reduziertes, elegantes und eigenständiges Erscheinungsbild.

The WC of the Inspire collection is characterized by its combination of organic flow and geometric precision. It creates a minimized, yet very elegant and distinct overall impression.

PRODUCT
APM-0812DH
Luftreiniger und Luftbefeuchter
Air purifier and humidifier

DESIGN
Coway
Hun-jung Choi, Dae-hoo Kim
Seoul, South Korea

MANUFACTURER
Coway
Seoul, South Korea

APM-0812DH ist mit einem Luftreinigungssystem, das Staub, Viren und schädliche Gase eliminiert, sowie eine natürliche Befeuchtung gewährleistet, ausgestattet. APM-0812DH passt in kleine Räume und in Kinderzimmer. Die Kombination von glatten Linien, Pastellfarben und weichen Materialien betont Stabilität. Universelles Design bewirkt der Farb-Licht-Luftqualität- Indikator. Der Wasserkasten befindet sich an der Seite, was zwecks Wartung für einen leichteren Zugang sorgt. Die innere Abdeckung besteht aus HIPS-Material, einem ebenfalls recycelbaren Kunststoff. Schließt die Verwendung von beschichteten Materialien oder Spray aus, was zur Minimierung von Kohlenstoff-Emissionen führt.

APM-0812DH is equipped with an air purifying system that eliminates dust, viruses and harmful gases, as well as a natural humidifying system. APM-0812DH is placed in the small room and children's room. Combination of smooth lines and pastel colors and soft materials, emphasizing stability and comfort. Universal design by a color-lighting air quality indicator. A water tank located on the side for easier access and maintenance. The interior cover is made from the HIPS material, which is a recycled plastic. Preclude the use of plated or spray to minimize carbon emissions.

PRODUCT
Reoclone
Jet-Händetrockner
Jet hand dryer

DESIGN
DAELIM DOBIDOS
Kim Jun, Byun Young-Min
Incheon, South Korea

MANUFACTURER
DAELIM DOBIDOS
Incheon, South Korea

Mit dem Reoclone-Jet-Händetrockner lassen sich die Hände viel schneller und hygienischer trocknen. Als Inspirationsquelle diente die Form einer Blütenknospe, dadurch strahlt das Gerät natürlichen Minimalismus aus. Reoclone ist ein hygienischer und umweltfreundlicher Händetrockner. Er hilft, den Standby- und Gesamtstromverbrauch sowie die Verwendung von Einwegtüchern zu reduzieren. Blaue, rote und grüne LEDs zeigen die Dauer des Trockenvorganges an und lassen nicht so schnell Langeweile aufkommen. Reoclone sorgt dafür, dass die Hände komplett getrocknet werden und ist auch für Kinder, Senioren und Menschen mit Behinderung leicht zu bedienen.

The Reoclone jet hand dryer can completely dry your hands faster and more hygienically in public toilets. The motivation behind the design is a flower bud, emphasizing natural minimalism. Reoclone is a hygienic and eco-friendly jet hand dryer. It can help to reduce standby electricity, total electricity consumption and the use of disposables. Blue, red and green LED indicators help users to recognize how long the drying process lasts, so they don't get bored easily. Reoclone ensures that users' hands are dried in full and is simple for children, the elderly and disabled people to use.

PRODUCT
INVENTIO II
Digitale Brausebatterie
Digital shower mixer

DESIGN
Daelim Trading Co., Ltd.
Kwi Hoon Ha
Incheon, South Korea

MANUFACTURER
Daelim Trading Co., Ltd.
Incheon, South Korea

Wassertemperatur und für Durchfluss / Wasserweiche
sind die Schlüsselfaktoren, die bequeme und intuitive
Nutzung ermöglichen. Die Griffe haben ein Steuerele-
ment für den Benutzer. Veränderungen von Durchfluss
und Temperatur werden in Farben und Helligkeit der
LEDs angezeigt. Dieses Das Design-Motto der INVENTIO II
ist Schlankheit und Glätte. Zwei Steuerpunkte für visuelle Feedback ermöglicht die intime Interaktion zwischen
Benutzer und Produkt, das sich durch Benutzerfreundlichkeit, visuelle Unterhaltung und Sicherheit auszeichnet. Zusätzlich ergänzt der große quadratische Dusch-
kopf das Gefühl einer frischen und angenehmen
Dusche.

The design motto of INVENTIO II is slimness and sleek-
ness. Two control handles for water flow / diverter and
On-Off / Temperature are the key factors allowing con-
venient and intuitive use. User's control of the handles to
change flow rate and temperature is displayed into the
LED's colors and brightness. This visual feedback enables
the intimate interaction between user and the product
effecting ease of use, visual entertainment and safety
enhancement. In addition, the wide square shower head
adds to the fresh and rich feeling of shower.

PRODUCT

SensoWash® Starck C
Dusch-WC-Sitz
Shower-toilet seat

DESIGN

Philippe Starck
Paris, France

MANUFACTURER

Duravit AG
Hornberg, Germany

Nichts ist so gründlich, so natürlich und so erfrischend wie die Reinigung mit Wasser – auch nach dem Toilettengang. Der Dusch-WC-Sitz SensoWash® Starck C bringt erstmals höchsten Designanspruch und Bidetkomfort miteinander in Verbindung. Dabei enthüllt sich die Duschfunktion ganz diskret erst beim Blick in das geöffnete WC. Denn alle technischen Komponenten wurden miniaturisiert, sodass die Anschlüsse für Wasser und Elektrik zwischen Keramik-Körper und WC-Sitz Platz finden und die klaren Designlinien nicht stören. Über eine ebenso reduzierte, kabellose Fernbedienung können Duscharten und Föhn-Einstellungen intuitiv gesteuert werden.

Nothing is as thorough, as natural and as refreshing as cleaning with water. After using the toilet, too. For the first time, the SensoWash® Starck C shower-toilet seat combines highest design requirements and bidet comfort. The shower function only becomes apparent when the toilet lid is opened. All the technical components were miniaturized so that the water and power connections could fit between the ceramic body and the toilet seat without detracting from the clear design lines. The different shower and dryer functions are operated intuitively via the similarly minimalist wireless remote control.

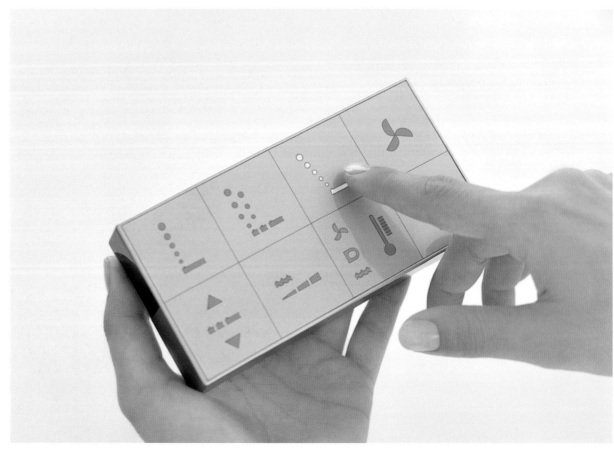

PRODUCT
St.Trop
Dampfdusche
Steam shower

DESIGN
Philippe Starck
Paris, France

MANUFACTURER
Duravit AG
Hornberg, Germany

Konsequent auf das Wesentliche reduziert präsentiert sich die Dampfdusche St.Trop als schlichtes Rechteck, das nicht mehr als einen Quadratmeter an Grundfläche beansprucht. Beim Design ließ sich Philippe Starck von einem Gemälde inspirieren: Die Tür zeigt einen Bilderrahmen wie bei einem großen Kunstwerk; der Hintergrund ist weiß und bildet die Leinwand. Zum Motiv wird der Duschende selbst und vollendet das Bild in seiner natürlichen Schönheit. Auch der aus temperaturfestem Material bestehende Hocker nimmt das künstlerische Motiv auf: Er ist eine Skulptur für sich. St.Trop verbindet eine vollwertige Dusche mit entspannendem Dampfbad in einem.

Consistently reduced to the essentials, the steam shower St. Trop is presented as a simple rectangle that takes up no more than one square meter of floor space. Philippe Starck's design is inspired by a painting: the door is akin to a frame adorning a large-scale artwork; the white background forms the canvas. The person taking a shower becomes the motif, creating a work of natural beauty. Continuing the artistic theme, the stool made of heat-resistant material is a sculpture in its own right. St. Trop combines wholesome showering with relaxing steam bathing in one.

PRODUCT

Easy Drain XS
Duschrinne
Linear shower drain

DESIGN

Easy Sanitary Solutions GmbH
Bad Bentheim, Germany

MANUFACTURER

Easy Sanitary Solutions GmbH
Bad Bentheim, Germany

Hightech und vor allem das schmalste Duschablauf-
system machen die Easy Drain XS einzigartig. Revolu-
tionär ist, dass das durch uns patentierte TAF-System
(Tile Adjustable Frame) auch hier Anwendung findet,
sodass Wasserdichtheit und eine perfekte Verarbeitung
100 % garantiert wird. Serienmäßig ist diese Duschrinne mit einem in der Höhe verstellbaren Siphon ausgestattet, der einfach zu reinigen ist und für eine sehr
hohe Ablaufleistung sorgt. Die XS ist in zahlreichen,
auch farbigen Variationen lieferbar. Wofür Sie sich auch
entscheiden: XS ist und bleibt „extra schmal". Mit dieser
Serie verbürgt sich ESS für Qualität, Design und Langlebigkeit.

*The Easy Drain XS is unique, high-tech and above all a
super small shower drainage system. With the revolutionary use of our patented TAF (Tile Adjustable Frame)
system we guarantee a beautiful, 100 % waterproof finish. The XS shower drain is equipped with an easy-to-
clean and height adjustable siphon, providing a very
high drainage capacity. The XS series is available in various and even colorful variations, but it is always "extra
small". With this series ESS guarantees quality, design
and durability.*

PRODUCT
New Water Jewels
Sanitär-Produkte
Sanitary ware

DESIGN
Eczacibasi Yapi Gerecleri
Inhouse Design Team
Istanbul, Turkey

MANUFACTURER
Eczacibasi Yapi Gerecleri
Istanbul, Turkey

New Water Jewels bietet diverse Farben, Töne und Gewebe, die die Gestaltung beispielloser Badezimmer ermöglichen. Die Becken beinhalten im Allgemeinen auffallende Details mit verschiedenen Farben und Mustern, wodurch das Badezimmer veredelt wird. Die Serien beinhalten außer Platin-, Kupfer- und Goldtönen auch andere Modelle für den Innenbereich mit einer Zwei-Ton-Farbauswahl. Neben ihren neuen Farben vervollkommnen die neuen „Vogue-Fliesen" (quadratisch oder rechteckig) die New Water Jewels-Becken.

VitrA offers you a wealth of colors, an exhilarating range of tones and textures with New Water Jewels that creates unique bathroom spaces possible. Washbasins are offered in variety of colors and patterns that enhance bathroom interiors with their eye-catching details. Besides platinum, copper and gold tones, the ranges include a variety of two-tone colors as well as inner sections designed with patterns that transform. Besides the colors in range, New Water Jewels washbasins with patterns can be complemented with "Vogue" wall tiles. Further enhancing the range is the selection of new sizes, washbasins have square and rectangular options.

PRODUCT

Sirius
Spülkasten-Kontrollpaneel
Concealed cistern control panel

DESIGN

Eczacibasi Yapi Gerecleri
Inhouse Design Team
Istanbul, Turkey

MANUFACTURER

Eczacibasi Yapi Gerecleri
Istanbul, Turkey

Inspiriert wurde das Paneel durch den glänzenden Hundsstern (Sirius) des Sternensystems. Das Kontrollpaneel besteht aus einfachen geometrischen Formen, die vollkommen übereinstimmen. Das Kontrollmodell besteht aus Doppelsiphon und tritt durch die funktionalen Knopfdimensionen in den Vordergrund. Sirius wird in vier verschiedenen Material- und Farbmöglichkeiten angeboten: glänzend weiß, matt schwarz, verchromt und matt verchromt. Durch diese Farb- und Materialmöglichkeiten können neue Variationen gebildet werden. Die kreativen Design-Arbeiten für die „VitrA"-Badezimmer beinhalten Anti-Fingerabdruck-Beschichtungen.

Sirius concealed system control panel is not only functional, but also adds value to your bathrooms. Design is influenced by binary star system, Sirius, appearing as the brightest star at night. Control panel composes of simple geometric forms joining in harmony. As its control type is dual flush; functionality is featured by button sizes. Sirius comes in four different material and color options: shiny white, matt black, chrome and matt chrome plated. Variations with color and material options are configurable. "VitrA's" innovative design studies created anti-fingerprint solution. Design individualized with functionality is carried to bathroom with Sirius.

PRODUCT

Legno Acqueo
Holzwaschschale
Wooden wash basin

DESIGN

Gino Pommerenke
München, Germany

MANUFACTURER

Flowood GbR
Dr. Martina Taubenberger, Gino Pommerenke
München, Germany

Legno Acqueo ist die Urform der Produktfamilie Legno, einer Waschschalen-Trilogie, die auf derselben Grundform beruht und nur durch die unterschiedlichen Außenradien jeweils einen völlig eigenen Charakter zeigt. Alle Flowood-Becken werden aus einem Mehrschicht-Massivblock geformt und in Handarbeit gefinished. Flowood arbeitet mit zwei Varianten der Oberflächenveredelung: Der traditionellen Behandlung mit natürlichen Ölen und Wachsen und dem revolutionären Verfahren „liquid glass", einer Tiefenimprägnierung mit flüssigem Quarzsand. Flowood empfiehlt die Verwendung von wassersparenden Armaturen mit weichem Wasserstrahl.

Legno Acqueo is the origin of the Legno product family, all of them based on the same basic form inspired by the natural flow of water. Only by changing the outside radius, each basin gets its own character. Every Flowood basin is formed from a solid block of multilayered wood and gets a handmade finishing. Flowood works with two types of finishing. Traditionally, we use natural oils and waxes and also the revolutionary procedure of liquid glass finishing. Target for 2013 is the series production of a solid wood bathtub.

PRODUCT
AquaClean Sela
Dusch-WC
Shower toilet

DESIGN
Matteo Thun & Partners
Milano, Italy

MANUFACTURER
Geberit International AG
Jona, Switzerland

Einzigartig ist dieses Dusch-WC durch integrierte Technik, minimale Aufbauhöhe sowie unsichtbare Befestigung und Anschlüsse an Strom und Wasser. Es erscheint wie ein normales WC. Dieses neuartige Konzept erfordert eine hochpräzise Fertigung. Trotz kompakter Außenmaße bietet es großzügigen Nutzraum. Sitz und Deckel aus stabilem Duroplast lassen sich mit Dämpfern leise schließen. Der ergonomische Sitz mit durchgehender Oberfläche ist einfach zu reinigen. Per Knopfdruck auf das intuitiv gestaltete Bedienfeld oder die Fernbedienung startet ein wohltemperierter, sanft reinigender Wasserstrahl.

Integrated functional components, minimal height, hidden fixations and concealed connections for power and water supply make this shower toilet unique. It looks like a conventional WC. This new concept requires high-precision production. Despite its compact size, it offers comfortable space. Its durable lid and the ergonomically designed seat made of Duroplast are equipped with dampers for silent closing. Cleaning is especially easy because the seat covers even the hinges. Pushing a button on the intuitively shaped control panel or the remote control initiates a warm and gentle water spray.

PRODUCT
FOX
Badewannenserie
Bathtub series

DESIGN
maKe design
Jörg Plehn
Darmstadt, Germany

MANUFACTURER
GKI - Sanitär-VertriebsgesmbH
Ebbs / Tirol, Austria

Die FOX-Badewannenserie verbindet eine klare, design-orientierte Formensprache mit einem hohen Anspruch an die Ergonomie der Innenform. Von der einsitzigen Wanne mit mehreren möglichen Überlaufpositionen, über die zweisitzigen Oval-, Rechteck- und asymmetrischen Eckwannen in Rechts- und Linksausführung bis zur Rundwanne bietet die Serie Gestaltungsmöglichkeiten für jede Badplanung. Die Ovalwanne mit bündig angeformter Schürze ergänzt das Sortiment durch eine frei stehende Lösung. Alle Wannenmodelle sind whirlpoolfähig und haben eine schmutzabweisende Oberflächenbehandlung.

The FOX bathtub series conveys a clear and design orientated formal expression with high level ergonomics of the inner shape. From the solo seat bathtub with different position options for the overflow, over the dual seat oval, rectangular and corner bathtubs, to the circular shaped bathtub, the range provides solutions for every bath planning. With the oval bathtub with the flush skirt there is also a solution for free-standing situations. All bathtubs can be equipped with whirlpool features and have a dirt-repellent finish.

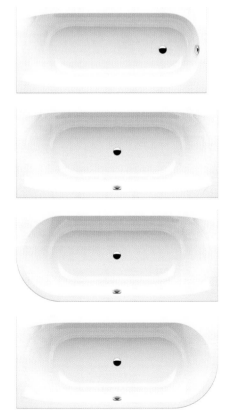

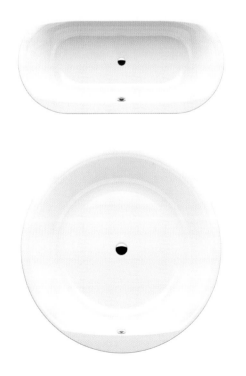

PRODUCT

Allure Aquastripe
Ablagelösung
Storage solution

DESIGN

Grohe AG
Düsseldorf, Germany

MANUFACTURER

Grohe AG
Düsseldorf, Germany

Als Erweiterung der preisgekrönten Allure-Kollektion entstand mit Aquastripe eine praktische und attraktive Ablagelösung, die Form und Funktion harmonisch verbindet. Ausgangspunkt war der Verbraucherwunsch nach mehr Platz für die griffbereite Aufbewahrung von Kosmetik- und Badprodukten genauso wie für die zeitweilige Ablage von Uhren und Schmuck. Die schlichte Streifenform bindet alle Allure-Elemente ein und wertet mit ihrer edlen Metalloptik den gesamten Waschtischbereich auf. Dabei gewährleisten die variablen Längen und die unsichtbare Wandbefestigung individuelle Lösungen für jede Badsituation.

To enhance our award-winning Allure collection we have delicately balanced form and function to create Aquastripe, a highly practical and beautiful storage solution. Inspired by the insight that consumers desire more space to store bathroom essentials, we designed an elevated shelf that is the perfect place to keep everything from watches and jewelry to cosmetics and SPA accessories. The simple metal shelf, which combines all the Allure components, is easily and discretely mounted to the wall. The geometric stripe creates harmony and transforms the washbasin zone. To ensure esthetic perfection, the shelves can be ordered in bespoke lengths.

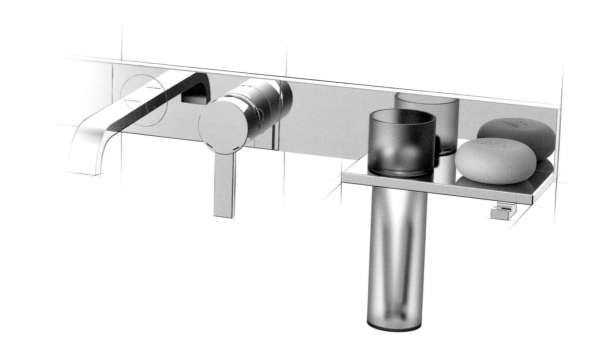

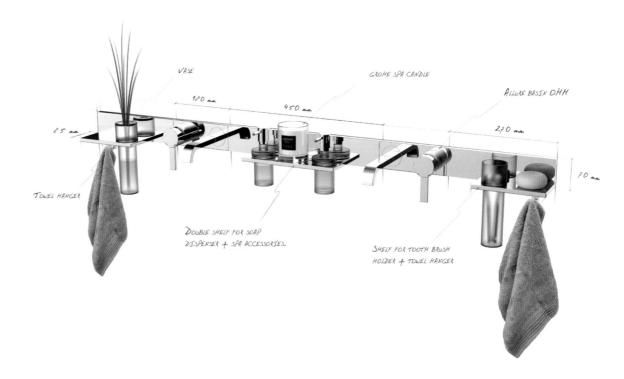

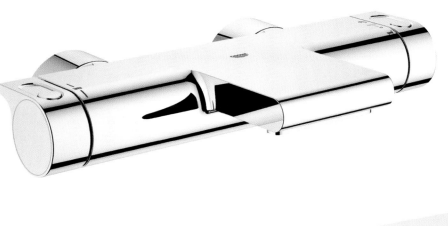

PRODUCT
Grohtherm 2000 new
Bad-Kollektion
Bath collection

DESIGN
Grohe AG
Düsseldorf, Germany

MANUFACTURER
Grohe AG
Düsseldorf, Germany

Ein minimalistisch gestalteter Thermostat mit innovativem Bedienkonzept. Seine ergonomisch geformten „Aqua Paddles" sind leicht zu greifen. Außerdem signalisieren sie sichtbar und fühlbar eine Über- oder Unterschreitung der voreingestellten Wassertemperatur von 38 °C. Aus dem Armaturenkörper erwächst nahtlos ein breiter Auslauf, der das Wasser weit und flächig im Stil eines Wasserfalls ausströmen lässt. Fortgesetzt wird die minimalistische Formgebung von der optionalen Duschablage, die die Lücke zwischen Armatur und Wand schließt. Intuitiv verständliche Farbpiktogramme regen zur aktiven Nutzung der Wassersparfunktion „Eco" an.

A minimalist thermostat with innovative "Aqua Paddles" which enhances the ergonomy of the product. Their unique sculpted form is easier to grip and clearly signifies when the temperature is above or below the preset 38 °C. The wide spout transitions seamlessly from the body and delivers an extra-large laminar flow, which is inspired by the width and powerful flow of a waterfall. The optional minimalist shelf simply attaches to the rear and provides easily accessible storage. The Eco function is clearly communicated through the introduction of intuitive colored graphic icons which guide the user to reduce water consumption when desired.

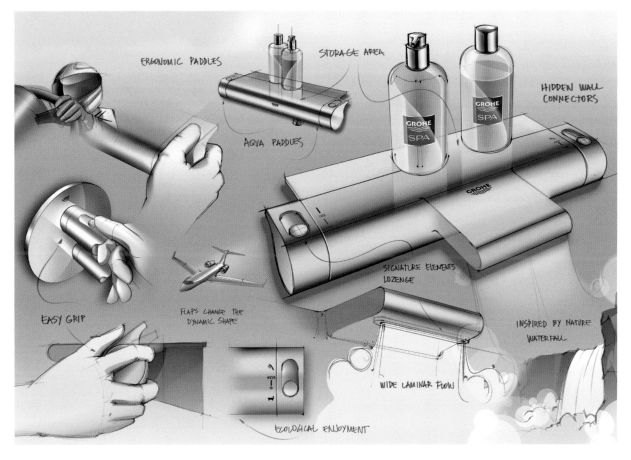

PRODUCT
F-Digital Deluxe
Brausen-Kollektion
Shower collection

DESIGN
Grohe AG
Düsseldorf, Germany

MANUFACTURER
Grohe AG
Düsseldorf, Germany

GROHE SPA™ bietet einen ultraschlanken Controller für die intuitive Steuerung eines einzigartigen Duscherlebnisses für alle Sinne. Über den extern platzierten Controller stellt man sein individuelles Wellnessprogramm aus Licht (Farbtherapie), Sound (Klangtherapie) und Dampf (Aquatherapie) zusammen. Damit realisiert GROHE seine ambitionierte Vision, das Bad von einem funktionalen Raum der Reinigung und Pflege in ein inspirierendes und emotional ansprechendes privates Spa zu verwandeln. Mit dieser digitalen Innovation kann jeder Benutzer sein individuelles Duschvergnügen im persönlichen Wohlfühlambiente gestalten und komfortabel steuern.

GROHE SPA™ introduces an intuitive and super-slim device that controls our unique new collection of products designed to stimulate the senses. With a simple touch of the "dry-zone" controller you can now choose your desired combination of lighting (chromotherapy), sound (audiotherapy) and steam (aquatherapy) – three vital elements that positively influence our physical, emotional and spiritual wellbeing. GROHE's ambitious vision of transforming the bathroom from a rational space for cleaning and grooming into an inspiring and emotional Home SPA is now a reality. F-Digital Deluxe is the perfect way to create a truly personalized experience.

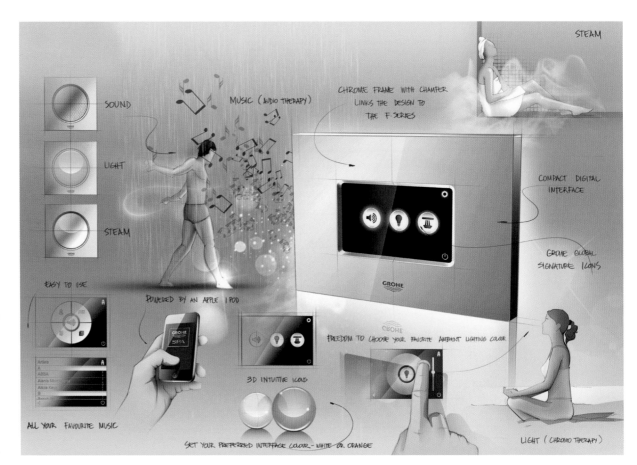

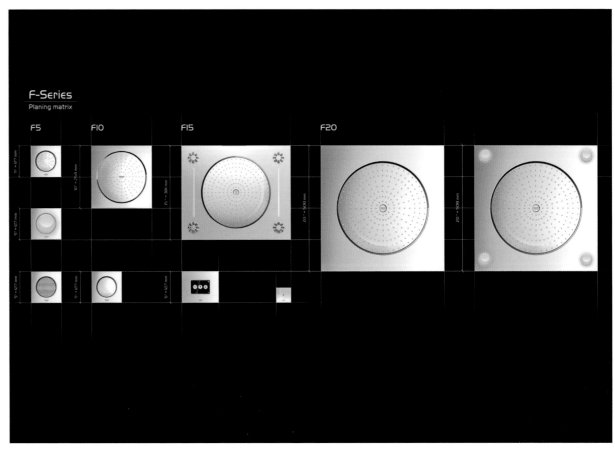

PRODUCT
Pump water heater
Wasserkocher
Water heater

DESIGN
Haier Innovation Design Center
Song Lei, Liu Haibo, Yang Sen, Dai Nanhai
Qingdao, China

MANUFACTURER
Haier Group
Qingdao, China

Dieses Produkt verbraucht sehr wenig Strom, sorbiert Wärme aus der Umgebungsluft ab, und transportiert diese durch den Kompressor in den Kondensator. Dann setzt es Wärme an dem Wassertank frei, um ihn zu erwärmen. Das passt zu den 24-Stunden-Bedürfnissen einer ganzen Familie, die Warmwasser in großer Menge, mit hohem Wasserdruck und konstanter Temperatur benötigt. Die Energieeffizienz ist dreimal höher als die herkömmlicher elektrischer Wasserkocher. In Verbindung mit der einzigartigen Haier-Anwärmung-3-D-Technologie, bei der die Heizstäbe partiell erwärmt werden, kann man jederzeit Warmwasser nutzen, ohne warten zu müssen.

This product consumes electric energy a little. In detail, it absorbs heat in surrounding air, transmits the heat to condenser through compressor and release the heat to water tank to heat it, which has the energy efficiency three times higher than electric heater and can meet various demands on hot water of big water volume, high pressure and constant temperature for a whole family for 24 h. It can release cold air as an air conditioner and can dehumidify to certain extent in partial space as balcony, storage room and garage. With the exclusive 3D heating technique of Haier that heats locally with heating rod.

PRODUCT
Raindance Select E 120
Handbrause
Hand shower

DESIGN
Phoenix Design GmbH + Co. KG
Stuttgart, Germany

MANUFACTURER
Hansgrohe SE
Schiltach, Germany

Die Raindance Select E 120-Handbrause verteilt zwei
Regenstrahlen, kräftig und sanft, großzügig über die
gesamte Fläche der Strahlscheibe. Hinzu kommt ein belebender Massagestrahl. Intuitiv einfach wechselt man
die Strahlarten mit einem Klick auf den großflächigen
Select-Knopf, der ergonomisch vorne in der Nähe des
Daumens positioniert ist. Soft-Cube-Design mit harmonisch abgerundeten Ecken prägt die Gestaltung. Der
120 mm große Brausekopf verschmilzt fließend mit
dem ergonomisch komfortablen Griff. Neben der reinen Chrom-Variante kombiniert der zweifarbige Weiß-
Chrom-Look eine weiße Strahlscheibe mit einem
chromglänzenden Gehäuse.

This hand shower generously distributes two forceful and
gentle streams of rain across the entire area of the shower
face. A third option is an invigorating massage jet. Switch-
ing from one type of jet to another is intuitively simple: a
single click on the large Select button ergonomically
placed at the front, close to the thumb. Harmoniously
rounded corners reflect the mixer's Soft-Cube design.
The 120 mm showerhead is joined to the ergonomically
shaped, comfortable handle in a seamless, fluid transition.
In addition to the all-chrome model, the two-tone white-
chrome look combines a white shower face with a shiny
chrome housing.

PRODUCT
Raindance Rainfall 150 Stream
Schwallbrause
Flood shower

DESIGN
Phoenix Design GmbH + Co. KG
Stuttgart, Germany

MANUFACTURER
Hansgrohe SE
Schiltach, Germany

Die neue Raindance Rainfall 150 Stream-Schwallbrause bringt mit ihrem innovativen RainStream-Strahl das Wasserfallgefühl ins Bad. Anders als bei herkömmlichen Schwallstrahlen, die sich häufig auf dem Weg nach unten verengen, teilt die neue Technologie den Schwall in viele Einzelstrahlen auf, die den Duschenden auf voller Breite benetzen. Dank ihres zeitlosen Designs lässt sie sich universell einsetzen und ganz einfach auf der Wand installieren. Der Strahl hat auch bei deutlich reduziertem Wasserverbrauch noch einen angenehmen Effekt – perfekt für Anwendungen mit belebender Wirkung, etwa nach dem Sport oder der Sauna.

With its innovative RainStream jet, the new Raindance Rainfall 150 Stream flood shower brings the sensation of standing under a waterfall into the bathroom. Unlike conventional flood jets, which often taper down along their trajectory, the new technology splits the stream into many separate jets which spread across the entire body of the person in the shower. Thanks to its timeless style, it is suitable for any setting, and it is easy to install on the wall. Even at significantly reduced water consumption, the jet still feels very pleasant – perfect for situations that call for an invigorating effect, such as after sporting activities or after a sauna.

PRODUCT

HÜPPE Design
Duschabtrennung
Shower enclosure

DESIGN

HÜPPE GmbH
Bad Zwischenahn, Germany
Phoenix Design GmbH + Co. KG
Stuttgart, Germany

MANUFACTURER

HÜPPE GmbH
Bad Zwischenahn, Germany

HÜPPE Design „elegance" und „pure" – moderne Glas-
duschen in exclusivem Design. Mit einem vielfältigen
Gleit- und Schwingtürprogramm bietet die Produktserie
HÜPPE Design transparente und intelligente Lösungen
für jeden Raum. Designed by Phoenix Design gibt es
den Alleskönner in zwei Designrichtungen: elegance
(soft, elegant) und pure (reduziert, puristisch). Preislich
attraktiv überzeugt diese Designlinie mit Bicolor-Aus-
stattung, barrierefreier Einstiegsmöglichkeit und technischen Highlights wie optionaler Soft-Close-Funktion
und innovativen Reinigungsfeatures. HÜPPE Design
elegance und pure – der designstarke Allrounder für
jedermann.

*HÜPPE Design elegance and pure – modern glass show-
ers in an exclusive design. With a diverse range of sliding
and swing doors HÜPPE Design offers transparent and
intelligent solutions for any room. Designed by Phoenix
Design, the all-rounder is available in two variants: elegance (soft, elegant) and pure (reduced, purist). Attractively priced, this design line impresses with Bicolor fittings,
barrier-free entry option and technical highlights such as
the optional Soft-Close function and innovative cleaning
features. HÜPPE Design elegance and pure – the well-
designed all-rounder for everyone.*

PRODUCT
HÜPPE Refresh pure
Duschabtrennung
Shower enclosure

DESIGN
HÜPPE GmbH
Bad Zwischenahn, Germany

MANUFACTURER
HÜPPE GmbH
Bad Zwischenahn, Germany

HÜPPE Refresh pure – Transparenz mit markanten Details und Persönlichkeit. Das neue Design der Schwing-
türserie HÜPPE Refresh pure präsentiert sich klar und
geradlinig. Durch den Verzicht auf horizontale Rahmen-
profile wirkt sie besonders transparent. Einen echten
Blickfang der neuen Designlinie bieten die markanten
Wandanbindungen mit klaren Linien und rechtwinkligen
Details. Technisch überzeugt die HÜPPE Refresh pure
mit einzigartiger Scharnierhaltetechnik, Innen- und
Außenöffnung, flächenbündigen Scharnieren, integrierter
Verstellmöglichkeit sowie der patentierten HÜPPE-Keder-
technik zur Wandleistenmontage ohne sichtbare Ver-
schraubungen.

*HÜPPE Refresh pure – transparency with striking details
and personality. The new design for the HÜPPE Refresh
pure swing door series presents itself with clarity and
clean lines. By dispensing with horizontal frame profiles
it comes across as strikingly transparent. The striking wall
connections with clear lines and rectangular details
provide the new design line with special visual appeal.
HÜPPE Refresh pure impresses you with unique hinge
technology, inward and outward opening, flush-mounted hinges, an integrated option for adjustment as well as
the patented HÜPPE sealing technology for fitting the
wall profile with no visible screws.*

PRODUCT
IDEALRAIN CUBE
Handbrausenserie
Hand shower series

DESIGN
ARTEFAKT industriekultur
Darmstadt, Germany

MANUFACTURER
IDEAL STANDARD INTERNATIONAL BVBA
Brüssel, Belgium

IDEALRAIN CUBE ist ein Handbrausenprogramm, welches in zwei mal zwei Ausführungen erhältlich ist. Durch das Gestalten nahe der „Quadratur des Kreises" wurde eine neue Duschkopfform mit reduzierter organischer Formsprache erzeugt. IDEALRAIN CUBE bietet nicht nur große Duschköpfe, sondern dazu den größtmöglichen Duschstrahl zu den einzelnen Modellgrößen. Die ultraflachen Ausführungen der Duschköpfe verlaufen fließend in die ergonomischen Griffbögen, zusätzlich erfolgt die Steuerung der verschiedenen Brauseprogramme bei den Modellen mit integrierten drei Funktionen durch den ergonomisch geformten „fin-handle".

IDEALRAIN CUBE is a hand shower system which is available in two by two versions. Designing close to "square of the circle" a new form of a shower head was made with a reduced organic design. IDEALRAIN CUBE offers not only large shower heads but also the greatest showering spout of each shower size. The very flat design of the shower head morphs into the ergonomical handle. Furthermore the versions which include three functions offer a control of different shower programs through an ergonomical designed "fin-handle".

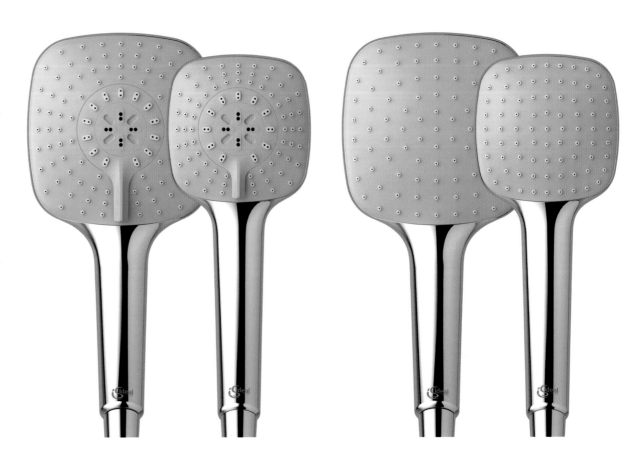

PRODUCT
STRADA
Armaturenserie
Fitting range

DESIGN
ARTEFAKT industriekultur
Darmstadt, Germany

MANUFACTURER
IDEAL STANDARD INTERNATIONAL BVBA
Brüssel, Belgium

Die Armaturenserie STRADA folgt mit ihrer Formsprache dem Trend der zeitgenössischen gradlinigen Architekturwelt. Mit ihrer puristischen Gestalt bietet sie viele Kombinationsmöglichkeiten bei der Badplanung, verliert jedoch dabei nicht ihren klaren formalen Charakter. Die Gestaltungsmerkmale wurden von der Armaturenserie für den Waschplatz konsequent auf ergänzende Armaturentypen für die Badewanne und den Duschbereich übernommen. Somit bietet die STRADA Serie ein urbanes zeitgemäßes Badprogramm, das durch seine Klarheit und Präzision hervorsticht.

The design of the fitting range STRADA follows the contemporary straight-lined trend of the architecture. With its pure form it offers a lot of combination possibilities in bathroom planning but in doing so it does not loose its clear formal character. The characteristic design features were applied consequently from the fitting range for wash stands to additional fittings for bath tubs and showers. Thus the STRADA series provides an urban contemporary bath system which stands out due to its clearness and precision.

PRODUCT

statthocker

Hocker

Stool

DESIGN

Beierarbeit GmbH

Bielefeld, Germany

phantastischlerei

Oliver Bahr, Bastian Demmer

Herford, Germany

MANUFACTURER

Identity Group

Bielefeld, Germany

Der statthocker ist eine ehemalige Straßenlaterne. Die seit Jahrzehnten bekannten „Pilzkopflampen" werden bundesweit durch energiesparende Diodenlampen ersetzt. Somit verschwindet ein Stück Kindheitserinnerung und Heimat. Wer erinnert sich nicht an die Zeitangabe der Eltern: Wenn die Laternen angehen, kommst Du nach Hause. Die Wiederverwendung als Hocker schont Ressourcen, bewahrt Stadt- und Designgeschichte. Der Hocker ist stapelbar, stabil und wasserresistent. Der Deckel aus Mineralstoff auf der ehemaligen Montageöffnung ist in diversen Farben wählbar.

Instead of stool is a former street lamp. The well-known for decades "mushroom lamps" are replaced by nationwide energy-saving lamps diodes. Thus disappears a piece of childhood memory and home. Who does not remember the time shown by the parents, if the lanterns tackle, you get home. Reuse as a stool saves resources, preserved city and design history. The stool is stackable, sturdy and water-resistant. The lid is made of minerals on the former installation opening can be selected in various colors.

PRODUCT
WHITE HOUSE
Badmöbelserie
Bathroom furniture

DESIGN
Kale, Design & Innovation Group (K. I. D.)
E. Sertaç Ersayın (VP Design & Innovation, CDO),
Özgür Alp (Product Design), Fatih Mintaş
(Product Design), Gözde Tüfekçi Mercan
(Strategic Design)
Istanbul, Turkey

MANUFACTURER
Kaleseramik Çanakkale Kalebodur Seramik Sanayi A.Ş
Istanbul, Turkey

Die WHITE HOUSE-Badmöbelserie von Kale besticht
durch ihr leichtes und minimalistisches Design. Dadurch
können perfekt passende Produkte für verschieden
große und individuell gestaltete Bäder geschaffen werden.
Die Produktfamilie zeichnet sich durch eine spezielle
Herangehensweise an ästhetische und funktionale Aspekte aus. Beim ästhetischen Bausteinprinzip werden
durch das markante Farbdekor alle Module zusammen-
geführt. Außerdem legt die Produktserie viel Wert auf
charakteristische Funktionseigenschaften wie den einheitlichen Aufbau der Bodenteile, um ein Maximum an
Benutzerfreundlichkeit zu gewährleisten.

*Kale's WHITE HOUSE bathroom furniture system, which
achieves a light and minimalist approach for baths, is
created with a concept that is based on the ability to
create suitable products that can fit a variety of different
sized and shaped bathroom spaces. The product family
has been designed with a flexible approach to both
esthetic and functional aspects; while the esthetic modularity of the range is sustained with the color splash
throughout the modules, distinctive functional properties
such as leveraged systems in the floor module allowing
easy use have been exploited by the range in order to
enhance the user's comfort to the maximum.*

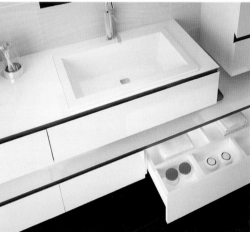

PRODUCT

NORDIC
Badezimmermöbel, Keramikfliesen
Bathroom furniture, tiling

DESIGN

Kale, Design & Innovation Group (K. I. D.)
E. Sertaç Ersayın (VP Design & Innovation, CDO),
Özgür Alp (Product Design), Fatih Mintaş
(Product Design), Gözde Tüfekçi Mercan
(Strategic Design)
Istanbul, Turkey
GIORGIO MINGARELLI ASSOCIATI srl
Modena, Italy

MANUFACTURER

Kaleseramik Çanakkale Kalebodur Seramik Sanayi A.Ş
Istanbul, Turkey

Die NORDIC-Collection-Badmöbelserie vermittelt mit
ihrer natürlichen Holzstruktur und passenden Fliesen
das Gefühl, mitten in der Natur zu sein. Sie richtet sich
an Kunden, die eine Oase inmitten des hektischen
Großstadtlebens suchen und dieses Konzept in ihren
Bädern umsetzen möchten. Die Serie zeichnet sich
durch eine deutliche Abkehr vom kalten Erscheinungsbild aus und verspricht stattdessen erholsame Entspan-
nung. Jede einzelne Fliese reflektiert die natürliche
Struktur des Holzes, besitzt jedoch die Langlebigkeit
von Keramik. Das Designkonzept wird auch von den
stimmigen Möbeln getragen, die den Kunden Stauraum und Ästhetik bieten.

*With its bathroom furniture enriched with the natural
texture of wood and complementary tiles, the NORDIC
Collection is a bathroom experience that feels set in nature.
The NORDIC Collection is for those who need an oasis in
the midst of a fast-paced metropolis lifestyle and carry
this concept into their bathrooms. By rejecting a cold
appearance, the series promises a relaxing experience
where every tile reflects the original texture of wood yet
integrates the durability of ceramics. The design concept
is supported with complementary furniture offering
both storage and esthetic benefits for the users.*

PRODUCT
Palomba Collection
Waschplatz
Washplace

DESIGN
palomba serafini associati
Milano, Italy

MANUFACTURER
LAUFEN Bathrooms AG
Laufen, Switzerland

Das Zusammenspiel geometrischer und organischer Linien individualisiert das Panorama im Badezimmer: Ein filigraner Waschtisch mit Lagunen-förmigem Becken, das in die keramische Ablage übergleitet. Möbel mit patentierten 45°- Kanten, schützende PVC-Folien-Oberfläche, eine interne Steckdose und atmosphärisches LED-Licht. Das mittig platzierte Becken, der Raumsparsiphon und die offenen Boxen bieten viel Ablagefläche. Die horizontal und kubisch geformten Module mit auswechselbarer Rückwand, ermöglichen individuelles Arrangement und eine Modularität innerhalb des gesamten Möbelsortimentes, welches nach einem repetitiven Raster aufgebaut ist.

The tension between geometric and organic lines individualizes the panorama of the bathroom: a slim ceramic washbasin with a lagoon-like bowl that blends into the flat countertop. Furniture with patented 45° edges, protective PVC foil surfaces, an internal socket and atmospheric LED-lighting. The central position of the bowl and the space-saving siphon in the furniture leave ample storage space. Further space is orchestrated with open modules. The rectangular or cuboid boxes with interchangeable rear walls allow individual arrangement and modularity with the complete furniture range that is designed in a repetitive grid.

PRODUCT
Saon 3905
Seifenspender
Soap dispenser

DESIGN
Mutelite Limited
Ningbo, China

MANUFACTURER
Lineabeta S. p. A.
Gambellara, Italy

Seifenspender mit einem Korpus aus ABS-Kunststoff
und einer 190-ml-Pumpe aus buntem weichem Silikon.

*Soap dispenser with ABS plastic body and 190 ml
smooth and colored silicon pump.*

PRODUCT
LaPreva P1
Dusch-WC
Shower toilet

DESIGN
brains4design GmbH
München, Germany

MANUFACTURER
Noventa AG
Diepoldsau, Switzerland

LaPreva P1: durchdacht bis ins Detail. Das Dusch-WC der neuen Generation vereint modernes Design, optimale Hygiene und größtmöglichen Bedienkomfort. Mit dem Controller oder der Fernbedienung können Wassertemperatur, Strahlstärke und Duschmodus individuell gewählt und in einem von vier Benutzerprofilen gespeichert werden. Die integrierte Entkalkungsfunktion, auswechselbare Düsen und Blenden, glatte Oberflächen und die selbstständige, thermische Reinigung garantieren Hygiene rundum. Dank Energiesparmodus und Ferienprogramm schont LaPreva P1 die Umwelt.

LaPreva P1: well thought out, down to the last detail. In addition to its modern design, the LaPreva P1, the new generation of shower-toilets, has an unmatched operating concept. The unique controller and the remote control allow adjusting water temperature, spray intensity and spray mode. The settings can be saved to one of the four user profiles. The hygienic requirements are met with an integrated decalcifying function, exchangeable nozzles and spray shields, an independent thermal cleaning process and smooth surfaces that are easy to clean. With its selectable energy-saving mode and holiday mode, the LaPreva P1 protects the environment.

PRODUCT

CAPELO
Elektrischer Wasserkocher
Electrical water heater

DESIGN

VESTEL
White Goods
VESTEL White Industrial Design Group
Serpil Sedef Yağcı
Manisa, Turkey

MANUFACTURER

Vestel Beyaz Eşya San. ve Tic. A.Ş.
Manisa, Turkey

Er verfügt über hervorragende Leistung seiner Klasse.
Der modern gestylte elektrische Warmwasserkocher
CAPELO verfügt über eine Drehknopf-Steuerung und
drei unterschiedliche Heizkapazitäten von 50, 65, 80 Litern, die den Anforderungen aller Verbraucher entsprechen. Der schlichte Design-Ansatz wird ergänzt durch
einen zylindrischen Körper und gekippte Kappen. Da
am Körper zylindrische Materialien verwendet wurden,
benötigt das Produkt weniger Platz und ist umweltfreundlicher in Bezug auf Materialien. Mit seiner reinen
Kontrolle, leicht montierbaren Teilen und minimalem
Materialeinsatz entspricht es dem höchsten Funktions-
standard und ist zudem ein kostengünstiges Produkt.

*It has the excellent performance of its class. Modernly
styled CAPELO electrical water heater features a knob
control and three different heating capacities of 50, 65,
80 liters that respond requirements of all consumers. The
simplistic design approach is followed that formed the
shape of the heater with a cylindrical body and tilted
caps. Since the body is cylindrical materials used are as
minimum as possible resulting in a product of both less
space equipping and more environmental-friendly in
terms of material. With its stark control, easy to assemble
parts and minimal material usage it serves the highest
standard features with a low cost product.*

PRODUCT
Moment
Waschbecken
Washbasin

DESIGN
ZEVA CORP.
In-house Design
Changhua, Taiwan

MANUFACTURER
ZEVA CORP.
Changhua, Taiwan

Waschbecken Moment, seine tanzenden Wellen sind Ausdruck der sanften Bewegung des Wassers. Zusammen mit der runden Form erfährt der Benutzer die Sinnlichkeit von Balance und Stabilität. Der Benutzer fühlt sich in die Arme der Natur aufgenommen und vergisst die täglichen Sorgen, um die innere Ruhe des Herzens wiederzufinden.

The washbasin, Moment, its dancing waves above expresses the smooth rhyme of water, together with the round shape brings customers sense of balance and stability. Customers casting away daily irritations and feel like returning to the nature where their hearts were full of original peace.

PRODUCT
Vortex
Wasserhahn für Waschbecken
Mixer for washbasin

DESIGN
ZEVA CORP.
In-house Design
Changhua, Taiwan

MANUFACTURER
ZEVA CORP.
Changhua, Taiwan

Vortex-Wasserhahn für Waschbecken. Durch die Anwendung von absorbierendem Luftstrom leitet er Wasser in einer einzigartigen Weise und stellt so eine visuelle Durchdringung mit einem surrealen Sinn dar. Die Innenstruktur mit Wassereinschränkung kann die Reinigungs- und Wassersparanfordungen erfüllen und gleichzeitig die Ziele von Waschspaß und Energieeinsparung erreichen. Separate Bedienhebel lassen eine freie Montageposition zu und erlauben so den Benutzern die Gestaltung eines Waschplatzes höchster Freude und höchsten Komforts.

Vortex, this mixer for basin, its unique innovation of hollow cyclic outlet applies the sucking-in airflow of the waterfalls, reaching a surreal sense of visual penetration. The limitation of water flow of internal construction effectively achieves functions of both cleaning and reserving, bringing fresh fun of washing for customers while reserving resources. The separable handler is ready to be assembled of the place at customers' will, promising customers a washing place of the utmost comfort and joy.

BUILDINGS

STEFAN GROBE

ANDREAS KALWEIT

JIM KRAIMER

PRODUCT
Berker Serie R.classic
Schalter und Steckdose
Switch and socket outlet

DESIGN
Studio Aisslinger
Prof. Werner Aisslinger, Nicole Losos
Berlin, Germany

MANUFACTURER
Berker GmbH & Co. KG
Schalksmühle, Germany

Mit sympathischem Radius und einer Ausführung mit pur-schlichtem Drehknebel interpretiert das Schalter-programm klassische runde Schalterserien zeitgemäß neu. Gefertigt wird die Berker Serie R.classic in vier Ma-terialitäten: in Kunststoff (schwarz oder weiß) mit einer Höhe von 10 mm oder in Kombinationen aus Kunststoff und Glas, Aluminium oder Edelstahl. Dabei werden auf einen 7 mm starken weißen oder schwarzen Grundträger aus Kunststoff, 3 mm hohe Echtmaterial-Platten aufge-setzt. Dadurch kommt die pur-schlichte Form optimal zur Geltung. Durch eine breite Auswahl an Funktionen lassen sich viele Anwendungen realisieren.

With its pleasant round shape and a design featuring a pure, straightforward rotary knob, the switch range con-stitutes a new and contemporary interpretation of classic round switch ranges. The Berker Serie R.classic is manu-factured in four material qualities: plastic (black or white) with a frame depth of 10 mm or a combination featuring a 3 mm thick frame made of genuine glass, aluminum or stainless steel mounted on a 7 mm thick white or black plastic base plate. This shows off the pure, straightforward form to its fullest advantage. A wide range of functions allows a variety of applications.

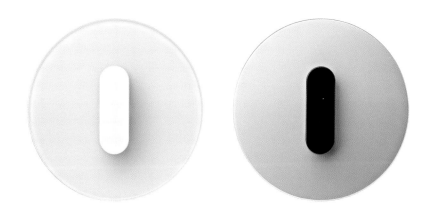

„Der Designer hat ein altes Muster in hervorragender Weise in die Moderne übertragen. Der Betrachter wird in alte Zeiten zurückversetzt. Die Nostalgie löst sich jedoch in dem zeitlosen, puristischen Design auf. Die Serie ist damit ein Beispiel für Universal Design."

"The designer has brought an old favorite right up to date with great skill. The beholder is brought back in time, but nostalgia ends at the timeless, purist design, making the series a great example of universal design."

JURYSTATEMENT

buildings

PRODUCT
Airlinq
Panel für Luftwechsel
Control panel for ventilation

DESIGN
design-people
Aarhus C, Denmark

MANUFACTURER
Airmaster A / S
Aars, Denmark

Das Airlinq-Panel sorgt mit einfacher und intuitiver Bedienung für frische Luft z. B. in Schulen. Dabei fügt sich das flache Panel optisch unauffällig ins Umfeld ein. Durch eine einfache Swipe-Geste auf dem kreisförmigen Bedienelement lässt sich der Luftwechsel im Raum entweder steigern oder verringern. Die Elemente des Kreises leuchten während der Swipe-Geste auf, um die Bedienung zu unterstützen. Danach tritt nur das unauffällige Einzelsegment in Erscheinung, um die gewählte Einstellung anzuzeigen. Per Knopfdruck lässt sich eine Abwesenheits-Betriebsart wählen, die den Energieverbrauch des Lüftungssystems begrenzt.

The Airlinq panel provides fresh air through a clear and intuitive interaction – empowering end-users in e.g. schools to control ventilation. At the same time, the sleek panel blends discreetly with its environment. By simply swiping clockwise or counterclockwise along the panel's distinctive, circular element, the air exchange in a room increases or decreases. The circle elements light up while swiping and settle into an unobtrusive single element indicating the setting that has been chosen. An away mode can be activated by the press of one button, limiting the energy consumption of the ventilation system at times when the room is not in use.

PRODUCT
Berker R.3 Touch Sensor KNX
Tastsensor
Touch sensor

DESIGN
Studio Aisslinger
Prof. Werner Aisslinger, Nicole Losos
Berlin, Germany

MANUFACTURER
Berker GmbH & Co. KG
Schalksmühle, Germany

Eine kantige Kontur und ein außergewöhnlicher Aufbau sind charakteristisch für den Berker R.3 Touch
Sensor KNX. Eine sanfte Berührung der makellosen
Oberfläche genügt und die gewünschte Funktion wird
ausgelöst. Der Tastsensor setzt sich zusammen aus
einer Trägerplatte (7 mm) in Kunststoff (schwarz / weiß)
und einer Glasabdeckung (3 mm) in schwarz oder polarweiß. KNX-Funktionen wie z. B. Licht, Jalousien, Heizung
und Klimaanlage lassen sich darüber steuern. Die
Betriebsbereitschaft und Schaltzustände werden über
LEDs angezeigt. Mittels WEB-Konfigurator lassen sich
die Bedienfunktionen kundenindividuell beschriften.

*An angular contour and an unusual design are charac-
teristic for the Berker R.3 Touch Sensor KNX. A gentle
touch of the flawless surface is all it takes to activate the
desired function. The push-button consists of a base plate
(7 mm) in black or white plastic and a glass cover (3 mm)
in polar white or black. It can control KNX functions such
as lighting, blinds, heating and air conditioning. LEDs
indicate operational readiness and switching states.
Operating functions can be individually labeled using
the Web configurator.*

PRODUCT
Berker R.1
Schalter und Steckdose
Switch and socket outlet

DESIGN
Studio Aisslinger
Prof. Werner Aisslinger, Nicole Losos
Berlin, Germany

MANUFACTURER
Berker GmbH & Co. KG
Schalksmühle, Germany

Charakteristisch für den Berker R.1 ist seine weiche
Rahmenkontur in Kombination mit dem runden Zentralstück. In der Basisvariante wird der R.1 in Kunststoff
(schwarz oder weiß) gefertigt. Durch Aufbau und Materialmix überzeugen auch die Varianten. Glas, Aluminium und Edelstahl werden in einer Stärke von 3 mm
auf einen 7 mm starken weißen oder schwarzen Grundträger aus Kunststoff aufgesetzt. Berker R.1 ist ein vollständiges Flächenschalter-Sortiment mit Unterputz-
Einsätzen inklusive KNX-Sensorik. Funktionsvarianten
und 1-fach- bis 5-fach-Rahmen machen das Programm
zum idealen, weil zeitlosen Begleiter für alle Einrichtungs-
projekte.

*The most striking characteristic of the Berker R.1 is the
soft frame contour combined with a round center plate.
In the basic version, the R.1 is manufactured in plastic
(black or white). The different versions feature impressive designs and material mixes. Three millimeter thick
glass, aluminum or stainless steel is mounted on a 7 mm
thick white or black plastic base plate. Berker R.1 is a full
switch range with flush-mounted inserts including KNX
sensors. Functional versions and the availability of 1-gang
to 5-gang frames make the switch range an ideal and
timeless solution for any interior design project.*

PRODUCT
Berker R.3
Schalter und Steckdose
Switch and socket outlet

DESIGN
Studio Aisslinger
Prof. Werner Aisslinger, Nicole Losos
Berlin, Germany

MANUFACTURER
Berker GmbH & Co. KG
Schalksmühle, Germany

Typisch für R.3 ist das bewusste Spiel von gegensätzlichen Formsprachen aus kreisförmigem Zentralstück und kantigem Rahmen. In der Basisvariante wird er in Kunststoff (schwarz oder weiß) gefertigt. Durch Aufbau und Materialmix überzeugen auch die Varianten. Glas, Aluminium und Edelstahl werden in einer Stärke von 3 mm auf einen 7 mm starken weißen oder schwarzen Grundträger aus Kunststoff aufgesetzt. Berker R.3 ist ein vollständiges Flächenschalter-Sortiment. Dank Funktionsvarianten, 1-fach- bis 5-fach-Rahmen und einer Grundform, die die Installation in Brüstungskanälen ermöglicht, ist das Programm gerade für Gewerbeobjekte geeignet.

Characteristic for R.3 is the deliberate play with contrasting designs where a circular center plate is combined with an angular frame. In the basic version, the R.3 is manufactured in plastic (black or white). The different versions feature impressive designs and material mixes. Three millimeter thick glass, aluminum or stainless steel is mounted on a 7 mm thick white or black plastic base plate. Berker R.3 is a full switch range. A variety of functional versions, 1-gang to 5-gang frames and a basic design that simplifies the installation process in dado trunking make the switch range ideal for use in commercial properties.

PRODUCT
Berker R.1 Touch Sensor KNX
Tastsensor
Touch sensor

DESIGN
Studio Aisslinger
Prof. Werner Aisslinger, Nicole Losos
Berlin, Germany

MANUFACTURER
Berker GmbH & Co. KG
Schalksmühle, Germany

Eine softe Kontur und ein außergewöhnlicher Aufbau sind charakteristisch für den Berker R.1 Touch Sensor KNX. Eine sanfte Berührung der makellosen Oberfläche genügt, um die gewünschte Funktion auszulösen. Der Tastsensor setzt sich zusammen aus einer Trägerplatte (7 mm) in Kunststoff (schwarz / weiß) und einer Glasabdeckung (3 mm) in schwarz oder polarweiß. KNX-Funktionen wie z. B. Licht, Jalousien, Heizung und Klima-anlage lassen sich darüber steuern. Die Betriebsbereit-schaft und Schaltzustände werden über LEDs angezeigt. Mittels WEB-Konfigurator lassen sich die Bedienfunk-tionen kundenindividuell beschriften.

A soft contour and an unusual design are characteristic for the Berker R.1 Touch Sensor KNX. A gentle touch of the flawless surface is all it takes to activate the desired function. The push-button consists of a base plate (7 mm) in black or white plastic and a glass cover (3 mm) in polar white or black. It can control KNX functions such as light-ing, blinds, heating and air conditioning. LEDs indicate operational readiness and switching states. Operating functions can be individually labeled using the Web configurator.

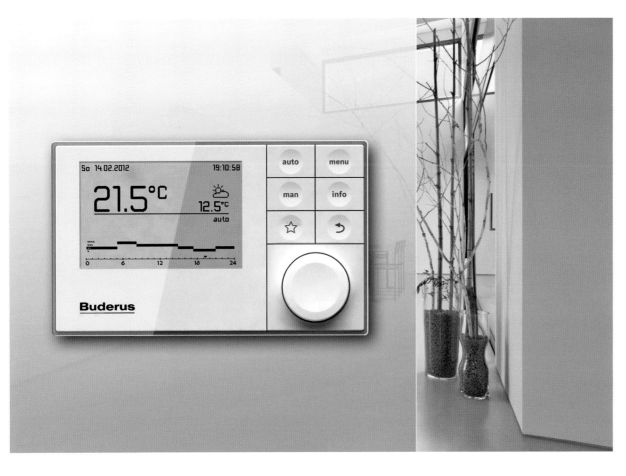

PRODUCT
Buderus RC Familie
Kontroll- und Regelsysteme
Boiler controls and modules

DESIGN
designaffairs GmbH
Erlangen, Germany

MANUFACTURER
Bosch Thermotechnik GmbH
Werk Lollar
Lollar, Germany

Die neue Regelsystemfamilie RC100, RC200 und RC300 bietet Buderus-Kunden zeitgemäßen Komfort und höchste Nutzerfreundlichkeit. Durch die Entwicklung einer Gerätefamilie entstand eine durchgängig logische, intuitive Bedienung für die Vielzahl an neuen Funktionen zur Effizienz- und Komfortsteigerung. Das Design im schlichten Weiß mit silbernen Rahmen ist bewusst zeitlos, elegant und präzise gehalten. Die Gestaltung unterstreicht Buderus-Markenwerte und ist in verschiedensten Wohnsituationen zu Hause. Langlebig und für alle Altersgruppen konzipiert besticht die Familie durch Bildschirme mit hohem Kontrast und deutlichen Druckpunkt der Tasten.

The new product family RC100, RC200 and RC300 offers state of the art user experience for Buderus customers. The devices are including new functions for efficiency and comfort paired with vastly improved intuitive operation and design. The design in gloss white with silver accent is timeless, elegant and precise to seamless fit for different living environments. Designed for longevity the device is aimed at all age groups and offers precision tactile button feedback and high contrast displays.

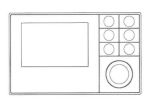

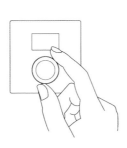

PRODUCT
Green Premium Switch
Schalter
Switch

DESIGN
DAEWOO E & C Co.
Seoul, South Korea

MANUFACTURER
CLIO Co., Ltd.
Seongnam-si, South Korea

Dieses Produkt ist ein schlaues Produkt, das Temperatur-regler, Beleuchtungsschalter, Notstromleistung, Sperr-schalter und Echtzeit-Überwachung in einem integriert hat. Am LCD-Fenster wird die Menge des Stroms der Innenbeleuchtung und der Stecker angezeigt, sodass man zu dem gesamten Energieverbrauch Bezug hat. Durch den Sperrschalter für Notstrom wird Energie ein-gespart. Durch die einfache Gestaltung mit blauem LED wirkt der Schalter mystisch.

Green Premium Switch is a product that integrates several functions such as a thermostat, a lighting switch, a standby power switch and monitoring in real time etc. LCD window displays the amount of consumed electricity for indoor lightings and outlets and alerts people to the use lesser energy and contributes the energy saving through the cutoff function of standby power. It is embodied in the mystic atmosphere with application of simple design and blue LED.

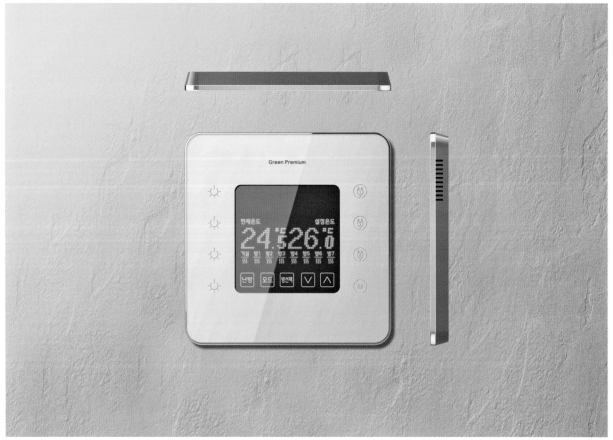

PRODUCT
Blue Crystal
Heimnetzwerk-System
Home network system

DESIGN
COMMAX
Jaesang Park, Yonghee Han
Kyunggi-Do, South Korea

MANUFACTURER
COMMAX
Kyunggi-Do, South Korea

Blue Crystal weitet den einheitlichen Look von Monitor und Kamera auf das ganze Heimnetzwerk aus. Dadurch zeigt sich konsequentes Produktdesign von A bis Z. Alle sichtbaren Geräteteile sind im Design der System-Familie von Monitor und Kamera gehalten. Abgesehen von der Beschichtung sind sämtliche Materialien, in diesem Fall Glas, Aluminium und Kunststoff, umweltfreundlich und recyclebar. Das Gehäuse aus Aluminium zeichnet sich durch eine klare und kantige Optik aus. Durch die sanften Kurven hebt es sich deutlich von den gewohnten, eher kastenförmigen Geräten ab. Die äußere Form verleiht dem Gerät Stabilität und einen hochwertigen Charakter.

Blue Crystal extends the uniform look of the monitor and camera to the entire home network, reflecting consistent product design from start to finish. It consists of main, window and bottom casing based on the family design of the monitor and the camera. All materials, except for the finish, are environmentally friendly and recyclable, including the glass, aluminum and plastic. The main casing, which is made of aluminum, has a rectangular look with clean edges. However, its subtle curves set it apart from other boxy-looking appliances, giving it an air of sophistication and providing stability.

PRODUCT
Corlo Touch
Touch-Schalter mit Display
Touch switch with display

DESIGN
Elsner Elektronik GmbH
Mathias Käfer
Gechingen, Germany

MANUFACTURER
Elsner Elektronik GmbH
Gechingen, Germany

Das Display Corlo Touch für das KNX-System ist so groß wie ein Wandschalter, bietet aber verschiedene Nutzungsmöglichkeiten: Durch das berührungssensitive, hochauflösende Display kann es wie ein normaler Schalter verwendet werden. Zugleich ist Corlo Touch eine Bedienzentrale für die automatische Raumklimaregelung. Einstellungen werden dabei über illustrierte Menüs vorgenommen. Das Corlo Touch ist modular aufgebaut und wird im Corlo 1-, 2- oder 3-Rahmen installiert. Die edle Glas-Touchoberfläche, der verchromte Rahmen und die einstellbare LED-Ambientebeleuchtung machen Corlo Touch zu einem Schmuckstück für hochwertige Interieurs.

The display Corlo Touch for the KNX system has the dimensions of a normal wall switch, but is suitable for different needs: thanks to the touch sensitive, high-resolution display, it can be used as a normal switch. At the same time, Corlo Touch is an operation unit for automatic control of room conditions. Settings are adjusted via illustrated menus. Corlo Touch is designed modularly and is installed in a Corlo 1-, 2- or 3-gang frame. The precious glass touch-surface, the chrome-plated frame and the adjustable LED ambient light turn Corlo Touch into a piece of jewellery for high-class interiors.

PRODUCT
LEO FS SERIES / COSMO PICOLLO
Lufterhitzer
Air unit heater

DESIGN
FLOWAR Głogowski I Brzeziński SPJ
(R&D Department)
Gdynia, Poland
Studio 1:1 Jarosław Szymański
Design team
Gdańsk, Poland

MANUFACTURER
FLOWAR Głogowski I Brzeziński SPJ
(R&D Department)
Gdynia, Poland

Die LEO FS-Produktgruppe bildet ein innovatives und geräuscharmes Heiz- und Lüftungssystem. Die Geräte haben hohen Benutzerkomfort und bieten clevere Lösungen für die Heizungsbauer und sind dazu noch optisch ansprechend. Die Strategie war ein Gerät im modernen Design zu entwickeln. Die Installation wurde komplett im ABS-Kunststoffgehäuse versteckt, die Montagekonsole ist bereits Bestandteil des Geräts. Das Gerät ist dadurch leicht, was die Montage erleichtert. Umweltfreundliche Lösungen bedeuten hier: wiederverwertbares Gehäuse und energiesparender EC-Motor (Energieverbrauch weniger als eine 60-W-Glühlampe).

LEO FS series is an innovative, silent heating and ventilation system. It combines comfort for end users and clever solutions for installers in an attractive design. The design strategy was to create a highly esthetic device. The ABS casing completely covers all necessary connections, its lightweight design and integrated mounting bracket make for quick and easy installation- no additional supporting structures needed. Green solutions include: fully recyclable casing and EC fan which provides significant savings in operation (power consumption is less than a 60 W lightbulb).

PRODUCT
Design-Regenwasserklappe
Design rainwater flap

DESIGN
Molldesign
Schwäbisch Gmünd, Germany

MANUFACTURER
GRÖMO GmbH & Co. KG
Marktoberdorf, Germany

Die neu designte Regenwasserklappe von GRÖMO hebt sich schon auf den ersten Blick von allen anderen Regenwasserklappen deutlich ab. Sie besitzt keinen Griff zum Öffnen des Klappmechanismus, sondern verfügt stattdessen über einen raffinierten Klickverschluss, welcher durch einmaliges Drücken aufspringt und durch nochmaliges Betätigen wieder verschlossen wird. Im Inneren befindet sich ein Schubfach mit Sieb, welches zur Reinigung einfach entnommen und gesäubert werden kann. Der edle schwarze Kunststoffrahmen sowie der charakteristische GRÖMO-Stern runden das optisch ansprechende Design der neuen Regenwasserklappe gelungen ab.

Already at a first glance, the new designed rainwater flap by GRÖMO stands out from all other rainwater flaps available on the market. Immediately noticeable is that this product does not have a handle for opening the flap mechanism. Instead, the rainwater flap has a sophisticated click fastening which opens simply by touching and closes in the same way. Furthermore there is also an insert inside with a sieve which can be easily removed for cleaning. The elegant black plastic frame, as well as the characteristic GRÖMO star successfully complete the attractive design of the new rainwater flap.

PRODUCT
My Smart Butler
Haussteuerungssystem
Home control system

DESIGN
GS Engineering & Construction
Naeun An, Yeon Taek Kwon
Seoul, South Korea
Design Mu
Jeoung Sik Yun, Woo Sung Lee, Hyun Dai Kim
Seoul, South Korea

MANUFACTURER
GS Engineering & Construction
Seoul, South Korea

Das innovative Haussteuerungssystem My Smart Butler steuert diverse Funktionen und überwacht die Sicherheit des Hauses bei Abwesenheit der Bewohner. Beleuchtung, Standby-Verbrauch, Heizung und Gaszufuhr können damit gesteuert werden. Fahrstühle und Alarmanlagen sind ebenfalls aktivierbar. Das System entspricht modernsten Technologie- und Sicherheitsstandards und besitzt einen Analogschalter mit ausgeklügelten Bildsymbolen. Die verschiedenen Funktionen sind benutzerfreundlich in blau und orange markierte Kategorien unterteilt. Durch Smart Control können unerwünschte Funktionen leicht abgeschaltet werden. Das System ist variabel montierbar.

My Smart Butler is an innovative home control system that controls home environment and monitors security when the house is unoccupied. It allows residents to control lights, standby power, heating systems and gas supply and also allows elevators and security alarms to be activated, guaranteeing unrivalled peace of mind. The cutting-edge technology also includes an analogue switch with an elaborate pictogram. To increase accuracy, the function types are categorized into orange and blue colors. Functions can be set to "out" mode with one touch of the smart control button. The system can be installed in a range of ways to fit with the interior.

PRODUCT

M-GAS water heater
Wasserkocher
Water heater

DESIGN

Haier Innovation Design Center
Dai Nanhai, Jiang Song, Liang Wenxin,
Li Lei, Sun Ke
Qingdao, China

MANUFACTURER

Haier Group
Qingdao, China

Das Front-Shell-Panel am Gehäuse der Gas-Wasser-Heizung besteht aus Edelstahl mit feiner Prägung. Für das UI-Display wurde Laser-Mikro-Bohrtechnik eingesetzt, womit ein einzigartiger Lichteffekt auf dem Edelstahl erzielt wird. Das hebt die High-End-Qualität. Das schön gestaltete Basisgehäuseteil verbirgt nach der Installation die komplexen Wasserleitungen. So fügt das Produkt sich in jede häusliche Umgebung ein. Die neue Technik der Kaltverdichtung benutzt den Wärmeverlust und ist so umfassend kohlenstoffarm und umweltfreundlich.

Due to the stainless steel fine punching technology for front shell panel and laser micro perforation technique used for UI display, this gas water heater has unique translucent effect of stainless steel material and has high-end quality. Complex water pipes installed are concealed under beautifully designed base housing, thus it is in harmony with home environment. The gas water heater can recycle the heat lost relying on the brand-new condensation technology to create an all-sided low carbon and environmental protection mode; zero-cold water technology is adopted to guarantee the gas water heater can offer hot water of constant temperature even.

PRODUCT
Huawei IPC SpeedDome
Überwachungssystem
Video monitoring

DESIGN
Huawei Technologies Co., Ltd.
Wei Feng
Hangzhou, China

MANUFACTURER
Huawei Technologies Co., Ltd.
Hangzhou, China

Die neue Philosophie für Videoüberwachung, die perfekt in ihr Umfeld passt. Es reduziert die Angst und die Menschen fühlen sich in Sicherheit. Das System ist mit einem intelligenten Licht-Sensormodul ausgestattet, das in die Umwelt passt. Es verfügt über eine Klarheit der Aufnahme, die das Bild in der Dunkelheit deutlicher macht als traditionelle Kameras. Wenn zu viel Licht auf Gesichter fällt, justiert die Haube automatisch den richtigen Winkel. Die Haube schließt automatisch, wenn die Kamera nicht arbeitet. Das schützt die Vorsatzlinse vor Staub.

A new philosophy for video monitoring, suits environment perfectly. It reduces monitoring fear and makes people feel more security. It's equipped with light sensing module which can intelligently matching the environment. It improves the shooting clarity and makes the image more clearly in darkness than traditional cameras. When the camera face glare, hood will automatically adjust the angle to make the amount of light control optimization state. The hood is automatically closed to avoid dust attachment lens window when it doesn't work.

PRODUCT
CITY EYE
Solarziegel-Beleuchtungskörper
Solar brick lighter

DESIGN
Two+Group
Cheng Hung
New Taipei City, Taiwan
Industrial Technology Research Institute
Hui-Hsiung Lin, Luan-Ying Chen, Tsung-Hsin Lin,
Ren-Huo Tsai, Chia-Jen Ting
Hsinchu, Taiwan

MANUFACTURER
Industrial Technology Research Institute
Hsinchu, Taiwan

CITY EYE ist der weltweit erste autostrom-reihengeschal-
tete Solarglasblock, der durch ein mikrostrukturiertes op-
tisches Leitsystem Sonnenlicht empfängt und durch seine
seitlich angebrachten stangenförmigen Siliziumkristalle
in eine Solarzelle leitet. Die umgewandelte elektrische
Energie produziert mittels einer transparenten LED-Glas-
platte Licht. Durch seine Lichtdurchlässigkeit erleuchtet
CITY EYE die Nacht. In Kombination mit herkömmlichen
Glasblöcken und verschiedenen zur Auswahl stehenden
Mustern und Modellen kann eine einfache Wand äußerst
variationsreich gestaltet werden.

*CITY EYE is the world's first power-generating cascading-
type glass solar brick. It's using a glass micro-structure
light-guiding system and absorbing sunlight through
strips of silicon solar cells on the side of glass brick. After
solar energy is converted to electricity, it generates light
through a transparent LED light-transmitting glass plate.
Its light absorption efficiency reaches 72 %, and its lu-
minosity efficiency 80 %. It will draw the most media
attention of eco building materials. It provides not only
brightness at night but, in combination with existing
glass bricks and selection of various modules, also an
enriched variety to walls.*

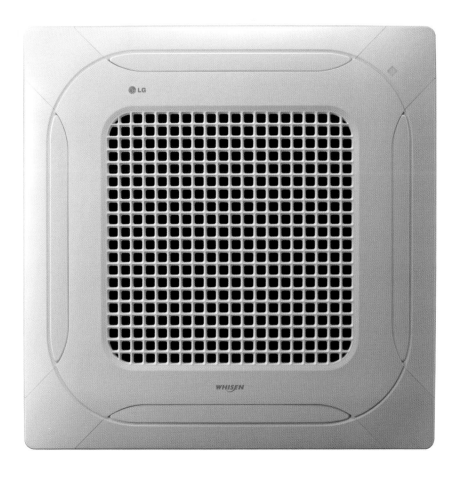

PRODUCT

N-style Cassette
Klimaanlage zur Deckenmontage
Ceiling mounted air conditioner

DESIGN

LG Electronics, Inc.
Corporate Design Center
Sang-moon Jeong, Myung-sik Kim, Hee-jae Kwon,
Yong Kim, Sun-young Jang
Seoul, South Korea

MANUFACTURER

LG Electronics, Inc.
Corporate Design Center
Seoul, South Korea

Diese 4-Wege-Kassette unterscheidet sich von der funktionellen Form der kommerziellen Klimaanlagen und passt sich an den Charakter der Innenausstattung an. Der Nutzer kann ein Gitter auswählen, das zu verschiedenen Umgebungen passt. Ein paneelartiges Gitter ohne Ansaugstutzen bietet ein klares Bild und das beleuchtete Gitter sorgt für eine besondere Atmosphäre. Der Bereich und die Ecken sind zur einfachen Reinigung abgerundet und die Ecke kann zur einfachen Installation separiert werden. Dieses 4-Wege-Kassetten-Design bietet verbesserte Qualität zur direkteren Präsentation.

This 4-way cassette deviates from the functional shape of commercial air conditioner and blends with the interior character. The user can select the grille that fits various environments rather than one typical grille. One panel type grille without front suction inlet provides clean image and lighting grille provides special atmosphere. The rounded edges of the air inlet area enable easy clean and each corner can be separated for easy installation. Such improved design aspects in the 4-way cassette design suggests better quality of the product itself.

PRODUCT
Flat Window
Fenster
Window

DESIGN
LG Hausys, Ltd.
Kim Hyung geun, Eom Youngmin
Seoul, South Korea

MANUFACTURER
LG Hausys, Ltd.
Seoul, South Korea

Die Besonderheit an Flat Window ist, dass sich hier Schiebefenster und fixiertes Fenster zu einer einzigen planen Fläche zusammenfügen. Dadurch gibt es keinerlei Schichtunterschiede beim geschlossenen Fenster, der Nutzer kann einen ungestörten Panoramablick genießen. Von innen sieht das Fenster wie eine flache Glastafel aus, wodurch es deutlich großflächiger wirkt. Obwohl es mit einer Schiebefunktion ausgestattet ist, minimiert die durchdachte Lösung den Spalt zwischen Fenster und Fensterrahmen. Die Dreifachverglasung sorgt für einen Wärmedurchgangskoeffizienten von 1 W / m² K.

In the flat window, the sliding window and the fixed window form a single flat surface when the window is closed, so there is no layer difference in the window. This allows the user to enjoy an optimal panoramic view. When viewed from indoors, the window looks like a single glass pane, making the space look more spacious. Although a sliding window, the design minimizes the gap between the window and window frame. The application of triple glazing results in insulation performance of 1 W / m² K.

PRODUCT
ceVo+
Schlüsselanhänger
Key fob

DESIGN
MADA Marx Datentechnik GmbH
Villingen-Schwenningen, Germany

MANUFACTURER
MADA Marx Datentechnik GmbH
Villingen-Schwenningen, Germany

Der neue Schlüsselanhänger ceVo+ wird für die berüh-rungslose Identifikation vornehmlich in den Bereichen der Zutrittskontrolle und Zeiterfassung eingesetzt. Der massive Rahmen aus poliertem Edelstahl schmiegt sich formschön an die Transponderkonturen an, wobei die Vorderseite ein individuell bedruckbares Deckelteil ent-halten kann. Der ceVo+ ist mit allen gängigen Chipva-rianten lieferbar.

Our new key fob ceVo+ is used for the contactless identi-fication primarily in the range of access control and time registration. The massive frame made of polished stain-less steel adapts shapely to the transponder outlines and the front side can contain an individually printed lid part. The ceVo+ is available with all common chip types.

PRODUCT

Arteso
Betonstein
Paving stone

DESIGN

Breimann & Bruun
Garten- und Landschaftsarchitekten
Hamburg, Germany

MANUFACTURER

Metten Stein+Design GmbH & Co. KG
Overath, Germany

Warum müssen Betonsteine eigentlich immer viereckig sein? Eine neue Formensprache zu entwickeln, die mit einem einzigen Format spannende und vollkommen neuartige Verlegemuster ermöglicht – das war das Entwicklungsziel. Durch die besondere Geometrie von Arteso, die mit Hilfe aufwendiger mathematischer Formeln und architektonischer Konzepte entwickelt wurde, wird dies möglich. Die Oberfläche ist mittels einer speziell entwickelten Oberflächenbearbeitung sehr fein und weich gestrahlt, sodass dieser Stein besonders trittsicher und durch die verwendete CleanTop-Technologie dauerhaft gegen Verschmutzungen geschützt ist.

Actually, why have concrete blocks always to be square? Our aim was developing a new design, which allows with only one size fascinating and completely new laying patterns. Now, this can be realized due to the special geometry of Arteso, which was developed by using complex mathematical formulas and architectural concepts. Based on a specially developed surface treatment the surface is very smooth blasted so that this stone is very non-slip and because of the CleanTop technology protected permanently against dirt.

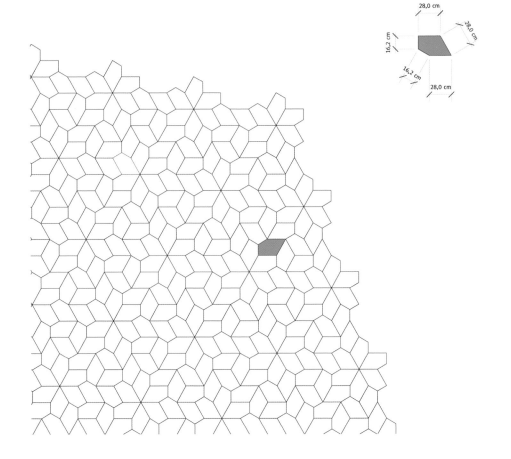

PRODUCT
NPE
Gaskondensations-Warmwasserbereiter
Gas condensing water heater

DESIGN
Navien Co., Ltd.
Seoul, South Korea

MANUFACTURER
Navien Co., Ltd.
Seoul, South Korea

Wir wollten uns deutlich vom schweren, düsteren Aussehen konventioneller Gaskondensations-Warmwasserbereiter mit ihrem kantigen Gehäuse distanzieren. Deshalb wurde die Front der Einheit im orientalischen Bambus-Stil gestaltet. Die kurvige Bambus-Form verleiht dem Gerät ein schmales und ebenmäßiges Erscheinungsbild. Wir verwenden Bambus zur Betonung der Aspekte Sauberkeit und Umweltfreundlichkeit. Die parallel angebrachten Wasseranschlüsse geben dem Gerät seinen speziellen Bambus-Look (CASCADE SYSTEM). Die Touch-Screen-Steuerung an der Vorderseite gewährleistet die Bedienfreundlichkeit und unterstreicht die luxuriöse Ausstattung.

We wanted to get away from the heavy, menacing look of conventional wall-hung gas condensing water heaters and their square casing, so we designed the front of the unit in an oriental bamboo style. The curved bamboo shape provides a slim and smooth design. We used bamboo because we wanted to emphasize the characteristics of cleanliness and environmentally friendliness. The parallel water connection gives the water heater that bamboo tree look (CASCADE SYSTEM). The touch screen controller on the front of the unit adds ease of use and luxury to the design.

PRODUCT

Bi2+
Ventilatorspirale
Fan coil with radiant panel

DESIGN

Olimpia Splendid
Gualtieri (RE), Italy

MANUFACTURER

Olimpia Splendid
Gualtieri (RE), Italy

Bi2+ ist die Inverter-Ventilatorspirale mit Strahlblende, entworfen von Dario Tanfoglio in Zusammenarbeit mit Olimpia Splendid. Die dem Produkt zugrunde liegende Idee war eine durch Wasser gespeiste Ventilatorspirale für Wohngebäude. Bi2+ liefert die Komfortvorteile einer Fußbodenheizung, die Flexibilität einer Ventilatorspirale und das Design eines Heizkörpers. Bi2+ liefert bei 12,9 cm Tiefe Kühlung, Entfeuchtung, Heizung und Luftreinigung. Dank einer international patentierten Technologie kann Bi2+ die normale Belüftungsheizung mit der Strahlungsheizung kombinieren. Eine professionelle Lösung mit hohem Wirkungsgrad für Wohngebäude.

BI2+ is the inverter fan coil with radiant panel, designed by Tanfoglio in collaboration with Olimpia Splendid. The idea behind the product was to design a water-powered fan coil for the household building construction. Bi2+ features the comfort advantages of a radiant floor, the flexibility of a fan coil and the design of a radiator. Bi2+, in only 12,9 cm depth provides cooling, dehumidifying, heating and air cleaning. Thanks to an international patented technology Bi2+ can integrate the normal ventilated heating with a radiation effect. This is a professional machine designed to bring a high efficiency solution for the residential housing.

PRODUCT
CS / RS series
Klimaanlage
Air conditioner

DESIGN
Panasonic Corporation
Design Company
Jun Yamano, Tan Chien Shiung
Tokyo, Japan

MANUFACTURER
Panasonic Corporation
Osaka, Japan

Highend-Klimaanlage zur Befestigung an der Wand für den Europäischen Markt. Hauptsächlich für das Wohnzimmer vorgesehen. Energiesparende Form – das Unterteil des Gerätes wirkt durch die kleinere Fläche äußerst kompakt. Das Oberteil ist größer und kann so mehr Luft ansaugen. Das Gerät ist schlicht und zeitlos und besitzt nur wenige Luftöffnungen und Leitungen, sodass man sich im Laufe der Jahre nicht daran sattsieht. Zwei Klappen ermöglichen die flexible Regelung der Luftströmung, das Gerät sorgt exakt für die von den Kunden bevorzugte Wohnatmosphäre – egal wie weit nördlich oder südlich sie in Europa wohnen.

Hi-end wall-mounted air conditioner for the European market. Mainly intended for use in living rooms. Energy-saving shape – the lower part of the product has a smaller surface area, which makes the product look extremely compact once installed, while the upper part is larger, enabling it to draw in more air. The product has a simple, timeless design with very few structural gaps and lines that users will not tire of as the years go by. Two flaps give flexible airflow control which means the product will deliver the living environment they prefer to the maximum number of customers, regardless of how far North or South in Europe they live.

buildings

PRODUCT

VISION series
Bedienteil
Wiring device

DESIGN

Panasonic Corporation
Design Company
Yasuhiro Akahori, Masaya Yoshioka
Tokyo, Japan
Panasonic Corporation
Eco Solutions Company
Kei Yamamoto
Tokyo, Japan

MANUFACTURER

Panasonic Corporation
Osaka, Japan

Sicherheit durch perfekte Anordnung. – Neue Anschluss-
geräte ermöglichen ein werkzeugloses Anschließen
und verringern fehlerhafte Anschlüsse. Die Haptik der
Schalter und die Töne, die diese erzeugen, beruhen auf
Studienergebnissen zur Benutzerpräferenz. Schlankes
und schlichtes Design – Ober- und Unterteile der Arma-
turentafel sind im selben Winkel ausgerichtet wie die
Schalter. Die laminierte Verpackung hält das Produkt
bei der Montage frei von Farbe und Staub und die
Oberflächen wurden so behandelt, dass sich tägliche
Gebrauchsspuren wie Fingerabdrücke usw. mühelos
abwischen lassen.

*Safety by design. – New terminals enable tool-free
connection and reduce faulty connections. The feel of
the switches and the sound they make are based on the
results of user preference surveys. Slim and simple design
– the upper and lower parts of the fascia are set at the
same angle as the switches. Laminated packaging keeps
product clean of paint and dust at time of installation
and surfaces have been treated to be easy to wipe clean
of the finger marks etc., that are a part of day to day living.*

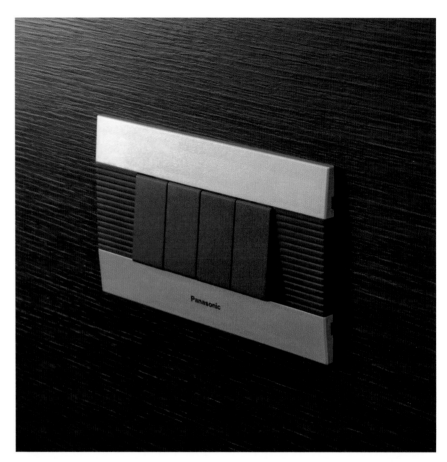

PRODUCT
Pluggit PluggLine
Bodenluftauslass
Ground air outlet

DESIGN
Pluggit GmbH
München, Germany

MANUFACTURER
Pluggit GmbH
München, Germany

Der Bodenluftauslass Pluggit PluggLine setzt neue Akzente bei der Integration einer Lüftungsanlage in ein modernes Wohnambiente. Das Basismaß (850 mm x 140 mm) orientiert sich an einer konventionellen Fensterbreite. Die Höhenverstellung passt das Gehäuse aus hochwertigem Edelstahl an die Stärke des Bodenbelags flächenbündig an. Pluggit PluggLine sorgt mit einem umlaufenden Luftaustritt (Breite 8 mm) für den notwendigen Frischluft-Volumenstrom – geräusch- und zugfrei. Das Design im Mittelbereich ist frei wählbar: Mit Naturstein, Fliese, Echtholz oder Teppich kann der umgebende Bodenbelag repliziert oder ein Kontrast dazu gesetzt werden.

The ground air outlet Pluggit PluggLine sets new accents by integrating a ventilation system into a modern residential ambience. The measurement (850 mm x 140 mm) is based on the width of a conventional window (900 mm). The vertical adjustment adapts the hight of the case – made from high-quality high-grade steel – to the size of the floor covering surface. Pluggit PluggLine provides every room with the necessary fresh air stream through a rectangular gap (width 8 mm) – noiselessly and draughtfree. The design in the middle area is freely eligible: the surrounding floor material can be replicated or a contrast can be put in addition.

PRODUCT

One-pass Card
Intelligente Zugangskarte
Smart card for access control

DESIGN

POSCO E&C
Gwangjong Kim, Haengho Lim, Myungho Sim
Incheon, South Korea
DESIGN K2L
Sooshin Lee, Yongtae Kim, Taehong Choi
Seoul, South Korea

MANUFACTURER

POSCO E&C
Incheon, South Korea

Diese Zugangskarte bietet Bewohnern von Appartement-
häusern eine Reihe von Funktionen. Die Inhaber können
verschiedene Bereiche, etwa das Parkdeck, betreten
oder die Karte verwenden, um den Lift in ihr Stockwerk
zu bestellen. Durch die dünne, flache Form unterscheidet
sie sich von anderen, sperrigeren Karten. Das schlanke
Design ermöglicht es, sie in Geldbörsen oder Taschen
unterzubringen oder an die Seite einer Handtasche zu
heften. Die Karte verfügt auch über eine Alarmfunktion
für Notfälle. Inhaber müssen lediglich einen Knopf drücken, um das Sicherheitspersonal zu benachrichtigen.
Dank kabelloser Ladefunktion ist kein Ladegerät nötig.

*This one-pass card provides a range of functions to resi-
dents in apartment blocks. Holders of the one-pass card
can enter various areas of the apartment block, such as
the parking lot, or use the card to call an elevator to their
floor. The slim-line shape sets this card apart from other,
chunky one-pass cards. The slender design means that
the card can be carried in wallets or pockets, or clipped
onto the side of a bag. The one-pass card also has an
emergency alarm function for urgent situations. All
cardholders need to do is slide a button and the security
personnel are notified. Wireless power charging means
that there is no need for a charger connector.*

PRODUCT

AQUA PLASMA

Vakuum-Röhrenkollektor

Evacuated tube collector

DESIGN

Ritter Energie- und Umwelttechnik
GmbH & Co. KG

Thomas Weidemann (Produktmanager),

Thomas Gorhan (Konstruktion)

Dettenhausen, Germany

Frank Neubert und Michael Müller

Pforzheim, Germany

Paradigma Italia S.r.l.

Luca Di Giorgi (Produktlogo)

Darzo, Italy

MANUFACTURER

Ritter Energie- und Umwelttechnik
GmbH & Co. KG

Dettenhausen, Germany

Der neue Kollektor AQUA PLASMA zeichnet sich durch seine innovativ einzigartige Plasma-Beschichtung der Vakuumröhren und Spiegel aus. Die Oberflächentechnik steigert den solaren Wärmeertrag zum derzeit höchsten am Markt. Das gilt besonders auch bei geringer Sonnenstrahlung oder Minusgraden. Die schlanke Form spart Material und verringert den CO_2 Fußabdruck um 15 %. Weniger Kanten verhindern Schmutzablagerungen, der niederere Sammelkasten führt zu weniger Selbstverschattung. Der Paradigma AQUA PLASMA arbeitet ausschließlich mit Wasser als Wärmeträger.

The new collector AQUA PLASMA convinces with its innovative and unique plasma coated evacuated tubes and mirrors. The coating technology increases the solar yield to the currently highest in the market. This is particularly true at low solar radiation or freezing temperatures. The slim form saves material and reduces the CO_2 footprint by 15 %. Fewer edges prevent dirt accumulation, the lower manifold results in less self-shading. The Paradigma AQUA PLASMA works exclusively with water as fluid transfer medium.

PRODUCT
SHS-6600
Smarter Türschließer
Smart door lock

DESIGN
Samsung SNS Co., Ltd.
Jae Hoon Kim, Jeong Hoon Ha, Sang Hyuk Kim
Seoul, South Korea

MANUFACTURER
Samsung SNS Co., Ltd.
Seoul, South Korea

Das RoHS zertifzierte, digitale Türschloss SHS-6600 erlaubt einfaches Drücken / Ziehen mit einfacher beschädigungsfreier Montage. Entwickelt für alle Altersgruppen und Fähigkeiten, erlaubt dieses ökofreundliche Produkt im Notfall schnelles und einfaches Verlassen. Die Merkmale sind: Touch-Passworteingabe und das eingebaute Handy- / Kreditkarten RFID- Autorisierungssystem; Einfachheit und Sicherheit durch Temperatur- und Infrarotsensoren, Feuer- und Eindringlingsalarm; Hochspannungsschutz und eine mit einer Legierung gekapselte, doppelschließende Verriegelung.

The SHS-6600 digital door-lock product enables users easy push / pull handle access. Designed for all ages, abilities and disabilities, this intuitive eco-friendly product efficiently sanctions quick and easy escape in case of emergencies. Utilizing a one-touch password input and built-in cell phone / credit card RFID authentication system, convenience and environment safety are enabled through temperature and infrared sensors, fire and intrusion alarms, high voltage electric shock prevention and an alloy-encased double locking device. This RoHS certified product is also easy to install without damaging existing structure.

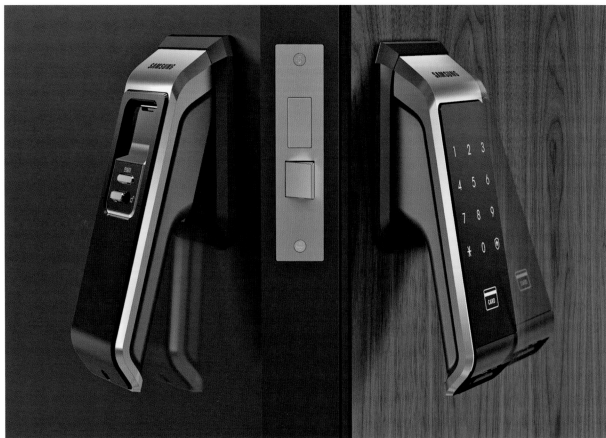

PRODUCT
markilux 8800
Wintergartenmarkise
Conservatory awning

DESIGN
kramerDesign
Wildeshausen, Germany

MANUFACTURER
Schmitz-Werke GmbH & Co. KG
Emsdetten, Germany

Die Wintergartenmarkise markilux 8800 integriert sich in die zeitgemäße Architektur durch die Verschmelzung weniger formaler Grundelemente. Gleichzeitig entsteht eine neue signifikante Gestalt, die gleichermaßen geschlossen und spannend wirkt, mit einem hohen Wiedererkennungswert. Das in das Schienensystem eingebaute „Zip-System" macht die Markise besonders windsicher: Das Tuch wird in den Schienen bündig in einer Art Reißverschluss geführt und ist somit weniger windanfällig. Die markilux 8800 kann aufgrund ihrer durchdachten Formgebung in einem erweiterten Größenraster bis zu 700 cm x 500 cm angeboten werden.

The conservatory awning markilux 8800 integrates into contemporary architecture by fusing a few formal basic elements. At the same time a new, significant shape comes to life with its exciting closed appearance and a high recognition value. The "zip system" integrated in the guide track system makes the awning particularly wind-resistant: the cover runs flush in the guide tracks in a kind of zipper and thus is less exposed to wind. Due to its sophisticated design the markilux 8800 can be offered in an extended size range of up to 700 cm x 500 cm.

PRODUCT

Concealed Door Lock

Türschloss

Door lock

DESIGN

Ssangyong Engineering & Construction

Inkuk Kim, Jonguk Shim, Sukki Kim

Seoul, South Korea

Dadam Design Associates Inc.

Sinhyung Cho, Kiyoung Kim, Kyuhyun Lee,

Jaeyoung Lim

Seoul, South Korea

MANUFACTURER

Ssangyong Engineering & Construction

Seoul, South Korea

Das verborgene Türschloss bietet mit einer Kombination aus Nummernschloss und verborgenem Türgriff unüberwindliche Sicherheit der Tür und ein pures äußeres Design. Das elektronische Touchpad ist das einzige exponierte Element bei verschlossener Tür. Der verborgene Türgriff tritt hervor, sobald der Geheimcode eingegeben oder eine Zugangskarte eingelesen wurde. Beim Verlassen des Raumes wird einfach der innere Griff leicht gedrückt. Dank der lückenlosen Struktur und einfachen Bedienung ist das verborgene Türschloss absolut sicher und gleichzeitig benutzerfreundlich.

The Concealed Door Lock provides impregnable door security and neat exterior design by combining a numeric lock and a concealed doorknob. The electronic touchpad is the only exposed element when the door is locked and the concealed doorknob protrudes once the secret code has been entered or an access card has been swiped. When exiting the room, the user simply pushes the inside handle lightly. Thanks to its gapless structure and simple operation, the Concealed Door Lock provides both watertight security and simply operation at the same time.

PRODUCT
Thanos
Raumbediengerät
Room operating unit

DESIGN
Thermokon
Sensortechnik GmbH
Polygon GmbH
Mittenaar, Germany

MANUFACTURER
Thermokon
Sensortechnik GmbH
Mittenaar, Germany

Als eines der weltweit ersten Raumbediengeräte mit innovativer Glas-Touch-Technologie verbindet das Thanos von Thermokon modernes Design mit intuitiv bedienbaren Funktionen. Über die berührungsempfindliche Glasoberfläche werden typische Anwendungen von energieeffizienten Green Buildings gesteuert. Eine integrierte Sensorik von Raumtemperatur und -feuchte ermöglicht individuelles Wohlfühl-Klima. Die Informationen werden per Funk versendet. Die berührungsempfindliche Funktionsspange aus Aluminium bildet den idealen Kontrast zur Glasfront. Hochwertige Materialien machen das Thanos zu einem exklusiven Designerlebnis in Wohn- und Büroräumen.

As one of the world's first room operating units with an innovative Glass-Touch-Technology, Thanos from Thermokon combines modern design with intuitive operation controls. Typical applications for energy-efficient green buildings can be controlled by a vitreous touch-screen-technology. Integrated temperature and humidity sensors transmit wireless signals to maintain a comfortable, controlled ambience. The aluminum operating clip, glass surface and high quality materials make Thanos an exclusive design orientated solution for living and working areas.

PRODUCT

ecoTEC plus
Gas-Wandheizgerät
Gas wall-hung boiler

DESIGN

Vistapark
Wuppertal, Germany

MANUFACTURER

Vaillant GmbH
Remscheid, Germany

Das Vaillant Gas-Wandheizgerät ecoTEC plus mit effizienter Brennwerttechnik sorgt für Warmwasserkomfort auf kleinstem Raum. Ein spezieller Heizungskeller oder ein separater Heizungsraum ist nicht erforderlich. Mit dem neuartigen, elektronischen Gas-Luft-Misch-System (ELGA) wird weniger Energie verbraucht. Damit werden Energiekosten eingespart sowie die Umwelt geschont. Im einfach zu bedienenden neuen Geräte-Interface mit Klartextanzeige kann der Vaillant System-Regler calor MATIC perfekt integriert werden. Konfiguration, Einstellung und Überwachung über das Internet ist durch Einsatz des Kommunikationsmoduls comDIALOG sehr einfach möglich.

The Vaillant ecoTEC plus gas-fired wall-hung appliance with efficient condensing technology ensures hot water comfort in the smallest space. A special heating basement or separate boiler room is not required. With the innovative electronic gas-air mix system (ELGA), less energy is consumed. This both saves energy costs and spares the environment. The Vaillant calorMATIC system control can be integrated perfectly in the easy-to-use new appliance interface with a plain text display. Configuration, setting and monitoring via the Internet is enabled very simply by the use of the comDIALOG communication module.

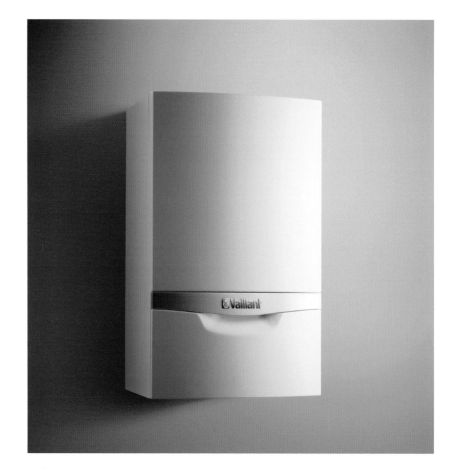

PRODUCT
SUAVE
Klimaanlage
Air conditioner

DESIGN
VESTEL
White Goods
VESTEL White Industrial Design Group
Burak Erbab
Manisa, Turkey

MANUFACTURER
Vestel Beyaz Eşya San. ve Tic. A.Ş.
Manisa, Turkey

SUAVE ist die neueste Klimaanlage von VESTEL mit höchster Technologie. Wenn sie nicht benutzt wird, bilden die kontinuierlichen reinen Linien den eleganten Ausblick von SUAVE. Wenn sie aktiviert wird, gleitet die Frontplatte nach oben und die Klappe öffnet sich, damit der alternierende Luftstrom strömt. Unter der Frontplatte befinden sich versteckte informative LED-Leuchten, die durch Reflektieren der entspannenden Eigenschaft des Lichts ein Lichtambiente im Raum schaffen. Diese LED-Leuchten werden verwendet, um dem Benutzer über Farbänderungen Informationen über die Modi der Klimaanlage zu geben.

SUAVE is the newest air conditioner of VESTEL with the highest technology. With the sliding front panel the purity has been reached. When it is not used the continuous pure lines form the sleek outlook of SUAVE. When it is activated front panel slides to top and flap opens to allow the alternating air current to flow. With the negative ion technology, air conditioner confines dust and bacteria. Under the front panel there are hidden informative LED lights creating light ambience in the environment reflecting the relieving feature of light. These LED lights are used to inform the user in terms of color changes for the modes of air conditioner.

PRODUCT
Ai1
Wärmepumpe
Heat pump system

DESIGN
industrialpartners GmbH
Beerfelden, Germany

MANUFACTURER
Waterkotte GmbH
Herne, Germany

Die neue Wärmepumpe Ai1 ist eine komplette Heizungs-
zentrale mit integriertem Warmwasserspeicher. Das
Produkt zeichnet sich durch optimale Schalldämpfung;
optimierten Wirkungsgrad und eine äußerst geringe
Aufstellfläche aus. Es ist deshalb jederzeit in Küchen
oder wohnnahen Wirtschaftsräumen zu integrieren.
Das Design unterstreicht diesen Anspruch und nimmt
die Formensprache von Produkten der sogenannten
„Weißen Ware" auf. Für den Gehäuseaufbau werden
ausschließlich hochwertige Materialien eingesetzt.
Alle Funktionen werden über ein intuitiv bedienbares
Touch-Display gesteuert, dessen Bedienführung ergonomisch optimiert wurde.

*The new heat pump Ai1 is a complete heating center with
a hot water storage tank included. The product is characterized by optimal soundproofing; an optimized efficiency
and a very small footprint. It is therefore at any time in
kitchens or living near areas to integrate. The design
underlines this claim and picks up the style of products of
the so-called "white goods". Only high-quality materials
are used to build up the case. All functions are controlled
via an intuitive-to-use touch display, its operating management has been ergonomically optimized. The heat pump
can also be controlled by a web interface via WLAN or the
internet.*

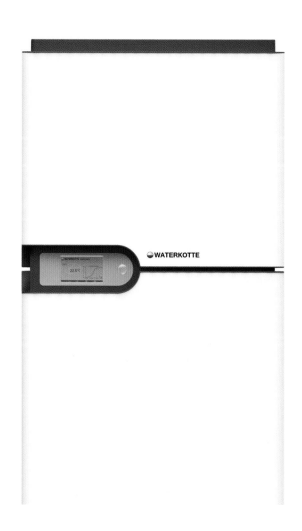

New Look FS12

New Look F9

PRODUCT
wodtke New Look
Kaminofen für Stückholz
Wood-burning stove

DESIGN
wodtke GmbH
Tübingen, Germany

MANUFACTURER
wodtke GmbH
Tübingen, Germany

Ein Kaminofen – zwei Varianten – drei Sichtfenster. In beiden Modellvarianten, New Look F9 und FS12, gewährleistet die wodtke HiClean-Filter®-Technik mit einem neuartigen Tiefenfilter aus Schaumkeramik den besonders emissionsarmen Abbrand bei gleichzeitig hohem Wirkungsgrad. Zusätzlich verfügt der FS12 über ein Wärmespeichermodul. Die Wärme kann über Stunden gespeichert werden, verlängert so die Wärmeabgabe und steigert die Wohlfühlwärme. Zukunftsweisend ist die raumluftunabhängige Betriebsweise des New Look, besonders wichtig für Gebäude mit dichter Bauweise und kontrollierter Wohnraumlüftung. Swarovski-Elemente veredeln den Türgriff.

One wood-burning stove – two versions – three viewing windows. With its novel ceramic foam depth filter wodtke's HiClean-Filter® technology ensures ultra-low emission combustion yet high efficiency in both of the two New Look model versions F9 and FS12. The FS12 is additionally equipped with a heat storage module which retains the heat for hours, providing sustained heat delivery with even cozier warmth. With a mind to future needs, New Look has been designed for room-air independent operation, an important feature in well-sealed residential buildings with controlled ventilation. Swarovski elements give the door handle a noble touch.

PRODUCT

RUNTAL FOLIO
Heizkörper
Radiator

DESIGN

King & Miranda Design S. R. L.
Milano, Italy

MANUFACTURER

Zehnder Group Boleslawiec Sp. z o.o.
Boleslawiec, Poland
Zehnder Group International AG
Gränichen, Switzerland

RUNTAL FOLIO erfüllt in perfekter Art und Weise die Erwartungen an einen leichten und gleichzeitig sehr rigiden Heizkörper. Kern dieses Designheizkörpers ist ein Heizregister aus Kupfer, eingebettet in eine Wabenkonstruktion aus Aluminium, welche von expandiertem Naturgraphit umschlossen ist. Dank dieser speziell entwickelten Konstruktion und einer neuartigen Fertigungstechnik konnte der sehr dünne und ultraleichte Heizkörper entwickelt werden, ohne Kompromisse an die Leistungsfähigkeit zu machen. Seine Designperformance ist beeindruckend. Er wirkt durch die durchgängig geschlossene Oberfläche sehr kompakt und gleichzeitig filigran und leicht.

RUNTAL FOLIO meets every possible expectation when looking for a lightweight yet extremely rigid radiator. At the heart of this designer radiator lies a copper heat registry. This is embedded in an aluminum honeycomb structure that is encased in expanded natural graphite. It was precisely this special new design and the innovative manufacturing technique that made it possible to develop an extremely thin and ultralight radiator without compromising on performance. The radiator offers impressive design performance and the fully enclosed surface creates an extremely compact yet sophisticated and lightweight look.

PRODUCT
Zehnder Fina
Design-Heizkörper
Design radiator

DESIGN
Tribecraft AG
Design Team
Zürich, Switzerland

MANUFACTURER
Zehnder Group Produktion
Gränichen AG
Gränichen, Switzerland

Der Design-Heizkörper Zehnder Fina wurde in seiner Formensprache äußerst dezent gestaltet. Die rückseitig angesetzten Blenden lassen die mit 20 mm extrem dünne Heizfläche optisch schweben und verbinden den Design-Heizkörper mit der Wand. Der Einsatz einer neuen Fertigungstechnologie im Zusammenhang mit der Ausrichtung auf eine funktionelle Verarbeitung bei der Installation ergab dieses innovative Konzept. Flexible Anschlüsse für die Installation auch im Niedertemperatursystem machen Zehnder Fina zu einem Design-Heizkörper für Neubau und Renovation. Eine oder mehrere Handtuchhalter tragen mit vorgewärmten Badetüchern zum Komfort im Bad bei.

The Zehnder Fina designer radiator utilizes a language of form with a striking simplicity. The side panels make the ultra-slim heating surface – 20 mm thick – stand out from the wall, forming the connection between the wall and the radiator whilst concealing the back of the radiator. This innovative concept combines new production technology with installation-friendly design. The flexibility of radiator connections, also allowing installation in low-temperature systems, makes Zehnder Fina ideal for new builds and renovation projects. For installation in the bathroom, it can be supplied with one or more towel rails for added convenience.

PUBLIC DESIGN / INTERIOR DESIGN

NEIL FRANKEL
MARTIN LOTTI
NIKO VON SAURMA

PRODUCT
VALLEY
Keramikfliesen
Ceramic tiles

DESIGN
AGROB BUCHTAL
Schwarzenfeld, Germany

MANUFACTURER
AGROB BUCHTAL
Schwarzenfeld, Germany

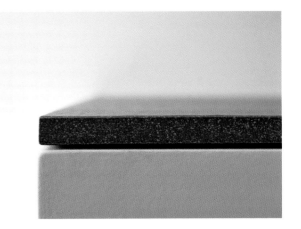

Verschiedenfarbige Tonminerale und Erden sind die natürlichen Rohstoffe der Feinsteinzeug-Bodenfliese VALLEY. Über die Materialverwendung im Herstellungsprozess hinaus, übersetzt die Fliese auch optisch ein mögliches Bild ihres Ausgangsorts. Das erdige, sattbraune Relief lässt an die fruchtbaren Böden einer Talsohle denken. Ähnlich der Entstehung mineralischer Steingefüge wird im Herstellungsprozess „Fliesenfertigung" das keramische Material feinteilig unter hohem Druck und Hitze verdichtet. Die hier während des Brennzyklus entstehende Glasphase bringt die zuvor matten Farben zum Leuchten, so wie wir es von Wasser auf Erde und Stein kennen.

Clay minerals and earths in diverse colors are the natural raw materials of the porcelain stoneware floor tile VALLEY. Apart from the material usage in the production process, the tile conveys a possible picture of its place of origin also visually. The earthy, deep-brown relief is reminiscent of the fertile soils of a valley bottom. Similar to the development of mineral rock fabrics, the fine-grained ceramic material is compacted under high pressure and heat in the production process of "tile manufacture". The glassy phase occurring during the firing cycle makes the previously matt colors shine as we know it of water on earth and stone.

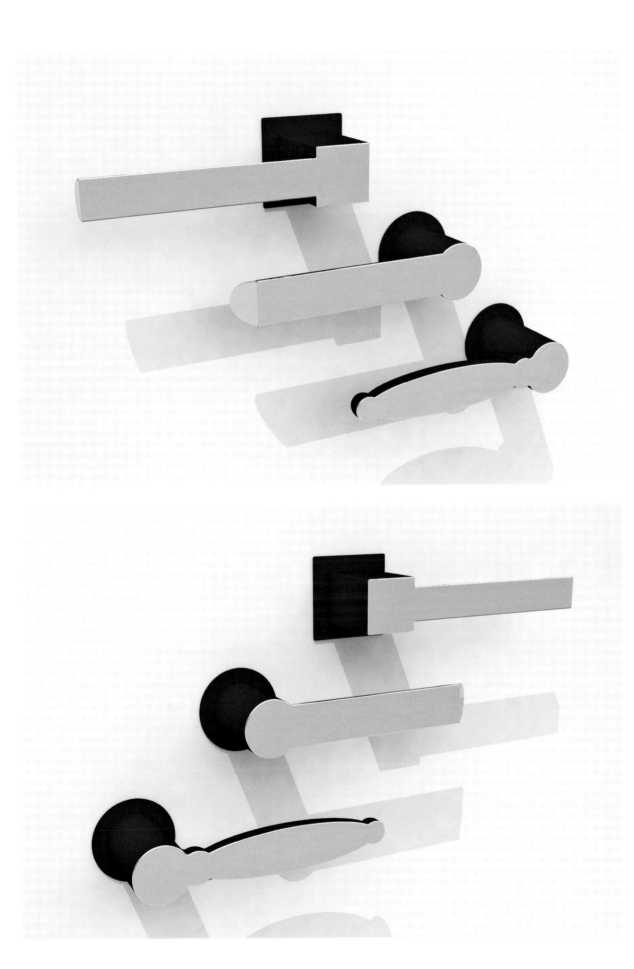

PRODUCT

Tagliato
Türdrücker
Lever handle

DESIGN

Doit & Beit
Arjan Moors (Designer)
Steijl, Netherlands

MANUFACTURER

Van Leeuwen International
Rhenen, Netherlands

Die Grundlage für diese Türdrückerserie sind Bauhaus-
artige, minimalistische Formen. Die ursprünglichen
Entwürfe bestehen meist aus zwei oder mehreren zu-
sammengesetzten Teilen, die zu einer Form zusammen-
fließen. Die Querschnittfläche mit abweichender Farbgebung macht den Türdrücker noch mehr zu einer Einheit
und gibt ihm ein elegantes und modernes Äußeres.

*This handle range is based on Bauhaus-inspired minimal-
ist shapes. The original designs generally consist of two
or more combined elements which merge together into
one shape. The sectional plane with a different coloring
lends greater unity to the handle and gives the handle a
sleek and modern appearance.*

PRODUCT
SANGO by AURES
Kassensystem
Point of sale system

DESIGN
AURES Technologies
Lisses, France
ID'S
Bertand Médas
Lyons, France

MANUFACTURER
AURES Technologies
Lisses, France

AURES präsentiert SANGO. Der IT-Hersteller AURES Technologies hat in Zusammenarbeit mit dem Designer Bertrand MEDAS (Agentur ID'S) SANGO geschaffen. SANGO unterscheidet sich deutlich von herkömmlichen EPOS-Konzepten. Anders als viele gängige Verkaufsstellensysteme (EPOS Systeme) wurde SANGO von Anfang an mit dem Ziel entworfen, den Raum unter dem Touch-Monitor zur freien Nutzung verfügbar zu halten. Der Monitor wird von einer Tragvorrichtung mit Ausleger gehalten, in der auch die Zentraleinheit untergebracht ist. Möglich wurde diese technische Spitzenleistung durch Verwendung eines nach dem Prinzip des Exoskeletts ganz aus Aluminiumguss bestehenden Monitorgestells. Das Gestell liegt zum Teil frei und ist teilweise mit jenen Farbwechselrahmen aus Polycarbonat verkleidet, die den EPOS-Systemen von AURES seit 2005 ihre einzigartige farbliche Eleganz verleihen. Dabei sorgt der Aluminiumspritzguss nicht nur für die Formbeständigkeit des Monitorgestells und seine fast schwerelos, nüchtern und funktional wirkenden Volumen, sondern gewährleistet auch die Ableitung der von der Zentraleinheit ausgehenden Wärme.

Introducing SANGO by AURES. Designed and developed by IT manufacturers AURES Technologies in collaboration with designer Betrand Médas from ID'S, SANGO is an original, groundbreaking EPOS terminal concept. Unlike existing EPOS terminals on the market, the foundational idea is to provide a point of sale terminal that frees up space beneath the touch screen. The monitor is suspended from an offset support that also houses the CPU. This technological feat has been made possible by using a structure made entirely out of cast aluminum – serving as a kind of exo-skeleton. Partly visible, partly concealed, this structure is clad in interchangeable colored polycarbonate sections – the next step in the EPOS color revolution first launched by AURES in 2005. Injected aluminum is strong and allows simple, graceful, functional esthetics – with the added bonus that it also acts as a heat sink for the CPU.

PRODUCT

QLOCKTWO CLASSIC
Wanduhr
Wall clock

DESIGN

Biegert & Funk Product GmbH & Co. KG
Schwäbisch Gmünd, Germany

MANUFACTURER

Biegert & Funk Product GmbH & Co. KG
Schwäbisch Gmünd, Germany

Die QLOCKTWO CLASSIC lässt innehalten und ermöglicht eine andere Sichtweise auf die Zeit. Ihre typografische Anzeige verbindet den Moment mit dem geschriebenen Wort und macht ihn zum Statement. „Es ist halb neun." Vier kleine Punkte in den Ecken sorgen für die genaue Minutenanzeige. Die 45 x 45 cm große Uhr besteht aus einem weiß lackierten, monolithischen Holzkörper. Das Frontcover aus pulverbeschichtetem Edelstahl mit gelaserter Buchstabenmatrix verleiht der QLOCKTWO CLASSIC POWDER-COATED, ob stehend oder an der Wand platziert, einen besonders eleganten Auftritt.

QLOCKTWO CLASSIC makes you stop and look at time in a different way. The typographical display combines the moment with the written word and turns it into a statement. "It is half past eight." Four small dots in the corners mean time is displayed down to the minute. The 45 x 45 cm clock is made of a white lacquered monolithic wooden casing. The front cover made of powder-coated steel with its laser cutted grid of letters gives the QLOCKTWO CLASSIC POWDER-COATED an elegant appearance, no matter if placed on a wall or stand-alone.

PRODUCT
Ai
Aluminum-Poller
Aluminum bollard

DESIGN
Design dada associates
Kwan joong Jeon, Chae wook Lim, Kwang hun Lee
Seoul, South Korea

MANUFACTURER
Design dada associates
Seoul, South Korea

Durch Aufbringen eloxierten Aluminiums an Poller wird ihr Gewicht verringert und Kosten werden reduziert. Sandstrahlen und das Härten der Oberfläche verringert die Korrosivität des Materials im Außenbereich. Die gummierte Rundung der Poller mildert die Auswirkungen von Unfällen mit hoher Elastizität und verbessert so die Sicherheit sowohl für das Auto als auch für den Poller.

By applying anodized aluminum to bollards, weight is lightened and cost is reduced. Sand blasting and anodizing finish decreases the corrosiveness of the material in outdoor environment. The rubber bar rounding the bollards softens the impact of crash with high elasticity and enhances safety for both car and bollard.

PRODUCT

Mountain & City
Verkaufsraum
Sales office

DESIGN

One Plus Partnership Ltd.
Hong Kong

MANUFACTURER

Forte Land Co., Ltd.
Chongqing, China

Um das Konzept von Mountain & City visuell zu verdeutlichen, sind Wände und Raumflächen mit einer Kombination aus dreieckigen Elementen und schrägen Linien in Grautönen dekoriert. Die Geometrie der Wandelemente setzt sich auf dem hochwertigen Marmorfußboden fort, wo ungleichmäßige dreieckige Muster aus Marmor aufgebracht wurden. Die vertikalen und horizontalen Flächen erinnern an eine Berglandschaft. Die braunen Edelstahltheken wirken wie eine Felsformation. Streifenförmig angebrachte LEDs simulieren die verträumte Atmosphäre eines Regentages. Die gedämpfte Beleuchtung steht im Kontrast zur zerklüfteten Optik der Raumflächen.

To visualize the concept behind Mountain & City, walls and rooms feature a collection of triangular planes and oblique lines in different shades of gray. Wall geometries extend to grand marble floors, where irregular triangular patterns of marble have been arranged in the same manner. Both vertical and horizontal planes create visuals reminiscent of mountain scenery. An array of brown stainless-steel counters is shaped like a series of rocks. Strings of LED lamps create a dreamy atmosphere of rain. The soft lighting forms a contrast with the rugged look of the interior design.

PRODUCT
Bubbles
Möbel für Wartebereich
Furniture for waiting areas

DESIGN
busk + hertzog
London, United Kingdom

MANUFACTURER
Globe Zero4 A / S
Aarhus C, Denmark

Mit der Einführung von Bubbles ist eine ganz neue Ebene dessen erreicht, was im Bereich der Polsterung möglich ist. Die spezielle Technik kombiniert mit der genial konzipierten Konstruktion erneuert diesen traditionellen Möbeltyp. Mit der Inspiration aus Seifenblasen haben die Designer spielerisch einen ganz neuen Ausdruck für kreisförmige Warte- und Lobby-Möbel geschaffen. Durch die endlose Auswahl an Oberstoffen und die Auswahl von drei verschiedenen Größen können Bubbles als zentrale Elemente in der Innenarchitektur, ob es eine Lobby, öffentliche Räume in Messezentren, Flughäfen, Museen oder Firmensitz ist, verwendet werden.

With the introduction of Bubbles a whole new level for what's possible in the field of upholstery has been reached. The special technique combined with the ingeniously designed construction revitalize a traditional type of furniture. With the inspiration from soap bubbles the designers have playfully created a whole new expression for the circular waiting / lobby furniture. Through the endless choices of fabric and the choice of three different sizes Bubbles can be used as a central element in the interior design whether it is a hotel lobby, public spaces in exhibition centers, airports, museums, spa or corporate headquarters.

PRODUCT
WIZBRICK
Fahrrad-Unterstand
Bicycle rack

DESIGN
GS Engineering & Construction
Sung-Hoon Kim
Seoul, South Korea
L'EAU DESIGN
Sang-Hak Lee, Han-Jun Kim
Seoul, South Korea

MANUFACTURER
GS Engineering & Construction
Seoul, South Korea

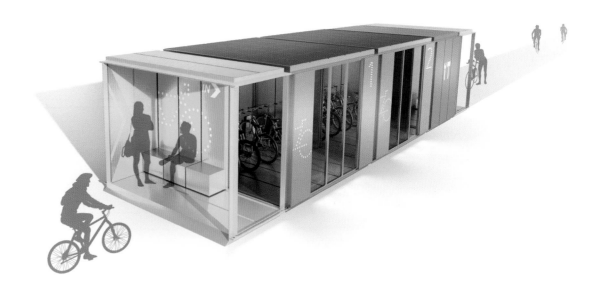

WIZBRICK ist ein umweltfreundlicher Fahrrad-Unterstand, der überall äußerst leicht aufgebaut werden
kann. Der Fahrrad-Unterstand misst 3,45 m x 0,65 m
und ist mit einer Verriegelung, Fahrradpumpe und Rad-
reinigungsvorrichtung ausgestattet. Durch das modulare
System kann der Stand variabel umgebaut werden, um
besser zur jeweiligen Umgebung zu passen. Er kann
außerdem vergrößert und verkleinert werden. Dadurch
ist er noch flexibler und komfortabler einsetzbar und
für die Langzeitanwendung geeignet. Außerdem nutzt
er Solarenergie und produziert den von ihm benötigten
Strom komplett selbst.

*WIZBRICK is an organic bicycle rack that can be easily
assembled in any location. The rack, which measures
3.45 m x 0.65 m, includes a lock device, bicycle pump
and wheel cleaning facility. The modular system can be
re-arranged into various configurations that may fit better to the surroundings. At the same time, it can also be
expanded or reduced in size, thus adding extra convenience and meaning that it's suitable for long-term use.
In addition, it is powered by solar energy and has a fully
self-generating power system.*

Small Tree Sign

Small Tree signage pillar design structure which apply twig pattern, so that keep the road for wind and sun light. It is symbiotic relationship with nature, shape, purpose.

not only information guide but also symbiotic relationship with nature : shape, purpose

What is different?

Pattern of the structure
: Overlap wood, leaf .

: Light & Shadow

Branches of a Tree

ECO friendly
: open mass.
wind & shine path.
promote plant growth.

Solar system
: solar panel back sheet

4 Hour

Day
accumulations of solar energy :

Night
: energy saving

well lighted

wind rise

WAY OUT

10

plants growth
open structure

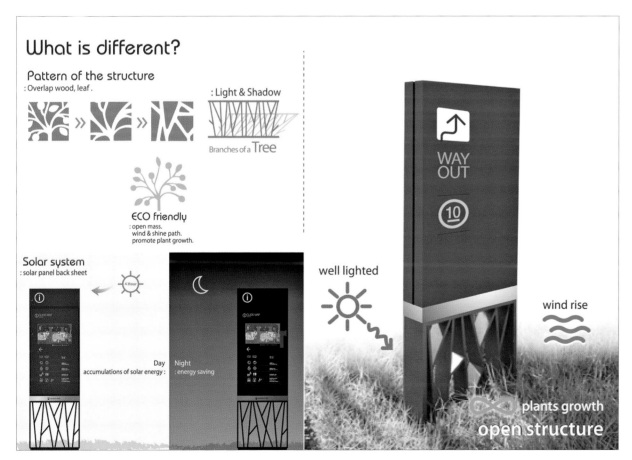

PRODUCT

Small Tree sign
Öffentliche Beschilderung
Public signage

DESIGN

Hanwha E & C
SunHee Choi
Seoul, South Korea
FLUX LAB
Sangill Kim
Seoul, South Korea

MANUFACTURER

Hanwha E & C
Seoul, South Korea

Small Tree ist eine umweltfreundliche Schildersäule, die mit ihrem Design in die unmittelbare Umgebung hinein wirkt. Bisher besteht umweltfreundliche Beschilderung oft aus ökologischem Material, aber die Umgebung wird nicht als Design-Element betrachtet. Das ist bei „Small tree" anders. Sie fügt sich perfekt in die Umgebung ein. Der untere Teil der Schildersäule ist als offene, zweigartige Struktur gestaltet. Die Schildersäule Small Tree wird neue Maßstäbe setzen – nicht nur als Informationsquelle, sondern auch in der symbiotischen Beziehung zwischen Natur, Form und Zweck.

Small Tree is an eco-friendly signage pillar that takes into its immediate surroundings in terms of its design. Existing eco-friendly signage is often made from eco-friendly materials, but the surroundings are frequently not considered as a design element. "Small tree" signage pillars are different. They have been designed to fit in in perfect harmony with their surroundings. The lower part of the signage pillar has been designed as an open structure with a twig-like pattern. The "Small tree" signage pillar will set new benchmarks – not only as an information guide, but also in the symbiotic relationship between nature, shape and purpose.

379

PRODUCT

Pixel Box Cinema
Kino
Cinema

DESIGN

One Plus Partnership Ltd.
Hong Kong

MANUFACTURER

Hubei Insun Cinema Film Co., Ltd.
Wuhan, China

Ein Pixel ist das Grundelement, aus dem Fotos bestehen. Mit „Pixel" erforscht der Designer die Beziehung zwischen Bewegung und dem Pixel. „Pixel" taucht in verschiedenen Bereichen des Kinos auf. Das Kinofoyer beherbergt einen riesigen geschwungenen Umschlag, der aus mehr als 6.000 Edelstahlplatten besteht. Die Hauptausstellungswand ist mit zahllosen quadratischen Streifen dekoriert, die aus der Wand herausragen und zusammen den Namen des Kinos bilden – Pixel Box. Im Kinosaal selbst wird durch das Zusammenwirken aller „Pixel"-Elemente eine großartige digitale Welt geschaffen, die jeder Einzelne genießen kann.

A pixel is the basic element of images. In "Pixel", the designer explores the relationship between movement and the pixel. "Pixel" pops up in different parts of the movie theater. The box office foyer houses a tremendous curved envelope made of over 6,000 stainless steel panels. The feature display wall is decorated with numerous square strips protruding from the wall that spell out the name of the movie theater – Pixel Box. Inside the movie theater, the cohesion of all "Pixel" elements creates a great digital world for everyone to enjoy.

PRODUCT
BETASIT
Modulares Banksystem für außen
Modular bench for outside

DESIGN
Nusser Stadtmöbel GmbH & Co. KG
Winnenden, Germany
rayerdesign
Andy Rayer
Esslingen, Germany

MANUFACTURER
Nusser Stadtmöbel GmbH & Co. KG
Winnenden, Germany

Stuhlcharakter für flexible Anordnungen: die modulare
Bankserie BETASIT. Einzelsitze mit oder ohne Rücken-
lehne; zu Reihenbank kombinier- und erweiterbar; zur
Ergänzung Grundelement mit Anbauelementen; beid-
seitige Anordnung der Lehne möglich; Gestell aus
Flachstahl feuerverzinkt und mit Pulverbeschichtung;
Standardfarbe „Anthrazit-Eisenglimmer"; Sitz- und
Lehnenfläche für komfortables Sitzen schalenförmig
ausgefräst; Ausführung der Holzleisten in FSC® Hartholz;
Länge pro Einzelsitz 55 cm.

*BETASIT: a flexible system of chairs. Seats with or without
backrest; to be arranged to a line of chairs; therefore just
add one or more seats to a basic-elements; backrest on
both sides of the seat possible; support made of hot dip
galvanized and powder-coated steel; color anthrazit-
grey; seat and backrest shaped in a very comfortable
way; timberslats in FSC® hardwood; length 55 cm per
seat.*

PRODUCT

Essential

Bett

Bed

DESIGN

Köhler and Wilms

Claudia Köhler, Irmy Wilms

Herford, Germany

MANUFACTURER

Royal Auping

Deventer, Netherlands

Mit dem Entwurf des Bettes Essential haben wir intelligente Technik in eine moderne, iconhafte und sinnliche Form gebracht. Durch die sensible Balance von Volumen und Leichtigkeit und seine organischen Modellierungen wirkt das Bett gleichermaßen einladend wie pur. Es war uns wichtig, dass das Essential in stilistisch unterschiedlichste Interieurs passt und somit eine lange Lebensdauer verspricht. Farben: warm-weiß matt, nachtblau, karbon-schwarz, yellow, skin.

With the design of the Essential we have combined diverse techniques with a very light and sensual design. Because of the delicate balance of size and organic forms the bed looks inviting and pure. With the design of the Essential we offer a bed that fits in every stylish bedroom. We offer the consumer a very diverse variety of colors. Safe colors like carbon black, pure white and night blue, but also yellow and skin.

MEDICINE / HEALTH+CARE

TORSTEN FRITZE
ANDREAS HAUG
MARKUS WILD

PRODUCT

Falck first-aid kit
Erste-Hilfe-Kasten
First-aid kit

DESIGN

Designit A/S
Aarhus C, Denmark

MANUFACTURER

Falck A/S
København V, Denmark

Falcks Redesign des Erste-Hilfe-Kastens verbessert die häusliche Sicherheit durch sein logisches und intuitives Design. Um den Benutzer schnell zu den relevanten Inhalten zu führen und Verwirrung zu vermeiden, ist das Kit in vier Kategorien unterteilt: Blutungen, Brandwunden, Prellungen und Zerrungen. Farbkodierungen und anleitende Bebilderungen liefern dem Benutzer einen schnellen Überblick und beruhigen dessen Handlung in einer angespannten Situation. Form und Material erfüllen eine optimale Funktion und ein ästhetisches und modernes Design, das einen sichtbaren Platz im Haus verdient und somit im Bedarfsfall immer zur Hand ist.

Falck's first-aid kit re-design innovates domestic safety through its logical and intuitive design, promoting user action when accidents occur. The kit is divided into four categories; bleeding, burns, bruises and strains to quickly guide the user to the relevant contents and avoid confusion. Color coding, conveying illustrations and the use of everyday terms provide the user with a swift overview in a stressed situation – providing reassurance to act. Form and material meet the need for optimal function and an aesthetically appealing and contemporary design worthy of keeping visible in the home – thus, just to hand when most needed!

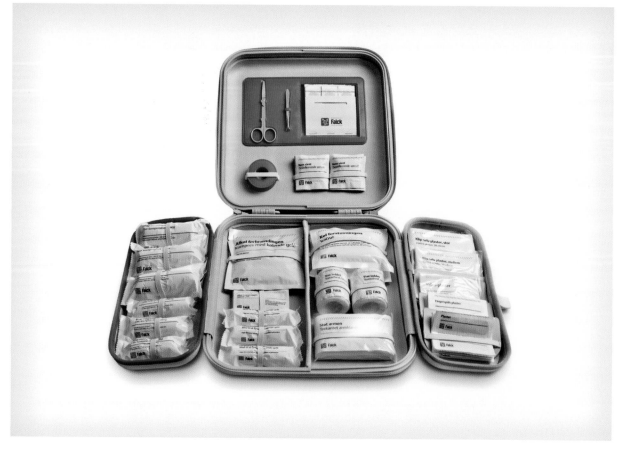

Falck

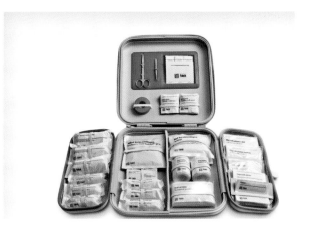

„Ein Erste-Hilfe-Kasten wie er sein sollte: übersichtlich und hervorragend organisiert. Vier Sparten – durch verschiedene Farben kenntlich gemacht – leiten den Benutzer. Die ausklappbaren Elemente machen es möglich, immer alles im Blick zu behalten und auch in schwierigen Situationen intuitiv zu den richtigen Dingen zu greifen. Ein Must-have für jeden Haushalt."

"A first-aid kit as it should be: clearly arranged and extremely well organized. Four sections, made immediately visible by their different colors, help the user find their way around. The fold-out elements make it possible to have an overview of the entire contents at all times, and to go for the correct products intuitively even in difficult situations. A must-have for every household."

JURYSTATEMENT

PRODUCT

HSL-001
Schlafdauer-Tracker
Sleep duration tracker

DESIGN

OMRON HEALTHCARE Co., Ltd.
Design Communication Department
Kyoto, Japan
C.Creative Inc.
Takashi Shigeno, Kazuya Andachi
Tokyo, Japan

MANUFACTURER

OMRON HEALTHCARE Co., Ltd.
Kyoto, Japan

Dieser Schlafdauer-Tracker überwacht die zum Einschla-
fen gebrauchte Zeit und die Zeitdauer bis zum Aufwachen. Er registriert außerdem anhand von Bewegungen
des schlafenden Körpers, wenn der Schlaf seichter wird
und lässt den Alarm dann klingeln, wenn der Benutzer
erfrisch aufwachen wird. Seine weiche Form und die
matte Oberfläche passen angenehm in eine Schlafum-
gebung, um stressfreie Messungen zu ermöglichen.
Durch NFC-Konnektivität kann eine visuelle Repräsen-
tation des Schlafs erzeugt und auf einem Smartphone
überprüft werden, um die Überwachung der Gesundheit zu unterstützen.

*This sleep duration tracker monitors the time taken to go
to sleep and the time elapsed until waking. It also senses
when sleep has become shallow from movements of the
sleeping body, and rings an alarm at a time when the
user will awake refreshed. The soft form and frost finish
fits comfortably into a sleeping environment to provide
stress-free monitoring. With NFC connectivity, a visual
representation of sleep can be created and checked on a
smart-phone to support health monitoring.*

„Er ist unauffällig und rund in seinen Formen. Das ist der Grund, weshalb man ihn gern am Körper trägt, obwohl der Tracker nachts benötigt wird. Seine Funktionen sind sofort verständlich. Auch auf dieser Ebene ergibt sich eine sehr angenehme Verbindung zwischen Produkt und Nutzer. Dass es sich darüber hinaus um ein modernes, sogar mit einem Smartphone kompatibles Produkt handelt, erstaunt bei dieser tollen Designleistung nicht."

"This product is inconspicuous, with its rounded shape, which means that the user is happy to wear it on the body although it is required at night. Its functions are immediately clear and on this level too there is a pleasant relationship between the product and the user. The fact that on top of this it is a modern product that is even smartphone-compatible is no surprise, given the product's great design."

JURYSTATEMENT

PRODUCT

seca mBCA 515/514
Diagnoseinstrument
Diagnostic instrument

DESIGN

npk design GmbH
Till Garthoff, Detlef Rhein
Hamburg, Germany

MANUFACTURER

seca gmbh & co. kg.
Hamburg, Germany

seca mBCA ermöglicht die Analyse der Körperzusammensetzung auf medizinischem Niveau. Das innovative
Diagnoseinstrument ist das einzige Body-Composition-
Analyzer-Gerät, das medizinisch präzise Messungen
durchführt und die BCA-Rohdaten nach medizinischen
Referenzen analysiert und interpretiert. So können viele
Krankheiten früher erkannt und Therapieverläufe exak-
ter verfolgt werden. Der medical-Body-Composition-
Analyser (seca mBCA) wird in Krankenhäusern, Reha-
kliniken oder Arztpraxen zur exakten Ermittlung der
individuellen Körperzusammensetzung des Patienten
eingesetzt.

*The innovative diagnostic instrument is the only Body
Composition Analyzer (BCA) which makes precise medical
measurements and analyzes and interprets the BCA raw
data against medical reference values. The results help
doctors to detect early signs of disease and to keep a close
watch on treatment progress. The seca medical Body Composition Analyzer 515/514 (seca mBCA) is ideally adapted
to the working conditions in hospitals, medical practices
and rehabilitation facilities to determine the exact body
composition of individual patients. Electrical impedance
is measured via electrodes to determine fat, muscle and
water components.*

product
design award

2013 GOLD

„Das Instrument analysiert die Zusammensetzung des menschlichen Körpers. Das einfache, schlichte Design nimmt dem Gerät jedoch den Charakter einer medizinischen Apparatur. Im Ergebnis fühlt sich der Patient der Maschine nicht ausgeliefert, sondern stets sicher. Eine reduzierte Formensprache, die im medizinischen Alltag absolut wünschenswert und daher mit einem iF gold award zu belohnen ist!"

"This product analyzes the composition of the human body. The simple, sleek design, however, means the device does not look like a conventional piece of medical equipment. The result is that the patient does not feel that he or she is at the mercy of the machine, but instead simply feels secure. This is minimalist design vocabulary that is highly desirable in the world of medicine and is therefore deserving of an iF gold award."

JURYSTATEMENT

PRODUCT
Breeze®Nebulizer
Vernebler
Nebulizer

DESIGN
digiO2 International Co., Ltd.
(Headquarters)
New Taipei City, Taiwan

MANUFACTURER
digiO2 International Co., Ltd.
(Headquarters)
New Taipei City, Taiwan
digiO2 International Co., Ltd.
(Factory)
Miaoli, Taiwan
SINBON Electronics Co., Ltd.
New Taipei City, Taiwan

Menschen mit Erkrankungen der Atemwege, wie COPD
oder Asthma, nutzen regelmäßig inhalative Medikamente, sodass andere Menschen den Eindruck haben,
sie seien kranke Patienten. Der Breeze®Nebulizer wurde
geschaffen, damit die Nutzer das Gefühl haben, auf na-
türlichem Wege zu atmen und, um die tägliche medizinische Versorgung auf eine entspannte Art und Weise
zu erreichen. Die Eigenschaften dieses Produktes beinhalten: portable Größe, kurvenreiches Design, das die
Tragfähigkeit vereinfacht. Das Gerät hat die Fähigkeit,
die Menge an vorhandenen Medikamenten zu ermitteln
und sich automatisch auszuschalten. Der Einschalt-
Knopf ist aus weichem Material.

*People suffering from respiratory diseases such as COPD or
asthma use inhaled drugs regular, and easy to leave to other
people the impression of patients. The Breeze®Nebulizer
design conception is to make the user feel "nature like
breathing", to have the daily medical care with relax. The
features of the product include: portable, convenient to get
hold, and is able to detect the amount of drugs and turn off
automatically. The open button is made of soft materials.
The ice blue light with elegant white overall makes people
feel calm. When you open it, the pharmacy will blow into
your chest like the breeze, bringing you health gradually.*

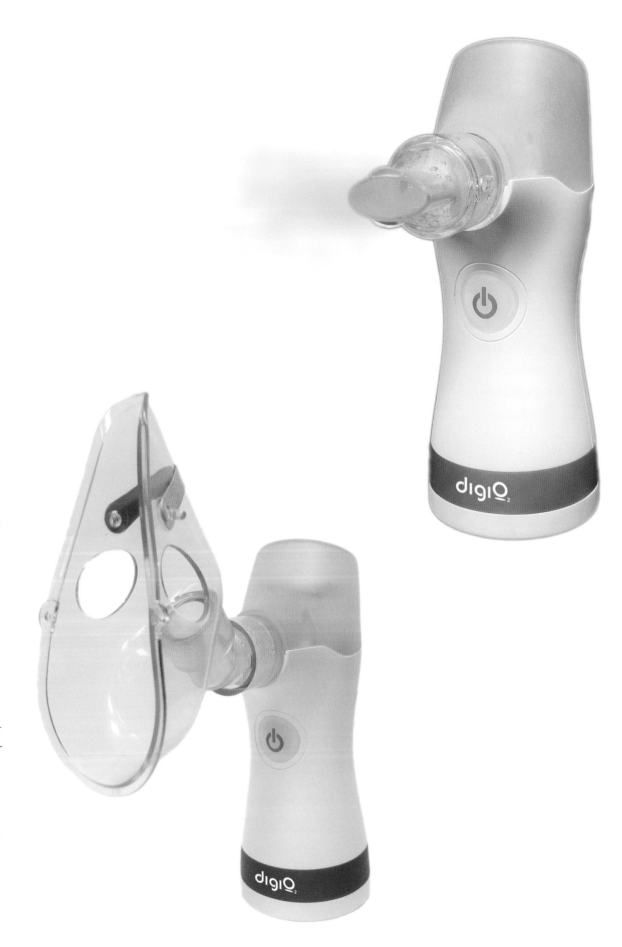

„Mit seinen frischen, hellen Farben liegt das Produkt voll im Trend einer neuen, freundlich gestalteten Generation medizinischer Geräte. Das funktionale Design lädt dazu ein, es intuitiv zu benutzen und unterstützt so seine medizinische Anwendung. Gerade im Bereich der Asthma- oder Atemwegspatienten ist es wichtig, eine Form für die ‚normale' Atemunterstützung zu finden, die einen entspannten Umgang von Patient und Umgebung ermöglicht."

"The fresh, light colors ensure that the product joins the trend of a new, friendlier generation of medical devices. The functional design encourages intuitive use and therefore supports the medical use of the device. It is particularly important for patients with asthma and respiratory problems to find a way of ensuring "normal" breathing support that allows relaxed handling of the patient and their environment."

JURYSTATEMENT

PRODUCT

Air Care-Light
Luftreiniger
Air cleaner

DESIGN

NOVA Design Co., Ltd.
New Taipei City, Taiwan

MANUFACTURER

AcoMo Technology
Hsinchu, Taiwan

Air Care-Light ist ein leichter, dünner und tragbarer
Luftreiniger für enge Räume. Er sterilisiert Bakterien mit
der Technologie von Kaltkathoden-Fluoreszenzlampen.
Die Luft gelangt durch die obere Öffnung hinein und
durchläuft den Desinfektionsbereich mit dem ultravio-
letten Licht der Lampe, bevor sie durch die untere Öffnung wieder entweicht. Das patentierte optische Panel
wandelt das UV-Licht in einen sicheren und sichtbaren
Lichtstrahl um. Die Beleuchtung der Lichtröhre zeigt an,
dass der Sterilisationsprozess läuft.

*The Air Care-Light is a lightweight, slim and portable air
purifier for use in confined spaces. It sterilizes bacteria
using CCFL (Cold Cathode Fluorescence Lamp) technology.
Air enters the system through the top vent and passes
through the disinfecting ultraviolet light area, before
being released out of the bottom vent. Ultraviolet light is
provided by the CCFL. The patented optic panel transfers
the ultraviolet light into a safe and visible light beam.
The illumination of the light tube indicates that the sterilization process is active.*

PRODUCT
StimRouter
Gerät zur Schmerzlinderung
Device for pain relief

DESIGN
Aran Research & Development
Shoham Zak, Tali Zichroni, Eitan Shiloh
Caesaeea Business Park, Israel

MANUFACTURER
Bioness Neuromodulation Ltd.
Ra'anana, Israel

Das StimRouter-System behandelt chronische Schmerzen. Das System besteht aus einem implantierbaren Blei, einem Externen Puls-Sender (EPT), Einweg-Elektroden und einer Fernbedienung. Der EPT generiert schmerzlindernde elektrische Signale und überträgt sie über die Elektrode und Haut auf die StimRouter-Führung. Der EPT ist das weltweit kleinste aufladbare Anregungsgerät seiner Art. Es wurde entworfen, um natürlichen Körperkonturen zu entsprechen. Das elegante Design behindert tägliche Aktivitäten nicht wie z. B. Ankleiden. Das „saubere" Design lässt andere Menschen nicht bemerken, dass der Benutzer ein medizinisches Gerät trägt.

The StimRouter system treats chronic pain. The system consists of an implantable lead, an External Pulse Transmitter (EPT), a Remote Control and disposable Electrodes. The EPT generates a pain relieving electrical signal and transmits it through the Electrode and skin to the StimRouter Lead. The EPT is the world's smallest rechargeable stimulation device of its kind. It was designed to conform to natural body contours. The sleek design does not impede on daily activities such as getting dressed and the "clean" design does not call attention to the fact that users use a medical device.

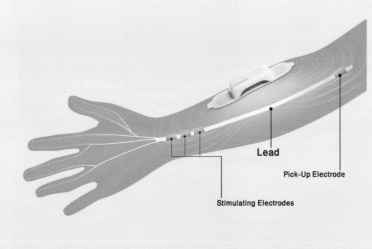

Lead

Pick-Up Electrode

Stimulating Electrodes

open the case

peel the disposable liner

Easily connect / disconnect the router

PRODUCT
AGUAMIX
Sensorarmatur
Sensor faucet

DESIGN
City GmbH
Sigmarszell, Germany

MANUFACTURER
City GmbH
Sigmarszell, Germany

AGUAMIX ist eine vollständig berührungslose Sensor-Armatur. Mit einer speziellen Innenkonstruktion beugt sie der Bildung von Biofilm vor und wehrt das Einnisten von Bakterien ab. AGUAMIX ist nach neuesten Hygiene-standards für den Gesundheitsbereich entwickelt. Weitere Vorzüge: mikroprozessorgesteuert, Temperatur-Anzeige mit Sensor zur einfachen Temperaturregelung durch kleine Handbewegungen, Verbrühschutz, flüster-leise, daher auch für Räume mit erhöhten Schallschutz-anforderungen geeignet, einfache Installation, energie- und wassersparend.

AGUAMIX is a completely touchless sensor-faucet. Its special construction inside prevents from growth of bio-film and attachement of bacteria. AGUAMIX has been developed in accordance with the latest guidelines for hygiene in health sector. Further advantages: micropro-cessor controlled, digital temperature indication with sensor, easy regulation of temperature caused by little movements of the hands, protection from scalding, ex-tremely quiet, suited for silent areas, easy installation, saving water and energy.

PRODUCT
Alta™ MLS
Modularer Dental-Laser
Modular dental laser

DESIGN
Product Insight Inc.
Acton, MA, United States of America

MANUFACTURER
Dental Photonics, Inc.
Walpole, MA, United States of America

Die Alta™ MLS ist vielseitig, kompakt und tragbar. Eine modulare Spule mit Handstück-Unterstützung kann für unterschiedliche Bedürfnisse der Chirurgen verändert werden. Soft-TPE schützt und verwaltet die optische Faser. Gezeigt wird nur das, was notwendig ist. Das leichte Design passt zu einem Tisch oder an die Wand in mehreren Umgebungen. Der Winkel der Anzeige wurde sorgfältig für eine optimale Anzeige in beiden Konfigurationen berücksichtigt. Eine saubere, reine Formensprache betont Einfachheit und Benutzerfreundlichkeit. Die Display-Oberfläche ist dominant, um visuelle Unordnung zu verringern und um die Konzentration auf den Touch-Screen zu richten.

The Alta™ MLS is versatile, compact and portable. A modular spool with handpiece support is interchanged to suit the surgeon's needs. A soft TPE material protects and manages the delicate optical fiber to expose only what is needed. The lightweight design easily and quickly attaches to a table or wall for optimal use in multiple environments. The display angle was carefully considered for optimal viewing in both configurations. A clean, pure form language was developed to emphasize the device's simplicity and ease-of-use. The display surface is purposefully dominant to reduce visual clutter and allows focus on the touch screen interface.

PRODUCT

Perseus A500
Anästhesiearbeitsplatz
Anesthesia workstation

DESIGN

Corpus-C Design Agentur
Sebastian Maier, Alexander Müller
Fürth, Germany

MANUFACTURER

Dräger Medical GmbH
Lübeck, Germany

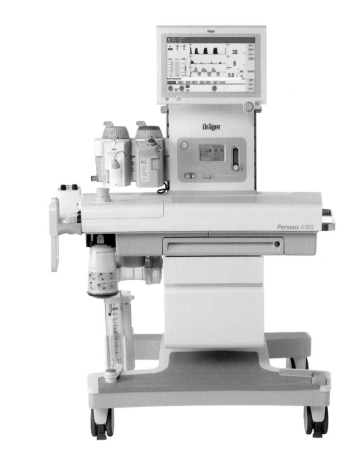

Der Dräger-Perseus A500 ist der erste konsequent
umgesetzte Anästhesiearbeitsplatz, der durch seine
ästhetische sowie funktionale Gestaltung modernste
Arbeitsplatzergonomie mit neuester Gerätetechnologie
verbindet. Gemeinsam mit den Anwendern weltweit ist
es gelungen, das Gerätekonzept mit einem hohen Maß
an Flexibilität auszulegen, das nun mehr als 120 individuelle Konfigurationsmöglichkeiten zulässt. Das neue
Designkonzept ermöglicht neben seinem charakteristisch großen Arbeitstisch hinaus, durch zusätzliche Ab-
lageflächen, Schubladen sowie integrierte Kabelmanage-
mentlösungen die Arbeitsplatzsituation weiterhin zu
optimieren.

*The Dräger Perseus A500 is the first anesthesia worksta-
tion, which was stringently designed to combine state-of-
the-art workplace ergonomics with the latest device technology taking both, esthetic and functional aspects into
account. Together with users from all over the world, a
highly flexible device configuration concept was created
to allow for more than 120 individual workplace set-ups.
Apart from the new, characteristical worktable the new
concept provides a choice of storage shelves, drawers as
well as an integrated cable management solution to further optimize the workplace.*

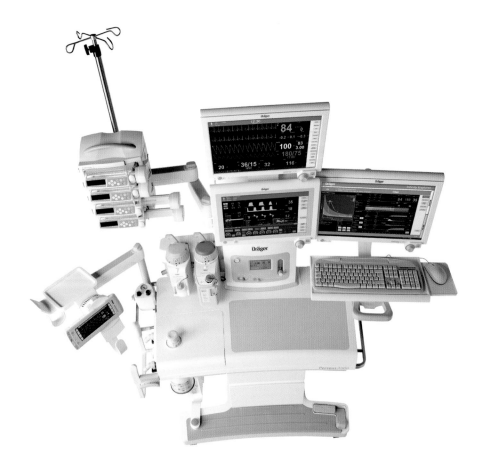

PRODUCT
F&P Pilairo™
Obstruktive Schlafapnoe-Maske
Obstructive sleep apnea mask

DESIGN
Fisher & Paykel Healthcare
Auckland, New Zealand

MANUFACTURER
Fisher & Paykel Healthcare
Auckland, New Zealand

Die F&P Pilairo™-Maske wurde speziell für Patienten-komfort und Benutzerfreundlichkeit entwickelt. Das klare Design wirkt warm, kompakt und federleicht. Die Maske wiegt 52 Gramm und ermöglicht dem Patienten uneingeschränkte Sicht. Die selbstaufblasende Kissen-Silikondichtung ermöglicht komfortable CPAP-Therapie für Obstruktive Schlafapnoe. Die Maske besteht aus drei einfach zerlegbaren Teilen, um sie einfach reinigen zu können. Das radikal neu designte Kopfband benötigt keine Anpassung und ist ein Novum im Markt. Die F&P Pilairo™ Maske ermöglicht dem Patienten bisher un-bekannten Tagekomfort, Benutzerfreundlichkeit und geruhsamen Schlaf.

The F&P Pilairo™ is designed for patient comfort and performance. The clean and simple design is warm, un-obtrusive, compact and lightweight. The mask weighs 52 grams and gives patients a clear field of view, reduc-ing claustrophobia and increasing patient comfort. The silicone seal inflates to comfortably deliver CPAP therapy to treat Obstructive Sleep Apnea. The mask has three separable components, making it easy to clean. The minimal headgear is light, easy to fit and doesn't need adjustment. These features allow the F&P Pilairo™ free-dom of movement giving patients a comfortable night's sleep.

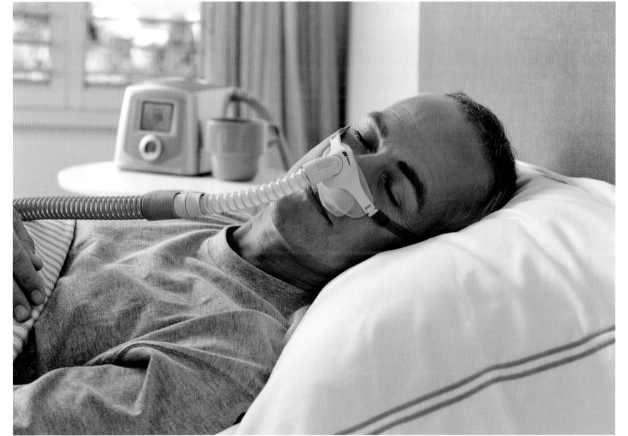

PRODUCT

Optiflow Junior
Nasenkanüle
Nasal cannula

DESIGN

Fisher & Paykel Healthcare
Auckland, New Zealand

MANUFACTURER

Fisher & Paykel Healthcare
Auckland, New Zealand

F&P's Optiflow Junior-Nasenkanüle ist die nächste Generation von Beatmungskanülen, um Patienten im Kindesalter, die unter Atemschwierigkeiten leiden, befeuchteten Sauerstoff zuzuführen. Während der intensiven Entwicklung wurden mehr als 500 Prototypen an Kindern getestet. Was ist Neu? - Das weltweit erste knickfreie und atmungsaktive Schlauch-System (reduziert die Atemkondensation um 87 % gegenüber konventionellen Schlauch-Systemen), vereinfachtes Anbringen und Entfernen der Nasenkanüle, sanfte Hautanpassung und kinderfreundliche Farben. Unsere Kunden sehen in Optiflow Junior die Evolution in der Optiflow-Therapie von Kindern.

F&P's Optiflow Junior nasal cannula system is a next-generation interface for delivering humidified oxygen to infant patients in respiratory distress, developed following extensive hospital-based research and over 500 prototypes trialed on real infants. Optiflow Junior incorporates substantial improvements over previous designs: the world's first kink-proof, breathable tubing (reducing condensation by 87 %), streamlined nasal cannula application / removal process, soft form integration with bright child-friendly colors. Optiflow Junior is viewed by customers as a treatment evolution in delivery of infant Optiflow therapy.

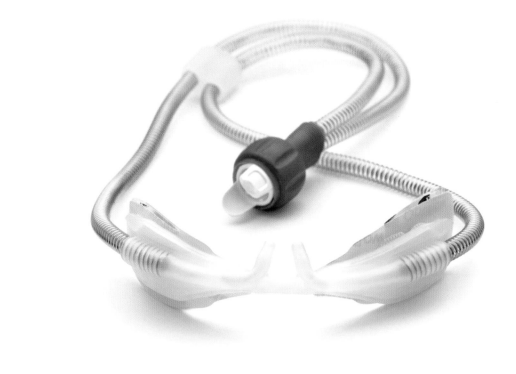

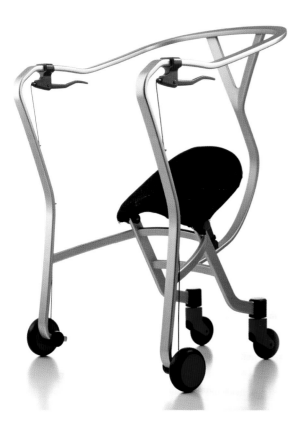

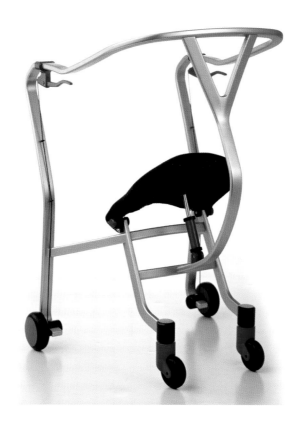

PRODUCT

SiTand Walker
Mobilitätshilfe
Mobility aid

DESIGN

435 CREATIVE Design Scenes Inc.
Taipei City, Taiwan

MANUFACTURER

Footwear & Recreation Technology Research Institute
Taichung, Taiwan

Dieser Stuhl ist Ihnen eine Stütze! Die hochbetagte Gesellschaft ist da und es gibt immer mehr Rentner. Ältere Menschen erleiden oft Unfälle, da ihre Kraft, Balance und Flexibilität abnehmen. Der SiTand Walker hilft, ihre Bewegungen zu stützen und Dinge wie z. B. Aufstehen oder Setzen zu erleichtern, um so Hinfallen zu verhindern. Der SiTand Walker kombiniert eine Gehhilfe und einen Stützstuhl. Sein Mechanismus bietet Hilfe für den Nutzer, um aus dem Sitzen aufzustehen, indem er den Druck auf Hüften und Gelenken vermindert. Der SiTand Walker hilft älteren und behinderten Menschen auch, sich rascher und sicherer zu bewegen.

Elderly people often suffer from accidents due to the reduction of their muscle strength, sense of balance, and body flexibility. The SiTand Walker is designed to assist their daily movement and for the actions like getting up and sitting down so a harmful fall will never happen again. The SiTand Walker combines the function of a walker and an assistive Chair. The assistant mechanism provides extra support for the user to get up from a seating position so it helps decrease the pressure in the hips and knees joints. The SiTand Walker also helps the elderly and disable user to move around more quickly in a safe way.

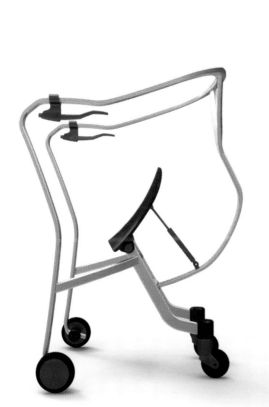

401

PRODUCT
MedSense
Hand-Hygiene-System
Hand hygiene system

DESIGN
WILDDESIGN
Gerhard Seizer, Yusheng Wu
Shanghai, China

MANUFACTURER
General Sensing
Hong Kong

MedSense, ein sensorbasiertes System der Firma General Sensing, verbessert die Hand-Hygiene von Mitarbeitern im Gesundheitswesen und überwacht die Einhaltung gemäß WHO-Richtlinien. MedSense besteht aus vier einfach bedienbaren, drahtlosen Komponenten: Badge, Beacon, Monitor und Base. Im Zusammenspiel erzeugen sie ein persönliches Abbild der Hand-Hygiene in Form von Echtzeit-Daten, welche mit der Cloud-basierten App ausgewertet werden. Die Einhaltung kann für Mitarbeiter, Stationen und Einrichtungen exakt gemessen werden. Unauffällig und einfach zu installieren, passt sich das MedSense nahtlos in die Krankenhaus-Umgebung und den Work-Flow ein.

MedSense by General Sensing is an electronic sensor-based system that monitors, incentivizes and improves hand hygiene practices of healthcare practitioners in accordance with WHO guidelines. The MedSense system consists of four easy-to-use wireless devices: badge, beacon, dispenser monitor, and base. Working together, the system provides real-time, accurate data to MedSense HQ – a cloud-based web application that tracks compliance and recognizes achievements for each user, department, and hospital. Designed to be unobtrusive, easy to use and install, MedSense fits seamlessly within any hospital environment and workflow.

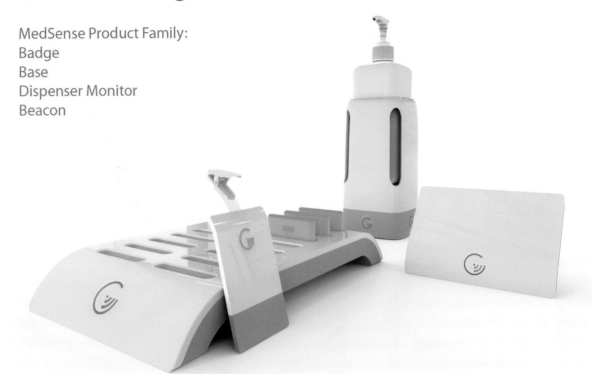

GeneralSensing

MedSense Product Family:
Badge
Base
Dispenser Monitor
Beacon

MedSense
Product Interaction

PRODUCT
Pirol + Skua
Medizinische Vakuumregler
Medical suction regulators

DESIGN
BAZARGANI | Design+Innovation
Hamburg, Germany

MANUFACTURER
Greggersen Gasetechnik GmbH
Hamburg, Germany

Die Produkte Pirol und Skua der Firma Greggersen sind für eine sichere regulierbare Absaugung von Körperflüssigkeiten im Krankenhaus und in Arztpraxen konzipiert. Das Gerät Pirol wird mit Vakuum, Skua mit Druckluft (Venturi-Prinzip) angetrieben. Beide verwenden eine Vielzahl von hochwertigen Aluminium- und Kunststoff-Gleichteilen, die auch gut recycelt werden können. Ihre ansprechende Erscheinung überzeugt durch die klare Formensprache mit präzisen, flächenbündigen Übergängen, die sich leicht reinigen lassen. Die konsequente Anwendung des Corporate Product Designs auf die Produkte Pirol und Skua kennzeichnet eindeutig die Marke Greggersen.

The products Pirol and Skua from the company Greggersen are designed for a securely controlled aspiration of body fluids in hospitals and office based physicians. The product Pirol is driven by vacuum whereby Skua uses the Venturi principle to create vacuum. Both use several carry-over parts build of high-quality aluminum and plastic, which can be recycled very well. Their clean shapes and precisely flush transitions between parts created a convincing appearance as well as easily cleaning. The consistent application of corporate product design to the products Pirol and Skua help uniquely identifies the brand Greggersen.

PRODUCT

Handicare Puma 40

Motorgetriebener Rollstuhl

Power wheelchair

DESIGN

VanBerlo B. V.

Eindhoven, Netherlands

MANUFACTURER

Handicare

Helmond, Netherlands

Mit dem Puma 40 führt Handicare eine neue Generation von motorgetriebenen Rollstühlen ein. Mit einer gelungenen Mischung aus Funktionalität, Komfort und Design setzt er einen neuen Standard im Gebrauch für innen und im Freien, mit der Gewährleistung höchstmöglicher Unabhängigkeit. Technisch ausgeklügelt und vielfältig, lässt er sich den spezifischen Anforderungen des Nutzers genau anpassen. Seine kompakten Maße und die hohe Wendigkeit schaffen optimale Voraussetzungen für die Verwendung im Innenraum. Das Sedeo-Sitzsystem garantiert besten Sitzkomfort. Die klare Gestaltung des Puma 40 ist bewusst funktional und gleichzeitig eigenständig.

With Puma 40, Handicare has introduced a new generation of power wheelchairs. A perfect blend of functionality, comfort and design, it sets a new standard for intensive use indoors and outdoors, ensuring maximum independence in daily life. Technically smart and truly modular, it is highly adaptable to suit the specific needs of the individual. High maneuverability and compact dimensions are particularly ideal for indoor use. The fully adjustable Sedeo seating system offers a new level of seating comfort. The clean design with subtle highlights is both contemporary and very refined, making Puma 40 stand out amongst competition.

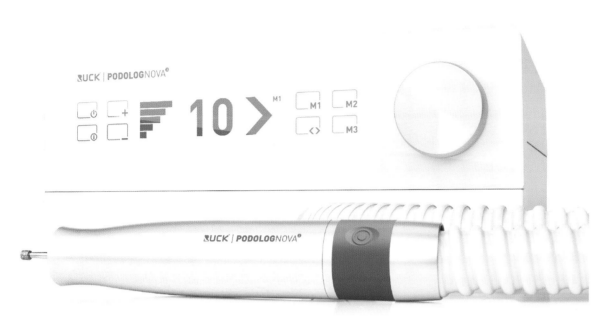

PRODUCT
PODOLOG NOVA 3
Fußpflegegerät
Podiatry device

DESIGN
crosscreative designstudios
Pforzheim, Germany
HELLMUT RUCK GmbH
Neuenbürg, Germany

MANUFACTURER
HELLMUT RUCK GmbH
Neuenbürg, Germany

Der PODOLOG NOVA 3 ist ein professionelles Fußpflege-gerät – formal an sein medizinisches Umfeld angepasst, ausgestattet mit einer patentierten, extrem wirkungsvollen Absaugung, wartungsfreien Mikromotoren mit langer Lebensdauer. Er ist das leiseste und leichteste Gerät seiner Art – wichtig für die Kommunikation zwischen Patient und Behandler sowie beim ambulanten Einsatz. Das ergonomische Handstück ist filigran und leicht. Das magnetische Drehrad ist abnehmbar – das Gerät dadurch leicht zu desinfizieren. Das Display informiert übersichtlich, führt Schritt für Schritt durch die Funktionen. Produktaussage: professionell für Fuß und Pflege.

The podiatry device PODOLOG NOVA 3 is a professional product designed according to its medical environment, equipped with a patented and extremely effective aspiration, maintenance-free micro motors for a long life cycle. It is the quietest and lightest device available – which is very important for the communication between patient and treating person and for mobile use. The ergonomic handpiece is filigree, and light. The magnetic jog dial is detachable so the device can easily be disinfected. The display is clearly structured, step-by-step instructions lead through various functions. Product statement: professional footcare.

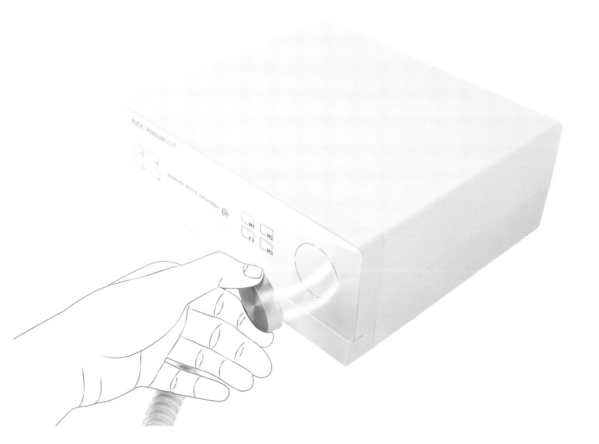

PRODUCT
LivOn
Telecare-System
Telecare service

DESIGN
LEED design & consulting
Lee Changsoo, Kim Jinsu, Lee Jaeho
Seoul, South Korea

MANUFACTURER
HIDEA Solutions Co., Ltd.
Seoul, South Korea

Das LivOn-Telecare-System besteht aus Basisstation, Aktivitätssensor und Alarmknopf. Es überwacht die Aktivitäten von Senioren durch Zimmerdeckensensoren in Räumen wie dem Bad, der Küche oder dem Schlafzimmer. Falls ein Notfall eintritt, informiert das System den zuständigen Betreuer oder Notdienst per Anruf oder SMS. Das Mobilteil hat eine gummierte Oberfläche und ein intuitiv nutzbares Bedienfeld. Es erfüllt damit höchste Komfortansprüche. Der wasserfeste Mini-Alarmknopf kann je nach Belieben als Kette oder Armband getragen werden. Dieses Telecare-System ist in Übereinstimmung mit dem hauseigenen Markenkonzept von LivOn entworfen worden.

The LivOn System is a telecare system consisting of a base unit, an activity sensor and a help trigger. The system monitors the activity of the elderly via sensors installed on the ceilings of bedrooms, bathrooms, kitchens and other rooms. In the event of an emergency, the system calls or sends a text message to caregivers or emergency services. The handset is made of rubber for easy use and comfort, and features intuitive PUI. The small, waterproof help trigger for making emergency calls can be worn as a necklace or bracelet depending on the user's preference. The system is designed to maintain LivOn's own identity as a set.

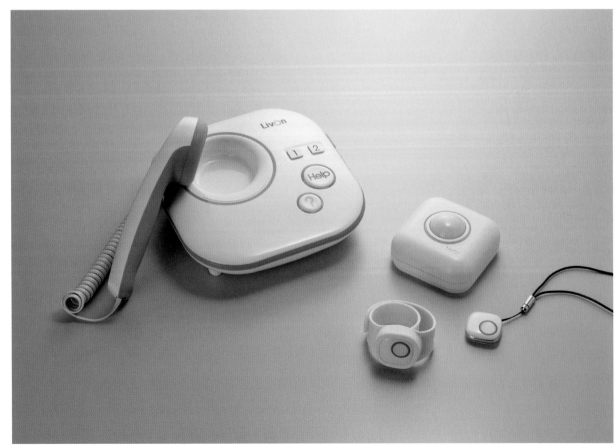

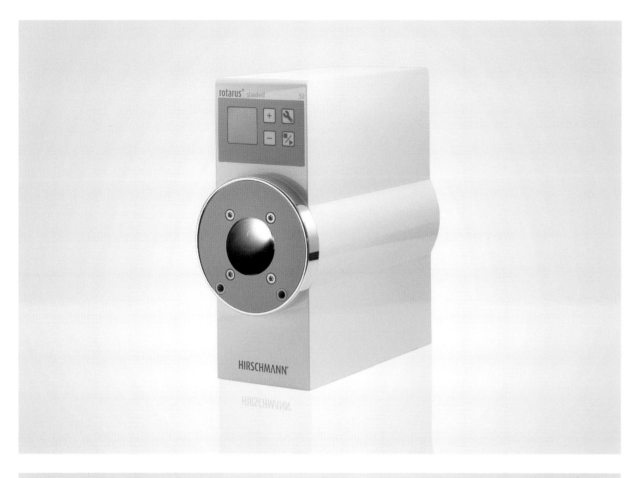

PRODUCT
rotarus®
Schlauchpumpe
Peristaltic pump

DESIGN
Phoenix Design GmbH + Co. KG
Stuttgart, Germany
Hirschmann Laborgeräte GmbH & Co. KG
Eberstadt, Germany

MANUFACTURER
Hirschmann Laborgeräte GmbH & Co. KG
Eberstadt, Germany

Mit der rotarus®-Schlauchpumpenserie macht Hirschmann den Schritt in die Welt der kontinuierlich fördernden Pumpen. Verschiedene Motoren, Gehäuse unterschiedlicher Schutzklassen und intelligente Steuerungstechnik der Fördermengen zeigen eine durchgängig geplante Produktfamilie, die ein breites Spektrum an Anwendungsbereichen im Labor und in der Industrie abdeckt. Die Kompetenz von Hirschmann im Liquid Handling ist auch bei rotarus® in durchdachten Funktionen und innovativen Details wieder zu finden. Damit können auch Medien hoher Viskosität exakt dosiert werden. RFID-Technologie kommt zur Erkennung des Pumpenkopfs und der Schläuche zum Einsatz.

The rotarus® peristaltic pump series sees Hirschmann taking the leap into the world of continuous dispensing pumps. Different motors, varying housing safety classes and intelligent control of delivery volumes distinguish a consistently planned product family which covers a broad spectrum of application areas in the laboratory and industry. Hirschmann's liquid handling competence is also evident in the sophisticated functions and innovative details of rotarus®. This means that media with a high viscosity can also be accurately dispensed. RFID technology is used to detect the pump head and tube.

PRODUCT

Ocean Life
Gerät zur Aufbereitung von Salzwasser
Desalination water dispenser

DESIGN

Two+Group
Cheng Hung
New Taipei City, Taiwan
Industrial Technology Research Institute
Yung-Jen Cheng, Hung-Cheng Yen,
Tung-Chuan Wu, Chan-Hsing Lo
Hsinchu, Taiwan

MANUFACTURER

Industrial Technology Research Institute
Hsinchu, Taiwan

Ocean Life ist das weltweit erste tragbare Gerät zur
Aufbereitung von Salzwasser in Trinkwasser. Eine Luft-
pumpe pumpt Salzwasser durch ein System von Auf-
bereitungsmembranen, die Salzwasser in Trinkwasser
umwandeln. Diese entzieht dem Meerwasser wirkungsvoll überzähliges Natriumchlorid und bitter schmeckendes
Magnesiumsulfat, hält aber eine angemessene Menge
Salz für die Erhaltung der vom Körper benötigten Menge
an Elektrolyten zurück. Verunglückte verfügen somit,
während sie auf Rettung warten, über genug Wasser
und Salz, was ihren Überlebenszeitraum verlängert und
damit den Erfolg der Rettungsaktivitäten steigert.

*Ocean Life is the world's first portable desalination water
dispenser. Through its air compressor filtering seawater
through the desalination membrane, it can effectively
remove excessive sodium chloride in seawater as well as
the bitter taste of magnesium sulfate which is rejected
by the body. It retains the electrolytes needed by the
human body, so as to supply victims plenty of water with
appropriate salts. This effectively extends victims' survival
time while waiting for disaster search and rescue. It will
become standard equipment in the future for navigation
and shipping life-saving systems.*

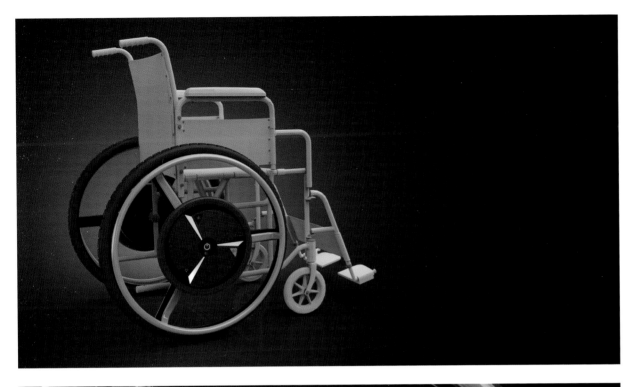

PRODUCT
LEAP
Zusatzleistung für Rollstühle
Auxiliary power unit

DESIGN
GIXIA GROUP Co.
Taipei, Taiwan
Industrial Technology Research Institute
Mechanical and Systems Research Laboratories
Yu-Yin Peng, Shih-ming Lo, Tseng-Te Wei,
Wen-Hsin Wu, I-Wei Lan, Shao-Yu Li
Hsinchu, Taiwan

MANUFACTURER
Industrial Technology Research Institute
Mechanical and Systems Research Laboratories
Hsinchu, Taiwan

LEAP ist ein intelligentes Zusatzstromversorgungsgerät der neuen Generation, das sich intuitiv einsetzen und einfach an herkömmliche Rollstühle anpassen lässt. Es verfügt über einen Leistungsmechanismus auf Torsions-basis, ein horizontaler Hebel erleichtert müheloses Steigen, eine Antikippvorrichtung dient zur Sicherheit beim Befahren von Gefällen. Das flache Energiemodul aus Kohlefasern lässt sich mit einem Knopfdruck entnehmen, die leichte Ausführung erleichtert Lagern, Tragen und Aufladen. Eine Signalbeleuchtung sorgt für mehr Sicherheit unterwegs. Ein Technik orientiertes Design mit hohem Wirkungsgrad auf professioneller Ebene!

LEAP is a new generation smart auxiliary power unit that is good for intuitive use and can be easily adapted to ordinary wheelchairs. It has a torsion-driven geared power mechanism and a horizontal lever to reduce effort when climbing and a stalling prevention device to act as a safety measure when going down a slope. The low-profile power module made of carbon fiber is easily removed by a single button push and the lightweight design facilitates storage, carrying and recharging. The alert lighting enhances the safety guarantee for users in mobile. A tech-oriented design that represents high efficiency and sophisticated professionalism!

PRODUCT

NUK Oral Care PATO

Beiß-Spielzeug

Teething toy

DESIGN

taliaYsebastian ID

Wien, Austria

Mapa GmbH

Bodo Warden

Zeven, Germany

MANUFACTURER

Mapa GmbH

Zeven, Germany

PATO unterstützt die gesunde Oralentwicklung von Babys. Durch die Verknüpfung von spielerischen und funktionalen Elementen können Kleinkinder langsam an die tägliche Mundhygiene herangeführt und vom oft als schmerzhaft und quälend empfundenen Zahnungsprozess abgelenkt werden. Die formale Gestaltung der Beiß-Elemente ist an Kauhölzer angelehnt, die seit Jahrhunderten als Zahnungshilfe genutzt werden; die weiche Interpretation der Grundgeometrien transportiert das Produkt in den markentypischen NUK Duktus. Der Einsatz verschiedener Materialien – PP und TPE – und Texturen erlaubt Babys intuitiv über die Nutzungsart zu entscheiden

PATO supports babies´ healthy oral development. Through a combination of playful and functional elements, toddlers are slowly introduced to daily oral hygiene and are distracted from teething, which is often perceived as painful. The formal design is based on miswaks, used for centuries as teething-support, the soft interpretation of the basic geometries transports the product into the NUK brand's characteristic design. The use of different materials – PP and TPE – allows the baby to decide intuitively which of the three ends matches its requirements best.

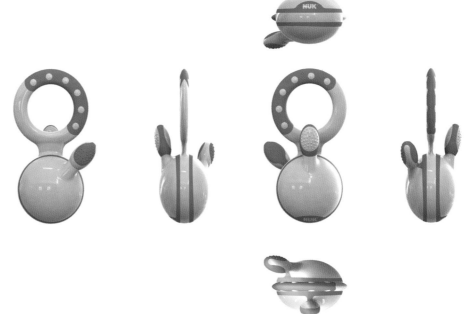

PRODUCT
mediven active
Medizinischer Kompressionsstrumpf
Medical compression socks

DESIGN
medi GmbH & Co. KG
Bayreuth, Germany

MANUFACTURER
medi GmbH & Co. KG
Bayreuth, Germany

mediven active ist ein robuster Kompressionsstrumpf für körperlich aktive Männer. Das Medizinprodukt im dezenten Feinripp-Design vereint medizinische Wirksamkeit, Tragekomfort und außergewöhnliche Weichheit. Der Strumpf hält dauerhaften Beanspruchungen stand und ist dabei durch sein außergewöhnliches Design in fünf attraktiven Farben nicht als Kompressionsstrumpf erkennbar. Erstmalig konnte durch ein spezielles Strickverfahren eine nicht spürbare und nicht sichtbare Naht im Zehenbereich ermöglicht werden. Die Komfortsohle, die verstärkte Ferse und der weiche sowie breite Abschlussbund mit grau eingestricktem Logo überzeugen zusätzlich.

mediven active is a robust compression sock for physically active men. The medical product with fine ribbed design combines medical effect, comfort and softness. The sock withstands unrelenting wear and tear and is never recognizable as a compression sock due to its extraordinary design with five attractive colors. For the first time a seam you can't feel and see at the toes was made possible due to a special knitting technique. The comfort sole, the reinforced heel and the soft and broad cuff with gray medi label convince the target group in addition.

PRODUCT

PureWhite
Medizinische Bedienelemente
Medical operating devices

DESIGN

at-design GbR
Tobias Kreitschmann, Christoph Tomczak,
Jan Andersson
Fürth, Germany

MANUFACTURER

medwork
medical products and services GmbH
Höchstadt, Germany

Instrumentarium für die flexible Endoskopie. Das Produktdesign visualisiert die Kernwerte Hochwertigkeit,
Reduktion und Sicherheit der global agierenden Marke
medwork. Die formale Betonung der Funktionsflächen
und Bedienelemente, bildet die Basis für eine charakteristische Formensprache. Die Vergrößerung der Griffbe-
reiche führt, ohne Erhöhung des Materialvolumens, zu
einer verbesserten Ergonomie und Funktionalität. Die
Sicherheit wird durch das optimierte taktile Feedback
erhöht. Weiße Hochglanzoberflächen assoziieren Sauberkeit und Sterilität. Zusätzlich zur formalen Neuaus-
richtung, wurde die Flexibilität im Fertigungsprozess
verbessert.

Medical devices for flexible endoscopy. The product de-
sign visualizes the core characteristics premium-quality,
reduction and safety of the global acting company med-
work. The formal emphasis of the functional surfaces
and operating device forms the basis for a characteristic
design idiom. The enlargement of the handle leads to
improved ergonomics and functionality without the in-
crease of material input. The safety is increased by the
optimized tactile feedback. Pure-white high gloss surfaces
associate cleanliness and sterility. In addition to the formal
reorientation, the flexibility of the manufacturing process
was enhanced.

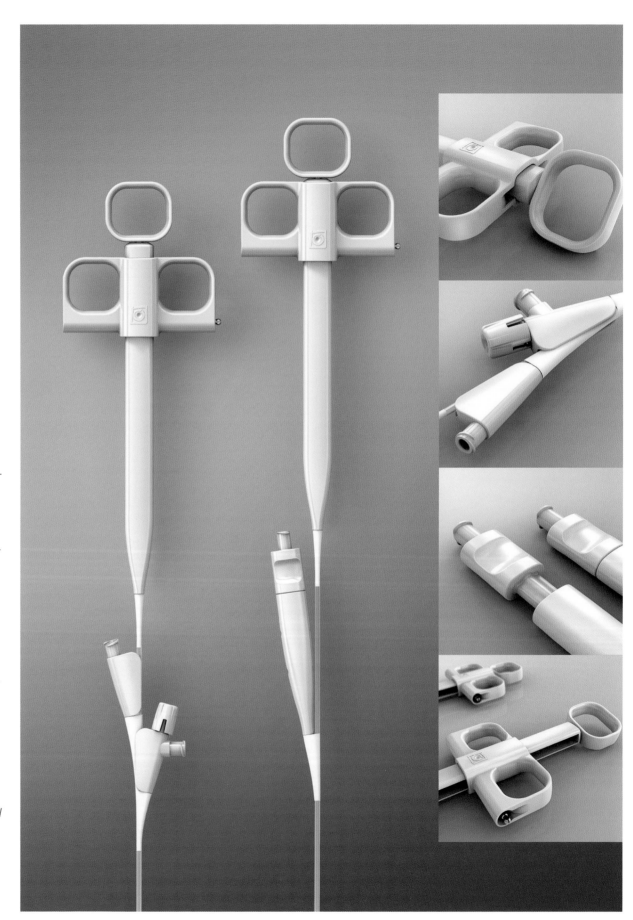

PRODUCT

Generation 2012
Temperierschrank-Serie
Series of thermal ovens

DESIGN

Oxxid GmbH
Ragnhild Albers, Jacqueline von Chelius,
Andrea Krüger, Stefan Reichl, Max Schmitt
München, Germany

MANUFACTURER

Memmert GmbH & Co. KG
Schwabach, Germany

Temperierschränke von Memmert finden sich im Bauwesen ebenso wie im hochsensiblen Bereich der Medizintechnik. Die durchgängige Verwendung von Edelstahl schafft Geräte mit überdurchschnittlicher Lebensdauer und höchster Präzision. Per Touch-Display und mit einem zentralen Drehregler bedient man die Geräte intuitiv und einfach. Ein neuartiges Schließsystem ermöglicht dem Benutzer erschütterungsfreies Öffnen und Schließen. Die klare Gestaltung erleichtert die Bedienung, unterstreicht den Markencharakter und erzeugt einen hohen Wiedererkennungswert. Die innovative Modulbauweise erlaubt mehr als 150 Varianten bei stark reduzierter Teilevielfalt.

Thermal ovens by Memmert can be found in the rough environment of construction plants as well as in clean medical applications. The consistent use of stainless steel establishes extremely long lasting appliances with high precision. The thermal ovens are controlled via touch display with a central control wheel, the Control COCKPIT. For this generation a new locking system was developed, featuring vibration-free opening and closing. The structured design and its clean appearance support an intuitive handling and result in a high brand recognition. A modular layout simplifies the creation of more than 150 models using less parts than before.

PRODUCT
D2R2 HRV
Herzschlag-Überwachungs-Sensor
Heart rate variability sensor

DESIGN
Metalligence Technology Corp.
Linyu Kao
New Taipei, Taiwan

MANUFACTURER
Metalligence Technology Corp.
New Taipei, Taiwan

Der „Metalligence D2R2 Heart Rate Variability Sensor (HRV)" lässt sich natürlich und glatt in der Hand halten. Seine farbenfrohe Gestaltung und ein einfaches Design verbindet Sicherheit und Komfort, basierend auf traditionellen Gesundheitsprodukten für die ältere Generation. Der HRV verbindet Überwachungs- und Bluetooth-Technologie in einem Gerät. Die zusätzliche Anwendung „UI" bietet eine Schnittstelle zur Gesundheitsüberwachung durch ein medizinisches Personal an.

Like holding a pebble in hands, "Metalligence D2R2 Heart Rate Variability Sensor (HRV)'s" smooth-and-harmonic touch makes you were surrounded by natural atmosphere. Unlike traditional health care products' aging and uncomfortable feel, HRV's gentle colorful and portable design links up safe and comfort feeling. Only needs few components, HRV integrates surveillance and Bluetooth technologies in one device. Additionally, its intelligent App UI with actual backend Cloud medical service team that support HRV reveals as a smarter and friendly health monitoring interface.

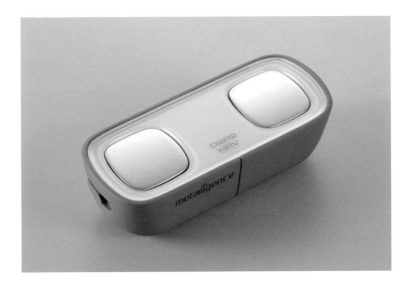

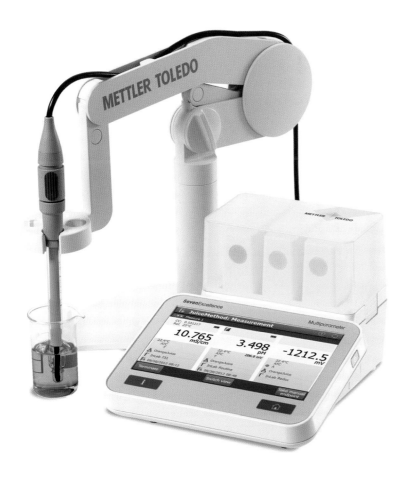

PRODUCT

Seven Messgeräte
Tisch-Messgerät
Benchtop meters

DESIGN

Multiple S. A.
Patrick Ammon, Yves Marmier, Paul Michel,
Sébastien Dassi
La Chaux-de-Fonds, Switzerland

MANUFACTURER

Mettler Toledo AG
Greifensee, Switzerland

Der universelle SevenCompact und leistungsstarke SevenExcellence sind die neuesten Tischgeräte in einer Reihe von eindrücklichen pH- / Ionen- und Leitfähig-keits-Messgeräten von METTLER TOLEDO. Während sich der vielseitige SevenCompact durch unvergleichliche Bedienerfreundlichkeit und intuitive Menüführung auszeichnet, offeriert das professionelle SevenExcellence-Gerät höchste Messgenauigkeit, Flexibilität und um-fassende Sicherheitsfunktionen für SOP/Compliance-Anforderungen. Beide Instrumente beeindrucken mit einem modernen Design, welches durch ein Farbdisplay im SevenCompact und einem kapazitiven Touch-Screen im SevenExcelence abgerundet wird.

SevenCompact and SevenExcellence are the new pH / ion meters from METTLER TOLEDO. While SevenCompact is characterized by easy operation and an excellent price / performance ratio, SevenExcellence is professional equipment for the laboratory based on a modular concept. The plug-in-modules allow the user to equip the meter with the desired functions. The touch screen operation adjusts automatically. The corresponding electrode holder with perfectly vertical displacement (uPlace™-kinematics) brings the electrode into the best work position. The complete system guarantees highly efficient, accurate and reliable measurements in the laboratory.

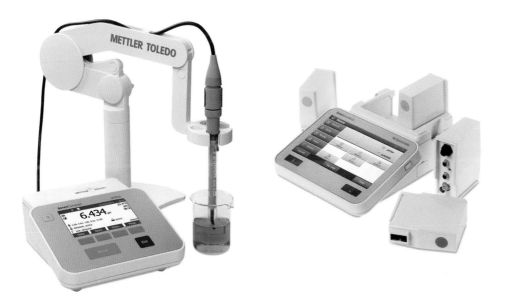

PRODUCT

HEM-6310 series
Handgelenk-Blutdruckmessgerät
Wrist blood pressure monitor

DESIGN

OMRON HEALTHCARE Co., Ltd.
Design Communication Department
Kyoto, Japan
Design Studio S
Fumie Shibata
Tokyo, Japan

MANUFACTURER

OMRON HEALTHCARE Co., Ltd.
Kyoto, Japan

Dieses kompakte Produkt – das leichteste und dünnste
Handgelenk-Blutdruckmessgerät der Welt – besitzt
ein innovatives Design. Seine Grafikfunktion und der
„Advanced Positioning Sensor", der anzeigt, wenn der
Träger die korrekte Körperhaltung für die Messung ein-
genommen hat, sind ideal für tägliche Blutdruckmessun-
gen und unterstützen die Überwachung der Gesundheit. Die Messung erfolgt lautlos, wodurch man immer
und überall diskrete Messungen durchführen kann.
Durch NFC-Konnektivität können auf einem PC Veränderungen des Blutdrucks als Graphik angezeigt und ein
Blutdruck-Tagebuch erstellt werden.

The world's lightest and thinnest wrist blood pressure
monitor, this compact product has an innovative design.
Its graphing function and "Advanced Positioning Sen-
sor", which indicates when the wearer has adopted the
correct posture for measurement, are ideal for daily
blood-pressure measurements to support health moni-
toring. It utilizes silent measurement for discrete readings
anywhere and any time. With NFC connectivity, changes
in blood pressure can be viewed as a graphic and a
blood pressure diary created on a computer.

PRODUCT

HBP-1300
Professionelles Blutdruckmessgerät
Professional blood pressure monitor

DESIGN

OMRON HEALTHCARE Co., Ltd.
Design Communication Department
Kyoto, Japan
YS design Inc.
So Noguchi, Shuji Tsuruta
Osaka, Japan

MANUFACTURER

OMRON HEALTHCARE Co., Ltd.
Kyoto, Japan

Dieses automatische Blutdruckmessgerät für den klinischen Gebrauch ist tragbar und verfügt über einfache Funktionen. Basierend auf einer Analyse, wie Krankenschwestern den Blutdruck von Patienten messen, wurde es im Hinblick auf Robustheit, einfache Bedienbarkeit und Langlebigkeit entworfen. Die umlaufenden Dämpfer schützen das Gerät vor Erschütterungen, wenn es fallen gelassen wird. Der integrierte Tragegriff verbessert die Tragbarkeit der Einheit, und die große Start-Taste erleichtert die Benutzung für jeden. Die Komponenten halten auch heftigem Gebrauch stand, wodurch die Wartungshäufigkeit sinkt.

This automatic blood pressure monitor for hospital use is portable and incorporates simple functionality. It has been designed for robustness, ease of use, and durability, based on an analysis of how nurses measure patients' blood pressure. The surrounding bumpers cushion the main unit against shock if it is dropped. The integral carrying handle and grip add to the unit's portability, and its large Start button means anyone can easily use it. Components capable of standing up to hard use reduce the frequency with which maintenance is required.

PRODUCT

Patella Pro
Patella-Rezentrierungs-Orthese
Patella re-alignment orthosis

DESIGN

Otto Bock HealthCare GmbH
Matthias Vollbrecht
Duderstadt, Germany

MANUFACTURER

Otto Bock HealthCare GmbH
Duderstadt, Germany

Die Patella Pro setzt aufgrund von einzigartiger Funktionalität neue Standards bei der Behandlung des vorderen Knieschmerzes. Dank ihrer dynamischen Rezentrierungstechnik sichert sie die Kniescheibe in allen relevanten Beugewinkeln. Die Führung der Kniescheibe ist explizit auf jeden Patienten einstellbar. Patella Pro erlaubt so dem Patienten eine schmerzfreie Bewegung. Die patentierte Textilkombination in Verbindung mit dem innenseitigen Vector-Grip-Effekt stellt den perfekten Sitz der Orthese sicher. Durch ihre leichte und schlanke Ausgestaltung ist sie unter Kleidung nicht wahrnehmbar und sorgt für höchsten Tragekomfort.

With its unique functionality, the Patella Pro sets new standards in the treatment of anterior knee pain. Thanks to its dynamic re-alignment technique, it secures the patella at all relevant flexion angles. Patella guidance is explicitly adjustable to the needs of each patient. Thus the Patella Pro makes pain-free movement possible for the patient. The patented textile combination in conjunction with the interior vector grip effect ensures the perfect fit of the orthosis. Due to its lightweight and slim design, it is imperceptible under clothing and ensures maximum wearer comfort.

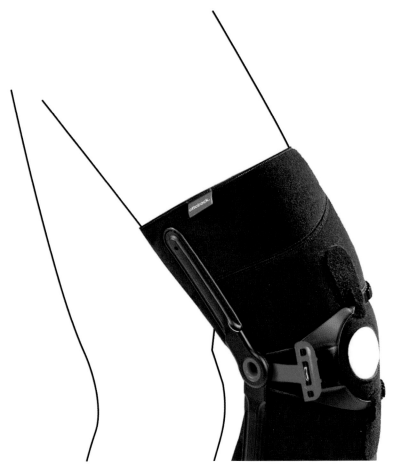

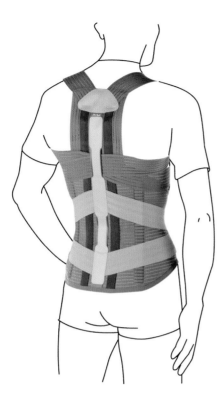

PRODUCT
Soft Backs
Rückenorthesen
Back orthoses

DESIGN
AWS Designteam
Adam Wehsely-Swiczinsky
Wien, Austria
Otto Bock HealthCare GmbH
Anke Lehmann, Boris Ljubimir
Duderstadt, Germany

MANUFACTURER
Otto Bock HealthCare GmbH
Duderstadt, Germany

Die OBO-Soft Backs ist eine Produktlinie textiler Rücken-orthesen, welche zur medizinischen Korrektur der Wirbelsäule eingesetzt wird. Besonderes Augenmerk wurde dabei auf selbsterklärende Handhabbarkeit und Reduktion auf das Wesentliche gelegt. Erweiterte Velourzonen an den Hauptverschlusstaschen bieten Platz zur Vorpositionierung der Kompressionsbegurtung im Anlegeprozess. Diese können im weiteren Schritt somit leicht gefasst und intensitätsgerecht repositioniert werden. Punktueller Überstand der fadenlosen Hochfrequenzschweißnaht kennzeichnet Griffelemente, welche besonders effektives Lösen des Mikrokletts vom Velour ermöglicht.

OBO Soft Backs is a product line of textile back orthoses used for the medical correction of the spine. Special emphasis was placed on intuitive handling and reduction to the essentials. Extended velour zones on the main closure pockets offer space for pre-positioning the compression belts while putting on the orthosis. In a subsequent step, this allows them to be grasped easily and repositioned according to intensity. Overhanging points of the threadless high-frequency welding seam identify gripping elements that facilitate highly effective loosening of the micro-hook-and-loop material from the velour.

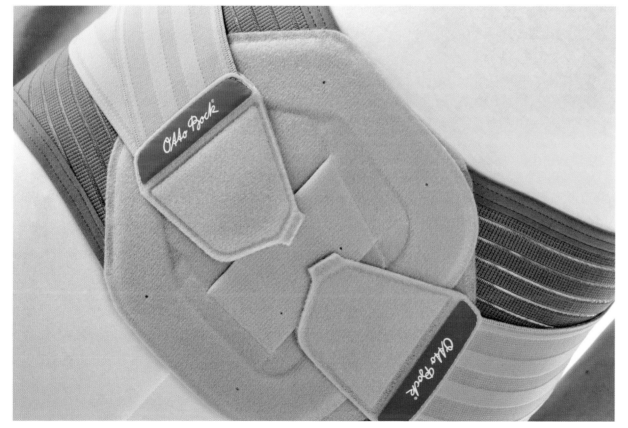

PRODUCT

Michelangelo Hand
Prothesenhand
Prosthetic hand

DESIGN

Otto Bock Healthcare Products GmbH
Wien, Austria

MANUFACTURER

Otto Bock Healthcare Products GmbH
Wien, Austria

Die Michelangelo Hand ist das Herzstück einer neuer
Prothesengeneration für Versorgungen der oberen Ex-
tremität. Michelangelo ist eine myoelektrisch gesteuerte Greifkomponente, deren komplexe Greifkinematik,
anatomisches Aussehen und geringes Gewicht den Anwender vielfältig unterstützen. Die Vielzahl der Funk-
tionalitäten ermöglicht sieben unterschiedliche Greif-
möglichkeiten. Die Michelangelo Hand überzeugt durch
ein außergewöhnliches Design mit verschiedenen harten
und weichen Strukturen. Der neue ovalförmige Hand-
anschluss wirkt sehr natürlich und beinhaltet ein Hand-
gelenk.

*The Michelangelo Hand is the heart of a new prosthesis
generation for upper limb fittings. Michelangelo is a
myoelectrically controlled gripping component with
complex gripping kinematics, an anatomical appearance
and low weight which supports the user in a variety of
ways. This versatile functionality offers seven different
gripping options. The Michelangelo Hand features an
unusual design with various hard and soft structures.
The new oval hand adapter appears highly natural and
incorporates a wrist joint.*

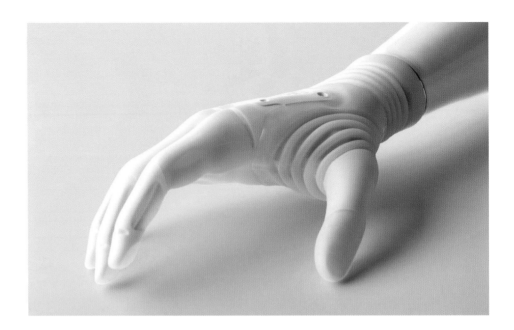

PRODUCT

CyFlow® CUBE 8
Blutanalyse-System
Cell analysis system

DESIGN

formfreun.de
Gestaltungsgesellschaft
Berlin, Germany
cyclos-design GmbH
Münster, Germany

MANUFACTURER

Partec GmbH
Roland Göhde CEO
Görlitz, Germany

CUBE – der Würfel. Egal aus welchem Blickwinkel man das innovative Blutanalyse-Ensemble betrachtet, es überzeugt. Die üblicherweise einzelnen Bausteine sind in zwei kompakten Gehäusen zusammengefasst. Der 19'-Bildschirm zeigt direkt am Ort des Geschehens die Fakten zur Messung. Die Führung erfolgt intuitiv durch die schwarz-weiße Farbgebung. Der CUBE ist nicht nur als Gerät bis ins kleinste Detail gestaltet, sondern auch grafisch. Das „C" im Logo leitet sich aus der Silhouette ab, während das „E" die drei Laserstrahlen aufgreift, mit denen die Datenverarbeitung erfolgt.

No matter which way you look at it – CUBE is an innovative cell analysis system that impresses from every perspective. In technical terms, there are countless sophisticated solutions. The normally separate modules are integrated in two compact housings. The 19' monitor shows the facts of the analysis directly at the point of care, while the black and white coloring ensures intuitive user guidance. The CUBE is attractively designed down to the last detail. This applies not only to the device proper but also to the graphic design. The "C" in the logo is derived from the silhouette, while the "E" refers to three laser beams used for data processing.

PRODUCT

CardioSecur pro
Professionelle EKG-Technologie
Professional ECG technology

DESIGN

Valerie Trauttmansdorff
Wien, Austria

MANUFACTURER

Personal MedSystems GmbH
Frankfurt, a. M., Germany

Um den Gesundheitszustand des Herzens festzustellen, ist das Elektrokardiogramm (EKG) essenziell. Ärzte mit mobilen Einsatzorten benötigen flexible, kleine und leicht handhabbare Systeme, die alle modernen Kommunikationsmöglichkeiten zulassen. CardioSecur pro ist das erste 12-Kanal EKG für smarte Endgeräte. CardioSecur pro besteht lediglich aus einem 200 Gramm leichten EKG-Kabel. Dieses wird mit dem Endgerät verbunden und aktiviert die dazugehörige App. Eine integrierte Kappe kann über die Kabel hochgezogen werden, um diese nicht zu verstricken. Minimalistische Formen unterstreichen den Bedienkomfort und revolutionieren das EKG-Geräte Design.

In order to assess the health condition of a human heart an electrocardiogram (ECG) is essential. Physicians that act mobile, either between different departments or on house call, are in need of flexible, small and easy to use systems that allow all modern communication options. CardioSecur pro is the first 12-lead ECG for smart terminal devices. CardioSecur pro comprises merely a 200-gram lightweight ECG cable. This connects with the terminal device and activates the corresponding App. An integrated cap may be pulled over the cables to prevent entanglement. Minimalistic shapes underline its ease of use and revolutionize ECG device design.

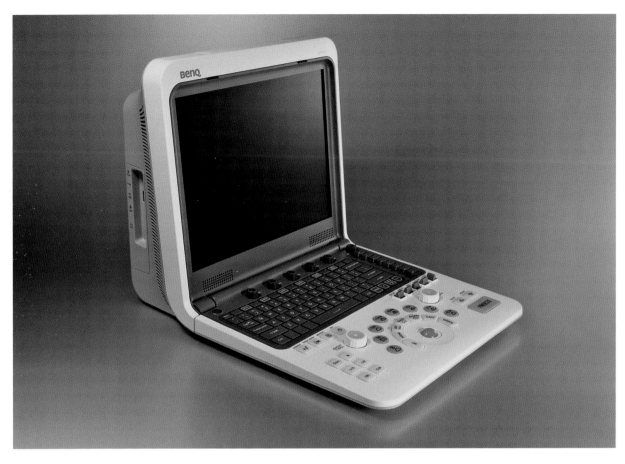

PRODUCT

QUS-101
Ultraschallscanner
Ultrasound scanner

DESIGN

Qisda Creative Design Center
Qisda Corporation
Taipei, Taiwan

MANUFACTURER

Qisda Corporation
Taipei, Taiwan

QUS-101 ist ein medizinischer Ultraschallscanner für
den professionellen Gebrauch. Mit seiner kleinen Oberfläche eignet er sich gut für Krankenhäuser, Kliniken
und Notaufnahmen. Er kann auf einem Tisch oder Fahr-
gestell eingesetzt werden. Ist die Klappe geschlossen
und der Griff herausgezogen, wird er als mobiles Ultra-
schallgerät genutzt. Ärzte erhalten fehlerfreie Daten
für Untersuchungen und Tests. Der Scanner wird in folgenden Bereichen eingesetzt: Kardiologie, Gastroente-
rologie, Gynäkologie, Psychiatrie, Urologie, Orthopädie,
Rehabilitation, Physiotherapie, Anästhesie, Notaufnah-
me, Intensivstation, Chirurgie usw.

*QUS-101 is a professional medical ultrasound scanner. Its
small surface has the function of a hospital mainframe,
making it the best choice for a hospital, small-mid clinics
or emergency room. It can be used on a table or on a
cart. Close the lid and pull out the handle to transform it
into an ultrasound machine, ideal for mobile medical
consultations. Thorough research and testings ensured
error-free use for physicians. Applicable divisions: cardi-
ology, gastrointestinal, gynecology, psychiatry, urology,
orthopedics, rehabilitation, physiotherapy, aenesthesia,
emergency, intensive care, general surgery, etc.*

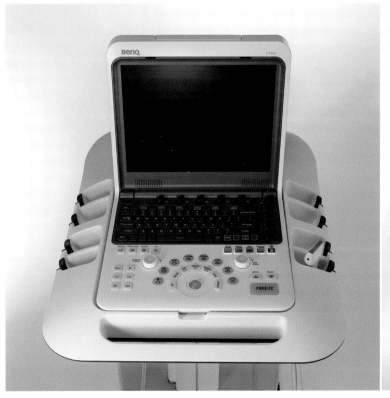

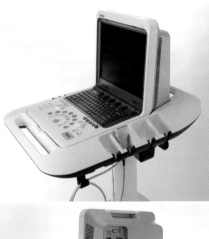

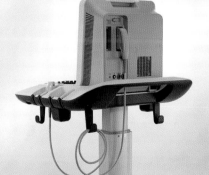

PRODUCT

Shark
Resektoskop
Resectoscope

DESIGN

designaffairs GmbH
Designteam
Erlangen, Germany

MANUFACTURER

Richard Wolf GmbH
Knittlingen, Germany

Schnell, präzise und effizient – das sind sie, die neuen
Shark-Resektoskope der Firma Richard Wolf. „Präzision
mit Biss" steht bei diesem High-End-Produkt für ein
durchgängig, ergonomisch gestaltetes Gesamtsystem
mit hervorragender Flow Charakteristik, intuitives
Handling, Kontrolle und Sicherheit. Neben der sogenannten „Shark-tip" und „Shark-fin" stellen die „Snap-on"-
Verschlüsse ein weiteres Key Feature dar, welche ein
Zusammenfügen und Trennen der Systemelemente
deutlich vereinfachen und damit zu einer deutlich ver-
kürzten Eingriffzeit beitragen. Komplettiert wird das
System durch den innovativen und am Markt einzigartigen
„PENDUAL®"-HD-Kamerakopf.

*Fast, precise and efficient – that's what they are, the new
Shark resectoscopes of Richard Wolf. "Precision with a
bite" stands for a consistently, ergonomically designed
system, with excellent flow characteristics, intuitive handling, control and safety of this high-end product. Besides
the so-called "Shark-tip" and "Shark-fin", the "Snap-on"
fasteners represent another key feature that clearly sim-
plify a connection and removing of the system elements
what contribute to a significantly shorter procedure
time. The system will be completed by the innovative
and unique „PENDUAL®" HD camera head.*

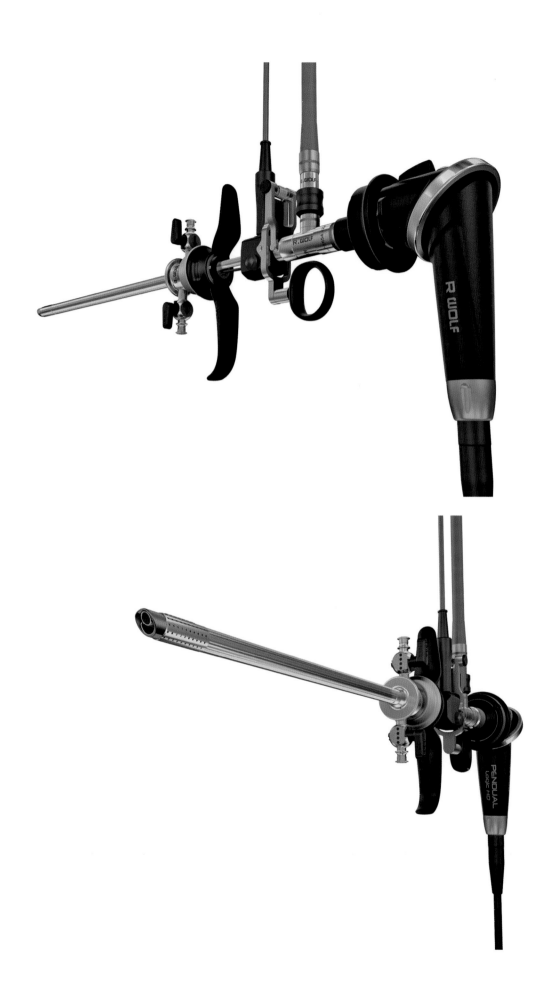

PRODUCT
Sparq
Hochmobiles Ultraschallsystem
Mobile ultrasound system

DESIGN
Philips Design
Eindhoven, Netherlands

MANUFACTURER
Royal Philips Electronics
Eindhoven, Netherlands

Das Philips Sparq ist ein kompaktes, flexibles und hochmobiles Ultraschallsystem, das das Scannen und Deuten
von Ultraschallbildern direkt am Patienten so einfach
wie möglich macht. Sparq wurde für Ärzte mit wenig
Ultraschall-Erfahrung entwickelt sowie für diejenigen,
die komplexe Funktionen benötigen und für den Einsatz
in einer Vielzahl klinischer Umgebungen. Sein ergonomisches Design und die intuitive, dynamische Benutzeroberfläche erhöhen die Effizienz und erleichtern die
Durchführung von Untersuchungen. Das Bedienfeld
verfügt über Touch-Funktionen auf einer Hartglasoberfläche, die leicht zu reinigen und hygienisch ist.

*The Philips Sparq is a compact, flexible and highly mobile
ultrasound system that makes scanning and interpreting
ultrasound images at the point of care as simple as possible. Sparq is designed to meet the needs of clinicians with
limited experience in ultrasound, as well those requiring
complex functions, and to be used across a variety of care
settings. Its ergonomic design and intuitive dynamic user
interface enhances efficiency and makes it easier to per-
form exams. The control panel features touch capabilities
on a sealed and tempered glass panel that is easy to clean
and hygienic.*

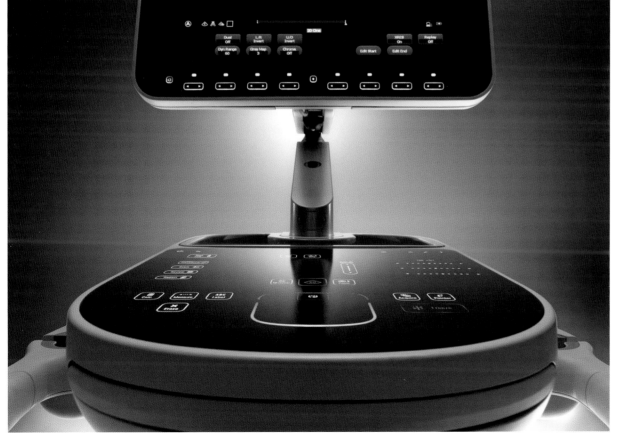

PRODUCT

NeoPAP
Atemwege-Behandlungssystem
Respiratory treatment system

DESIGN

Philips Design
Eindhoven, Netherlands

MANUFACTURER

Royal Philips Electronics
Eindhoven, Netherlands

NeoPAP ist ein hoch entwickeltes CPAP-System zur
Behandlung von Neugeborenen und Säuglingen mit
Atemnot-Syndrom. Leckage-Kompensationstechnik
verbunden mit Low-Profile-Interface und Haubenaus-
führung ermöglichen eine lockere Passform und reduzieren den Druck auf das Gesicht des Babys. Mit der als
Baby-Trak bezeichneten Leckage-Kompensationstech-
nologie kann das Gerät den Druck an der Nase des Neugeborenen messen und regelt ihn nach CPAP-Vorgabe.
Haube, Nasenkanüle und Maske reduzieren den Anpas-
sungsbedarf und durch weniger Störungen wird eine
Umgebung geschaffen, in der sich Babys erholen und
ihre Energie auf ihre Entwicklung fokussieren können.

*Designed to be used in neonatal intensive care units, the
Philips NeoPAP provides respiratory treatment for pre-
mature infants cared for in incubators. It delivers CPAP
(continuous air pressure) and oxygen through a nasal
cannula and head hood attached to the infant's head that
is designed to be more comfortable for the child. A seamless
integration of display and controls helps care-givers adjust
treatment in a fast and intuitive way. The overall design
aims to convey trust, clarity and confidence in the product
performance, making it seem less threatening and more
sensitive towards the feelings of worried parents visiting
a neonatal ward.*

PRODUCT
HeartStart FR3
AED-Gerät
AED device

DESIGN
Philips Design
Eindhoven, Netherlands

MANUFACTURER
Royal Philips Electronics
Eindhoven, Netherlands

Der Philips HeartStart FR3 unterstützt Ersthelfer dabei, eine kritische, lebensrettende Therapie bei Menschen mit plötzlichem Herzstillstand (SCA) in Sekundenschnelle einzuleiten. Dieser professionelle automatische externe Defibrillator (AED) visualisiert den Ablauf einer SCA-Rettung und automatisiert viele Schritte bei der Notfall-hilfe. Der HeartStart FR3 schaltet sich automatisch beim Öffnen ein* und gibt den Helfern visuelle und akustische Anweisungen, sodass sie nicht nach Bedienelementen suchen müssen. Bereits angeschlossene Pads sparen wertvolle Sekunden. *Diese Option ist nur mit dem Koffer verfügbar.

The Philips HeartStart FR3 helps responders to start critical life-saving therapy for victims of a sudden cardiac arrest (SCA) in mere seconds. This professional-grade automatic external defibrillator (AED) helps visualize the workflow of an SCA rescue and automates many steps in the rescue process. The HeartStart FR3 automatically turns on when opened and gives users visual and audio instructions so they do not have to look for controls. Pre-connected defi-brillation pads save valuable seconds.*This option is only available with the hard case.*

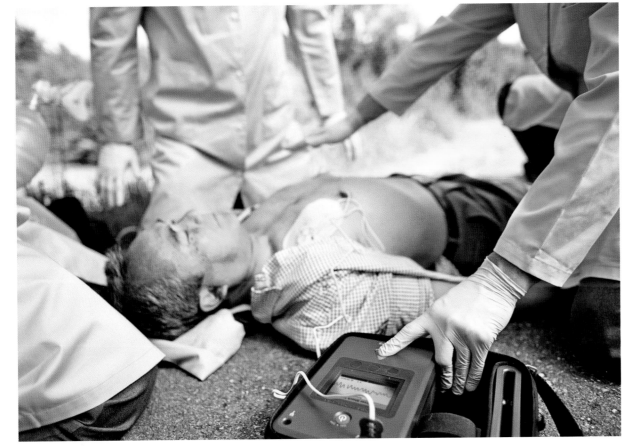

PRODUCT

LABGEO PT10

Blutanalysegerät

Blood analyzer

DESIGN

SAMSUNG Electronics Co., Ltd.

Seoul, South Korea

MANUFACTURER

SAMSUNG Electronics Co., Ltd.

Gyeonggi-do, South Korea

Hauptziel der Formgebung des LABGEO PT10 war, eine einheitliche Designsprache zu finden, die perfekt zu den anderen Blutanalyse-Produkten von SAMSUNG passt. Die raffinierte Linienführung und abgerundete Form zeichnen das äußerlich schlichte und digitalisierte Hightech-IT-Produkt aus. Die glänzende Oberfläche ermöglicht einen maximalen Betrachtungswinkel. Das weiße Farbschema betont das elegante Design des Produktes.

The main goal in designing the PT10 was to have the family look of other SAMSUNG blood test products through unified design language. Refined lines and rounded shape are designed to convey the appearance of a simple but digitized high-tech IT product. The glossy surface makes it possible for users to have a wide view angle and the black and white color scheme reinforces the sleek design of the product.

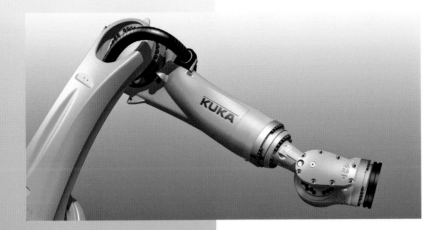

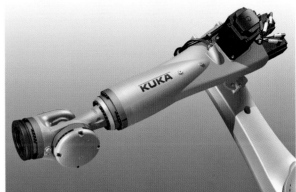

„Dieser Roboter weist fast menschliche Züge auf. Denn die Kraftlinien bringen die Bewegungen des menschlichen Körpers zum Ausdruck und entsprechen den Muskeln. Art und Engineering gehen hier eine sehr gelungene Fusion ein, die zudem ein äußerst präzises Werkzeug bei gleichzeitig geringem Gewicht und somit Energieverbrauch erschaffen haben. Eine tolle offene Konstruktion sorgt auch für optisch designästhetischen Genuss!"

"This industrial robot has almost human traits; its lines of force express the movements of the human body and are consistent with the muscles. Art and engineering come together very well here, resulting in an extremely precise tool that is nonetheless lightweight, thus saving energy. Great construction also leads to a very pleasing design esthetic."

JURYSTATEMENT

PRODUCT
Olympus DSX Series
Opto-digitale Mikroskope
Opto-digital microscopes

DESIGN
Olympus Corporation
Tokyo, Japan

MANUFACTURER
Olympus Corporation
Tokyo, Japan

Die DSX-Serie mit den drei Modellen DSX100, DSX500 und DSX500i setzt Maßstäbe für die opto-digitale Industriemikroskopie und die berührungslose Messtechnik. Ergonomisches Design und hohe Bedienungsfreundlichkeit treffen auf fortschrittlichste Optik. Durch den Verzicht auf Okulare ist das DSX-Inspektionssystem besonders ergonomisch. Volle Flexibilität und individuelle Anpassungsmöglichkeiten bieten zudem verschiedene Benutzermodi und die Option zum Anlegen von Nutzerprofilen und Protokollen. Über die Vorschau des intuitiven Touch-Screens lässt sich schnell die beste optische Technik für präzise und hoch aufgelöste Bilder wählen.

The DSX series with its three models, the DSX100, DSX500 and DSX500i, sets new standards for opto-digital industrial microscopy and non-contact measuring techniques. An ergonomic design and high level of user-friendliness is matched with the most advanced optics. With no binoculars, the DSX inspection system is especially ergonomic. Various user modes and the facility to create user profiles and protocols ensure full flexibility and individual adjustment possibilities. Previews displayed on the intuitive touch screen enable a swift selection of the best optical technique for obtaining precise, high-resolution images.

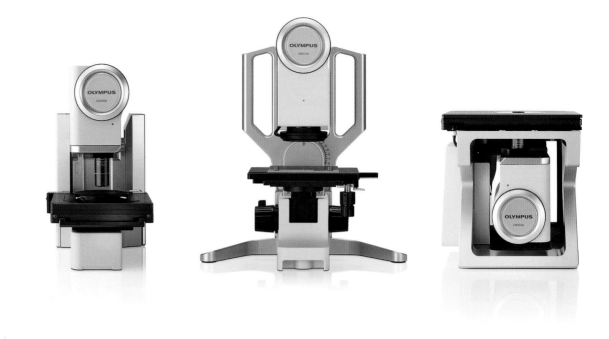

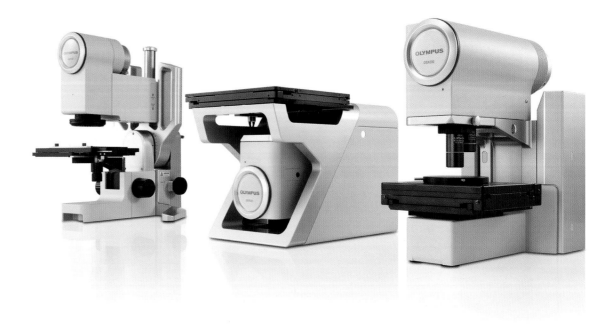

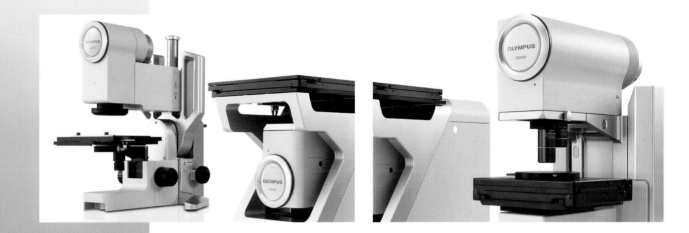

„Durch die exakte und zeitgemäße Linienführung präsentiert sich dem Benutzer ein junges Produkt im Bereich Industriemikroskopie. Das Gerät muss komplexe Aufgaben mit absoluter Präzision erfüllen. Dieser Anspruch wurde auf exzellente Weise auch im Design umgesetzt, so dass die berührungslose Messtechnik mittels Touchscreen intuitiv möglich ist."

"The exact, contemporary design of this product makes it an interesting emerging product in the industrial microscopy field. This device must carry out complex tasks with total precision, a requirement that has been extremely well implemented in the design, so that the non-contact measurement technology via touchscreen is intuitive to use."

JURYSTATEMENT

PRODUCT
3M Speedglas 9100 FX
Schweißmaske
Welding shield

DESIGN
Veryday
Oskar Juhlin, Martin Birath, Stefan Strandberg,
David Crafoord, Erik Wahlin
Bromma, Sweden

MANUFACTURER
3M Svenska AB
Gagnef, Sweden

9100 FX ist ein Schild für Premium-Schutz beim Schweißen und Schleifen. Das Designteam hat aus 20 Jahren Benutzer-Erfahrung Erkenntnisse aus der Schweißtechnik, die es in diesem idealen Schild umgewandelt hat. Sie haben ein völlig neues Konzept, den geteilten Schild, erstellt. Eine neue Stufe, die hervorragenden Schutz, Flip-up-Kombination aus einem Automatikschweißfilter, Schild und Schutzvisier bietet, hilft dem Anwender, jederzeit geschützt zu bleiben. Auf der Innenseite ist der Schild mit überlegener Ergonomie und abgerundeten Kanten ausgestattet. 9100 FX erfüllt alle Bedürfnisse. Seine Passform wurde verfeinert, der Schutz wurde verstärkt und die Stabilität optimiert.

9100 FX is a shield for premium protection during welding and grinding tasks. The design team has transformed 20 years of experience and user insights from the welding industry into this ideal shield. They have created a totally new concept, the split shield. This offers a new level of outstanding protection, a flip-up combination of an auto-darkening welding shield and a protective visor, help the user stay protected at all times. On the inside it is designed with superior ergonomics and rounded edges on all surfaces. 9100 FX meets all needs. Its fit has been refined, the protection has been strengthened and the stability optimized.

PRODUCT
SRB1021
Batterie-Modul
Battery module

DESIGN
ads-tec GmbH
Matthias Bohner, Roman Molchanov
Leinfelden-Echterdingen, Germany

MANUFACTURER
ads-tec GmbH
Leinfelden-Echterdingen, Germany

Die SRB1021 ist ein Batterie-Modul. Regenerative Ener-gie steht nicht gleichmäßig zur Verfügung. Man muss Energie zwischenspeichern. Für leistungsstarke, echt-zeitfähige, elektrische Speicher sind Li-Ion-Systeme die erste Wahl. ads-tec hat größten Wert auf Sicherheit gelegt, mit drei unabhängigen Sicherheitskreisen, stän-diger Temperaturüberwachung und beispielsweise einer Konstruktion, die losen Schrauben die Kurzschluss-gefahr nimmt. Das Design ist bestimmt von der hoch-wertigen Front, in der die eigens entwickelten Sicher-heitsstecker dominieren: Plus und Minus zeigen an wie montiert wird und worum es sich bei dem Produkt handelt.

The SRB1021 is a battery module. Renewable energy is not a constant source. We have to store the energy. For powerful storages reacting in real time, Li-Ion-systems are the right choice. ads-tec made the point on savety: three safety-circles, permanent scanning for all relevant signs und a design which passes the loose screw test are some of the safety features. The design accentuates the high end front dominated by the ads-tec safety-plugs "plus" and "minus". The safety-plugs show how to mount the system and explain the product by itself.

PRODUCT

ADVANTECH SPC Series
Industrie-PC
Industrial PC

DESIGN

Union Design & Development Corp.
Liu YiPo, Ma Richard, Bacon Hsu
Taipei, Taiwan
Advantech Co., Ltd.
Taipei, Taiwan

MANUFACTURER

Advantech Co., Ltd.
Taipei, Taiwan

HMI-Bedien-Panels für den Schaltschrank-Einbau zum
Einsatz in maschinennahen Umgebungen. Kapazitives
16 : 9 Widescreen-Multi-Touch-Display, 15.5´´ bis 21.5´´,
gestaltet Nutzerverhalten intuitiver und ergonomischer.
Das schlanke Aluminium-Gehäuse bietet Dank der M12-
Anschlussverbindungen rundum IP65 und widersteht
auch hohem Wasserdruck und dauerhaft feuchter Umgebung. Zudem wird eine praktische Handhabung über
den integrierten VESA-Arm ermöglicht. Die intelligente
Auto-Setup-Taste ermöglicht noch mehr kundenspezifische Möglichkeiten und ein flexibel anpassbares Bedienszenario, um individuell den Bedürfnissen der Anwendung nachzukommen.

*A series of HMI operating panels for cabinet installation
for use in a variety of machine environments. Embedded
with 15.5" to 21.5" capacitive multi-touch displays with
16 : 9 wide screen ratio the purpose was to change existing HMI user behavior into being more intuitive and ergonomic. A slender, aluminum housing offers all-around
IP65 protection and M12 connectors with an integrated
VESA arm allows the device to withstand high water
pressure and extremely humid environments. The intelligent key brings more customized possibilities and a flexible user scenario to satisfy individual industry's needs.*

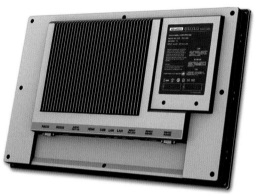

PRODUCT

ADVANTECH TPC Series
Industrie-PC
Industrial PC

DESIGN

Union Design & Development Corp.
Liu YiPo, Ma Richard, Bacon Hsu
Taipei, Taiwan
Advantech Co., Ltd.
Taipei, Taiwan

MANUFACTURER

Advantech Co., Ltd.
Taipei, Taiwan

Serie von HMI-Bedien-Panels für den Schaltschrank-Einbau zum Einsatz in verschiedenen Maschinen nahen Umgebungen. Kapazitives Multi-Touch-Display mit 16 : 9 Widescreen und Diagonalen von 15.5´´ bis 21.5´´, was bisheriges Nutzerverhalten intuitiver und ergonomischer gestaltet. Das elegante Aluminium-Gehäuse betont Modernität, bietet frontseitig IP65 und Dank neuem Design die Möglichkeit des werkzeugfreien Panel-Einbaus. Die intelligente Auto Setup Taste ermöglicht noch mehr kundenspezifische Möglichkeiten und ein flexibel anpassbares Bedienszenario, um individuell den Bedürfnissen der Anwendung nachzukommen.

A series of HMI operating panels for cabinet installation for use in a variety of machine environments. Embedded with 15.5" to 21.5" capacitive multi-touch display with 16 : 9 wide screen ratio. The purpose was to change existing HMI user behavior into being more intuitive and ergonomic. Elegant aluminum housing emphasizes modernity and offers front IP65 protection and a tool free installation design allows workers to panel mount the HMI without any tools. The intelligent key brings more customized possibilities and a flexible user scenario to satisfy individual industry's needs.

PRODUCT

Scraper Holder Libel

Tapezier-Werkzeug

Paperhanging tool

DESIGN

Hotswap AB

Huskvarna, Sweden

MANUFACTURER

Anza AB

Bankeryd, Sweden

Dieses erste Produkt seiner Art kombiniert mehrere Werkzeuge in einem. Mit seinem ergonomischen Design und seiner innovativen Funktion hilft es dem Tapezierer effizienter zu arbeiten. Die eingebaute Wasserwaage verhindert Unregelmäßigkeiten beim Zuschneiden der Tapete. Aus robustem ABS – Kunststoff, mit einer Klinge aus rostfreiem Stahl und aufgedruckten Maßangaben, besteht es auch in rauem Milieu.

This first of its kind product combines many tools into one. With its ergonomic design and innovative function it helps the decorator become a more efficient worker. The built in spirit level leaves you no worries about tearing an uneven edge on the wallpaper. Made from durable ABS plastic with a stainless steel blade that has dimensions printed upon it can take on the roughest environment.

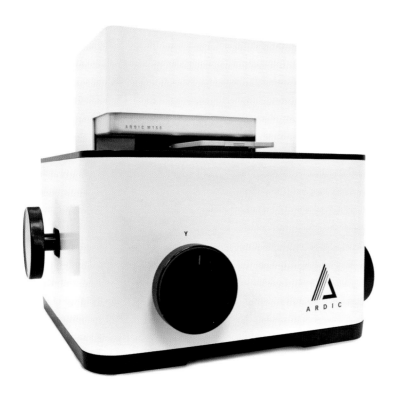

PRODUCT
M150 MEMS Analyzer
Laborgeräte
Lab equipment

DESIGN
KAMIA
Taipei, Taiwan

MANUFACTURER
ARDIC INSTRUMENTS
Taipei, Taiwan

Das M150 ist ein MEMS-Messsystem zur Charakterisierung der mechanischen Eigenschaften von Mikrostrukturen. Durch die Verwendung einer einfachen Point-and-Shoot-Laseroptik, kann der Benutzer mittels Breitband-Frequenzabtastung und Echtzeit-Fourier-Transformation (FFT) schnell Resonanzspitzen einer Mikrostruktur erfassen. Das M150 wurde von Grund auf für eine intuitive Bedienung konzipiert. Die nutzerfreundliche Bedienoberfläche erlaubt dem Anwender, nach nur minimaler Einarbeitungszeit, Messungen durchzuführen. Die berührungslose optische Messung macht das M150 zu einem grundlegenden Instrument für die MEMS-Entwicklung.

The M150 is a MEMS Analyzer used for characterizing microstructural mechanical properties. Using a simple point-and-shoot laser optical system, the user can quickly obtain resonant peaks of a microstructure through wide bandwidth frequency scanning and real-time Fourier transform (FFT). Designed from the ground up to be a highly intuitive instrument, the M150 employs tactile interfaces that allow users make measurements with minimal training. By using non-contact optical measurement, the M150 is an essential instrument for MEMS development.

PRODUCT
ADYTON
Hardware-Sicherheitsmodul
Hardware security module

DESIGN
Achilles Design
Design Team
Mechelen, Belgium

MANUFACTURER
Atos Worldline SA / NV
Brussels, Belgium

Das kompakte Hardware-Sicherheitsmodul vereint Eleganz mit funktionaler Perfektion. Die schwarze Glasfront bildet einen deutlichen Kontrast zu den hellen Tönen des Gehäuses. Das Gehäuse aus gegossenem Aluminium erlaubt eine passive Kühlung, wodurch Energieverbrauch sowie Geräuschentwicklung verringert werden. Dank der soliden Führungsschienen auf beiden Seiten, gleitet ADYTON leichtgängig in den Spezialrahmen zur einfachen und sicheren Installation in IT-Schaltschränken. Das Design birgt zeitgemäße Technologien, wie hinterleuchtete, berührungsempfindliche Tasten, einen Fingerabdruckleser, Kartenleser und ein hochauflösendes Farbdisplay.

The compact hardware security module, ADYTON, combines fashionable elegance with functional perfection. Its black glass panel creates a clear contrast to the light tones of the housing. The cast aluminum housing allows for passive cooling, which improves the energy footprint and noise load. Thanks to robust guide rails on each side, ADYTON slides easily into the special rack for simple, secure installation in IT-cabinets. The design also holds modern technology, like backlit capacitive keys, a fingerprint-reader, card-reader and a high-resolution color display.

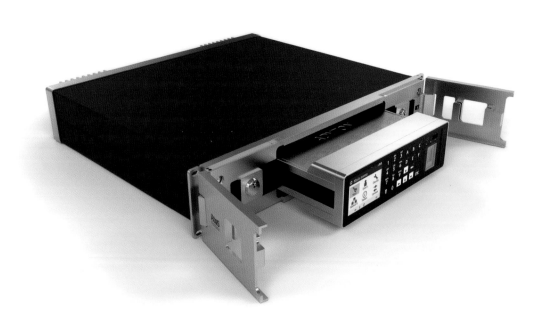

PRODUCT
CleverLevel LFFS
Sensor zur Füllstanderkennung
Level detection sensors

DESIGN
Baumer A/S
R&D department
Århus V, Denmark

MANUFACTURER
Baumer Group
Frauenfeld, Switzerland

Mit dem CleverLevel LFFS hat Baumer eine wirklich clevere Alternative zum Schwinggabel-Füllstandsschalter entwickelt. Hier kommen Design und Funktionalität zusammen und bieten dem Kunden einen echten Mehrwert. Am Kopf des Gehäuses, das aus poliertem Edelstahl besteht, sind Mulden, die eine 360-Grad-Sicht der integrierten blauen LED-Schaltzustandsanzeige ermöglichen. Diese Mulden sind so gestaltet, dass Flüssigkeitsanhaftungen oder Bakterienansammlungen ausgeschlossen sind und der Sensor für die Lebensmittelproduktion geeignet ist. Selbst bei einer Installation des Sensors auf hohen Tanks ist der Schaltzustand durch die LED Anzeige zu sehen.

With the CleverLevel LFFS, Baumer has developed a truly clever alternative to vibrating fork level switches. Design and functionality come together to create real value for customers. On the top of the polished stainless steel housing are recesses which provide for a 360 degree view of the integrated blue LED output indicator. These recesses are designed to prevent the adherence and collection of fluids and bacteria, making the sensor suitable for food production. The output is visible through the LED display even if the sensor is installed on high tanks.

PRODUCT

Bolzen
Universalbolzen
Universal bolt

DESIGN

Selic Industriedesign
Mario Selic
Augsburg, Germany
Bernd Siegmund GmbH
Evelyn Bergmann, Bernd Siegmund
Großaitingen, Germany

MANUFACTURER

Bernd Siegmund GmbH
Großaitingen, Germany

Der Bolzen erzeugt eine kraftschlüssige Verbindung zwischen Bauteilen, z. B. Anschlagwinkel mit dem Schweißtisch, mit einer Tragkraft von bis zu 12 t. Seine ausgeklügelte und zuverlässige Schnellspannmechanik erlaubt sekundenschnelles Fixieren und Lösen und spannt dabei Bauteile verschiedenster Materialstärken. Die Rändelung am Bolzenkopf sorgt für Griffigkeit. Die Funktionstransparenz trägt zur einfachen Handhabung bei. Der Bolzen kann zudem mit Inbusschlüssel gespannt werden. Er wird mit hoher Präzision aus gehärtetem hochlegiertem Stahl gefertigt und sorgt für hohe Festigkeit. Die brünierte Oberfläche dient der Korrosionsbeständigkeit.

The bolt creates a force-fit connection between component parts, like for example stop squares and welding table and guarantees a bearing capacity of up to 12 tons. It can be fixed and dissolved in a matter of seconds due to its smart and safe mechanism. It clamps components of different material thicknesses. The milling at the top of the bolt enables grip and the transparency of the function is responsible for the easy handling. Besides the bolt can be fixed with an Allen key. The bolt is produced with highest precision out of hardened high-alloyed steel and guarantees high solidness and accurateness. The burnished surface is corrosion resistant.

PRODUCT
GK 600 PN
Spannwinkel
Clamping square

DESIGN
Selic Industriedesign
Augsburg, Germany
Bernd Siegmund GmbH
Evelyn Bergmann, Bernd Siegmund
Großaitingen, Germany

MANUFACTURER
Bernd Siegmund GmbH
Großaitingen, Germany

Der 600 mm hohe Anschlagwinkel mit seiner plasmani-
trierten Oberflächenveredelung ist für den stark beanspruchten Einsatz konzipiert und bietet optimale Ver-
schleißfestigkeit und Korrosionsbeständigkeit, günstig
für eine lange Lebensdauer. Plasmanitrieren ist ein umweltfreundliches Härteverfahren, da es nur auf Sauerstoff, Wasserstoff und Stickstoff basiert. Verwendet
wird der Anschlagwinkel in der Schweiß- und Spann-
technik zum definierten Positionieren und Fixieren von
Werkstücken. Die durchgespannte Strebe stemmt sich
kraftvoll dem Werkstück entgegen und visualisiert Stärke. Aussparungen reduzieren das Gewicht für gutes
Handling auf 22,5 kg.

*The vacuum nitrided stop square with its height of 600 mm
and its wear-free tight surface is designed for heavy
claimed application and ensures protection from corrosion and a long lifetime. Moreover, the plasmanitriding is
one of the most ecological hardening processes as only
nitrogen, hydrogen and oxygen are used. It is used in
welding and clamping technics for accurately defined
positioning and fixing of working parts. The strained bar
mortises powerful against the working piece and visualizes strength. Cavities at the whole square decrease the
weight to 22,5 kg and therefore improve the daily handling.*

PRODUCT

GK 800 PN

Spannwinkel

Clamping square

DESIGN

Selic Industriedesign

Mario Selic

Augsburg, Germany

Bernd Siegmund GmbH

Evelyn Bergmann, Bernd Siegmund

Großaitingen, Germany

MANUFACTURER

Bernd Siegmund GmbH

Großaitingen, Germany

Der 800 mm hohe Anschlagwinkel mit seiner plasmani-
trierten Oberflächenveredelung ist für den stark beanspruchten Einsatz konzipiert und bietet optimale Ver-
schleißfestigkeit und Korrosionsbeständigkeit, günstig
für eine lange Lebensdauer. Plasmanitrieren ist ein umweltfreundliches Härteverfahren, da es nur auf Sauerstoff, Wasserstoff und Stickstoff basiert. Verwendet
wird der Anschlagwinkel in der Schweiß- und Spann-
technik zum definierten Positionieren und Fixieren von
Werkstücken. Die durchgespannte Strebe stemmt sich
kraftvoll dem Werkstück entgegen und visualisiert Stärke. Aussparungen reduzieren das Gewicht für gutes
Handling auf 28,5 kg.

*The vacuum nitrided stop square with its height of 800 mm
and its wear-free tight surface is designed for heavy
claimed application and ensures protection from corrosion and a long lifetime. Moreover, the plasmanitriding is
one of the most ecological hardening processes as only
nitrogen, hydrogen and oxygen are used. It is used in
welding and clamping technics for accurately defined
positioning and fixing of working parts. The strained bar
mortises powerful against the working piece and visualizes strength. Cavities at the whole square decrease the
weight to 28,5 kg and therefore improve the daily handling.*

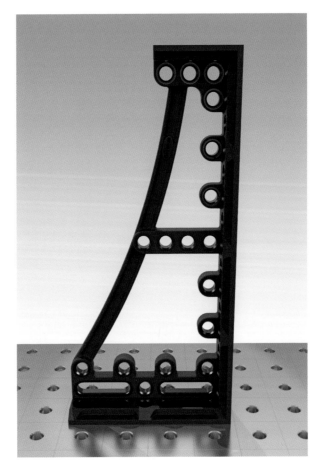

BP-80
Minimalism Design
Professional Rugged Look

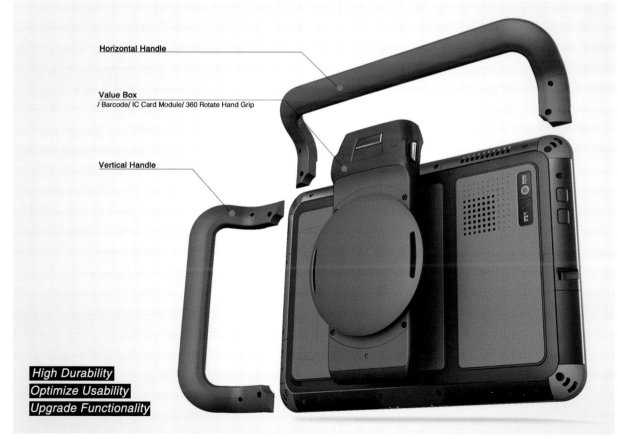

Horizontal Handle

Value Box
/ Barcode/ IC Card Module/ 360 Rotate Hand Grip

Vertical Handle

High Durability
Optimize Usability
Upgrade Functionality

PRODUCT

BP80
Tablet PC

DESIGN

Bluebird Soft
JungSik Park, SeBin Park, JiSeok Heo
Seoul, South Korea

MANUFACTURER

Bluebird Soft
Seoul, South Korea

BP80 ist ein Windows XP/7 basierter Tablet PC, der mit IP65-Code und 1,2 m Fallresistenz in verschiedenen Sektoren wie in den öffentlichen Einrichtungen, Groß-und Einzelhandel, Healthcare-Bereichen, Konstruktionsarbeiten und Märkten seine Anwendung erfährt. Durch das vertikale oder horizontale Anbringen eines Schultergurtes oder eines Griffes an den Ecken der Hinterseite kann man das Gerät an unterschiedlichen Arbeitsumfelder und Nutzzwecken anpassen. Die Funktionalität und Nutzbarkeit konnte weiterhin durch die modulweise an- und absetzbaren Wertefelder wie Barcodescanner, IC-Kartenleser und 360° rotierbaren Scharnier-Griff verbessert werden.

The BP80 is the brand new business tablet pc with Windows OS (Windows XP/7). With IP65 Rate and 1.2 m drop resistance, the BP80 serves government and public sector, retail, healthcare, and CAD engineering sector. The front looks elegant like a consumer device. The back looks professional and rugged as different module types may be attached. The shoulder-strap and handle can be attached horizontally and vertically with mini screws at each corner on the back. The functionality have been greatly enhanced since different types of modules like barcode scanner, IC card reader, 360 rotating hinge handle have become available.

PRODUCT

d'Weaver
Probenahme-Webstuhl
Sampling loom

DESIGN

Otsuka Information Technology Corp.
Creative Aesthetics Center
Carlos Hsu, Chris Chuang, Bruce Wang, Chiayi Cho
Taipei County, Taiwan

MANUFACTURER

CCI TECH Inc.
Taipei County, Taiwan

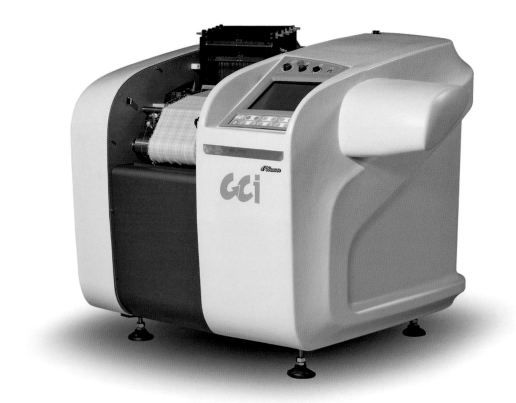

d'Weaver ist eine spezielle Webmaschine für Mode-Designer, die leicht zu bedienen ist und umfangreiche Funktionen bietet, sodass die verschiedenen Anforderungen der Bemusterung bewältigt und die Effizienz der Neuentwicklung der Tücher erhöht werden können. d'Weaver vermittelt ein neues Image einer Werkzeugmaschine, wobei die Maschine sich mehr in der Arbeitsumgebung des Anwenders integriert hat. Das Gehäuse ist aus Kunststoff durch Spritzgusstechnik gefertigt, wodurch die Vielfältigkeit der Produkte sich erhöht und die Kosten und die Zeit der Herstellung sowie das Gewicht sich stark reduzieren.

d'Weaver gives very careful consideration to interaction between user and the working environment. The characteristics of the fabric, its texture and the flexibility of the fibers are used as an expression of the exterior design. Then, to reduce the machine operator's workload and increase their confidence in the operation of the equipment, d'Weaver also provides an imported FRP Process and Plastics to substantially increase the possibilities of styling. This decreases costs, reduces weight, and also shortens both production time and time to market.

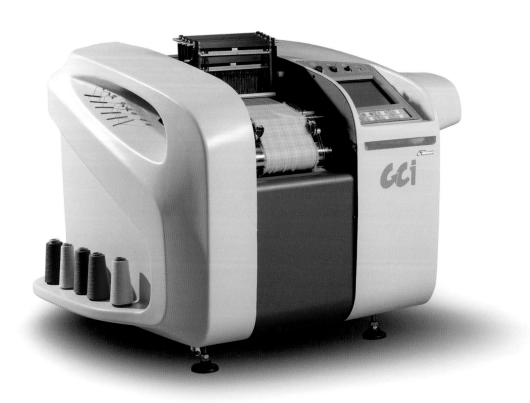

PRODUCT
Cairen F10
Sauerstoff-Maske
Oxygen mask

DESIGN
2rabbit Co., Ltd.
Seoul, South Korea

MANUFACTURER
CIJ Co., Ltd.
Daejeon, South Korea

Cairen F10 ist die weltweit erste selbstatmende Sauerstoffmaske, die in Notfallsituationen verwendet wird. Ein austauschbarer Sauerstofftank ist im Nasenbereich versteckt, der mit einem On / Off – Griff versehen ist. Sie schützt das ganze Gesicht und der eingebettete Sauerstofftank bietet Luft für schnelle und sichere Entnahme. Die Maske wird durch ein vierarmiges System eng am Gesicht gehalten, das leicht angepasst werden kann und so das unbeabsichtigte Entweichen von Sauerstoff verhindert. Polycarbonat und hitzebeständiges Silikon sind angenehm zu tragen und schützen den Anwender vor Gefahren. Die allgemeine Form ist ästhetisch und sein futuristischer Look liefert einen Mehrwert für das Produkt.

Cairen F10 is the world's first self-breathing face type oxygen mask used for emergency situations. The Cairen F10 protects the whole face and the embeded oxygen tank provides air for quick and safe extraction. A replaceable oxygen tank is hidden in the nose area and it is also used to grip for easy on and off action. The mask is held by 4 way mesh type adjustable strip and is designed to fit tight to prevent any gas leak. Polycarbonate and thermal resistant silicone are used to protect and relax the user from any dangerous situations. The overall shape is aesthetically pleasing and its futuristic look adds value to the product.

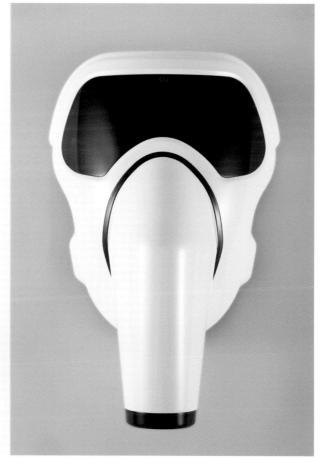

PRODUCT
DATRON M8Cube
CNC-Fräsmaschine
CNC milling machine

DESIGN
DATRON AG
Frank Wesp
Mühltal, Germany

MANUFACTURER
DATRON AG
Mühltal, Germany

Hochleistungs-CNC-Fräsmaschine deren Designkonzept von der Würfel-Form inspiriert wurde. Die klare äußere Form- und Farbsprache minimiert die visuelle Ablenkung von den wichtigen Funktionen und fokussiert somit auf den Fräs-Bereich. Ein neu entwickeltes Bedienterminal mit einer auf Touch-Bedienung optimierten Software-Oberfläche schafft eine geordnete Übersicht und vereinfacht die Bedienung. Die Integration von Signalleuchten in Bedienterminal und Portalgehäuse erleichtern die Wahrnehmung des aktuellen Maschinenstatus. Das optimierte Türkonzept und der großzügige Spänewagen ermöglichen ein ergonomisches, ermüdungsfreies Arbeiten.

High performance CNC milling machine, its design inspired by a cube. Its pure shape and color language minimize the visual distraction from key functions, thus focusing on the milling device. A newly developed operator terminal with a software interface optimized for touch screen usage provides a structured overview and simplifies operation. Signal lights integrated into the operator terminal and system cabinet indicate the current machine status. The enhanced door concept and the large chip carriage provide an ergonomic and fatigue-free working environment.

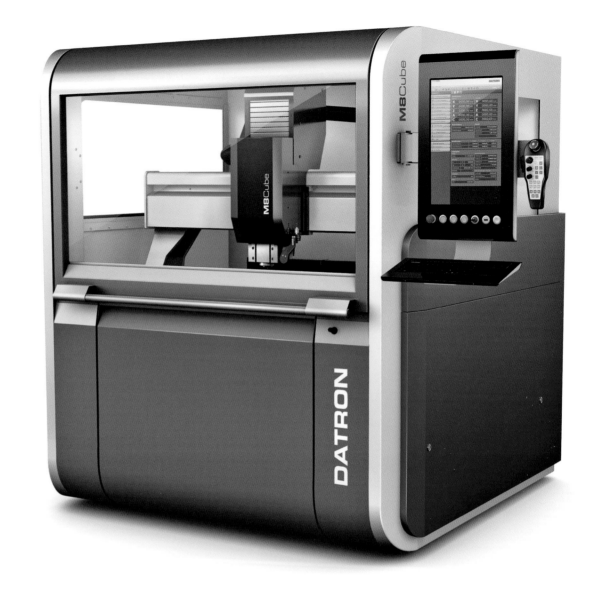

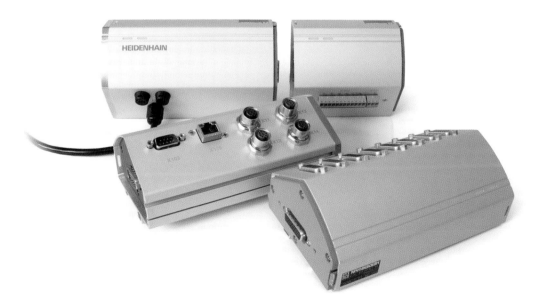

PRODUCT
MSE 1000
Ethernet-Bussystem
Ethernet bus system

DESIGN
zweigrad GmbH & Co. KG
Hamburg, Germany

MANUFACTURER
Dr. Johannes Heidenhain GmbH
Traunreut, Germany

Die MSE 1000 ist ein modulares Ethernet-Bussystem für Mehrstellen-Messplätze zur Anwendung in der Automatisierung und Qualitätssicherung. Die dort erforderlichen hohen Messgenauigkeiten werden durch das klare und präzise Design sowie die sehr hohe Verarbeitungsqualität der MSE 1000 auf den ersten Blick kommuniziert. Hochwertige Materialien und Oberflächenveredelungen sowie das lückenlose Erscheinungsbild unterstützen die elegante Gestaltung. Die werkzeuglose Montage durch ein innovatives Stecksystem der Einzelmodule unterstreicht den hohen Gebrauchswert des Bussystems.

The MSE 1000 is a modular ethernet bus system with support for multiple measuring stations. It can be used for automation and quality assurance purposes and even at first glance it can be seen that the high level of accuracy required for such applications is provided by the MSE 1000, with its clear and precise design and excellent manufacturing quality. High quality materials and surface finishing, as well as the uniform appearance throughout, also contribute to the elegant design. An innovative plug-in system for the individual modules enables tool-free assembly and highlights the high utility value of the bus system.

PRODUCT
e.sybox
Elektronisches Druckregelungssystem
Electronic pressure system

DESIGN
DAB Pumps S. p. A.
Mestrino (PD), Italy

MANUFACTURER
DAB Pumps S. p. A.
Mestrino (PD), Italy

Ein integriertes elektronisches Kompaktsystem zur
Wasserdruckerhöhung und Druckbeaufschlagung.
Das Produkt eignet sich besonders für Privathaushalte,
Wohngebiete und die Leichtindustrie sowie für Bewässe-
rung und Gartenbau. Das System verfügt über eine
mehrstufige, selbstansaugende Pumpe, einen drehzahl-
variablen Umrichter (Aufrechterhalten eines konstanten
Drucks bei veränderter Durchflussmenge), Druck- und
Durchflusssensoren, einen 2-Liter-Druckbehälter, ein
Rückschlagventil und eine einfache, benutzerfreundliche
Schnittstelle mit einem hochauflösenden LCD-Display.
Die Installation zusätzlicher Geräte ist nicht notwendig.
Diese Gesamtanlage kann als einzige All-in-One-Lösung
auf dem Markt sowohl vertikal als auch horizontal ins-
talliert werden. Sie ist außerdem mit einem drahtlosen
Kommunikationssystem ausgestattet, mit dem Sie
Druckerhöhungsanlagen mit bis zu vier Einheiten ohne
externe Steuerkästen oder Leitungen erzeugen können.

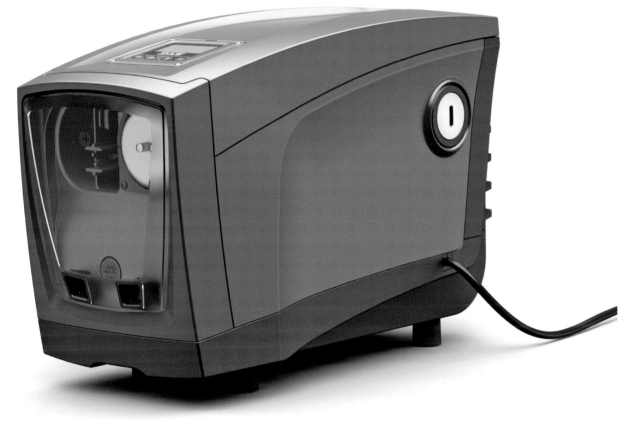

A compact integrated electronic system for water boosting and pressurization. This product is particularly suitable for domestic, light residential and light industrial use as well as for irrigation and gardening purposes. The system includes a multi-stage self-priming pump, variable speed inverter (maintaining constant pressure in relation to variations flow rate), pressure and flow sensors, a 2 l pressure vessel, non return valve and a simple, user-friendly interface with a high resolution LCD display. This complete unit doesn't need any other additional devices to be installed. It's an all-in-one solution that's unique on the market, as it can be installed either vertically or horizontally. It's also fitted with a wireless communication system which allows you to create booster sets consisting of up to four units without any external control boxes or wires.

PRODUCT

EOL Transmission Test

EOL-Getriebeprüfstand

EOL transmission test rig

DESIGN

Braake Design

Stuttgart, Germany

MANUFACTURER

ZF Friedrichshafen AG

Passau, Germany

Der neue ZF-Getriebeprüfstand übernimmt die Befüllung und Endkontrolle von Automatikgetrieben für
quer eingebaute Motoren. In unterschiedlichen Prüf-
modi werden die Getriebe akustisch, hydraulisch und
elektronisch getestet. Die grundlegend neu entwickelte
Schallschutzverkleidung mit ihrem markanten Design
dient der akustischen Entkoppelung und dem Bediener-
schutz während des Prüfvorgangs. Die großen Sicher-
heitsglastüren ermöglichen einen optimalen Zugang
und hervorragenden Einblick für die visuelle Kontrolle
der Testkomponenten. Der Monitorarm ist schwenkbar
linear verfahrbar und bietet so perfekte Ergonomie für
Service und Bedienung.

*The new ZF Transmission Test rigs are designed to per-
form final tests and oil filling of state of the art power
shift transmissions. For this purpose the gearbox is tested
acoustically, electrically and hydraulically. The basically
new developed noise protection booth with its significant design reduces background noises and ensures the
machine operators safety. Large security glass doors give
optimal approach and outstanding view for the visual
control of the test components. The operator system is
turnable, linear moved and provides a perfect ergonomic solution for service and operating of the test stand.*

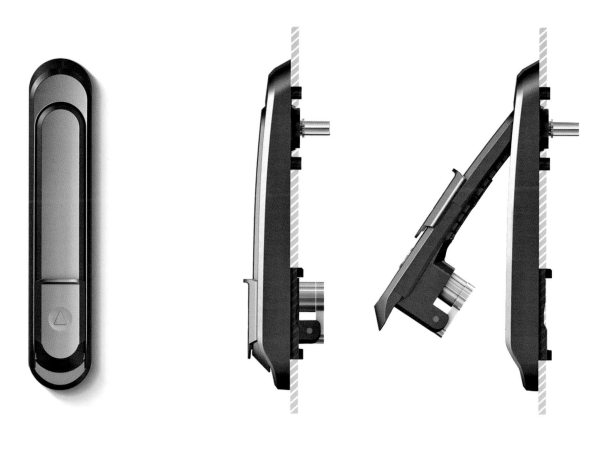

PRODUCT
Schwenkgriff 1325
Schwenkgriff
Swing handle

DESIGN
EMKA - Beschlagteile GmbH & Co. KG
Stefan Mostert, Andreas Schütz
Wuppertal, Germany

MANUFACTURER
EMKA - Beschlagteile GmbH & Co. KG
Wuppertal, Germany

Ausgangsform einer neuen Produktfamilie:
– ergonomische Griffgestaltung,
– alle gängigen Betätigungen sind modular austauschbar,
– anpassbar an verschiedene Blechstärken,
– neuartige Gelenkdornlagerung erleichtert die Montage,
– keine Verspannungskräfte zwischen Gelenkdorn und Stangenschloss,
– optimale Kraftübertragung, der Gelenkdorn durchgreift das Ritzel vollständig,
– Schnellmontage mit Hakenfixierung (Schutzklasse IP 40),
– Staub- und Feuchtigkeitsschutz durch Kappenfixierung (Schutzklasse IP 65).

Die Gestaltung verhindert ein Verkratzen der Mulde durch den Griff. Der Griff ist federnd gelagert und bewegt sich selbsttätig aus der Mulde.

Form giving to a new product family:
– *ergonomically shaped handle,*
– *all commonly used inserts can be manually replaced on demand,*
– *the newly developed shaft fastener simplifies assembly,*
– *no tension forces between the shaft and latch,*
– *perfect force transmission,*
– *full penetration of the shaft though the sprocket-wheel,*
– *fast mounting with hook fixation (Protection class IP 40),*
– *dust and moisture protection by protective cover on the inside (Protection class IP 65).*

Integrated guides prevent the swing handle to scratch the rim of the dish. The spring loaded handle separates automatically from the dish upon unlocking.

PRODUCT
SAMH-S
Befestigungsbausatz
Mounting kit

DESIGN
Festo AG & Co. KG
Karoline von Häfen
Esslingen, Germany

MANUFACTURER
Festo AG & Co. KG
Esslingen, Germany

Mit dem Zubehör SAMH-S werden Zylinderschalter in der Nut pneumatischer Antriebe entsprechend der Maschinenrichtlinie sicher befestigt: formschlüssig, unverlierbar und manipulationssicher. Der Bausatz SAMH-S kommt damit zur Anwendung bei der binären Abfrage der Antriebstechnik in Sicherheitskreisen, beispielsweise der Rückmeldung von Schutztüren, die pneumatisch betätigt werden. Somit entfällt die zusätzliche Abfrage über bisher extern an der Schutztür montierte Tasten. Das Design des transparenten Sicherungsclips bildet mit dem Sensor eine funktionale Einheit und ist durch die gelbe Kennzeichnung eindeutig als Sicherheitsbauteil markiert.

The mounting kit SAMH-S is used to secure proximity sensors in the slot of pneumatic drives. It provides a captive, positive-locking connection that is protected against manipulation and so meets the requirements of the Machinery Directive. It can be used for binary sensing of the drive technology in safety circuits, for example for receiving feedback from pneumatically actuated safety doors. This does away with the need for additional sensing via pushbuttons mounted externally on the safety door. The design of the transparent circlip forms a functional unit with the sensor and the yellow marking clearly identifies it as a safety component.

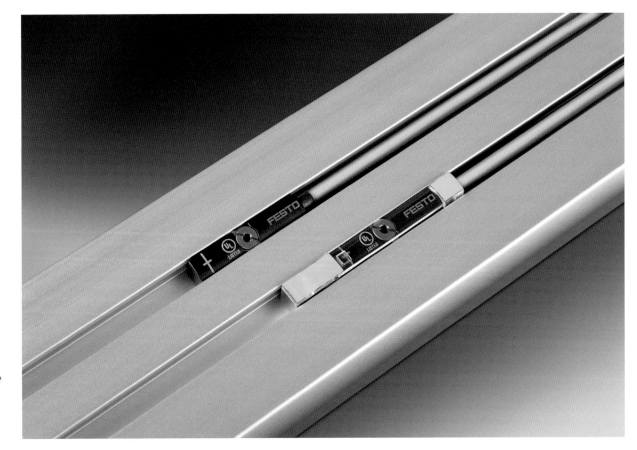

PRODUCT
HE DB Mini
Handeinschaltventil
Manual on-off valve

DESIGN
Festo AG & Co. KG
Jörg Peschel, Robert Jachmann
Esslingen, Germany

MANUFACTURER
Festo AG & Co. KG
Esslingen, Germany

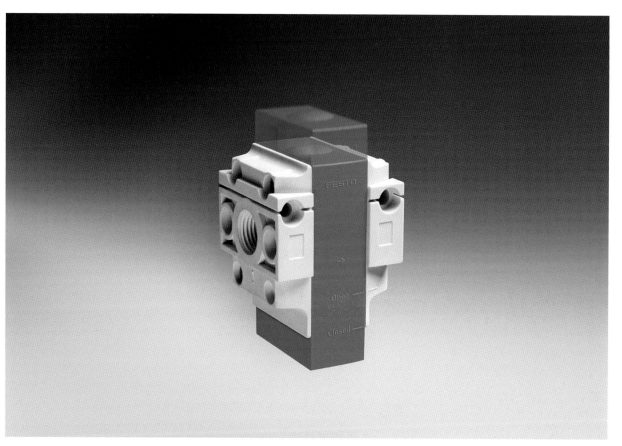

Das Handeinschaltventil ergänzt die bestehende DB Mini-Baureihe. Das Ventil regelt auf einfache Weise das Be- und Entlüften von druckluftbetriebenen Maschinen. Die Zielanwendung des Ventils sind Produktionsanlagen, bei denen Einfachheit und Kosten im Fokus stehen. Durch die Gestaltung des Schiebers wird eine intuitive Bedienung erreicht. Blau steht für handbetätigte Teile. Der Schieber selbst bildet einen Rahmen, der das Gehäuse umgreift, gleichzeitig aber auch Bestandteil des Gehäuses ist. Das Ventil kann mit einem Vorhängeschloss gegen unbeabsichtigtes Verstellen gesichert werden.

The manual on-off valve is an addition to the DB Mini series. It provides an easy way of regulating the pressurization and exhausting of machines operated using compressed air. It is designed for use in production systems where the focus is on simplicity and costs. Intuitive operation is achieved with the blue coloring and the shape of the slide. This forms a frame that both encompasses the housing and is part of it. When the valve is closed, the frame also enables the valve to be locked.

PRODUCT

EMCA
Positionierantrieb
Motor for positioning tasks

DESIGN

Festo AG & Co. KG
Simone Mangold, Thomas Kehrer
Esslingen, Germany

MANUFACTURER

Festo AG & Co. KG
Esslingen, Germany

Der EMCA vereint in einem kompakten Gehäusekonzept einen verschleißfreien EC-Motor, Leistungselektro-
nik mit Positioniercontroller, optionale Haltebremse
und Feldbusanschluss. Der Anbau verschiedener Getriebe ist in einem modularen Baukasten vorgesehen. Eine
ausgeklügelte Anschlusstechnik sowie hohe Schutzklassen gegen Wasser und Schmutz prädestinieren ihn
für den industriellen Einsatz. Das Design unterstreicht
die kompakte Bauweise und bildet den Rahmen für die
gesamte Einheit. Ein klar definierter Anschlussbereich
unterstützt die intuitive Bedienung durch den Nutzer.

*The EMCA combines a wear-free EC motor, power elec-
tronics with position controller, optional holding brake
and fieldbus connection in a compact housing concept.
A modular product system provides the attachment of
various gear units. Cleverly thought-out connection
technology as well as high protection classes against water and dirt make it ideal for industrial use. The design
underlines the compactness and provides the framework for the entire unit. Intuitive operation by the user is
supported with a clearly defined connection area.*

PRODUCT
CLEANTEX CT 48 AC
Absaugmobil
Dust extractor

DESIGN
Schirrmacher Product Design
Roland Schirrmacher
Landsberg, Germany

MANUFACTURER
FESTOOL Group GmbH & Co. KG
Wendlingen, Germany

Große Staubmengen sind für den CLEANTEX CT 48 AC kein Problem. Durch sein Fassungsvermögen von 48 Litern ist er ideal für die Werkstatt. Mit seinen großen Rädern und dem Schubbügel ist der CT 48 AC leicht über Treppen zu ziehen. Das Schlauchdepot und die Kabelaufwicklung sorgen für Ordnung und die Feststellbremse für einen sicheren Stand. Mit vollautomatischer AUTOCLEAN-Hauptfilterabreinigung wird für konstante Saugkraft gesorgt. Eine kompakte Hochleistungsturbine garantiert dabei die hohe Absaugleistung. Der CT 48 AC fügt sich optimal in die CT-Serie ein. Durch einen modularen Steckplatz lässt er sich individuellen Bedürfnissen anpassen.

High volumes of dust are no problem for the CLEANTEX CT 48 AC. Its 48 l capacity makes it ideal for workshop applications. With its large wheels and push bar, the CT 48 AC is easy to transport on stairs. The hose caddy and cable reel help maintain order while the locking brake keeps the unit securely in place. Fully automatic AUTO-CLEAN main filter cleaning maintains consistent suction. A compact high-performance turbine guarantees outstanding extraction performance. The CT 48 AC is a perfect addition to the CT series. It can be adapted to individual requirements thanks to a modular slot.

PRODUCT

LEX 3 150 / LEX 3 77
Pneumatischer Exzenterschleifer
Pneumatic orbit sander

DESIGN

Schirrmacher Product Design
Roland Schirrmacher
Landsberg, Germany

MANUFACTURER

FESTOOL Group GmbH & Co. KG
Wendlingen, Germany

Der LEX 3 150 und der LEX 3 77 sind die beiden pneumatischen Exzenterschleifer der neuen LEX-Generation, eingebettet in ein Druckluftsystem mit geringem Druckluftverbrauch optimaler Absaugung und Zubehör. Sie sind sehr kompakt, leise und vibrationsarm und liegen dadurch optimal in der Hand und das in jeder Arbeitshaltung. Das Absaugsystem mit den IAS 3-Schläuchen sorgt für staubfreie Luft. Die Motoren laufen ölfrei und dadurch gibt es keine Fehlstellen und Nacharbeit wegen ölhaltiger Abluft. Durch den hohen Wirkungsgrad der energieeffizienten Motoren spart man bis zu 30 % Druckluftverbrauch.

The LEX 3 150 and LEX 3 77 are the two pneumatic eccentric grinders of the latest LEX generation, embedded in a pneumatic system with low compressed-air consumption, optimum extraction and accessories. They are extremely compact and quiet, and minimize vibrations, making them very ergonomic – in any working position. The extraction system with IAS 3 hoses ensures the air is free of dust. Motors that run without oil eliminate defects and rework caused by exhaust air containing oil. Thanks to the high effectiveness of the energy-efficient motors, compressed air consumption is decreased by up to 30 %.

PRODUCT
FE35
Rundläufer Tablettenpresse
Rotary tablet press

DESIGN
Dominic Schindler Creations GmbH
Lauterach, Austria

MANUFACTURER
Fette Compacting GmbH
Schwarzenbek, Germany

Flexibilität und hohe Anlagenverfügbarkeit sind entscheidende Faktoren für eine erfolgreiche und effiziente Pharmaproduktion. Die FE35 verbindet sämtliche Vorteile der neuen FE-Baureihe von Fette Compacting mit der kürzesten Produktwechselzeit ihrer Klasse. Anwender profitieren von höchster Anlagenverfügbarkeit und maximaler Investitionssicherheit. Die FE35 ist die erste Maschine ihrer Klasse, die konsequent auf einfachste Bedienung ausgerichtet ist. Dazu stellt Fette Compacting den Anwender in den Mittelpunkt und ermöglicht so den einfachen und sicheren Betrieb – weltweit und unabhängig vom Qualifikationslevel der Bediener.

Flexibility and high equipment availability are becoming crucial factors for efficient pharmaceutical production. The FE35 combines all the advantages of the new FE range of models from Fette Compacting with the shortest product changeover times of its class. Users benefit from maximum equipment availability and from maximum investment security. The FE35 is the first machine of its class to have been so thoroughly designed for the simplest possible operation. Fette Compacting therefore puts its central emphasis on the user. That is how it provides easy, reliable operation anywhere in the world, regardless of the operators qualification level.

PRODUCT
PRISMO MIRAGE
Spektrophotometer
Spectrophotometer

DESIGN
Kyoto Institute of Technology
Department of Design
Prof. Kentaro Yamamoto
Kyoto, Japan

MANUFACTURER
FUSO PRECISION Co., Ltd.
Kyoto, Japan

PRISMO MIRAGE ist ein kompakt und einfach zu bedie-
nendes Farb-Messinstrument. Anwendbar ist das Gerät
jederzeit, überall und durch jede Person.

*PRISMO MIRAGE is compact and easy operation color
measuring instrument. It's available anytime, anywhere
and for anybody.*

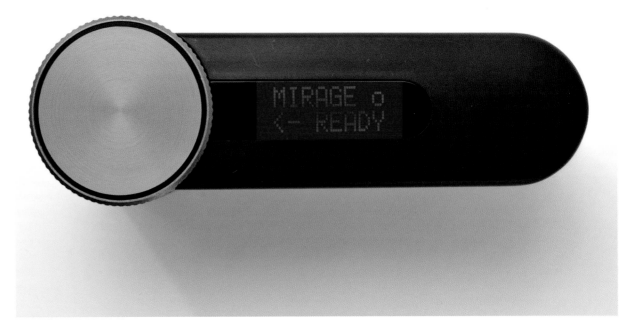

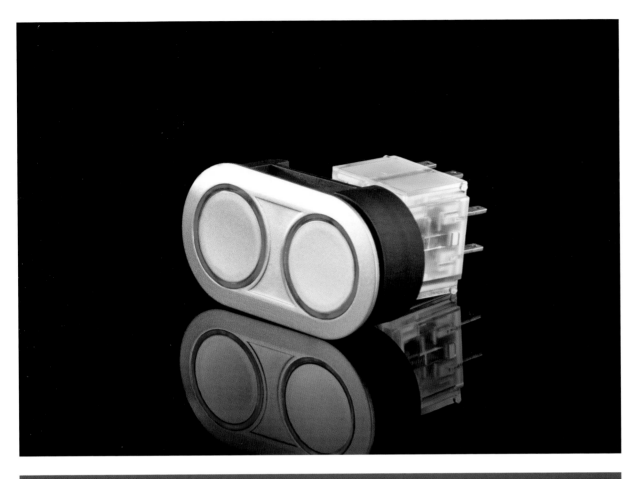

PRODUCT
RRJDTLR/RRDTLR
Elegante Doppeldrucktaste
Elegant double pushbutton

DESIGN
Georg Schlegel GmbH & Co. KG
Dürmentingen, Germany

MANUFACTURER
Georg Schlegel GmbH & Co. KG
Dürmentingen, Germany

Dabei handelt es sich um zwei in einer Hülse kombinierte, titanlackierte Drucktasten (laserbeschriftbar) mit Ringbeleuchtung und nur einem Kontaktelement. Als Einbauöffnung wird eine ovale Spezialbohrung oder eine Kombination aus drei überlappenden 22-mm-Bohrungen benötigt. Mit dem passenden Unterlegring kann der Betätiger auch in eine 16-mm-Bohrung montiert werden. Die Doppeldrucktaste funktioniert über ein geteiltes Druckstück und kann daher nur mit Kontaktelementen mit zweigeteilten Stößeln kombiniert werden, z. B. Baureihe BZ oder mit CT/CZT-Kontaktgebern (CT2, CTL2, CZTP2, CZTLP2).

Two titanium-lacquered pushbuttons with ring illumination are combined in one housing, requiring only one contact unit and one mounting hole – provide either one oval borehole or a combination of three overlapping 22 mm round holes. Using a suitable washer, allows the actuator to be mounted also in a 16 mm hole. The lenses are suitable for laser printing. The double pushbutton has a two-part plunger, thus, can only be combined with contact units being equipped with two-part plungers as e.g. the BZ type series or some of the CT/CZT contact units (ref. CT2, CTL2, CZTP2, CZTLP2).

PRODUCT
KOMBITAST-R-JUWEL
Flache Befehlsgeräte
Flat control units

DESIGN
Georg Schlegel GmbH & Co. KG
Dürmentingen, Germany

MANUFACTURER
Georg Schlegel GmbH & Co. KG
Dürmentingen, Germany

Mit der neuen Baureihe KOMBITAST-R-JUWEL bietet die
Firma Schlegel auch für den 30- mm-Bereich sehr flache
(2,7 mm) runde Betätiger (D = 36 mm) mit großer Betä-
tigungsfläche (D = 26 mm). Der schmale, titanlackierte
Frontring unterstreicht das elegante Design. Alle Schal-
terarten wie Drucktasten, Kipp-, Wahl-, Schlüsselschalter,
Notaus- und Meldeleuchten sind lieferbar sowie reich-
haltiges Zubehör. Die Betätiger können mit den zuverlässigen Schlegel-Kontaktgebern kombiniert werden, je
nach Anforderung mit Schraub- oder Cage-Clamp-An-
schlüssen oder mit Cage-Clamp-Schnellanschlüssen
(Steckanschlüsse).

*The new Schlegel KOMBITAST-R-JUWEL series offer very
flat (2.7 mm) round actuators (d = 36 mm) in the 30 mm
range, featuring a large touch surface of 26 mm diameter. A slim titanium-lacquered front ring gives the actuators that elegant look. All types of switches, such as
pushbuttons, toggle, selector and key switches, emergency stops and pilot lights are available, as well as a
wide range of accessories. The actuators can be combined with the reliable Schlegel contact blocks: depending on the requirements, select between screw or cage-
clamp terminals and cage-clamp fast connections (push
in).*

PRODUCT
Bedienerführung
Operator guidance system

DESIGN
Ottenwälder und Ottenwälder
Schwäbisch Gmünd, Germany

MANUFACTURER
Gerhard Schubert GmbH
Verpackungsmaschinen
Crailsheim, Germany

Die Bedienerführung für Gerhard Schubert GmbH-Verpackungsmaschinen repräsentiert ein neues Bewusstsein für Gestaltungsqualität im Maschinenbau. Ein flaches Aluminiumgehäuse mit rahmenlosem Glasdisplay und intuitiver Touch-Bedienung vermitteln einen hohen Gebrauchswert und eine professionelle Ästhetik. Der Bildschirm und die PC-Einheit sind im Servicefall einzeln abkoppelbar. Die ergonomisch vorteilhafte Gestaltung und angenehme Haptik der Bedienelemente optimieren das Handling. Die hochwertige Formensprache des Designs fördert die Identifikation mit der Arbeit und erhöht damit auch die Sicherheit und Produktivität am Arbeitsplatz.

The operator guidance system for Gerhard Schubert GmbH-Packaging Machines represents a new awareness in the design quality of machinery. A flat aluminum housing with frameless glass-display and intuitive touch handling connects a high practical value and professional esthetics. The screen and the pc can be disconnected separate for service. Ergonomic design and the comfortable haptic of the operator guidance system optimize the handling. The high-grade form language of the design supports the identification of the users with their work and increases the security and productivity at the workstation.

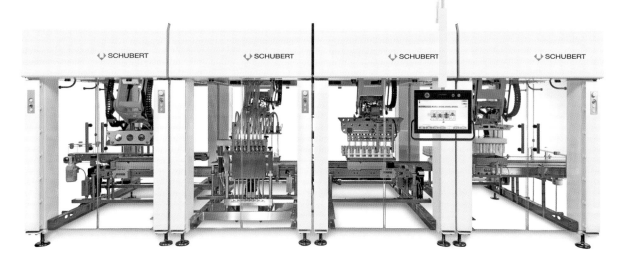

477

PRODUCT
BDS SC-100
Banknotenvernichtungsanlage
Banknote destruction machine

DESIGN
N+P Industrial Design GmbH
Christiane Bausback
München, Germany

MANUFACTURER
Giesecke & Devrient GmbH
München, Germany

Die BDS SC-100 gehört zur neuen Generation der Bank-
notenvernichtungs-Anlagen BDS®, entwickelt von
Giesecke & Devrient. Das System saugt geschredderte
Banknoten ab und presst diese in handliche Briketts.
Sicherheit, Qualität und Langlebigkeit der innovativen
Anlagen stehen genauso im Vordergrund wie eine
hohe Bedienerfreundlichkeit und Modularität. Strukturiert, elegant und hochwertig – die neue BDS-Linie
zeigt deutlich die Markenzugehörigkeit und besticht
durch eine neue, eigenständige Designidentität.

*The BDS SC-100 is part of a new generation of banknote
destruction machines BDS®, developed by Giesecke &
Devrient. The machine is suctioning shredded banknotes
and compacting them into handy briquettes. The main
focus of these innovative systems lies on the safety, quality and durability, as well as on a high level of usability
and modularity. Structured, elegant and sophisticated –
the new BDS-line clearly shows the brand affiliation and
captivates with its new, unique design identity.*

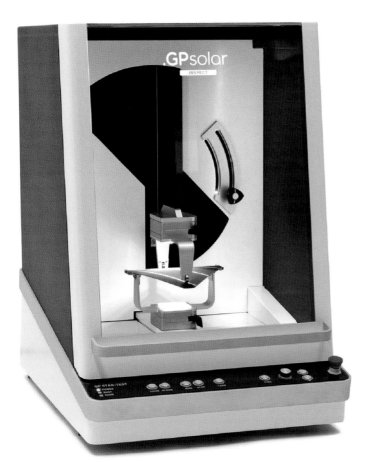

PRODUCT

GP STAB-TEST .Pro 2.0
Solarzellenprüfgerät
Solar cell testing system

DESIGN

defortec GmbH
design for technology
Christoph Keller, Stefan Grobe
Tübingen / Dettenhausen, Germany

MANUFACTURER

GP Solar GmbH
Konstanz, Germany

Labormessgerät zur Qualitätssicherung von Solarzellen und Wafern. Das Labormessgerät GP STAB-TEST .Pro 2.0 ist für das Testen der mechanischen Stabilität von Wafern und Solarzellen entwickelt worden. Einfach zu wechselnde Prüfmodule bieten sieben unterschiedliche Testverfahren, um Qualität und Effizienz von Solarzellen sicherstellen zu können. Das System analysiert Elastizität und Eigenspannung der Zellen sowie die Adhäsionskraft der gelöteten Kontaktbänder. Die innovativen Prüfmodule bieten einfache, intuitive Handhabung, hohe Genauigkeit und ein besonderes Lichtcodierungssystem, das einen schnellen und sicheren Prüfablauf gewährleistet.

Laboratory instrument for quality control of solar cells and wafers. The GP STAB-TEST .Pro 2.0 has been designed for testing the mechanical stability of solar wafers and cells. Easy to change test modules offer seven different test methods to secure the quality and efficiency of modern solar cells. The system analyzes elasticity, the solar cell bow after the firing process and the adhesion force of the soldered ribbon. The innovative test modules provide easy, intuitive operation, higher accuracies and a special light coding system, which ensures a quick and reliable test sequence.

PRODUCT
HMA Lift 25
Tragarm
Suspension system

DESIGN
Design Tech
Ammerbuch, Germany

MANUFACTURER
HASEKE GmbH & Co. KG
Porta Westfalica, Germany

Das Industriedesign des Lift 25 besticht durch eine funktionale Vereinfachung, die ihn vom gesamten Wettbewerb differenziert. Es sorgt für eine einmalig „cleane" Optik und ein deutlich reduziertes Fugenbild: Ein heller Ausleger verbindet dunkel abgesetzte Kopf- und Fußlager. Die bogenförmige, horizontale Abschluss- form des Auslegers wirkt dynamisch. Der farblich abge- setzte Ring am Kopflager unterstreicht den „Plug and Play"-Charakter des Lifts sowie seine hohe Modularität. Das akzentuierte Industriedesign der Details spiegelt die hohe Qualität der HASEKE-Produkte wider – und eignet sich somit hervorragend für den Einsatz im Me- dizin- und Industriebereich.

The appeal of the industry design of the HMA Lift 25 lies in its uniquely minimalist appearance and functionality which significantly set it off from all competitors. A light gray cantilever connects the dark head and base bearing. The curved, horizontal shape of the cantilever looks dy- namic. The ring at the head bearing with its different color underlines the „plug and play" character of the lift and its high popularity. The accentuated industry design of the details mirrors the high quality of the HASEKE products – a definite plus for use in medicine and industry. With the HMA Lift 25 the team of engineers and design experts have succeeded in creating a big jump ahead.

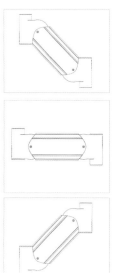

PRODUCT

TE 30-A36
Akku-Kombihammer
Cordless combihammer

DESIGN

Hilti Corporation
Schaan, Liechtenstein
Proform Design
Winnenden, Germany

MANUFACTURER

Hilti Corporation
Schaan, Liechtenstein

Der weltweit erste Akku-Kombihammer, der die volle Leistung eines vergleichbaren Kabelgerätes mit der Autonomie eines Akku-Gerätes verbindet. Durch die zusätzliche Meißelfunktion bietet das Gerät ein breites Anwendungsspektrum. Bei Serienbohrungen von Dübellöchern (Ø 10–20 mm) in Beton sorgt die patentierte automatischen Schnellabschaltung ATC (Active Torque Control) für maximale Sicherheit auch in schwierigen Untergründen. Der TE 30-A36 überzeugt zudem durch ein optimales Gewicht-Leistungsverhältnis. Der Geräteschwerpunkt im Zentrum beider Griffe ermöglicht eine optimale Balance und Handhabung.

The TE 30-A36 is the world's first cordless combihammer to successfully combine cordless mobility with the full power of a comparable corded tool. Its chiseling function also makes it suitable for a wide range of applications. Featuring Hilti's patented automatic cut-out system known as ATC (Active Torque Control), this tool ensures maximum safety in repetitive drilling applications (10–20 mm dia.) on concrete, even in tricky situations. With its center of gravity ideally positioned between the two grips, the TE 30-A36 is not only well balanced and easy to handle, it also offers an impressive power-to-weight ratio.

PRODUCT

HDE 500-A22 /HDM 500
Auspressgerätefamilie
Line of dispensers

DESIGN

Hilti Corporation
Schaan, Liechtenstein

MANUFACTURER

Hilti Corporation
Schaan, Liechtenstein

Die Produktplattform ist als ganzheitliche Systemlösung konzipiert und setzt sich aus den neuen schadstofffreien Hilti-Injektionsmörteln und Brandschutzschäumen sowie den dazugehörigen Auspressgeräten HDM und HDE zusammen. Treiber der Lösung war die sichere Anwendung: Durch eine erklärungsfreie Farbcodierung der Systemkomponenten ist eine Verwechslungsgefahr nahezu ausgeschlossen. Beide Auspressgeräte verfügen über eine Mengenregulierung für die präzise Bohrlochfüllung sowie einen automatischen Entspannmechanismus für geringen Mörtelverbrauch. Das ergonomische Design verhilft zu einem mühelosen Auspressen auch bei großen Verankerungstiefen.

This product platform is designed to present an all-embracing system solution consisting of the HDM and HDE dispensers and the new pollutant-free Hilti injectable adhesive mortars and firestop foams. Development of the solution was driven by the need for reliable, error-proof operation: the self-explanatory color coding of system components virtually rules out the risk of confusion. Both dispensers feature a volume control for accurate hole filling and an automatic pressure release mechanism that reduces mortar consumption and wastage. Ergonomic design helps ensure effortless dispensing even in deep anchor holes.

PRODUCT
TE-CD / TE-YD
Hohlbohrer
Hollow drill bits

DESIGN
Hilti Corporation
Schaan, Liechtenstein
Proform Design
Winnenden, Germany

MANUFACTURER
Hilti Corporation
Schaan, Liechtenstein

Die konzeptionell neuartigen Hohlbohrer Hilti TE-CD und TE-YD machen das bisher erforderliche nachträgliche Reinigen des Bohrlochs überflüssig. Das Bohrmehl wird bereits während der Bohrphase in das Staubabsaugsystem gesaugt. Der Anwender profitiert von einem schnelleren Bohrvorgang und einer Arbeitsumgebung, die so gut wie staubfrei ist. Das bedeutet ein Höchstmaß an Zuverlässigkeit, Sicherheit hinsichtlich der Haltekraft des einzusetzenden Ankers und einer gesundheitsbewussteren Arbeitssituation. Das neue Bohrer-System ist ausgelegt für die größtmögliche Effizienz und Effektivität speziell bei Serienanwendungen.

Featuring an entirely new concept, Hilti TE-CD and TE-YD hollow drill bits make the previously essential step of hole cleaning after drilling entirely unnecessary. Drilling dust is extracted by the vacuum system while drilling is in progress. Users also benefit from faster drilling and a virtually dustless working environment. This results not only in maximum reliability and security in terms of the hold obtained by the anchor installed in the hole, it also improves health and safety at the workplace. The new drill bit system is designed to achieve greatest possible efficiency and effectiveness, especially in repetitive drilling applications.

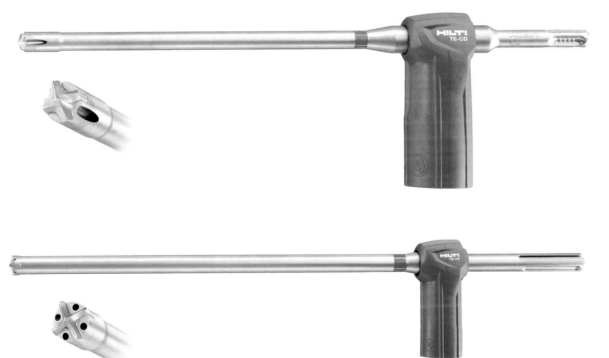

PRODUCT

DD 150-U / DD 160

Diamant-Kernbohrsystem

Diamond core drilling system

DESIGN

Hilti Corporation

Schaan, Liechtenstein

Busse Design & Engineering

Elchingen, Germany

MANUFACTURER

Hilti Corporation

Schaan, Liechtenstein

Das neue Diamant-Kernbohrsystem Hilti DD 150-U / DD 160 stellt eine optimale Lösung für vielfältige Anwendungen in Beton und Mauerwerk dar. Hand- oder ständergeführte Nassbohrungen in Beton können ebenso mit Leichtigkeit durchgeführt werden wie handgeführte Trockenbohrungen in Mauerwerk. Der 360° justierbare Seitengriff mit integrierter Staub- und Wassermanagementfunktionalität garantiert höchsten Arbeitskomfort. Dank der LED-Leistungsanzeige verleiht das kraftvolle 3-Gang-Getriebe dem Anwender kontrollierte Bohrleistungen und hilft auch ungeübten Anwendern, die optimale Bohrgeschwindigkeit und maximale Bohrkronen-Lebensdauer zu erzielen.

The new Hilti DD 150-U / DD 160 diamond core drilling system provides the optimum solution for a wide range of applications on concrete and masonry. Ideal for use with the wet drilling technique, hand-held or mounted on the drill stand, it's equally easy to use for hand-guided dry drilling on masonry. The side handle with built-in dust and water management functions can be adjusted through 360° and guarantees top working comfort. Thanks to the LED performance indicator, even inexperienced users can make best use of the power transmitted by the 3-speed gearing and thus achieve the optimum rate of drilling progress and maximum core bit life.

PRODUCT

TE 2-A22
Akku-Bohrhammer
Cordless rotary hammer drill

DESIGN

Hilti Corporation
Schaan, Liechtenstein
Matuschek Design & Management
Aalen, Germany

MANUFACTURER

Hilti Corporation
Schaan, Liechtenstein

Kompakt, leicht und komfortabel – das beschreibt den neuen Akku-Bohrhammer TE 2-A22 am besten. Der Bohrhammer wurde für leichte Bohrungen in Beton und Mauerwerk entwickelt. Er ist das ideale Gerät für den professionellen Innenausbau und Metallarbeiten. Das integrierte LED-Arbeitslicht verhilft zur besseren Sicht in schlecht beleuchteten Räumen. Aufgrund seines ausgeklügelten Kühlluft-Zirkulations-Konzeptes konnte im Design eine sehr kompakte Bauform realisiert werden, die nicht nur der Reduzierung des in der Hand liegenden Gewichts, sondern auch der Eckenzugänglichkeit des Gerätes zugute kommt.

Compact, light and comfortable to hold and use – that's the new TE 2-A22 cordless rotary hammer in a nutshell. This convenient tool has been specially designed for drilling small-diameter holes in concrete and masonry and is thus ideal for use in the interior finishing and metal fabrication trades. An interesting feature is the built-in LED lamp that helps provide a better view of the job in poorly lit areas. Thanks to the clever cooling air circulation concept it has been possible to achieve a very compact design that not only reduces the weight of the tool but also allows easier access in tight corners.

PRODUCT

CS 33EDTP
Motor-Kettensäge
Engine chain saw

DESIGN

Hitachi Koki Co., Ltd.
Yoshiki Aoki
Hitachinaka-City, Ibaraki-Pref, Japan

MANUFACTURER

Hitachi Koki Co., Ltd.
Hitachinaka-City, Ibaraki-Pref, Japan

Die Kettensäge besitzt einen umweltfreundlichen Motor der über einen katalytischen Schalldämpfer die Abgase deutlich reduziert. Das neue Design garantiert eine stabile Balance und durch die Optimierung der Griffform eine sichere Bedienbarkeit auf hohem Niveau. Darüber hinaus stellt die konkave Daumenauflage eine stabile Verbindung zwischen hinterem und vorderem Griff her, sodass ein sicherer Betrieb in jede Richtung gewährleistet ist. Die installierten Federn im Gelenk des Gehäuses, sowie der Anti-Vibrations-Handgriff reduzieren die Vibration zu Gunsten des Anwenders um ein Vielfaches. Zum sicheren Ablegen oder Hängen dient der serienmäßige Haken.

Each of the models CS33EDTP and TCS33EDTP is an environmentally-friendly engine chain saw that reduces gas emissions with a catalytic muffler. In addition, I included certain operability and stable balance characteristics at a high level by the optimization of the handle shape. Moreover, a thumb rest (concave portion) is provided at the joint between the rear handle and the front handle to ensure stable operation in any direction. I installed a spring in the joint of a body and the handle to reduce vibration and a shock to burden the worker. And the (hanging) hook is convenient for the work at the high place.

PRODUCT
e-spool
Energiekettensystem
Energy chain system

DESIGN
igus® GmbH
plastics for longer life®
Köln, Germany

MANUFACTURER
igus® GmbH
plastics for longer life®
Köln, Germany

Die neuartige Alternative zur Kabeltrommel verknüpft auf einzigartige Weise zwei Energiezuführungen: Eine Standard e-kette® ist auf einer Spule aufgetrommelt und sorgt durch eine integrierte Rückholfeder jederzeit für die richtige Länge und Spannung. Das „twisterband" verbindet die rotierende Spule mit der statischen Aufhängung – die Schnittstelle zu den fest verlegten Leitungen. So kommt die e-spool – anders als Kabeltrommeln – ohne Schleifring oder spezielle Zugseilleitungen aus. Die Neuauslegung des Schleifrings beim Ändern der Befüllung fällt somit weg und neben Daten und Energie können hier auch Medien unterbrechungsfrei geführt werden.

The new alternative to the cable drum is a unique combination of two energy supply systems: a standard e-chain® is rolled up on a spool, always ensuring the correct length and tension by means of an integrated retaining spring. The "twisterband" connects the rotating spool to the static suspension – the interface to the permanently laid cables. In contrast to cable drums, the e-spool is able to operate without a slip ring or special draw wire guides. A redesign of the slip rang can therefore be omitted when changing the filling, also allowing for the uninterrupted guidance of media in addition to data and energy.

PRODUCT
triflex® TRLF
Zu öffnende 3-D-Energiekette
Snap-open 3D EnergyChain®

DESIGN
igus® GmbH
plastics for longer life®
Köln, Germany

MANUFACTURER
igus® GmbH
plastics for longer life®
Köln, Germany

Schneller befüllen bei dicken Schläuchen und Leitungen: Maßgleich mit der triflex® TRL, bei der die Leitungen per easy chain®-Verfahren eingedrückt werden, lassen sich die Kettenglieder der TRLF aufklappen. Dadurch wird das Einlegen großer Befüllungsdurchmesser deutlich erleichtert, z.B. für Roboter mit Zuführungen von Schrauben oder Nieten. Dank des speziellen triflex® R-Verbindungsprinzips der Kettenglieder kann dieses System hohe Zugkräfte aufnehmen, bleibt dabei aber beliebig kürz- und verlängerbar. Die Version TRLF vereint Gewichts- und Kostenvorteile mit maximaler Flexibilität und der Sicherheit mechanisch verriegelter Verschlüsse.

Faster filling of thick hoses and cables. Dimensionally equivalent to the triflex® TRL, where the cables are pressed in using the easy chain® process, the chain links of the TRLF can be snapped open. This greatly simplifies inserting large filling diameters, for instance for robots with screw or rivet feeds. Thanks to the special triflex® R linkage principle of the chain links, this system can absorb high tensile strengths, and can still be shortened and lengthened at will. The TRLF version combines weight and cost advantages with a maximum flexibility and the reliability of a mechanical lock.

PRODUCT
Baureihe XMS
Maschinenbausystem
Machine building kit

DESIGN
item Industrietechnik GmbH
Carsten Schulz, Guido Gabler
Solingen, Germany

MANUFACTURER
item Industrietechnik GmbH
Solingen, Germany

Der neue XMS-Baukasten von item bietet ausgewählte Features für den Bau hochwertiger und individuell skalierbarer Maschinengehäuse: Aluminiumprofile mit integrierten Kabel- und Medienkanälen bilden den tragenden, modularen Rahmen der Konstruktion. Gehäuse aus XMS-Bauelementen stellen im Innern die technische Infrastruktur klar und aufgeräumt bereit. Das Konzept trennt die Funktions- klar von Versorgungsbereichen. Dichtungen in allen Türöffnungen verhindern Lärm- und Partikelemissionen. Außen bildet das Gehäuse unabhängig von den Dimensionen eine glattflächige, gradlinige Gesamtform und schafft damit eine Harmonie zwischen Design und Technik.

The new XMS building kit system from item is ideal for building high-quality, scalable machine housings. Aluminum profiles with integrated conduits create the perfect load-bearing, modular framework for constructions. Housings built from XMS components have a ready-made and clearly laid out infrastructure built in. The concept ensures a clear separation between functional areas and areas that house supply lines. Seals on all door openings prevent noise and particle emissions. Regardless of size, the outside of the housing features smooth, straight lines and brings design and technology into harmony.

PRODUCT

Trijet

Hammerbohrer

Hammer drill bit

DESIGN

ITW Heller GmbH

Dinklage, Germany

MANUFACTURER

ITW Heller GmbH

Dinklage, Germany

Das Trijet-Design folgt einem ausgesprochen innovativen Konzept und setzt Akzente in einer Branche, die ihre Vermarktung sonst ausschließlich auf funktionell-technischen Aspekten aufbaut: Durch seine drei geschwungenen Hartmetallschneiden erzielt der Trijet außergewöhnliche Leistungen. Sowohl die Lebensdauer bei Betonbohrungen wie auch die Stabilität bei Armierungstreffern sind unvergleichlich hoch. Ein gelungenes Design in Verbindung mit überzeugenden Anwendungsergebnissen lassen den Trijet-Hammerbohrer zum einzigartigen Problemlöser für jeden Handwerker werden.

The Trijet design follows a highly innovative concept and sets accents in an industry that otherwise bases its marketing concepts only on technical and functional oriented aspects: thanks to its three-winged carbide tip the Trijet hammer drill bit achieves extraordinary performance. Both the concrete drilling life and the durability if the user hits reinforcement bars are unrivalled. A distinct design combined with convincing application results makes the Trijet a unique product for any tradesman.

PRODUCT
IFM-5/10
Solar-Wechselrichter
Solar inverter

DESIGN
DINAMO
Iñigo Echeverria
San Sebastian, Spain
DINAMO
Miguel Sanchez
Köln, Germany

MANUFACTURER
JEMA
LASARTE-ORIA, Spain

JEMA-Solarwechselrichter stellen den Stand der Technik hinsichtlich Ergonomie und Sicherheit dar. Außerdem bringen sie Leistungssteigerung sowie Konstruktions-, Betriebs- und Instandhaltungsverbesserungen. IFM-5/10 stellt dabei eine Produktreihe für den nicht-professionellen Einsatz im privaten Bereich dar, sowohl im Innen- als auch Außen-Betrieb. Ausgestattet mit einem intuitiv zu bedienenden Display, sind die Modelle geräuschlos zu betreiben und durch ein kompaktes, selbstkühlendes Gehäuse mit praktischen, abgesicherten Verbindungs-stücken und Griffen sehr einfach zu installieren.

JEMA solar inverters embody the state of the art in the sector bringing ergonomics and safety criteria together with performance improvement and construction, operation and maintenance simplification. The IFM-5/10 models conform the low-power end of the product range and have been designed to suit the residential market needs. In accordance, they are prepared for non-professional use, both indoors and outdoors, feature an easy to use graphic display to customize optimal working conditions, are ultra-noiseless and have a compact sized self-cooling enclosure with built-in connections protector and handles for extremely easy installation.

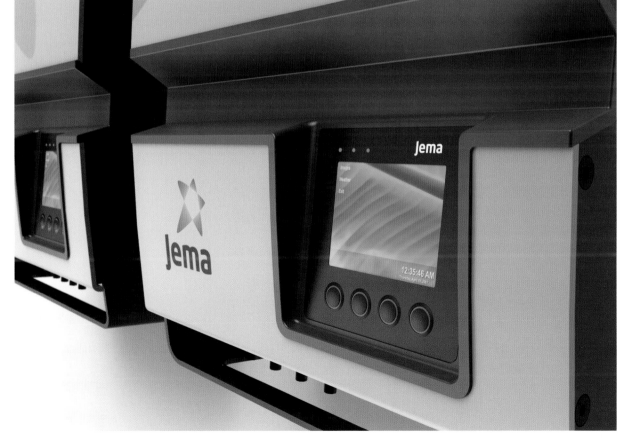

PRODUCT
Installationszange
Elektro-Installationszange
Installation pliers

DESIGN
KNIPEX-Werk
C. Gustav Putsch KG
Wuppertal, Germany

MANUFACTURER
KNIPEX-Werk
C. Gustav Putsch KG
Wuppertal, Germany

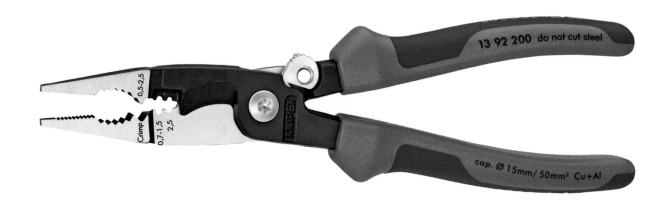

Die Installationszange ist als ideale Ergänzung zum unersetzbaren Seitenschneider konzipiert. Sie hat die Grundfunktionen der übrigen Basiswerkzeuge, die in der Elektroinstallation unentbehrlich sind. Ideal für Bau- und Industrieelektriker, die in ihrem Arbeitsumfeld viel unterwegs sind. Kombination der wesentlichen Funktionen, die Elektroinstallateure im täglichen Einsatz benötigen: Kabel schneiden und abisolieren, Flach- und Rundmaterial greifen, Durchführungslöcher entgraten und Aderendhülsen vercrimpen. Die Ausführungen mit Öffnungsfeder und intelligenter Sperrklinke ermöglichen es zu greifen und gleichzeitig die Schneiden zu schützen.

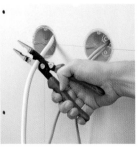

The installation pliers are designed as an ideal complement to the indispensable diagonal cutters. They are equipped with the basic functions of the other basic tools, which are essential in the electrical installation. Ideal for construction and industrial electricians who often have to travel around from one site to another. A combination of the essential functions that electricians apply every day: cutting and stripping cables, gripping flat and round material, deburring of feed-through holes and crimping end-sleeves. The spring assisted versions with intelligent latching mechanism enable to grip while the cutting edges are protected.

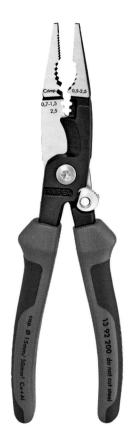

PRODUCT
X-Cut
Kompakt-Seitenschneider
Compact diagonal cutters

DESIGN
KNIPEX-Werk
C. Gustav Putsch KG
Wuppertal, Germany

MANUFACTURER
KNIPEX-Werk
C. Gustav Putsch KG
Wuppertal, Germany

Der X-Cut hat das Talent zum Alleskönner. Er ist kompakt und leicht, kraftvoll, hochpräzise und mit robusten Schneidkanten ausgestattet. Er schneidet feinste Drähte ebenso wie mehrdrähtige Kabel und harten Pianodraht und bietet somit eine vielseitige Verwendbarkeit in Industrie und Handwerk. Für das Trennen eines mittelharten Drahts (Ø 3 mm) benötigt der X-Cut rund 40 % weniger Kraft als mit einem konventionellen Seitenschneider gleicher Größe. Weitere Vorteile: durchgesteckte, außermittige Gelenkkonstruktion mit leichtem, spielfreien Gang und großer Öffnungsweite; schlanke Kopfform für gute Zugänglichkeit auch in beengten Arbeitssituationen.

The X-Cut is a multi-talented all-rounder. It is compact and light, powerful and highly precise and provided with robust cutting edges. It cuts through finest strands as well as multi-stranded cables and hard piano wire, providing a versatility in industry and crafts. When cutting a medium-hard wire (diameter 3 mm) the X-Cut requires about 40 % less effort than a conventional diagonal cutter of the same size. Further user-friendly benefits are provided by the eccentric box-joint construction with easy, zero-backlash movement and large jaw opening as well as a slim head shape for easy access even when working in confined areas.

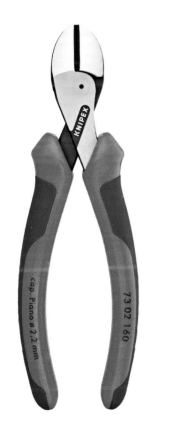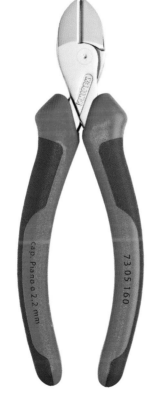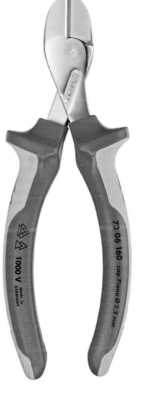

493

PRODUCT

KR 240 ultra K
Konsolroboter
Shelf-mounted robot

DESIGN

Selic Industriedesign
Mario Selic
Augsburg, Germany
KUKA Roboter GmbH
Günther Merk, Joachim Markert
Augsburg, Germany

MANUFACTURER

KUKA Roboter GmbH
Augsburg, Germany

Auf einem Sockel montiert kann der Roboter aufgrund seines langen Vorbaus problemlos und kollisionsfrei in die Tiefe arbeiten und überbrückt bis zu 3.100 mm große Distanzen zum Montieren, Handhaben, Bearbeiten und Schweißen. Organisch gestaltete, kraftvolle Bauelemente geben ihm ein lebendiges Erscheinungsbild und zeigen visuell die Leistungsfähigkeit und Beweglichkeit der Maschine. Zugleich sorgen sie mechanisch für hohe Biegefestigkeit und Torsionssteifigkeit, wichtig für präzises, zuverlässiges Arbeiten, Wiederholgenauigkeit ± 0,06 mm. Fließende Formübergänge begünstigen den mechanischen Kraftfluss und erhöhen die dynamischen Eigenschaften.

Thanks to its projecting front end, the robot can be mounted on a pedestal and work downwards without problems or collisions, bridging distances of up to 3,100 mm for assembly, handling, machining and welding tasks with a repeatability of ± 0.06 mm. Organically formed, high-strength components give the robot a dynamic appearance and give visual expression to the performance capability and agility of the machine. Mechanically they also ensure high torsional and bending stiffness – important for precise, reliable operation. Smooth transitions between structural shapes improve the mechanical force transmission and increase the dynamic properties.

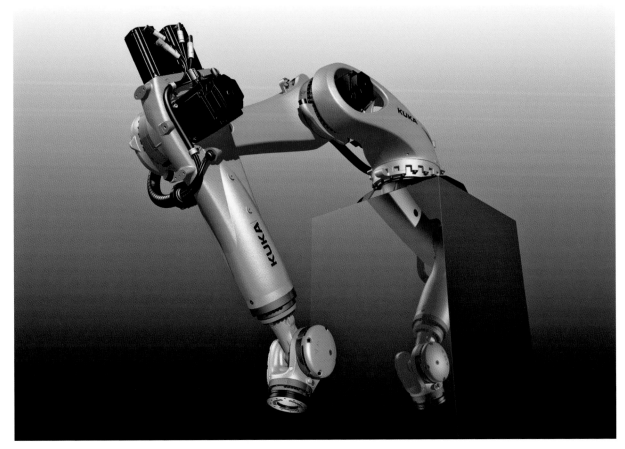

PRODUCT

MiraLux 360
Optische Inspektionseinheit
Optical inspection unit

DESIGN

ksp. Kay Saamer Produktgestaltung
Ober Ramstadt, Germany

MANUFACTURER

Laetus GmbH
Alsbach-Hähnlein, Germany

Die 360°-Prüfung von Objekten wird durch „INSPECT"
mit der Beleuchtungseinheit MiraLux 360 perfekt ausgeführt. Vier Kameras, deren Daten zu einem homoge-
nen Bild zusammengefügt und ausgewertet werden,
prüfen unter anderem Position und Druckqualität von
Etiketten sowie den korrekten Inhalt. Der Abstand der
vier Kameras zum Produkt wird durch nur einen skalierten
Drehknopf reguliert. So können Objekte unterschiedlichster Größen ohne aufwendigen Umbau geprüft
werden. Die automatische Korrektur der Beleuchtung
garantiert durch die integrierten LED-Elemente eine zuverlässige Prüfung: funktionelles Design gepaart mit
ausgefeilter Mechanik.

*A 360° inspection of objects can be done perfectly by
"INSPECT" combined with the MiraLux 360° light box.
The data collected by four cameras is assembled into one
homogeneous picture, evaluating and testing for position, presence, printing quality of labels and accuracy of
content. The distance between cameras and objects can
be easily adjusted by just one central scaled turning button, allowing for a large range of different sized products to be inspected without performing any system
modification. The automatically adjusted lighting with
integrated LED elements guarantees a reliable inspection. These mechanics are located in functional design.*

PRODUCT

Inductive 600 Series
Drehgeber
Rotary encoder

DESIGN

Avalon Innovation AB
Mathias Stavervik
Stockholm, Sweden

MANUFACTURER

Leine & Linde AB
Strängnäs, Sweden

Die neue 600-Serie mit Absolutdrehgebern zum vorwiegenden Einsatz in Singleturn- und Multiturn-Anwendungen bietet eine völlig neue Sichtweise auf Maschinenteile in der Branche. Wo bisher beim Produktdesign die ästhetischen Gesichtspunkte größtenteils außer Acht gelassen wurden, hat man nun Absolutdrehgeber entwickelt, die nicht nur ergonomisch, sondern auch optisch ansprechend sind. Das Ergebnis lässt sich sehen: Sein Äußeres unterstreicht einerseits die Weltklasse seiner Innenkonstruktion und stärkt andererseits die Markenidentität – nicht unwichtig auf einem Markt mit einer großen Anzahl ähnlicher Produkte.

The new 600 Series absolute encoders, mainly used to position single-turn or multi-turn motion, gives a completely new perspective on machine parts within the industry. On a market where product design from an esthetical viewpoint has been more or less neglected, each characteristic of these encoders has been both ergonomically designed and made esthetically appealing. The result is a presentable product where the exterior strongly radiates the interior's world class quality and dramatically strengthens the brand identity, which is an issue on a market with numerous similar products.

PRODUCT

LORCH i-Torch
WIG-Brenner mit Bedienpanel
TIG torch with controlpanel

DESIGN

LIO Design GmbH
Klaus Schindler, Sebastian Dröge, Christian Strohal
Braunschweig, Germany

MANUFACTURER

LORCH Schweißtechnik GmbH
Auenwald-Mittelbrüden, Germany

Der i-Torch-Brenner bietet extrem kompaktes Design mit hervorragender Bedienergonomie und integriertem Multifunktionsdisplay. Die besondere Anordnung von Bedienelementen und Display ermöglicht die optimierte Bauweise und verkürzt den Abstand von Bedienhand zu Schweißlichtbogen. Die geringeren Hebelwirkungen bewirken eine bessere Kontrolle des Schweißvorgangs. Die Schweißparameter sind stets im Blick und direkt regelbar. Per Tastendruck wird die Anzeigerichtung im Display für Links- und Rechtshänder angepasst und sorgt zusammen mit der ergonomischen Formgebung und der Konturführung der Tasten für optimale Einsatzbedingungen in der Praxis.

The i-Torch features an extreme compact design with excellent ergonomics and an integrated multifunctional display. An unique arrangement of all operational elements helps to reduce the distance between welder's hand and the arc, allowing a better control of the welding process. The torch can be easily switched from right to left-handed mode. All welding parameters are visible in every torch position and can be adjusted straight at the torch itself. The control keys provide a max. of haptic feedback. In summary, the i-Torch guarantees a more efficient workflow whilst achieving higher degrees of precision, thanks to improved ergonomics.

PRODUCT
bks+6
Ultraschall-Bahnkantensensor
Ultrasonic edge sensor

DESIGN
stephan gahlow produktgestaltung
Maria Sofia Schaake, Stephan Gahlow
Hamburg, Germany

MANUFACTURER
microsonic GmbH
Dortmund, Germany

Ultraschall-Bahnkantensensoren zeigen die Spurtreue
von Rollenmaterial in der Papier- und Folienindustrie
an. Der 40 mm Messbereich des bks+6 ist Weltrekord,
seine platzsparende Rechteckform ein Alleinstellungs-
merkmal. Das Diodenfeld nimmt diese Form auf: Die
intuitive Zuordnung der Diodeninfo zur realen Kanten-
position wird so möglich. Glatte, eng geführte Flächen
und versenkbare Schrauben ergeben ein nur 23 mm
breites Gehäuse. Der große Eckradius erlaubt eine ver-
größerte Folientastatur. Er erzeugt eine klare Geräte-
orientierung (wichtig in staubigem Umfeld). Bedien- /
Anzeigeelemente sind so groß wie möglich, somit leicht
auffind- und bedienbar.

*Ultrasonic edge sensors detect whether coil material is
running in line or not. The bks+6s` 40 mm measuring area:
world record, its compact rectangular shape a novelty.
This shape is echoed by the diode interface on top: an
intuitive matching of diode info and real edge position is
achieved. Introducing the plane silver metal surface and
blue zero-marker-line as key visuals, the design underlines
microsonic core values: precision and durability. A clear
top-bottom orientation (needed in dusty paper production) is created by the corner radius. It also allows an en-
larged keyboard foil: user interface and logo are presented in maximum size.*

PRODUCT

Shuttle4
Intralogistik
Intralogistics

DESIGN

I DESIGN AG
Michael Koch, Pascal Amacker
Biberist, Switzerland

MANUFACTURER

montratec AG
Gerlafingen, Switzerland

Ein Monorail-Transportsystem für die Produktion und Beförderung innerhalb von Firmen. Bisher gab es einerseits Transportsysteme, welche die Bearbeitung / Montage während des Transports ermöglichen und andererseits Transportsysteme, welche die Logistik des Endproduktes unterstützen. Mit dem Monoschienen-Konzept Montrac bieten wir jedoch ein Transportsystem, welches sowohl in der Produktion als auch in der Logistik eingesetzt werden kann. Das neue Shuttle4 wurde mit einem starken Aluminium-Chassis mit einem neuen Reinraum tauglichen Design gebaut.

A monorail transport system to produce and dispatch products within companies. Until now there have always been handling lines that allow for transport of the products during the phase of assembling / machining and other transport systems that deal with the logistics of the finished product. The new concept is to use a monorail transport system, more reliable and flexible than traditional air transport and its great advantage is that it can be used both in production and logistics, then your product will be handled one time. The new Shuttle4 was built with a strong aluminum chassis with a new cleanroom suitable design.

PRODUCT
INGENIA
PVD-Beschichtungsanlage
PVD coating system

DESIGN
Design Form Technik
J. Peter Klien
Triesenberg, Liechtenstein

MANUFACTURER
OC Oerlikon Balzers AG
Balzers, Liechtenstein

Die Beschichtungsanlage INGENIA von Oerlikon Balzers bringt maximale Leistung und herausragende Ingenieurs-leistung auf kleinstem Raum und übertrifft damit bisherige Anlagen in punkto Schnelligkeit, Präzision und Flexibilität. Zudem ist INGENIA mit den neusten Errungenschaften der PVD-Technologie ausgestattet. Sie besticht durch eine klare Formgebung, einfache Volumen und wertvermittelnde Materialien. Die Kombination von eloxiertem Aluminium mit den dunkel beschichteten Oberflächen verleiht der INGENIA eine zeitgemäße Präsenz im Hightech Bereich. Die großzügig angeordneten Griff- und Bedienelemente erlauben ein einfaches Handling der Anlage.

Oerlikon Balzers' INGENIA coating system delivers maximized performance and superb engineering expertise on a compact footprint. It outclasses conventional systems with respect to speed, precision, and flexibility. Moreover, INGENIA embodies the very latest state of PVD technology. It stands out with impressively sleek lines, appealing volumetric proportions, and high-grade materials. The combination of anodized aluminum and dark coated surfaces underscores the INGENIA's contemporary presence in hightech environments. Handling convenience is enhanced with intelligently configured operating elements.

PRODUCT
E5CC/E5EC Series
Temperaturausgleicher
Temperature controller

DESIGN
TAC design Inc.
Osaka, Japan

MANUFACTURER
OMRON Corporation
Kyoto, Japan

Die E5CC/E5EC-Produktfamilie stellt die nächste Generation von Temperaturreglern dar, die wir nun mit großer
Zuversicht anbieten. Sie verfügen über die beste Ables-
barkeit (aus größerer Entfernung und aus jedem Blickwinkel) auf dem Markt mit einem großen, außergewöhnlichen LCD-Display und weißer Hintergrundbeleuchtung.
Außerdem wurde die besondere Kundenvorliebe von
abgerundeten Kanten erstmalig designerisch umgesetzt. Ihre Regeleigenschaften sind trotz geringer Bau-
größe hervorragend. Die E5CC/E5EC-Produktfamilie
lässt sich über eine rastende Schnellmontage sogar
unter stark beengenden Einbauverhältnissen sehr einfach montieren.

*The E5CC/E5EC Series is the next-generation tempera-
ture controller, which we release with confidence. They
have the best visibility (visible from large distances and
from any angle) throughout the trade by big LCD with
the font peculiar to us and white backlight. Moreover,
we raised the affinity with the user's device by the round
design, which we adopted for the first time. Their control
performance is well and the size is small nevertheless.
The E5CC/E5EC series allow quick snap-mounting and
easy installation even under very cramped conditions.
And, use is very comfortable in the setting being simple
by Omron's CX-Thermo support software.*

PRODUCT
ToolCase
Werkzeugkasten
Tool case

DESIGN
raaco A / S
Nykøbing F., Denmark
Artlinco A / S
Horsens, Denmark

MANUFACTURER
raaco A / S
Nykøbing F., Denmark

Der raaco-ToolCase bietet kompromisslose Qualität von A bis Z. Die Kombination aus neuen Design- und Konstruktionsprinzipien, hochwertigen Materialien, umfassender Funktionalität und moderner Optik ist Garant für eine überlegene und nachhaltige Komplettlösung. Der Koffer ist mit Werkzeugpaneelen ausgestattet: Ein oder zwei austauschbare sind im Deckel montiert, ein festes Paneel im Unterteil. Die mehrfach kombinierbaren Paneele sind ein- oder beidseitig mit Einsteckfächern – entweder flexiblen Open-ToolFix-Werkzeughaltern oder strapazierfähigen Gummilaschen – versehen. Die Bodenschale kann durch raaco-Einsätze oder Trennwände unterteilt werden.

With raaco ToolCase you get outstanding quality from top to bottom. The combination of new principles in design and construction, high-quality materials, end-to-end functionality and streamlined design ensures a sustainable solution that´s ahead of the pack. The raaco ToolCase features tool panels – one or two detachable panels mounted in the lid and one permanent bottom panel. The tool panels are available in both single and double options and can be mixed across the various product types: with flexible Open ToolFix tool holders or open elasticized tool holders. The tray can be divided into small compartments using raaco inserts or dividers.

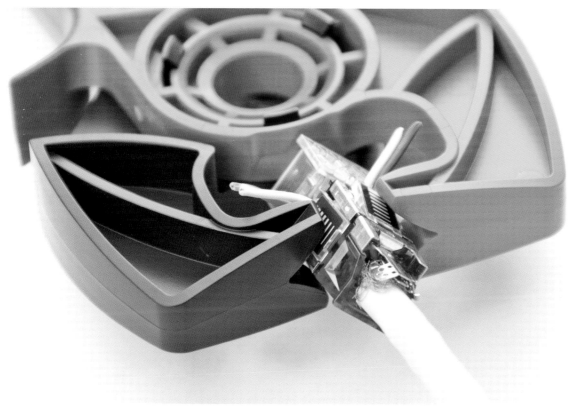

PRODUCT

Termination Tool
Ethernet-Beschaltungswerkzeug
Ethernet wiring tool

DESIGN

IPEK Institut für Produktdesign,
Entwicklung und Konstruktion
Ein Institut der Hochschule für Technik Rapperswil
Urs Egger
Rapperswil, Switzerland

MANUFACTURER

Reichle & De-Massari AG
Wetzikon, Switzerland

Beim Termination Tool handelt es sich um ein Spezial-werkzeug zur komfortablen Feldkonfektionierung von Ethernet Steckerbuchsen. Die prismenförmigen Zangen-backen erlauben die effiziente Beschaltung von allen acht Drähten gleichzeitig. Die frontale Anwendung und die großen Handgriffe ermöglichen langfristig ein ent-spanntes Arbeiten, selbst an schwer erreichbaren Stellen. Dank guter Balance von Form und Werkstoff konnte auf zusätzliche Verbindungselemente verzichtet wer-den. Das bringt ökonomische Vorteile und erleichtert späteres Recycling. Die Elemente rot und schwarz fügen sich gut ins Sortiment und Corporate Design des Her-stellers ein.

The Termination Tool is a special instrument for comfort-able tailoring of ethernet jacks. The prism shaped jaw allows efficient connection of all eight wires simultane-ously. Frontal appliance and large handles enable stress-free installation over long terms, even in demanding space situations. Thanks to a good balance of shape and material, no additional mechanical fastening elements were required. This is an economical advance and subse-quently facilitates recycling. The red and black elements integrate well into the product line and corporate design of the manufacturer.

PRODUCT

Ultra Slide Tools

Manuelles Werkzeug zur Rohrverbindung

Manual pipe joining tool

DESIGN

Intovision

Ron Cafri, Alexey Rubinchick

Petach-tikva, Israel

MANUFACTURER

Sagiv Ltd.

Kibbutz Mashabei Sade, Israel

Manuelles Rohrverbindungs-Tool für Innovative. Ultra Slide Fitting-System eignet sich für alle Arten von PEX und PE-RT Rohren. Viel Aufmerksamkeit wurde auf die Ergonomie hinsichtlich Benutzerfreundlichkeit gelegt. Kalibrierung oder vorheriges Abfackeln bzw. Bördeln sind nicht notwendig und sparen Zeit bei der Installation. Ein einziges Werkzeug kann für 16 - 32 mm große Rohre verwendet werden. Das Werkzeug ist aus widerstandsfähigen Materialien produziert und ausgewählt, um sowohl schonendes Handling zu gewährleisten als auch für extreme Betriebsbedingungen ausgelegt zu sein. Das Werkzeug hat weiche und starke Linien.

Manual pipe joining Tool for innovative. Ultra Slide pipe fitting system for all PEX & PE-RT pipe types. Much of attention was given to ergonomics for easy use with no need for calibration and pre-expansion of pipe edges and to save time on installation – a single tool is used for 16-32 mm pipes. Soft and strong materials, along with soft and strong lines, were chosen to suit both gentle handling and extreme operating forces.

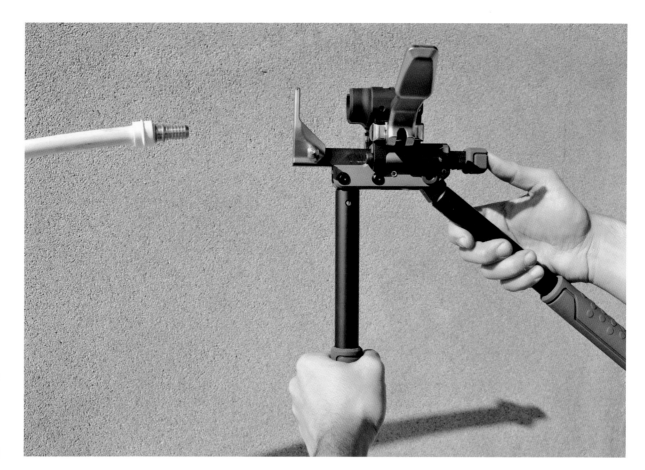

PRODUCT
RECS
Ladegerät für Elektrofahrzeuge
Electric car charger

DESIGN
SAMSUNG C & T
Seoul, South Korea

MANUFACTURER
SAMSUNG C & T
Seoul, South Korea
KODI-S
Kyungki-Do, South Korea

Die S-förmige Ladestation geht über das gewohnte Aussehen einer kastenförmigen Ladestation hinaus und spiegelt das Nutzerverhalten wider. Sie hat nicht nur eine elegante, stromlinienförmige Form mit einer formativen Vorder- und Seitenansicht, sondern bietet auch höchsten Bedienkomfort. Der Kontrast von hochglänzendem Schwarz und haarfeinem Silber vermittelt futuristische Sensibilität. Der LCD-Bildschirm auf Augenhöhe macht das Überprüfen des Ladezustands und des aktuellen Status in Echtzeit möglich.

This S-shaped charging station design goes beyond a conventional crude box shape and reflects the behavior of users. It has not only an elegant streamlined shape with a formative front and sides, but also provides convenient usability. The contrast between the high-glossy black and the hair-lined silver harbors futuristic refined feelings. The LCD screen at eye level allows users to check the charge level and the current status in real time. The RF card authentication function in the S-shaped folding section naturally guides behavior such as making payment.

PRODUCT

Floor air outlet
Belüftungssystem
Ventilation system

DESIGN

Shanghai BLLC Environment
Technology Co., Ltd.
Shanghai, China

MANUFACTURER

Shanghai BLLC Environment
Technology Co., Ltd.
Shanghai, China

Der Bodenluftauslass dient dazu, eine sinnvolle Luft-
verteilung von unten nach oben zu erzielen. Der Auslass-
kasten ist mit einem statischen Druckkasten versehen,
dank dem eine geringere Luftgeschwindigkeit und Geräuschentwicklung am Bodenluftauslass möglich sind.
Der Insektenschutz verhindert effektiv das Eindringen
von Fremdkörpern in die Luftleitung. Die Tiefe des Aus-
lasskastens kann je nach Bedingungen vor Ort geändert
und somit gut an die Anforderungen verschiedener
Kunden angepasst werden. Anders als bei herkömmlichen
metallischen Materialien wird hier durch verschleiß-
feste weiche Materialien die Verletzungsgefahr von
Personen vermieden.

*The floor air outlet is so designed to achieve reasonable
air distribution of bottom admission and top expulsion.
The outlet box is provided with a static pressure box,
which allows a lower air velocity and lower noise at floor
air outlet. The design of the mosquito screen effectively
prevents foreign objects from entering into the vent
tube. It is allowed to change the depth of outlet box
based on site conditions so as to adapt it to the demands
of different customers. Instead of traditional metallic
material, personal injury can be avoided by using wear-
resistant soft material.*

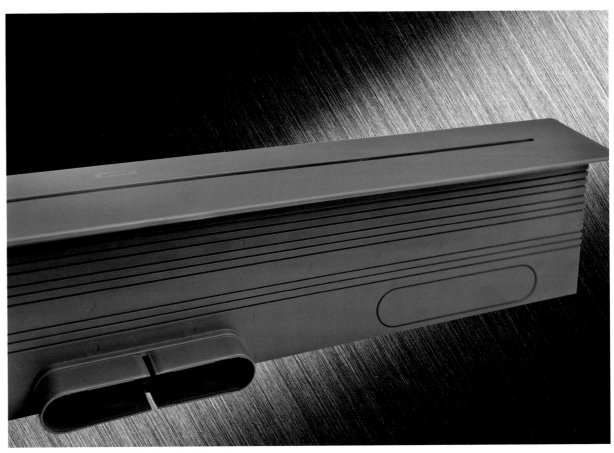

PRODUCT
VESTA
Sinterofen
Sintering furnace

DESIGN
Shimadzu Corporation
Kenji Asai (General Manager),
Jun Kawai (Industrial Design),
Yoshizako Mitsutomo (GUI Design),
Yurika Ichimaru (Graphic Design)
Kyoto, Japan

MANUFACTURER
Shimadzu Mectem, Inc.
Shiga, Japan

VESTA ist ein revolutionärer Druck-Vakuum-Sinterofen, der als Einstiegsmodell vorgesehen und auch von Anfängern leicht zu verstehen ist. Er wurde entworfen, um das Image von Sinteröfen als schmutzige und ölverschmierte Industriemaschinen zu beseitigen. Das simple und glatte Design ermöglicht den Transport in jeden Raum ohne Zerlegung, und die großen Temperaturanzeigen sowie der intuitive Sensorbildschirm gestatten die Überwachung des gesamten Betriebs auf einen Blick. Dank dem voll verstellbaren Monitor und der automatischen Tür kann nahezu jede Person in jeder möglichen Position mit diesem Gerät arbeiten.

VESTA is a revolutionary pressure vacuum sintering furnace, aimed as entry model and easy to be understood even by beginners. It was designed to overcome the image of sintering furnaces as dirty industrial machinery, covered in oil. The simplistic and smooth design makes it possible to move it into any room without disassembly, and the large temperature indicators as well as the intuitive touch screen allow to manage the entire operation at a single glance. The fully adjustable monitor and the automatic door make it be suitable to work with for just anybody in every possible position.

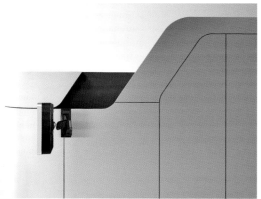

PRODUCT
deTec4
Sicherheits-Lichtschranke
Safety light beam device

DESIGN
2ND WEST | design for public
Michael Thurnherr, Manuel Gamper
Rapperswil, Switzerland

MANUFACTURER
SICK AG
Waldkirch, Germany

deTec4 – Hightech, auf das Wesentliche konzentriert.
Der Sicherheits-Lichtvorhang sichert auf höchstem
Schutzniveau Personen an Maschinen und Anlagen ab.
In modularen Schritten von 150 mm wird eine Schutz-
feldhöhe von 300 mm bis zu imposanten 2.100 mm
abgedeckt. Die Form des Profils ermöglicht eine un-
erreicht schnelle und intuitive Installation (stufenlose
Ausrichtung +/- 15°, freie Ausrichtung und Platzierung
der universellen Halter an beliebiger Stelle, Endkappe
als Anschlag). deTec4 bietet über die gesamte Profillänge
blindzonenfreien Schutz, ist extrem kompakt gebaut,
was eine problemlose Integration erlaubt – auch an
bestehenden Anlagen.

deTec4 – Hightech, focused on the essentials. The safety
light curtain protects persons at machines on a top safety
level. In modular steps of 150 mm height a protective
field height of 300 mm up to an impressive 2,100 mm
are covered. The shape of the profile allows an unmatched
quick and intuitive installation (smooth alignment +/- 15°,
free orientation and positioning of the universal brackets
at any spot, end cap as end stop). deTec4 gives you a
blind-zone-free protection over the entire profile length
and it is extremely compact. That allows a trouble-free
integration – as well in existing machines.

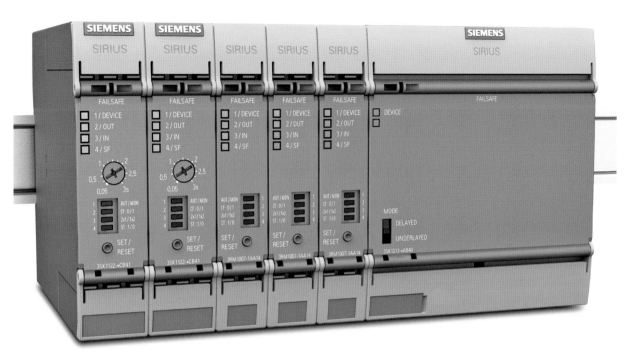

PRODUCT

SIRIUS F-Relais
Funktionale Sicherheitstechnik
Functional safety

DESIGN

at-design GbR
Christoph Tomczak
Fürth, Germany
Siemens AG, Industry Sector
Design Management
Frank Zeitler
Nürnberg, Germany

MANUFACTURER

Siemens AG, Industry Sector
Nürnberg, Germany

Das neue Gehäusekonzept für SIRIUS-Funktionsrelais verbindet neue Funktionen, hohe Automatisierungsfähigkeit und optimierte Bedienbarkeit bei kostenoptimierter Herstellung. Ziel des Industrial Design war es, die technischen Herausforderungen in ein systemübergreifendes, einheitliches Erscheinungsbild zu integrieren. Die Formgebung und Produktgrafik unterstützt die Bedienbarkeit der Produkte. Technische Innovationen wie Laserschneiden, sowie Laserbeschriftungsfonds optimieren den Herstellungsprozess und schaffen beste Bedienbarkeit auf kleinstem Raum.

The new housing concept for SIRIUS function relays combines new functions, a high automation capability, and optimized operability with cost-optimized production. The aim of the industrial design was to integrate the technical challenges into a uniform appearance for the entire system. The design and product graphics also support the operability of the products. Technical manufacturing innovations, such as laser cutting and special laser etching fonts, optimize the production process and create best operability in the smallest possible space.

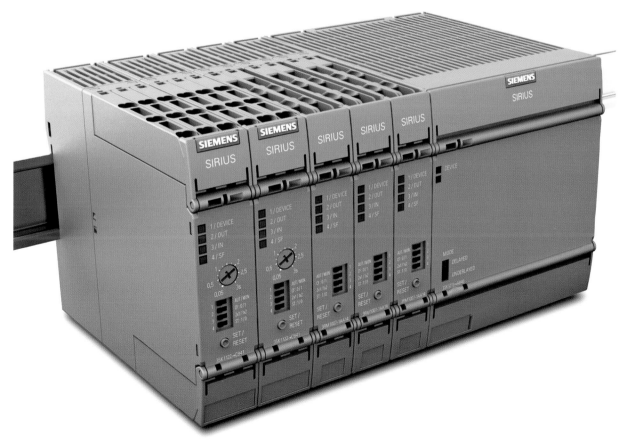

509

PRODUCT

SIMATIC ET 200SP

Automatisierungssystem

Automation system

DESIGN

at-design GbR

Jan Andersson

Fürth, Germany

Siemens AG, Industry Sector

Design Management

Birgit Leutner

Nürnberg, Germany

MANUFACTURER

Siemens AG, Industry Sector

Nürnberg, Germany

Die Siemens SIMATIC ET 200SP ist ein multifunktionales, modulares, fein skalierbares und äußerst kompaktes System für die dezentrale Automatisierung. Das Corporate Design konforme Industrial Design integriert das System schlüssig in die Produktlandschaft der Siemens Automatisierungslösungen. Um den geringen Platz in Schaltschränken optimal zu nutzen, sind die Module in ihrer Größe auf ein Minimum reduziert. Besondere Herausforderungen waren die Realisierung einer lesbaren Modulbeschriftung und die hohe Modulvarianz. Die Beschriftung wurde als „Tag-Nacht-Design" ausgeführt. Dadurch sind nur die benötigten Beschriftungen sichtbar.

The Siemens SIMATIC ET 200SP is a multifunctional, modular, finely scalable and extremely compact system for distributed automation. Its corporate design compliant Industrial Design logically integrates the system into the product portfolio of Siemens automation solutions. To make optimum use of the confined space in control cabinets, the size of the modules has been minimized. Special challenges were implementing legible module labeling and high module variance. The Product Graphics was implemented as a day-and-night design. In this way, only the necessary labels are visible.

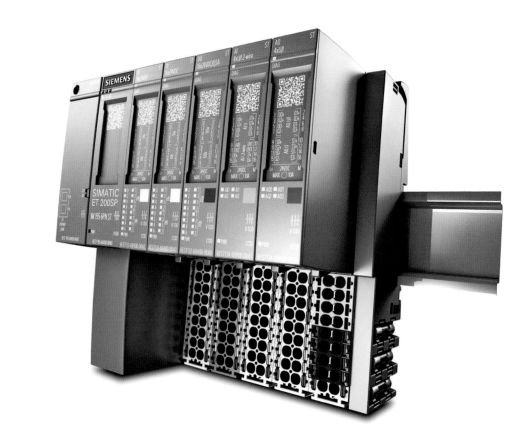

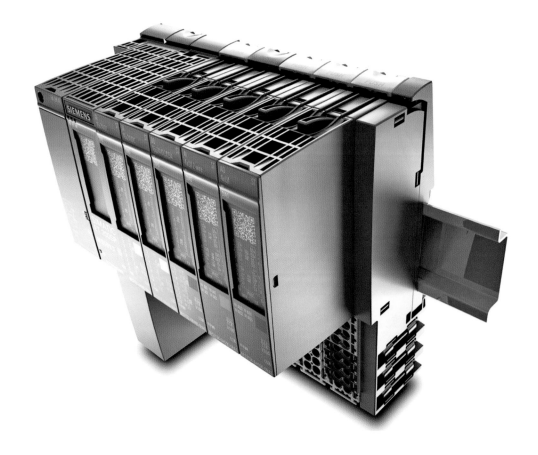

PRODUCT
SIMOGEAR
Grauguss-Kegelstirnradgetriebe
Cast iron bevel helical gear

DESIGN
at-design GbR
Jan Andersson
Fürth, Germany
Siemens AG, Industry Sector
Design Management
Birgit Leutner
Nürnberg, Germany

MANUFACTURER
Siemens AG, Industry Sector
Nürnberg, Germany

SIMOGEAR – das komplette Spektrum von Getriebe-
motoren in allen gängigen Getriebearten (Stirnrad-,
Kegelstirnrad-, Stirnradschnecken- und Flachgetriebe).
Ziel war es, dem Produktsystem durch präzise, technisch
orientierte Gestaltung ein deutliches Alleinstellungs-
merkmal zu verleihen. Durch gemeinsame Gestaltungs-
merkmale werden die unterschiedlichen Getriebetypen
über alle Baugrößen und Fertigungsverfahren hinweg
formal verbunden. Sie wirken durch feingliedrige und
trotzdem kraftvolle Gestaltung. Der Verlauf des Momen-
tums innerhalb der Gehäuse entlang des Antriebsstran-
ges wird durch charakteristische Flächen dargestellt.

*SIMOGEAR – the complete range of geared motors with
all common types of gear types (helical, helical bevel, helical worm, and parallel shaft gearing). The aim was to
give the product system a clear unique selling point by
the use of precise industrial aesthetics. Formally, the different types of gearing are connected across all frame
sizes by the specific use of design features. They impress
by their delicate but powerful design. The progression of
the momentum following the drive shaft in the housing
is represented by unique surface treatment.*

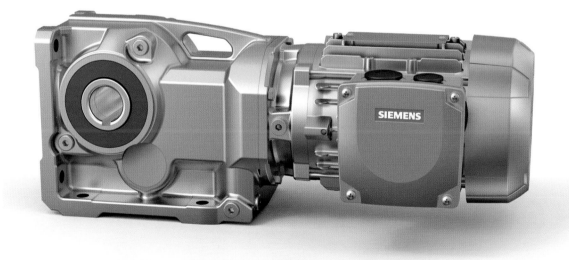

PRODUCT

SIMATIC S7-1500
Programmierbare Steuerung
Programmable logic controller

DESIGN

at-design GbR
Jan Andersson
Fürth, Germany
Siemens AG, Industry Sector
Design Management
Stephan Hühne
Nürnberg, Germany

MANUFACTURER

Siemens AG, Industry Sector
Nürnberg, Germany

Die SIMATIC S7-1500 ist das innovative Steuerungssystem für den Maschinen- und Anlagenbau. Mit bester Usability ist es bei höchster Performance künftig das Flaggschiff der Industrieautomation. Die Komponenten des Systems sind trotz variierender Funktion durchgängig gestaltet. Unverkennbar SIMATIC, aber charaktervoll eigenständig. Auf dem speziellen Trägersystem reihen sich die volumenoptimierten Bauteile side-by-side. Horizontal betonen die straff gewölbten Fronttüren das Ensemble. Vertikal sind die Bedien- und Anzeigeelemente pro Gerät angeordnet. Alle Schnittstellen sind sauber verdeckt.

The SIMATIC S7-1500 is the innovative control system for machine and plant assembly. With superlative usability and top performance, it will be the future flagship of Industry Automation. The components of the system are designed in an integrated way despite their varying functions. Unmistakably SIMATIC, but with a unique character. The volume-optimized components are lined up side by side on the special rack system. Horizontally, the tightly convex front doors emphasize the equipment as a unit while numerous operating and display elements of each device are arranged vertically. The interfaces are covered to provide a clean impression.

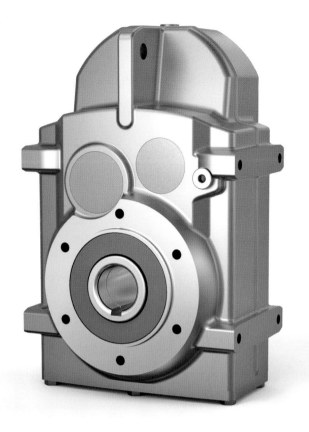

PRODUCT
SIMOGEAR
Grauguss-Flachgetriebe
Cast iron parallel shaft gear

DESIGN
at-design GbR
Jan Andersson
Fürth, Germany
Siemens AG, Industry Sector
Design Management
Birgit Leutner
Nürnberg, Germany

MANUFACTURER
Siemens AG, Industry Sector
Nürnberg, Germany

SIMOGEAR – das komplette Spektrum von Getriebe-motoren in allen gängigen Getriebearten (Stirnrad-, Kegelstirnrad-, Stirnradschnecken- und Flachgetriebe). Ziel war es, dem Produktsystem durch präzise, technisch orientierte Gestaltung ein deutliches Alleinstellungs-merkmal zu verleihen. Durch gemeinsame Gestaltungs-merkmale werden die unterschiedlichen Getriebetypen über alle Baugrößen und Fertigungsverfahren hinweg formal verbunden. Sie wirken durch feingliedrige und trotzdem kraftvolle Gestaltung. Der Verlauf des Momen-tums innerhalb der Gehäuse entlang des Antriebsstran-ges wird durch charakteristische Flächen dargestellt.

SIMOGEAR – the complete range of geared motors with all common types of gear types (helical, helical bevel, helical worm, and parallel shaft gearing). The aim was to give the product system a clear unique selling point by the use of precise industrial aesthetics. Formally, the dif-ferent types of gearing are connected across all frame sizes by the specific use of design features. They impress by their delicate but powerful design. The progression of the momentum following the drive shaft in the housing is represented by unique surface treatment.

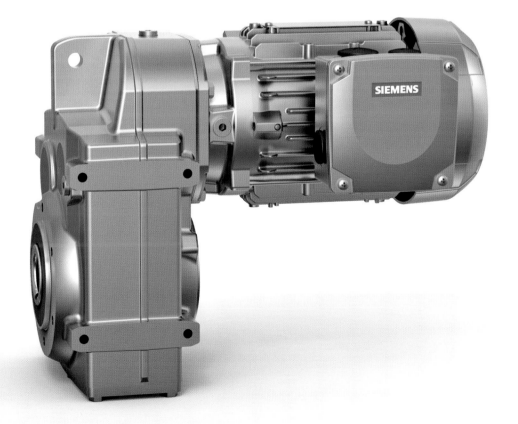

PRODUCT
RexcanCS
Industrieller 3-D-Scanner
Industrial 3D scanner

DESIGN
Korea University
MinSung Kwon
Seoul, South Korea

MANUFACTURER
Solutionix
Seoul, South Korea

Er ist einfach, smart, aber kräftig! Solutionix bringt eine neue 3-D-Scanning-Solution mit hoher Exaktheit zu einem ausnahmsweise vernünftigen Preis auf den Inspektions- und Metrologiemarkt. Rexcan CS ist als ein alleinstehender Typ erhältlich und kompakt, aber kräftig und ermöglicht Benutzern, ein exakteres und detaillierteres Daten-Set zu erhalten. Mit der aktuellsten blauen LED-Technologie und dem eingebauten Kontroller versehen, ist Rexcan CS für Qualitätskontrolle optimiert und verwendet eine Vielzahl von Applikationen wie reverse Engineering und Design. Sein Scanning-Volumen ist durch auswechselbare Linsen-Sets bis zu 400 mm flexibel.

It's simple, smart, yet powerful! Solutionix launches new high accuracy 3D scanning solution for inspection and metrology markets at an exceptionally reasonable price. Rexcan CS is available as a stand-alone type and compact yet powerful, enabling users to obtain more accurate and detailed scan data set. Equipped with the latest blue LED technology and built-in controller, Rexcan CS is optimized for quality control and use in a wide variety of applications such as reverse engineering and design. Its scanning volume is flexible up to 400 mm (diagonal) through interchangeable lense-sets.

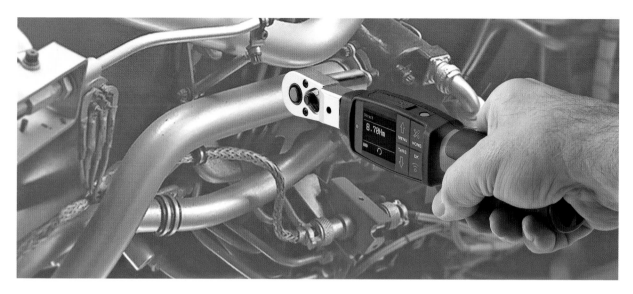

PRODUCT

MANOSKOP 714
Drehmoment- und Drehwinkelschlüssel
Torque and angle wrench

DESIGN

STAHLWILLE
Eduard Wille GmbH & Co. KG
Marco Theißen
Wuppertal, Germany

MANUFACTURER

STAHLWILLE
Eduard Wille GmbH & Co. KG
Wuppertal, Germany

Im MANOSKOP 714 vereint STAHLWILLE die Vorteile seiner elektromechanischen Drehmomentschlüssel und seiner präzisen Drehwinkelschlüssel mit einer komfortablen Softwarelösung zur individuellen Konfiguration und Dokumentation. Für eine benutzerfreundliche und sichere Bedienung können die Menüs per Software anwenderspezifisch aufgebaut werden. Die realisierten Schraubfalldaten werden im selbstleuchtenden Farbdisplay mit großem Ablesewinkel angezeigt und ermöglichen eine sofortige Bewertung. Eine extrem kompakte Bauform in Verbindung mit seitlichen Signalgebern unterstützt das präzise Anziehen auch in schwer zugänglichen Montagesituationen.

The MANOSKOP 714 by STAHLWILLE unites the advantages of electromechanical torque wrenches and the accuracy of angle wrenches with the convenience of user-friendly software for configuring the tool and documenting work processes. For user-friendly, safe operation, menus can be individually configured via the software. The readings for the current joint are displayed on the backlit color screen, which has a generous reading angle, to enable the joint to be immediately evaluated. This is an extremely compact construction, coupled with side-mounted signal transmitters to support accurate tightening even in hard-to-reach assembly sites.

PRODUCT
CenFlex1
Bandfinish-Maschine
Bandfinish machine

DESIGN
Design Tech
Ammerbuch, Germany

MANUFACTURER
Supfina Grieshaber GmbH & Co. KG
Wolfach, Germany

Das minimalistische Maschinendesign der CenFlex unterstützt die unternehmerischen Ziele, folgt dem ökologischen Gesamtkonzept und ist ergonomisch durchdacht bis ins Detail. Es macht den Superfinishing-Prozess markant sichtbar: Die geschwungene Form verleiht der Maschine hohe Wiedererkennbarkeit und differenziert sie gezielt und punktgenau vom Wettbewerb. Die versenkbaren Schiebetüren, eine Weltneuheit, fügen sich nahtlos in die Front aus dunklem Echtglas ein. Das Bedienpanel wird zum industrial Designmerkmal. Das Hydraulikaggregat erhielt eine technische Textilie mit geringem Gewicht und Materialeinsatz, die den Hightech-Charakter der Maschine unterstreicht.

The minimalist machine design of the CenFlex supports company goals, follows the overall ecological concept and is ergonomically thought-out down to the smallest detail. It is a striking visualization of the super finishing process. The flowing shape makes for high product identification and pointedly sets the machine off from competitors' products. The flush sliding doors – a world first – seamlessly fit into the front made of dark real glass. The operating panel becomes part of the industrial design. The hydraulic unit was fitted with a low-weight, material-saving textile casing that underlines the high-tech character of the machine.

PRODUCT
TKA55
Energieführungskette
Cable carrier system

DESIGN
TSUBAKI KABELSCHLEPP GmbH
Wenden-Gerlingen, Germany

MANUFACTURER
TSUBAKI KABELSCHLEPP GmbH
Wenden-Gerlingen, Germany

Das neue Designkonzept mit einer rundum geschlossenen Konstruktion, der TKA55, verhindert wirkungsvoll das Eindringen von Fremdkörpern. Eine optimierte Seitenband- und Deckelkontur verhindert effektiv Funktionsbeeinträchtigungen durch das Anhaften oder Eindringen von Spänen und Schmutz. Die formschlüssig neu gestalteten Deckel fügen sich nahtlos ineinander, ragen bis über die Seitenbänder und schließen mit ihnen ab. Dadurch bieten sie einen sicheren Halt, auch bei starken mechanischen Belastungen. Die glatte, schmutzabweisende Kontur der Seitenbänder lässt ebenfalls keine Fremdkörper eindringen. TKA – Design und Funktion im Einklang.

The new design concept features complete enclosure of the TKA55, effectively preventing foreign bodies from entering. An optimized sideband and cover shape effectively prevents functional impairments caused by chips and dirt entering into or sticking to the cable carrier. The compact new design of the covers allows them to fit seamlessly into one another, protruding over the sidebands to form a compact, closed unit. This ensures a secure grip even in the case of extreme mechanical loads. The smooth, dirt-repellent shape of the sidebands also prevents the intrusion of any foreign bodies. TKA – design and function at one.

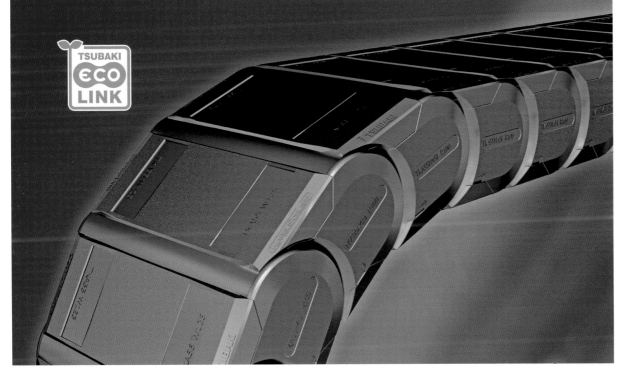

PRODUCT
UVEX Pheos Alpine
Kletter- und Arbeitschutzhelm
Safety and climbing helmet

DESIGN
LIO Design GmbH
Klaus Schindler, Sebastian Dröge, Christian Strohal
Braunschweig, Germany

MANUFACTURER
UVEX ARBEITSSCHUTZ GmbH
Fürth, Germany

Extrem leichter Multifunktionsschutzhelm für Höhen-
arbeit und Rettung. Der weltweit erste Helm, der sowohl die Anforderungen für Industrieschutzhelme (EN
397), als auch für Kletterhelme (EN 12492) erfüllt. Sport-
liches, schlankes Design reduziert Gewicht, entlastet
den Nacken und macht den UVEX Pheos Alpine zum
idealen Helm für Arbeiten in Höhe, engen Schächten
und Räumen. Ein umfassendes Zubehörprogramm von
Kopflampen, diversen Kinnriemen für unterschiedliche
Einsätze, eine Auswahl an Clips zum Anbringen von z. B.
Brillenband, Stift, Lampenkabel über Reflektorstreifen
bis hin zu abgestimmtem Gesichts- und Gehörschutz
vervollständigt den Helm.

*Extremely lightweight, multifunctional safety helmets for
working at heights and rescue work. The world's first helmet to fulfill the requirements of the certification for industrial safety (EN 397) and mountain climbing (EN 12492).
The sporty, sleek design reduces the weight and strain on
the neck, making the UVEX Pheos Alpine helmet perfect
for working in high areas and tight shafts or rooms. The
comprehensive range of accessories for the helmet includes
head lamps, chin straps for different applications, various
clips for holding and attaching eyewear cords, pens, lamp
cables, reflective strips and coordinated face and hearing
protection.*

PRODUCT
UVEX Pheos
Arbeitschutzhelm mit Brille
Safety helmet with spectacle

DESIGN
LIO Design GmbH
Klaus Schindler, Sebastian Dröge, Tim Schuhmann,
Christian Strohal
Braunschweig, Germany

MANUFACTURER
UVEX ARBEITSSCHUTZ GmbH
Fürth, Germany

Der UVEX Pheos ist weltweit der erste Arbeitsschutz-
helm mit patentierter Systemintegration einer bestehenden Schutzbrille. Die integrierte Brille erhöht den
Tragekomfort bei verbesserter Augenabdeckung
gegenüber Visieren und reduziert Augenverletzungen.
Der Quickrelease-Clip ermöglicht die schnelle Entnahme
der Schutzbrille zur Reinigung. Komplett von außen zu
bedienende Belüftungselemente sorgen für gutes
Helmklima und anwenderorientiertes Zubehör, wie
Stifthalter, Lampe, Gehörschutz passen den Helm den
Erfordernissen an. Optimierter Materialeinsatz reduziert Gewicht und macht den UVEX Pheos zu einem der
leichtesten Schutzhelme im Markt.

*UVEX Pheos is the world's first industrial safety helmet
with patented integrated safety eyewear. This increases
wearer comfort while providing better eye protection
than integrated visors and reducing risk of injury. The
quick release clip allows safety eyewear to be cleaned
swiftly. Climate inside the helmet can be regulated with
ventilation slits from the outside. User-oriented extras
such as pen holder, torch and hearing protection can be
fitted to meet requirements. The lower weight through
optimum material selection makes the UVEX Pheos one
of the lightest safety helmets on the market.*

PRODUCT
Mag-System
Bodenreinigungsgerät
Floor cleaning tool

DESIGN
Vermop Salmon GmbH
Michael Egger
Gilching, Germany

MANUFACTURER
Vermop Salmon GmbH
Gilching, Germany

Das Mag-System ist ein modulares, handgeführtes Boden-
reinigungssystem, das auf Grund seiner Einfachheit und
Vielseitigkeit für weltweites Aufsehen in der Reinigungs-
branche sorgt. Magnete im Halter und Metallplättchen
im Mop verbinden sich praktisch wie von selbst. Dies reduziert sowohl die erforderlichen Schulungsmaßnahmen
wie auch die Rüstzeit in den Räumlichkeiten. Das multifunktionale System ermöglicht dem Anwender mit nur
einer Stielaufnahme vier Moptypen aufzuspannen und
so diverse Reinigungsanwendungen abzudecken. Die
Reinigungskraft arbeitet stets rückenschonend und
kommt nicht in Kontakt mit dem verunreinigten Mop.

*The magnetic system is a modular, hand-operated floor
cleaning system, which furor due to its simplicity and
versatility for worldwide attention in the cleaning business. Magnets in the holder and metal disks in the mop
come together practically by themselves. This significantly reduces both the training necessary and the set-up
time in the premises. This multifunctional system allows
users to connect four types of mop for different cleaning
applications with only one handle. The cleaning staff
works always back-friendly and does not come in contact with the contaminated mop.*

PRODUCT
VOSS-Cap pro
Anstoßkappe
Bumpcap

DESIGN
raus+weber design
Simone Raus, Gabriel Weber
München, Germany

MANUFACTURER
VOSS-HELME GmbH & Co. KG
Burgwedel, Germany

Anstoßkappen sind durch integrierte Hartschalen die leichteste Art des professionellen Industriekopfschutzes, wo ein Schutzhelm nach EN 397 nicht vorgeschrieben, aber der Kopf durch scharfe und harte Kanten verletzungsgefährdet ist. Die VOSS-Cap pro erfüllt die erweiterte EU Richtlinie EN 812:1997+A1:2001 und schützt im Scheitel- und Schläfenbereich sicher vor Stoßverletzungen. Eine optimierte Verschlussführung und große Lüftungsquerschnitte führen neben dem eigenständigen Design, das die Schutzfunktion der VOSS-Cap pro betont, zu höchstem Tragekomfort und Produktakzeptanz dieser persönlichen Schutzausrüstung (PSA).

Its integrated hard shell makes the bump cap the lightest type of professional protective head gear not requiring a protective helmet in line with EN 397, but calling for head protection in order to prevent injuries from exposure to sharp and hard edges. The VOSS-Cap pro complies with the regulations of the extended EU Directive EN 812:1997+A1:2001 safely protecting skull and temples against impact injuries. Complimented by a distinct design visually emphasizing the protective features of the VOSS-Cap pro, the improved alignment of the lock system and large vent slots provide extremely comfortable fit and make for high product acceptance.

PRODUCT

WM4 NEXT
Photovoltaik-Steckverbinder
Photovoltaic plug connector

DESIGN

Weidmüller Interface GmbH & Co. KG
Detmold, Germany

MANUFACTURER

Weidmüller Interface GmbH & Co. KG
Detmold, Germany

Design in Funktionalität: stecken, drehen, fertig – Der vormontierte, einteilige Steckverbinder WM4 NEXT von Weidmüller ist intuitiv bedienbar. Speziell für die Direkt-verkabelung im Feld entwickelt, ermöglicht er eine schnelle und kostensparende Montage ohne zusätzliches Spezialwerkzeug. Hochwertige Verarbeitung und sichere Leistungsfähigkeit kombiniert mit intuitiver Bedienung garantieren zuverlässige Verbindungen von Wechselrichtern und Photovoltaikmodulen im Feld. Das Design verbindet technische Leistungsmerkmale mit effizienter Handhabung. Maximale Funktionalität – außergewöhnlich designt. Let's connect.

Design with functionality: plug in, rotate, done - The pre-assembled, single-component WM4 NEXT plug connector from Weidmüller is easy to operate. Developed especially for direct cabling in the field, the connector enables rapid and cost-saving assembly without the need for other special tools. High-quality workmanship and reliable performance, combined with intuitive operation, guarantee reliable connections for inverters and photovoltaic modules in the field. The design combines technical features with efficient handling. Maximum functionality – exceptional design. Let's connect.

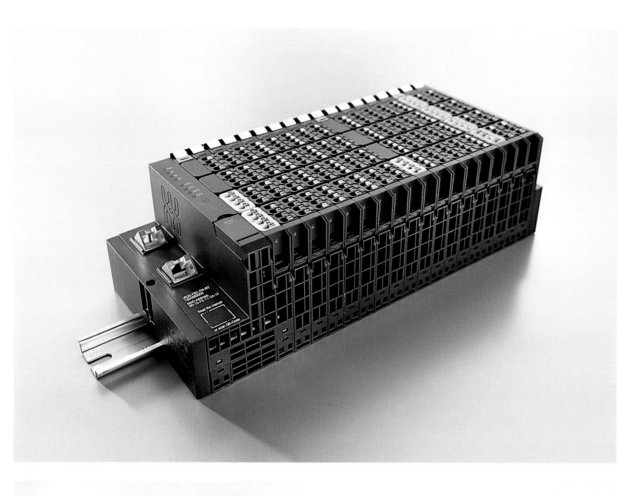

PRODUCT
u-remote
Remote System

DESIGN
Weidmüller Interface GmbH & Co. KG
Detmold, Germany

MANUFACTURER
Weidmüller Interface GmbH & Co. KG
Detmold, Germany

Das innovative Designkonzept von u-remote vereint Spitzen-Leistungsfähigkeit mit höchster Verdrahtungs-dichte und unerreichten Vorteilen zur Handhabung eines Remote I/O-IP20-Systems. Kleinere Schaltschränke, höhere Anlagenperformance und schnellere Installati-ons- und Wartungsarbeiten sind das Ergebnis des intelli-genten Konzeptes. Ob dreiteiliger Sandwichaufbau, werkzeuglose Installation, einreihige Anschlussleiste mit Status-LEDs oder das funktionsspezifische Farbkon-zept – bei u-remote sind alle Details auf Optimierung hin getrimmt. So wird Produktdesign als wesentlicher Treiber für spürbare Produktivitätssteigerungen wirk-sam.

The innovative design concept behind u-remote combines leading technical performance with highest-density wir-ing for a remote I/O IP20 system, along with unrivalled handling advantages. This intelligent concept results in smaller cabinets and higher system performance, as well as faster installation and maintenance work. Be it the three-part sandwich structure, the installation without tools, the single-row terminal block with status LEDs, or the function-specific color concept – with u-remote, all details are trimmed for optimization. The product design thus acts as an essential driver of tangible increases in pro-ductivity.

PRODUCT

JOKER (4er Satz)
Maul-Ringratschenschlüssel
Ratcheting combination wrench

DESIGN

Wera Werk Hermann Werner GmbH
Wuppertal, Germany

MANUFACTURER

Wera Werk Hermann Werner GmbH
Wuppertal, Germany

Alles, was ein Schlüssel können muss und noch viel mehr. Die Haltefunktion durch Metallplatte im Maul reduziert die Gefahr des Verlierens von Schrauben und Muttern. Anti-Abruthscheffekt: Die Doppelsechskant-geometrie sorgt für die formschlüssige Verbindung mit Schraube oder Mutter, zusätzlich sichert die auswech-selbare Metallplatte im Maul Schrauben und Muttern mit extra harten Zähnen. Der integrierte Endanschlag kann das Abrutschen vom Schraubenkopf nach unten verhindern und ermöglicht das Aufbringen hoher Dreh-momente. Der kurze Rückschwenkwinkel von nur 30° auf der Maulseite vermeidet das zeitintensive Wenden des Schlüssels beim Schrauben.

Everything that a wrench has to do, and a whole lot more: unique holding function, thanks to the metal plate in the jaw, reduces the risk of dropping nuts and bolts. Replaceable metal plate in the jaw secures nuts and bolts with its extra hard teeth and reduces the danger of slipping. Integrated limit stop prevents any slipping around the bolt head and allows higher torque to be applied; double-hex geometry makes for a positive con-nection with nuts or bolts and reduces the risk of slip-ping. Return angle of only 30° at the open end to avoid time consuming flipping of the wrench during fastening jobs.

PRODUCT

Wiha MagicFlip
Universal-Bithalter
Universal bit holder

DESIGN

Wiha Werkzeuge GmbH
Schonach, Germany

MANUFACTURER

Wiha Werkzeuge GmbH
Schonach, Germany

Durch seinen starken Neodym-Ringmagnet hält er selbst schwere Schrauben sicher fest. Er kann aber noch mehr: Ist der Schraubenkopf sauber versenkt, dann springt die Ringmagnethülse automatisch zurück und gibt die Sicht auf den Schraubenkopf frei. Der Anwender hat so die Wahl, ob er die Schraube gezielt weiter versenken möchte. Nicht bei jeder Anwendung ist die Ringmagnet-Funktion erforderlich. Falls gewünscht, kann der Ringmagnet manuell nach hinten geschoben und somit deaktiviert werden.

With its strong Neodym ring magnet it even securely holds heavy screws. But that's not all it can do. If the screw head is cleanly recessed, then the ring magnet sleeve automatically springs back, allowing a view of the screw head. Users can thus recess the screw further if desired. Not all applications need the ring magnet function. If desired, the ring magnet can be manually pushed back and in this way deactivated.

PRODUCT

Wiha BitBuddy

Bit-Box

Bit box

DESIGN

Wiha Werkzeuge GmbH

Schonach, Germany

MANUFACTURER

Wiha Werkzeuge GmbH

Schonach, Germany

Der BitBuddy ist die perfekte Ergänzung zu den neuen MaxxTor-Bits von Wiha. Er bietet sowohl dem 29er Torsionsbit als auch dem 49er Impact-Bit Platz. Der Bitwechsel mit nur einer Hand wird zum Kinderspiel. Die Bits werden direkt aus der Box in den Bithalter entnommen und wieder zurückgelegt – schnell, einfach, effizient. Zudem wird der Bit beim Wechsel des Abtriebs „automatisch" wieder in die „richtige Stelle" in der Box abgelegt. Der positive Nebeneffekt: mehr Ordnung, weniger verlorene Bits. Mit dem neuen Aufbewahrungssystem können die Bits direkt aus der Box in den Halter entnommen werden, was maximale Effizienz ohne Umwege garantiert.

The BitBuddy is the perfect complement to the new MaxxTor bits from Wiha. Changing bits with a single hand is child's play. It's impressive that the bits are removed directly from the box and inserted into the bit holder and replaced in the same way – quickly, easily, and efficiently. In addition, when exchanging the output, the bit is "automatically" returned to the "right spot" in the box. The positive side effect is more order and fewer lost bits. With the new storage system, the bits can be directly removed from the box and inserted into the holder, which guarantees maximum efficiency without any problems.

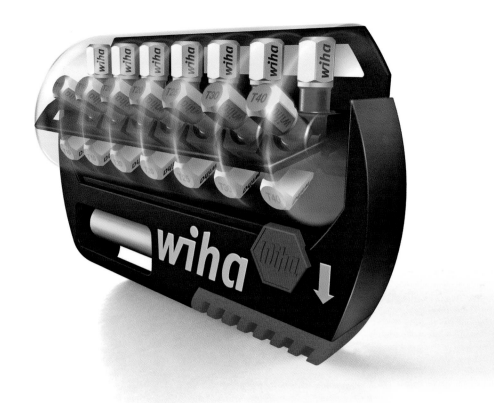

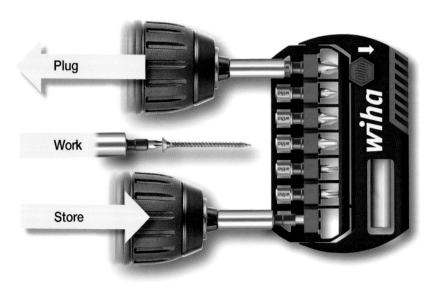

PRODUCT
Wiha MaxxTor-Bits
2-Komponenten-Bits
2-component bits

DESIGN
Wiha Werkzeuge GmbH
Gerd Heizmann
Schonach, Germany

MANUFACTURER
Wiha Werkzeuge GmbH
Schonach, Germany

Dank innovativer Zwei-Komponenten-Technologie gerüstet für steigende Anforderungen: Die MaxxTor-Bits bieten ein nie gekanntes Maß an Sicherheit und Lebensdauer. Leistungsstarke Bohr- und Schlagschrauber stellen hohe Ansprüche an Bits – beispielsweise durch veränderte Belastungsverläufe bei Impact-Schlagschraubern oder speziell harte Schraubfälle. Standard-Bits sind hier rasch überfordert. Nicht so die MaxxTor-Bits! Durch ihre maximale Torsionszone (MaxxTor) wird die Lebensdauer der Bits entscheidend verlängert. Ein weiterer Vorteil: Mit der Längenerweiterung von 25 auf 29 mm erreichen die Bits nun selbst tief liegende Schraubelemente gut.

Thanks to innovative 2-component technology, equipped for increasing demands: the MaxxTor bits offer a level of safety and service life unknown until now. High-performance drill and impact screwdrivers place tough demands on bits, for example via changing loads with impact screwdrivers or especially tough fastenings. Thus standard bits are quickly unable to meet the challenge. That's not the case with MaxxTor bits! With their maximum torsion zone (MaxxTor), the service life of the bits is significantly increased. A further plus factor: with length extension from 25 to 29 mm the bits now reach low-lying fastening elements.

PRODUCT

Wiha iTorque
Drehmomentschraubendreher
Torque screwdriver

DESIGN

Henssler & Schultheiss
Fullservice Productdesign GmbH
Schwäbisch Gmünd, Germany

MANUFACTURER

Wiha Werkzeuge GmbH
Schonach, Germany

Der erste Drehmomentschraubendreher seiner Art. Das „i" im iTorque repräsentiert die Eigenschaften dieser Novität: intelligent, innovativ und individuell. Als mechatronische Ausführung verbindet er eine hohe Präzision mit einer einfachen Handhabung. Der integrierte Zähler registriert jede Anwendung und zeigt deren tatsächliche Anzahl an. Zusammen mit der speziell festlegbaren Alarmfunktion wird dadurch die Prüfmittelüberwachung so leicht und individuell wie nie zuvor. Kunden können sowohl eine dauerhafte Belaserung mit individuellen Kundeninformationen sowie eine zuverlässige Rekalibrierung durch Wiha-Services in Anspruch nehmen.

The first torque screwdriver of its type. The "i" in iTorque stands for the new product's properties: it's intelligent, innovative and individual. As a mechatronic model, it combines high precision with simple handling. The integrated counter records each application and displays its actual number. In conjunction with the specially adjustable alarm function, testing equipment monitoring is now easier and more individual than ever before. Customers can use both permanent lasering with individual customer information and reliable recalibration by Wiha Services.

PRODUCT
Altendorf 2
Holzbearbeitungsmaschine
Woodworking machine

DESIGN
jojorama produktgestaltung GbR
Hannover, Germany

MANUFACTURER
Wilhelm Altendorf GmbH & Co. KG
Minden, Germany

Die Zeit ist reif für eine neue Altendorf – die Altendorf 2. Ein neues Sägen-Konzept, das das Beste aus drei Säge-systemen vereint: Von der Längsschnittsäge übernimmt die Altendorf 2 das komfortable Besäumen und Auf-trennen von Massivholz. Das verfahrbare und extrem leistungsstarke Sägeaggregat macht's möglich. Von der Plattensäge übernimmt sie das präzise Aufteilen von Plattenwerkstoffen. Die hohe Effizienz entsteht durch das verfahrbare Sägeaggregat, das integrierte Platten-aufteil-Programm und die zahlreichen Hilfsanschläge. Die Altendorf 2 ist die 3-in-1-Säge!

The time is ripe for a new Altendorf – for the Altendorf 2. A new cutting concept which unites the best of three types of saw in a single machine: Like a rip saw it trims and rips solid wood easily thanks to the movable and ex-tremely powerful saw unit. Like a beam saw it divides up panels precisely. And, thanks to the moveable saw unit, integral panel sizing program and many auxiliary fences, it does all of this highly efficiently. The Altendorf 2 is the 3-in-1 saw!

PRODUCT

TIMOS
Integrierte Post-Versand-Lösung
Integrated mailoutput solution

DESIGN

Braake Design
Stuttgart, Germany

MANUFACTURER

Winkler + Dünnebier GmbH
Neuwied, Germany
W+D Direct Marketing Solutions GmbH
Löhne, Germany

Die neue W+D-TIMOS (Totally Integrated Mail Output
Solution) ermöglicht die personalisierte und indivi-
dualisierte Briefumschlagherstellung, Bedruckung und
Kuvertierung (enveloped-on-the-fly), so schnell (15.000
Mails / h) und effizient wie eine E-Mail. Das neue modular aufgebaute Housing mit den signifikanten Designele-
menten spiegelt dabei den Prozesslauf der einzelnen
Produktionsschritte nach außen wider. Hervorragenden Einblick in den gegenläufigen Prozessfluss auf zwei
Ebenen bieten die großen Glashauben und partielle
Glasfronten. Die neu entwickelten Bedienterminals gewährleisten die intuitive Prozesskontrolle an jedem Bereich der Maschine.

*As the world's leading technology solution partner W+D
offers a wide range of integrated systems for the mail industry. The new W+D TIMOS (Totally Integrated Mail Output Solution) is designed for the personalized production
of envelopes, printings and enveloped-on-the-fly, as fast
(15,000 mails / h) and efficient as an e-mail. The new
modular housing with its significant design reflects the
workflow of the innovating production process. The large
transparent glass hoods and glass fronts give ideal view to
the complex two-level reverse process engineering. The
new interfaces (HMI) allow an intuitive control at every
area of the machine.*

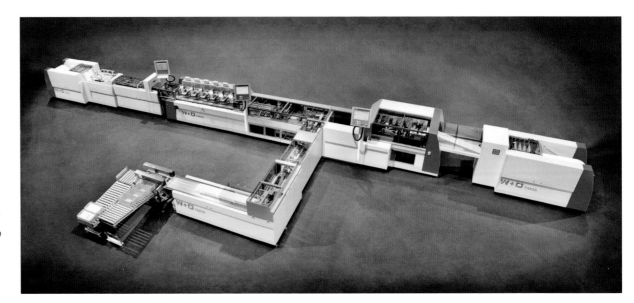

PRODUCT
i1Pro 2
Spektralphotometer
Spectrophotometer

DESIGN
formmodul
Guido Max Franzke, Detlef Fischer
Sassenberg, Germany

MANUFACTURER
X-Rite GmbH
Neu-Isenburg, Germany

Das universelle Farbmessgerät dient der Kalibrierung und Profilierung von Druckern, Displays oder Projektionen, unterstützt die Digitalisierung von Farbmustern oder misst das Umgebungslicht in der Fotografie. Das Messsystem besteht aus dem eigentlichen Spektralfotometer sowie einer Reihe von Zubehörteilen. Die Gestaltung zeigt eine klare Formensprache, durch die das Messgerät und die zahlreichen Zubehörteile visuell als Einheit erscheinen. Der konsequente Einsatz von Aluminium, die mattierten Oberflächen, aber auch die sachlich reduzierte Formgebung unterstreichen den Anspruch auf Präzision und Qualität.

This versatile color-measurement device, which is used for the calibration and profiling of printers, displays and projectors, supports the digitalization of color samples and the measurement of ambient light in photography. The system consists of a spectrophotometer and various accessories. The design features a clear language of form that turns the measurement device and its numerous accessories into one visual entity. The consistent use of aluminum and matte surfaces, together with the reduced and serene design, emphasize the high demands of precision and quality.

PRODUCT

stripperdriver

Schraubendreher

Screwdriver

DESIGN

YIH CHENG FACTORY Co., Ltd.

Nantuo, Taiwan

MANUFACTURER

YIH CHENG FACTORY Co., Ltd.

Nantuo, Taiwan

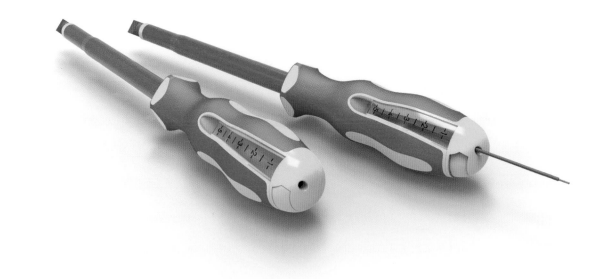

Der VDE-geprüfte sog. „Abisolier-Schraubendreher"
vereinigt drei verschiedene Werkzeuge für den Elektriker:
Schraubendreher, Draht-Abisolierer und Drahtbieger.
Abisolieren: Draht bis zur gewünschten Länge in den
Griff schieben (Maßskala benutzen) und durch Knopf
am Griffende fixieren. Durch Drehen und gleichzeitiges
Drücken des Griffes wird der Draht abisoliert. Draht aus
dem Griff nehmen, das abgeschnittene Isolierteil fällt
heraus. Biegen: Der Abisolierknopf kann zum Biegen
eines Drahtes benutzt werden (siehe Skizze). Mit diesem
Werkzeug können Sie drei Arbeitsgänge ausführen, was
Überkopfarbeiten sehr erleichtert.

*The VDE screwdriver stripperdriver combines three prac-
tical tools for the electrical work: screwdriver, wire stripper, and wire bender. With the special ruler and blade
design, it's ideal to strip wire: insert the wire into the
handle until reaching the certain scale, fix it by the stripper button, rotate the handle while applying pressure to
the button in order to make a cut around the insulation.
Once the device is clamped on, the remainder of the
wire can simply be pulled out. The stripper button can
also be used to fix and bend the wire. With this 3 in 1
tool, it can be light and portable as far as the overhead
work is concerned.*

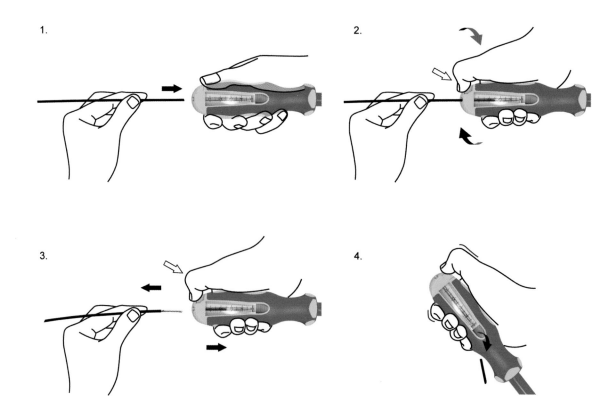

1.

2.

3.

PRODUCT
Non-touch
Werkzeugkasten
Tool box

DESIGN
YIH CHENG FACTORY Co., Ltd.
Nantuo, Taiwan

MANUFACTURER
YIH CHENG FACTORY Co., Ltd.
Nantuo, Taiwan

Non-touch ist eine neu entwickelte Werkzeugbox, die infolge seines ästhetischen und ergonomischen Designs sicher und bequem in der Hand gehalten werden kann. Wird der Deckel geöffnet, stehen die Bits senkrecht und können mittels einer speziellen Verriegelung am Bithalter durch Drehen einfach und schnell aus der Bitleiste entnommen und danach wieder in die Bitleiste zurückgesteckt werden. Der Bithalter wird vorn in die Box gelegt, so dass beim Schließen des Deckels zwei Klinken den Bithalter verriegeln. Ist der Bithalter nicht so eingelegt, kann der Deckel nicht geschlossen werden. Damit kann das Werkzeug nicht versehentlich verloren gehen.

Non-touch is an innovative tool box. With the esthetic and ergonomic design, it can fit in the palm and stay comfortable while holding. When the lid is open, the bits fixture rises along with it. With the special latch design, the user can easily grip the bit upright by rotating the tool handle and after use, the bit can be simply pulled out by putting back to the storage. The front end of the box has a storage space for the handle. When closing, the two latches inside of the lid firmly withhold the handle as a locking device. If the handle is not in place, the lid can't be closed. It will remind the user not to loose the product after use.

SPECIAL VEHICLES / CONSTRUCTION / AGRICULTURE

WERNER AISSLINGER
SYLVIA FEICHTINGER
SAM LIVINGSTONE
CHARLOTTE SJÖDELL
ACHIM STORZ

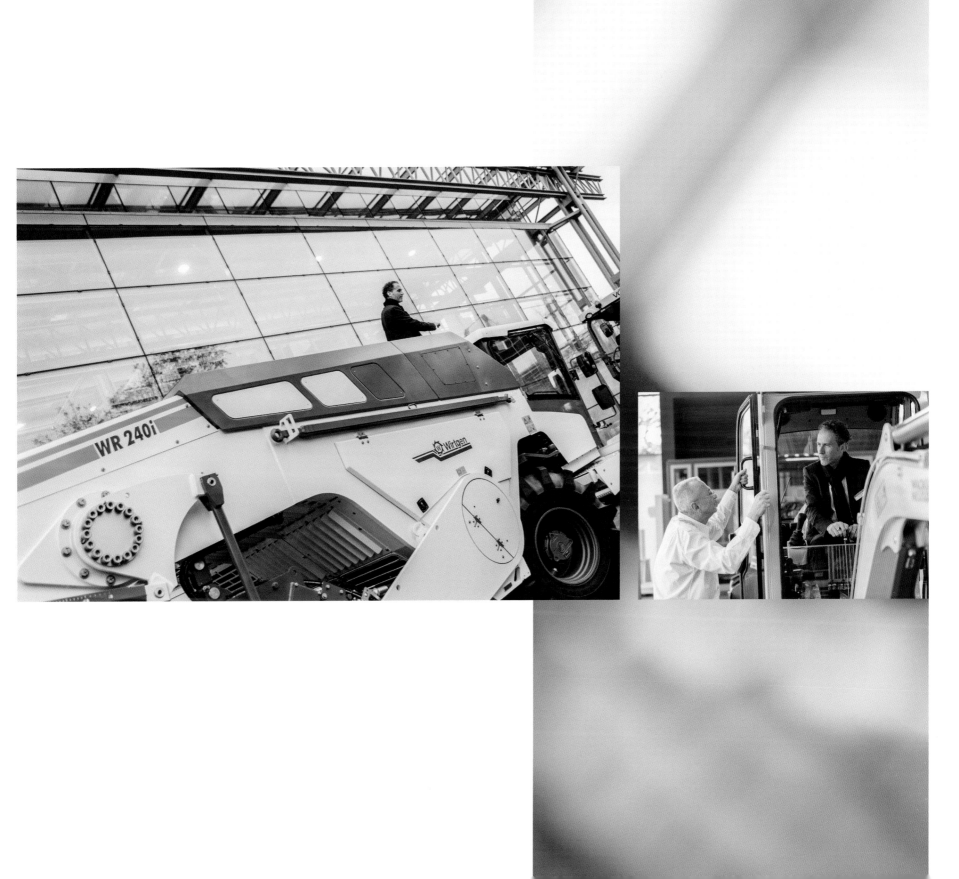

PRODUCT
WIRTGEN WR 240
Kaltrecycler
Cold recycler

DESIGN
Budde Industrie Design GmbH
Münster, Germany

MANUFACTURER
WIRTGEN GmbH
Windhagen, Germany

Die WR 240 ist ein Kaltrecycler, der selbst im schwierigen Gelände in der Lage ist, den Boden so zu stabilisieren, dass dieser als Piste auch für schweres Gerät dienen kann. Alle Baugruppen sind auf optimale Arbeit und Wartungsfähigkeit ausgelegt. Die Kabine vor der Vorderachse der Maschine ist um 400 mm nach rechts aus der Maschinenkontur heraus verfahrbar, um in Kombination mit dem um 90° schwenkbaren Fahrerstand beste Sicht auf die Arbeitsaggregate zu bieten. Die Kabine ist eine Neuentwicklung, bei der die Ergonomie und der Fahrerkomfort höchste Priorität hatten. Die ganzheitliche Gestaltung lässt die Leistungskraft und Variabilität spüren.

The WR 240 is a cold recycler and soil stabilizer, capable of converting soil of poor bearing capacity into fully pre-compacted construction material, carrying even heavy vehicles. All components have been optimized with work and maintainability in mind. The cabin in front of the leading axle can be moved 400 mm beyond the right edge of the machine. In combination with a swiveling of the driver's seat of 90°, the best view of the working components is achieved. The spacious cabin has been completely redesigned, focusing on ergonomics and operator comfort. The holistic design conveys the machine's power and its multitasking-abilities.

„Es ist erstaunlich, wie sehr bei diesem Gerät auf Details geachtet wurde, zumal es sich um eine Arbeitsmaschine handelt – ein bisher immer noch sehr benachteiligter Bereich. Alle Einzelteile sind sehr schön gestaltet, die Zusammensetzung der verschiedenen Materialien ist innovativ und ergonomisch bis in die letzte Anordnung durchdacht. In der Kategorie der Arbeitsmaschinen sticht der Kaltrecycler einfach heraus und verdient einen iF gold award!"

"The attention to detail in this appliance is striking, particularly since it is a special vehicle, an area that is still largely neglected. All of the individual elements are very handsome, while the configuration of the different materials has been thoroughly thought through to ensure the innovative and ergonomic nature of the product. In the category of special vehicles machines, the cold recycler simply stands out among the rest and deserves an iF gold award!"

JURYSTATEMENT

PRODUCT

AL-KO

Kotflügel-System

Mudguard system

DESIGN

designship

Thomas Starczewski, Michael Fürstenberg

Ulm, Germany

MANUFACTURER

ALOIS KOBER GmbH

Kötz, Germany

Das System ist ein Novum im Markt! Zentrale Kompo-
nente ist der multifunktionale Kotflügel, an dem unterschiedliche Systemkomponenten angedockt werden.
Gängige Kunststoffkotflügel sind, als Trittstufe zweck-
entfremdet, gefährlich! Sie halten dem Körpergewicht
nicht stand. Verletzung droht durch Verformung des
Kotflügels und Abrutschen auf der glatten Oberfläche.
Mit den additiven, solide ausgeführten Systemkomponenten „Trittfläche", „Aufstiegshilfe" und „Infofläche"
schafft AL-KO ein Plus an Sicherheit und Komfort.
Stilelemente wie überspannte Flächen und markante
Fasen charakterisieren die dynamische neue AL-KO-
Produktlinie.

*The system is a novelty in the market! Central component
is a multi-functional mudguard, which different system
components are docked to. Common plastic mudguards
are often misused as a step: dangerous! They don´t stand
a human weight. With the risk of deformation of the
mudguard and slipping on the smooth surface. With the
additive, solid system components „tread", climbing aid"
and „branding area" AL-KO creates a plus on safety and
comfort. Style elements such as spanned surfaces and
distinctive chamfers characterize the dynamic new AL-KO
product line.*

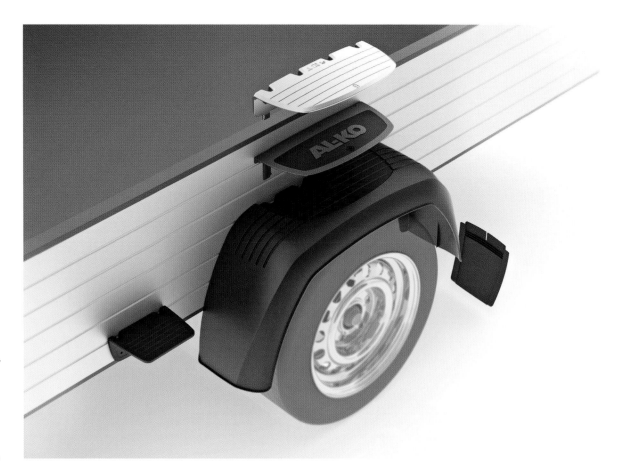

PRODUCT

CLAAS LEXION 780

Mähdrescher

Combine harvester

DESIGN

Budde Industrie Design GmbH

Münster, Germany

MANUFACTURER

CLAAS SE GmbH

Harsewinkel, Germany

Neue Generation des leistungsstärksten Mähdreschers der Welt jetzt mit „Tier IVi"- Motorentechnik. Sein innovatives Kühlsystem baut einen Luftschleier zwischen der Arbeitsstaubwolke und der Frischluftansaugung auf und hält sich so fit für neue Rekorde. Die formintegrierten seitlichen Luftaustritte stehen hierfür Pate. Die Karosserie ist komplett überarbeitet und zeigt trotz seiner sehr kompakten Breite von nur drei Metern, dass der LEXION der Primus ist. Den knapp 1,7 m großen Hinterrädern wurde durch entsprechende Freischnitte der Bewegungsraum gegeben um auch auf schwierigstem Terrain eine gute Figur zu machen.

The next generation of the world's most powerful combine harvester, now meeting "Tier IVi" requirements. Its ground-braking cooling system separates the cloud of dust at work and the fresh air intake by means of an air-curtain, keeping in shape for new records. The lateral air outlets visualize this innovation. The body has been completely redesigned, highlighting LEXION's role as the leader, despite its narrow width of just three meters. The designers have foreseen sufficient space for the movement of the rear wheels, each measuring nearly 1.7 meters, helping LEXION to make a good appearance even in the most demanding terrain.

PRODUCT

Serie H ROPS
Walzenzug
Single drum roller

DESIGN

Dialogform GmbH
Ulrich Ewringmann, Boris Eickhoff
Taufkirchen, Germany

MANUFACTURER

HAMM AG
Tirschenreuth, Germany

HAMM H-Serie als ROPS-Version. Das Erscheinungsbild der neuen H-Serie wird durch die ROPS-Version nachhaltig mitgeprägt. Für die offene Version wurde deshalb neben der Kabinenversion ein adäquat einprägsames Erscheinungsbild entwickelt. Der ROPS-Walzenzug mit ECO-Mode entspricht den strengsten US-Emissionsnormen (Tier 4). Der offene Fahrerstand wurde in Einklang mit den US-Sicherheitsnormen entwickelt. Alle Bedien- und Anzeigenelemente entsprechen der Kabinenversion, sie sind nach aktuellen ergonomischen Gesichtspunkten Fahrer orientiert, intuitiv und sprachneutral bedienbar, sodass man im Betrieb problemlos und sicher damit zurechtkommt.

Open ROPS version of HAMM H Series compactors. It is specifically the ROPS version that will significantly influence the image of the new H-Series. A unique design was developed for the open version too, distinguishing the machines as HAMM compactors. The ROPS compactors with ECO Mode complies with US norms (Tier 4). The open driver's platform has been developed in conformity with current US specifications, all safety aspects have been implemented. The operation and display elements are equivalent to the cab version, designed ergonomically with intuitive and language-neutral symbols. Drivers will easily operate this without difficulty.

PRODUCT
SUPER 2100-3
Asphaltfertiger
Road paver

DESIGN
Dialogform GmbH
Ulrich Ewringmann, Boris Eickhoff
Taufkirchen, Germany

MANUFACTURER
Joseph Vögele AG
Ludwigshafen, Germany

Mit der neuen „Strich 3"-Generation wird die Arbeit für das Bedienpersonal noch einmal wesentlich vereinfacht. Das Antriebssystem sorgt mit mehr Leistungsreserven für stark reduzierte Geräusch- und Schadstoffemissionen (erfüllt TIER 4i). Das intuitive ErgoPlus-Bediensystem wurde um viele ergonomisch funktionale Details erweitert (z. B.: neues Interface-Design). Ein „PaveDock Assistent" übernimmt mit Signalampeln die Kommunikation zwischen Bediener und dem Fahrer des Mischgut-LKW. Das Maschinendesign ist, bis hin zu den Bohlen, fertigungsoptimiert und unterstreicht die kraftvolle Dynamik der neuen Maschinenreihe.

The new "Dash 3" generation simplifies the work of the operating team. The drive system ensures higher efficiency, lower noise levels and lower exhaust emissions (TIER 4i). Its Ergo Plus-system is developed with numerous additional ergonomic and functional advantages, including a new interface design. With its signal lights the new developed "PaveDock Assistant" simplifies the communication between paver operator and driver of the feed lorry. The overall design – including the screed – is production-optimized and shows the powerful dynamic of the new machine range.

PRODUCT
P4001 V-FLOW
Milchmengenmessgerät
Milk meter

DESIGN
Indes
Enschede, Netherlands
N.V. Nederlandsche Apparatenfabriek NEDAP Agri
Groenlo, Netherlands

MANUFACTURER
N.V. Nederlandsche Apparatenfabriek NEDAP Agri
Groenlo, Netherlands

Die derzeitigen Geräte zur Erfassung des Milchertrags messen die Milchleistung einzelner Tiere (Kühe, Ziegen, Schafe und Büffel) volumetrisch anhand konventioneller Methoden wie Füllen und Leeren von Messkammern oder Füllstandsmessung mittels Leitfähigkeitssonden. Nachteile dieser Methoden: relativ großes Messgerät, schmutzempfindlich, Verschleiß durch bewegliche Teile, Behinderung von Luft (Vakuum) und Milchfluss. Das neue V-Flow Milchmengenmessgerät von Nedap nutzt optische Abtasttechnologie sowie intelligente Software und eliminiert all diese Nachteile. Ergebnis: ein kleines, wartungsfreies Gerät mit tollem Design.

Actual milk yield recording devices measure milk production of individual animals (cows, goat, sheep and buffalo) volumetrically using conventional technologies such as fill and dump measuring chambers and / or level measuring using arrays of conductivity probes. Disadvantages using these technologies: relatively large size of the meter, sensitivity for pollution, wear due to moving parts, obstruction of both air (vacuum) and milk flow. The new Nedap V-Flow milk meter uses optical sensing technology combined with smart software and eliminates all these disadvantages. Result: a small, nicely designed and maintenance free flow device.

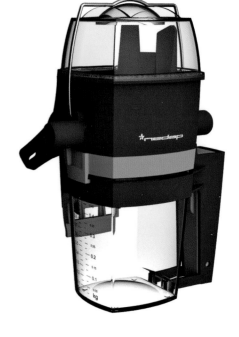

ALT / OLD

NEU / NEW

ELi2 Euro**Landträger** –
Freie Sicht nach vorne
ELi2 Euro**Fork**Carrier
Unobstructed front view

PRODUCT
ELI2
Euro-Landträger
Euro fork carrier

DESIGN
VETTER Umformtechnik GmbH
Burbach, Germany

MANUFACTURER
VETTER Umformtechnik GmbH
Burbach, Germany

Bisherige Palettengabeln für Frontlader haben sehr volu-
minöse Aufhängungen und bieten nur schlechte Sicht
auf Gabelzinken und transportiertes Gut. Der ELI2 Euro-
Landträger hingegen hat ein nach modernsten Gesichtspunkten optimiertes Design. Die Aufhängung als
Schmiedeteil bietet höchste Festigkeit und Tragfähigkeit der Palettengabel. Die Ausführung erfolgt in Indus-
triestandard: mit 3-facher Sicherheit, dynamisch getestet und höchster Schweißqualität nach DIN 18800-7.
Nach Einführung zur Agritechnica im November 2009
ist der ELI2 mit geschmiedeter Aufnahme zum Quali-
tätsmerkmal und Markenzeichen der VETTER-Paletten-
gabeln geworden.

Conventional pallet forks for front loaders have volumi-
nous suspensions and a poor visibility on forks and trans-
ported loads. The ELI2 Euro fork carrier, on the other
hand, has an advanced and optimized design. The sus-
pension as forged component offers highest stability
and load capacity of the pallet fork. The design complies
with industry standard: triple safety, dynamically tested
and highest welding quality acc. to DIN 18800-7. After
launching at the Agritechnica in November 2009, the
ELI2 with forged adapter has quickly become a quality
feature and trademark of VETTER pallet forks.

PRODUCT
A40F
Knickgelenkter Dumper
Articulated hauler

DESIGN
Volvo Construction Equipment
Brussels, Belgium

MANUFACTURER
Volvo Construction Equipment
Brussels, Belgium

Der A40F bringt die einzigartige Flexibilität eines Volvo-Dumpers zum Ausdruck. Das beeindruckende Äußere dieser Baumaschine spiegelt unmittelbar die hohe Leistung, Produktivität, Stärke und Langlebigkeit wider. Mit dem niedrigsten Kraftstoffverbrauch seiner Klasse, hervorragender Rundumsicht und einem ergonomisch gestalteten Arbeitsplatz des Fahrers mit leicht erreichbaren Bedienelementen ist es offenkundig, dass Volvos Kernwerte Qualität, Sicherheit und Umweltschutz bei dieser Konstruktion von ausschlaggebender Bedeutung waren.

Volvo Construction Equipment's A40F articulated hauler maneuvers, travels and dumps its load in the most efficient and safest way. The machine features improvements in design, functionality and maintenance and expresses the unique speed, balance and flexibility of a Volvo hauler. The A40F's imposing appearance is a direct reflection of its high performance, productivity, strength and durability. With class-leading low fuel consumption, all-around visibility and an ergonomically designed operator station featuring easy to reach controls, it's clear that Volvo's core values of quality, safety and environmental care have driven this design.

PRODUCT

HSG II
Schienenschleifzug
Rail grinding train

DESIGN

zweigrad GmbH & Co. KG
Hamburg, Germany

MANUFACTURER

Vossloh Rail Services GmbH
Seevetal, Germany

Der HSG II von Vossloh Rail Services ist ein Schleifzug zum Hochgeschwindigkeitsschleifen von Eisenbahnschienen. Durch seine weltweit einzigartige Technologie schleift der HSG II mit einer Betriebsgeschwindigkeit von 80 km / h Schienen, hält das Schienennetz instand und verhindert somit die Entstehung von Schienenfehlern - und das bei laufendem Fahrplan. Mit dem betont kraftvollen und dynamischen Design werden die Kerneigenschaften des Zuges, Leistungsfähigkeit und Geschwindigkeit, eindrucksvoll visualisiert. Darüber hinaus ermöglicht die flächige Formensprache die Anforderungen der Kleinstserienproduktion auf ökonomische Art und Weise.

The HSG II from Vossloh Rail Services utilizes a unique technology in order to enable the grinding of rails at a speed of 80 km / h, which is approx. 10 times faster than with conventional grinding trains. So called preventative grinding ensures that rail faults which could require expensive maintenance measures do not arise. Because of its high grinding speed, HSG II can fit into existing train timetables. The accentuated powerful and dynamic design expresses the key characteristics of the train – efficient performance and speed – in a striking way. The two-dimensional stylistic elements meet the requirements of small series production.

PRODUCT
ET20
Kompaktbagger
Compact excavator

DESIGN
Wacker Neuson Linz GmbH
Hörsching, Austria

MANUFACTURER
Wacker Neuson Linz GmbH
Hörsching, Austria

Der ET20 zeichnet sich durch geringste Abmessungen bei maximalem Kabinenkomfort aus. Ein breiter, niedriger Einstieg sowie großzügige Platzverhältnisse im Inneren machen das Arbeiten zum Vergnügen. Mit einem sehr eigenständigen Charakter präsentiert sich das Design des ET20: Kabinenrahmen und Chassis bilden eine Art „schwungvolles Exoskelett", das vor Beschädigung schützt, die Flächen sinnvoll strukturiert und einen robusten Eindruck vermittelt. Der Heckdeckel öffnet weit und gibt den Wartungsbereich großzügig frei. Die seitlichen Blenden sowie die darunter liegenden Chassisabdeckungen sind mit wenigen Handgriffen demontierbar.

The ET20 distinguishes itself through its small dimensions coupled with maximum cabin comfort. A wide, low entrance, as well as generous interior space, make work a pleasure. With its very distinct character, the design of the ET20 presents itself: The cabin frame and chassis create a kind of "bold exoskeleton," which protects the machine from damage, structures the surfaces sensibly, and conveys a robust appearance. The rear hood opens wide, amply exposing the maintenance area. The side panels, as well as the chassis covers below these, are easily removable by hand.

PRODUCT
650
Radlader
Wheel loader

DESIGN
Kramer Werke GmbH
Pfullendorf, Germany

MANUFACTURER
Kramer Werke GmbH
Pfullendorf, Germany

Der kompakte Radlader 650 besticht durch seine markante Linienführung. Der Schwung der Haube findet seine Fortsetzung in der Kabine. Die voluminösen, in der Breite verstellbaren Kotflügel verleihen ihm ein stämmiges Auftreten. Das Heck der Maschine wird dominiert durch einen v-förmigen Kühlergrill, der in Kombination mit den schräg stehenden Leuchten-Vertiefungen eine kraftvolle Heckansicht erzeugt. Massive Guss-Stoßfänger an den hinteren Ecken schützen vor Beschädigung. Sie sind zu den Ecken hin hochgezogen, um einen maximalen Böschungswinkel zu ermöglichen. Die Befestigungsschrauben verstecken sich im Radhaus und in den Leuchtenhöhlen.

The compact wheel loader 650 impresses with its distinctive lines. The flywheel of the hood continues to be in the cabin. The ample mudguards, adjustable in width, give it a sturdy appearance. A large, v-shaped radiator grill dominates the rear of the machine, which, in combination with the angular light recesses, creates a powerful rear view. Massive cast iron bumpers on the rear corners protect the machine from damage. These are raised up at the corners in order to allow a maximum angle of approach. The fastening screws are concealed in the wheel housing and in the light sockets.

RESEARCH+DEVELOPMENT / PROFESSIONAL CONCEPTS

JAMES AUGER
FRANZISKA KOWALEWSKI
OSCAR PEÑA

PRODUCT

Opel RAK e
Elektroexperimentalfahrzeug
Electric experimental vehicle

DESIGN

Adam Opel AG
Rüsselsheim, Germany

MANUFACTURER

Adam Opel AG
Rüsselsheim, Germany

Zur IAA präsentierte Opel sein RAK e -Konzept. Durch intelligenten Leichtbau und innovatives Design präsentiert es eine neue Art von Mobilität, die sogar für eine Zielgruppe ab 16 Jahren möglich wäre. Charakteristik: RAK e ist wegweisend zur Erforschung alternativer Antriebe. Besonders hervorzuheben sind: attraktives Experimentalfahrzeug für Stadt und Autobahn; Konzept für bezahlbare batteriebetriebene Null-Emission-Leichtbaufahrzeuge; hocheffizienter flinker Tandem-Zweisitzer jenseits von Auto und Motorrad; maximale Mobilität bei minimaler Umweltbelastung; Opel's 1-Euro / 100 km-Leichtfahrzeug; 100 km Reichweite; Vmax: 120 km / h.

At the IAA Opel presented the RAK e concept. With its light weight and ground-breaking design, the vehicle could give a new form of mobility to a new group of customers already starting at age of 16. RAK e continues Opel's pioneering spirit in the search of alternative propulsions. The highlights are: sexy experimental vehicle for city and autobahn; concept for an affordable lightweight zero emission fun-BEV; the "1 Euro / 100 km" vehicle; highly efficient and agile tandem two-seater beyond cars and motor-bikes; potential performance data: 120 km / h top speed, 100 km range; maximum mobility with minimum effect on the environment.

PRODUCT
Sigma Shuttle
Wasser-Fahrzeug
Water craft

DESIGN
Buffon Wang
Taipei, Taiwan

MANUFACTURER
Ship and Ocean Industries R & D Center
New Taipei, Taiwan

Das Sigma Shuttle kombiniert das Breitenmaß von Schiffen mit der längsgerichteten Beweglichkeit von U-Booten zu einem neuen Konzept für den Seetransport. Das Sigma Shuttle besitzt die Gestalt eines dreiflügeligen Katamarans. Unterhalb der Wasseroberfläche hat es die Form eines schmalen, tränenförmigen U-Boots, die sich in einem Trimaran-Überwasserschiff fortsetzt. Stahlketten, Gelenke und Hydraulikgelenkköpfe dienen zum Aus- oder Einfahren der Flügel, um in der Kajüte möglichst viel Platz zu schaffen. Dieses Design bringt zusätzlichen Nutzen hinsichtlich der Belastbarkeit und Stabilität der Flügelkonstruktion.

The Sigma Shuttle combines the planar dimension of ships with the longitudinal mobility of a submarine to deliver a new concept in marine transportation. The Sigma Shuttle features a winged triple catamaran design that expands from a slim, underwater tear drop-shaped submarine into a trimaran surface vessel. Steel chains, hinges and hydraulic rods are used to expand or contract the wings to maximize the internal cabin space. Such a design also offers benefits in terms of wing structure strength and stability.

PRODUCT
LYKOR®
Thermoplastisches Kunststoffmaterial
Thermosetting polymer

DESIGN
Marco Goffi
Milano, Italy

MANUFACTURER
ALPAS S. R. L.
Solero (Alessandria), Italy

Das innovative thermoplastische Kunststoffmaterial LYKOR® greift auf gewohnte Gusstechniken zurück und ist speziell auf das Design von Möbeln, Lichtquellen, Medizinprodukten etc. zugeschnitten. Dieses neuartige Material ist um 40 % leichter als herkömmliche Materialien, aber hart und widerstandsfähig genug, um für komplexe, ansprechende und variabel strukturierte Objekte geeignet zu sein. Neun Vollfarben und drei Beschichtungen sind in der Standardversion wählbar. Andere Farben sind auf Anforderung verfügbar. LYKOR® kann je nach Kundenwunsch auch UV-beständig und feuerfest gestaltet werden. Als massegefärbtes Material ist es zu 100 % wiederherstellbar und benötigt keine spezielle Beschichtung, was eine Produktionskostensenkung erlaubt. Die beliebtesten Bearbeitungstechniken wie Bohren und Fräsen sind anwendbar.

Durch die Herkunft des Materials aus zu mehr als 50 % erneuerbaren natürlichen Ressourcen und dessen volle Recycelbarkeit ist es ökologisch und ökonomisch nachhaltig. Die Gusstechnik, die Serienproduktion auch kleiner und mittlerer Mengen und die Umweltfreundlichkeit des Materials führen zu effizienter Preisgestaltung und sparen primäre Umweltressourcen.

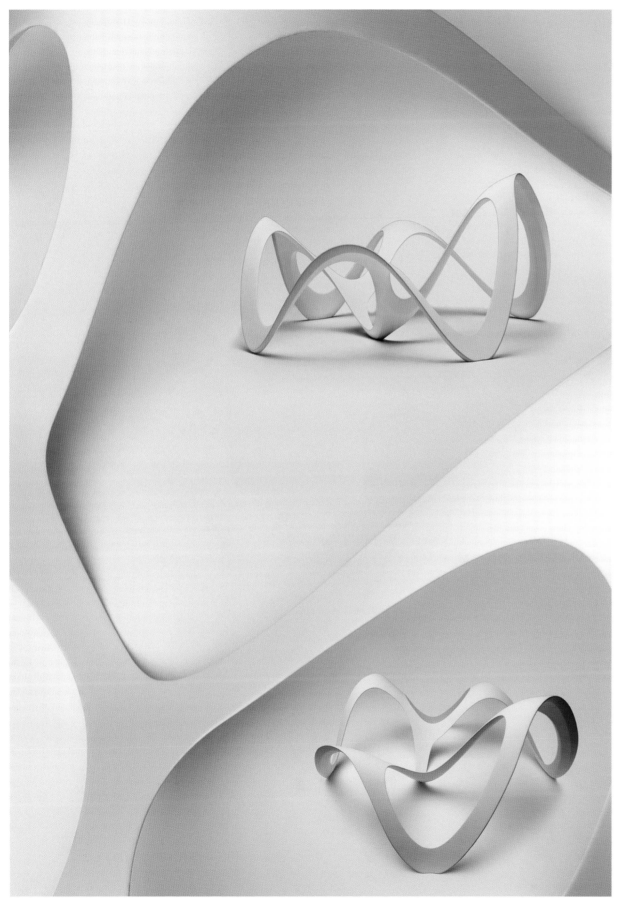

LYKOR® is an innovative thermosetting polymer that utilizes existing casting technology and is specifically formulated for design applications including furniture, lighting, medical and product design. This new material is 40 % lighter than standard solid surfaces, but strong and rigid enough to allow for the design of complex and appealing "free-form" structural objects. Nine full colors (other colors available on request) and three finishing effects are available for the standard version. LYKOR® is customizable, enabling it to become UV and fire-resistant. As a "mass-colored" material, it is 100 % restorable and needs no special finishing, limiting production costs and permitting the use of the most popular processing techniques, such as drilling, milling, etc.

Because the material is made from more than 50 % natural renewable resources, it is both ecologically (100 % recyclable) and economically sustainable. Basic molding technology and serial production (including small / medium volumes), combined with LYKOR®'s eco-friendly life cycle, leads to price efficiency and ultimately preserves primary environmental resources.

PRODUCT

Gentle Tug
Führungssystem für Blinde
Blind guiding system

DESIGN

Automotive Research & Testing Center
Chen-Hsun Huang, Maggie Sheu,
Tzi-Wei Ou, Mien-Chih Chen, Yi-Feng Su
Changhua County, Taiwan

MANUFACTURER

Automotive Research & Testing Center
Changhua County, Taiwan

Ein Gentle Tug ist ein Stock für Blinde, bei dem sich das Gewicht vor Hindernissen verschiebt, um das Berühren zu vermeiden. Gentle Tug verwendet die „Stereo-Visions-Kollision-Vermeidungs"-Technologie, die von der ARTC in Taiwan entwickelt wurde. Dabei wird ein virtuelles Bild des Ansteuerungsraums erstellt. Die Technologie des "Stereo-Visions-Kollisions-Vermeidungssystem" erfordert nur zwei Sensorkameras zum Erkennen der Straßen und der Hindernisse. Die verarbeiteten Informationen werden an die Smartphone-Anwendung übertragen, um den Benutzer darüber zu informieren, wie das Ziel zu finden ist.

A Gentle Tug is a blind stick which shifts the weight of the stick to tug users away from obstacles, thus naturally avoid the impending object. A Gentle Tug used "Stereo-Vision-Collision-Avoidance-System" technology developed by the Automotive Research and Testing Center (ARTC) in Taiwan to construct a virtual image of the approaching space. "Stereo-Vision-Collision-Avoidance-System" technology only requires two sensor cameras to recognize road environment and detect obstacles. Processed information is transferred to users' smart phone application informing user how to reach his or her destination.

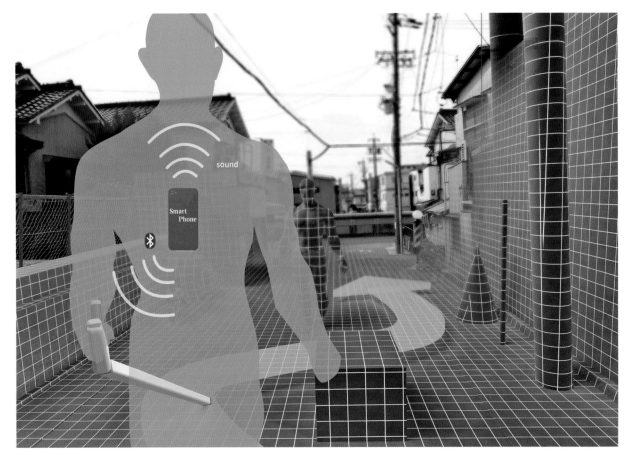

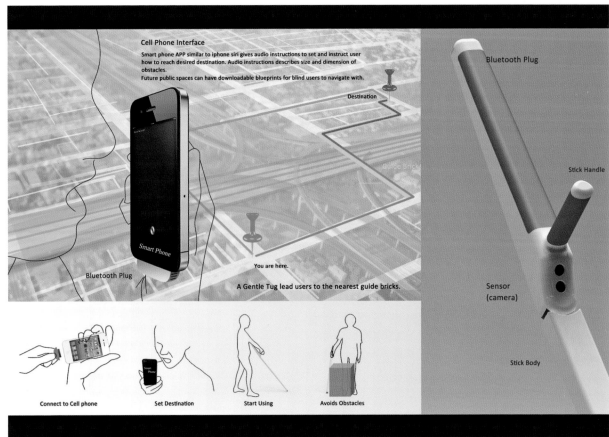

PRODUCT

NIL PraiseMetal+
Umweltfreundliche Metallbearbeitung
Eco metal surface tech

DESIGN

Compal Experience Design
Taipei City, Taiwan

MANUFACTURER

Compal Electronic, Inc.
Taipei City, Taiwan

Die Nanoprägelithografie ist eine hochmoderne Techno-logie zur alternativen Metallbearbeitung. Sie ermöglicht eine innovative Oberflächenbehandlung von Metallge-häuseteilen. Diese Methode ist einfach, schnell, benötigt wenig Energie und bietet einen hohen Qualitätsstandard. Im Gegensatz zum Eloxal-Verfahren oder der kathodischen Tauchlackierung sind alle Bestandteile wiederverwendbar, da chemikalienfreie Materialien eingesetzt werden. Hier wird eine außerordentlich erfolgreiche Kombination von Nanotechnologie, ästhetischem Empfinden, umwelt-freundlichen Herstellungsverfahren und großem Zukunfts-potenzial geschaffen.

Nanoimprint lithography is state-of-the-art technology that offers alternative metal finishing. It provides an ad-vanced surface finish for metal enclosure applications. It is simple, fast, requires low energy consumption and achieves a higher quality standard. In contrast with anod-izing and ED processes, all the substances are reusable due to the use of chemical-free materials. This extraordinary series delivers a successful combination of nanotechnology, esthetic sensibilities and green manufacturing processes with future market potential.

PRODUCT
Smart
Vorrichtung zur Wasseraufbereitung
Water filtration appliance

DESIGN
Coway
Hun-jung Choi, Seung-woo Kim
Seoul, South Korea

MANUFACTURER
Coway
Seoul, South Korea

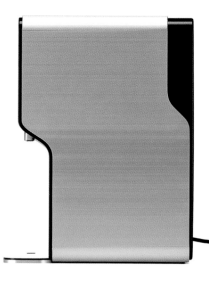

Dieses Produkt dient der Aufbereitung von verunreinig-
tem Leitungswasser und der Bereitstellung von sauberem
Trinkwasser in der Küche. Über die Smart-Touch-Benut-
zeroberfläche kann die gewünschte Wassermenge in
der gewünschten Temperatur einfach und präzise be-
zogen werden. Die intuitive und einfach zu bedienende
Benutzeroberfläche bietet höchsten Bedienkomfort.
Zudem werden nützliche Informationen zu Rezepten,
dem Wetter, der Uhrzeit usw. bereitgestellt. Die neue
Bedienoberfläche ermöglicht faszinierende Interaktio-
nen und eine vollkommen neue Benutzererfahrung.

*This product has been designed to be installed in a kitch-
en, purify polluted tap water and provide clean drinking
water. Smart touch GUI allows users to set the precise
amount of water at the precise temperature easily and
exactly. The intuitive and simple interface provides simple usability. In addition, it provides useful information
such as recipes, the weather, the time, etc. for additional
functionality. When touching this product, users can enjoy interesting interactions. A new interface has been
adopted to create a new user experience.*

PRODUCT

Home Control Center
Smart-Home-Benutzeroberfläche
Smart home user interface

DESIGN

DAI-Labor / TU Berlin
Florian Weingarten, Eva Burneleit
Berlin, Germany

MANUFACTURER

DAI-Labor / TU Berlin
Berlin, Germany

Wer auch in Zukunft den Überblick über seine vernetzten Geräte im Haushalt nicht verlieren möchte, braucht angesichts der steigenden Anzahl an vernetzbaren Gerätetypen und Funktionen eine einfach zu bedienende Steuereinheit. Das Home Control Center bietet hierfür eine klar strukturierte Oberfläche und ein einheitliches Bedienkonzept für Beleuchtung, Unterhaltungselektronik und unterschiedlichste Hausgeräte. Diese sind über eine eigens entwickelte Plattform hersteller- und technologieunabhängig ansteuerbar. Ausgelegt für mobile Endgeräte mit Touch-Screen, bildet das Home Control Center eine zentrale und dennoch mobile Schnittstelle.

With the increasing number of networked devices in households and their variety of functionality, a great challenge will be to offer a possibility to handle this network in a transparent and comprehensible way. Optimized for portable devices with touch capability, the Home Control Center offers a ubiquitous easy-to-use interface for device monitoring and control.

PRODUCT

Concept Style Coupé

Viertüriges Coupé

Fourdoor coupé

DESIGN

Daimler AG

Sindelfingen, Germany

MANUFACTURER

Daimler AG

Stuttgart, Germany

Das seriennahe Coupé ist der neue Maßstab für avantgardistisches Design in der Mittelklasse. Sportliche Proportionen und die kraftvoll-dynamische Designsprache mit dem Wechselspiel konkaver / konvexer Flächen machen das viertürige Coupé unverwechselbar. Ein großes Zierteil aus Echtcarbon zieht sich über die ganze Breite des Interieurs und vermittelt die Eleganz eines Coupés. Edle Materialien ergeben zusammen mit der hochwertigen Verarbeitung einen neuen Qualitätsmaßstab.

The almost production-standard coupé sets a new benchmark for avantgarde design in the executive segment. Its sporty proportions and powerfully dynamic design idiom, featuring the interplay between concave and convex surfaces give this four-door coupé its unmistakable look. A large carbon-fibre trim panel spans its full width, giving it the elegance appeal of a coup. Fine materials combine with high-grade workmanship to set a new benchmark for quality.

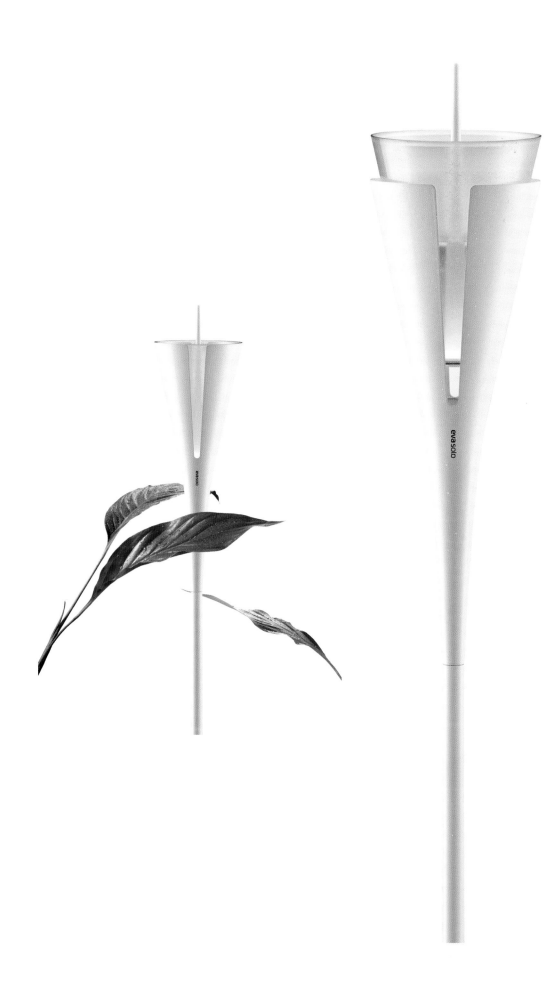

PRODUCT
Rain gauge
Niederschlagsmesser
Rain gauge

DESIGN
Tools Design
Copenhagen, Denmark

MANUFACTURER
Eva Solo A/S
Maaloev, Denmark

Der Niederschlagsmesser von Eva Solo ist ein skulpturelles und praktisches Produkt, mit dessen Hilfe man leicht verfolgen kann, wie viel Niederschlag fällt. Der Pegelstand ist durch die Schlitze an der Seite des Außenteils aus weiß lackiertem Metall leicht abzulesen. Das Innenteil aus klarem Kunststoff kann an dem Stäbchen leicht herausgenommen und entleert werden. Der Niederschlagsmesser ist frostbeständig.

The Eva Solo rain gauge is a sculptural and practical product which helps you keep an eye on how much rain has fallen. The water level is easy to read through the slits in the side of the outer holder, which is made of white-painted metal. The inner rain collector is made of transparent plastic and is easily removed for emptying. The rain gauge is frost-proof.

PRODUCT

Growing Basin
Blumentopf
Flower pot

DESIGN

Hoyidea Design Co., Ltd.
Zhao Lin, Lin Wenjie, Zhao Wendi, Lu Gangliang
Shunde, China

MANUFACTURER

Hoyidea Design Co., Ltd.
Shunde, China

Dieser Blumentopf ist dehnbar, entweder durch den kontinuierlichen Gebrauch oder aber auch durch künstliche Dehnung, wenn es etwas schneller gehen soll. Durch das Wachstum der Pflanzen wird der Boden gestreckt und der Blumentopf kann sich der Pflanze anpassen. Damit ist ein Höchstmaß an Funktionalität und Visualität erreicht. Der „wachsende" Blumentopf ist aus polymerem Material hergestellt. Farbe und Größe des Topfes passen sich den Präferenzen des Menschen an. Mussten Sie bislang im Leben eine Pflanze drei verschieden große Blumentöpfe kaufen, reicht nun der eine. Damit ist eine Kostenersparnis erreicht.

This flower pot is expandable, either by continuous use, or ahead of time it can be stretched artificial. By the growth of plants, the flower pot can adapt the size. The ultimate in functionality and visuality is reached. The „growing" pot is made of polymeric material. Color and size of the pot are adjustible to the preferences of the people. If you used to change the flower pot 3 times during the life of a plant, now you need only one pot. Cost saving is also achieved.

1 Months ········▶ 6 Months ················▶ 2 Years

PRODUCT

bamboo words
Artikel für den täglichen Bedarf
Articles for daily use

DESIGN

Hangzhou Paradise Umbrella Group Co., Ltd.
Chen Xiaolei, Xiong Xinbin, Dong Ying
Hangzhou, China
Zhejiang University City College
Li You, Zhang Fan, Yang Cheng
Hangzhou, China
TEAK Cultue & Creative Co., Ltd.
Li You, Xu Xiaofeng, Qiu Bohui, Ruan Lu, Li Chen
Hangzhou, China

MANUFACTURER

Hangzhou Paradise Umbrella Group Co., Ltd.
Hangzhou, China

Wir haben für den Regenschirm ein grünes Design gewählt. Um traditionelle Produktion mit fortschrittlicher
zu vereinen, verwenden wir für den Regenschirm-
Rahmen den lokal produzierten Bambus als Rohmaterial.
Daneben wird die völlig neue Technologie "Pressvorgang
für Verbundbambusfasern" verwendet. Der entstandene
Regenschirmrahmen hat so einen bessere Struktur als
die traditionellen chinesischen Regenschirme aus Bambus.
Das Bambus-Spaltungshandwerk wird mit der maschi-
nellen Produktion verbunden, damit eine Batch-Produk-
tion möglich wird.

*Bamboo Words (Qiantang) umbrella develops a localized
green design for manufacture. To adapt traditional material and crafts to contemporary manufacture, the umbrella
frame uses bamboo, an abundant local resource, as the
main material and uses a new technique called composite
bamboo technique to meet requirements of manufacture.
In addition, the frame develops the structure of traditional
Chinese bamboo umbrella and adapts bamboo-split craft
to manufacture. The umbrella re-interprets the relation
between tradition and manufacture. It explores a better
relationship among green design, traditional craft, traditional culture and new material.*

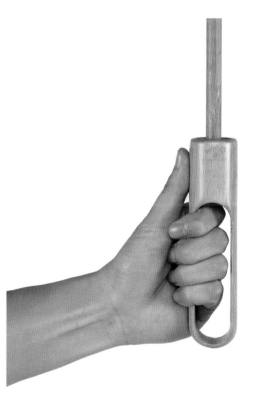

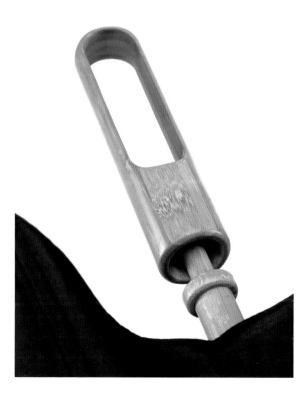

PRODUCT

SEIL-bag
Bluetooth-LED-Rucksack
Bluetooth LED backpack

DESIGN

Lee Myung Su DesignLab
Seoul, South Korea

MANUFACTURER

Lee Myung Su DesignLab
Seoul, South Korea

SEIL-Rucksack ist so gestaltet, dass sich der Radfahrer durch die Bedienung eines drahtlosen Kontrollers auf der hinteren Oberfläche des Rucksacks Verkehrszeichen (Fahr-, Stopp-, Notzeichen) wie „nach links"- und „nach rechts"-Richtungszeichen zeigen lassen kann. Der Rucksack besteht aus einem abnehmbaren drahtlosen Kontroller und einem innerhalb des Rucksacks eingebauten LED-Display. Die Teile werden durch Bluetooth miteinander verbunden. Mit der Smartphone-App kann der Benutzer auch selbst Images und Texte fertigen und sie durch Bluetooth zum Rucksack übertragen. Wird die App ausgeführt, können die aktuell auf dem Rucksack gezeigten Images rechtzeitig erkennbar sein.

SEIL-bag is designed in order to illustrate traffic signals such as proceed signal, stop signal and emergency signal on the back pack. It is composed of detachable wireless controller and LED display which is built in the back pack. Bicycle riders could operate wireless controller to show left and right turn signal. Bluetooth-enabled device can connect between controller and back pack. Furthermore, user could make any texts and images they want through smartphone App and transmit data to LED display. Whenever App is running, user can make sure contents on the SEIL-bag in real time and wireless controller do not practice during walking.

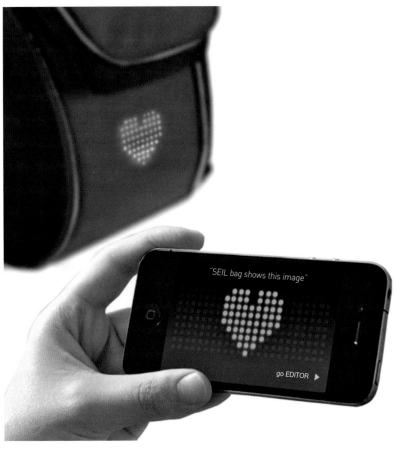

PRODUCT

Bike Zone
Fahrradzubehör
Bike peripherals

DESIGN

Lite-On Technology Corp.
Stuart Morrow, Frank Guo, Hung Wang
Taipei, Taiwan

MANUFACTURER

Lite-On Technology Corp.
Taipei, Taiwan

Im Dunkeln Rad zu fahren ist gefährlich. Es ist eine anerkannte Tatsache, dass an beiden Seiten des Fahrrades eine Sicherheitszone von mindestens einem Meter eingehalten werden muss. Leider fällt es Autofahrern oft schwer, diese Zone einzuhalten oder auch nur daran zu denken. Außerdem birgt ein Spurwechsel oder das Abbiegen in der Dunkelheit ein noch höheres Gefahrenpotential, auch wenn der Radfahrer seine Absicht durch Handzeichen signalisiert. Zur Risikominimierung schafft Bike Zone mit zwei Laser-Projektoren eine ein Meter große Sicherheitszone rund um das Fahrrad. Außerdem zeigen animierte Pfeile die Abbiegeabsicht an.

Cycling at night is dangerous. It is widely accepted that a safety zone of at least one meter is required on either side of a bicycle, but this is difficult for car drivers to accurately gauge, or even remember to do. Additionally, changing lanes or turning when cycling in the dark has its own dangers, even when the cyclist indicates with an arm signal his or her intentions. To help minimize the risks, Bike Zone is a pair of laser projectors that create a one-meter safety zone around your bicycle during normal use. It also features animated arrows to indicate when you intend to turn.

PRODUCT

Safe Guard

Wasserrettungsausrüstung

Water rescue equipment

DESIGN

Lite-On Technology Corp.

Taipei, Taiwan

Zhejiang University

Liu Yi, Xu Wei, Meng Luhua, Li Ke

Zhejiang, China

MANUFACTURER

Lite-On Technology Corp.

Taipei, Taiwan

Safe Guard wird zur Wasserrettung eingesetzt. Die Vorrichtung mit integrierter Rettungsboje wird an wassernahen Zäunen angebracht. Der Retter hebt den oberen Teil der Vorrichtung ab und wirft ihn der ertrinkenden Person zu. Sobald die noch flache Rettungsboje die Wasseroberfläche berührt, pumpt sie sich automatisch auf. Hat der Ertrinkende die Boje erreicht, kann der Retter ihn und die Boje mit dem daran befestigten Seil an Land ziehen und den Menschen somit vor dem Ertrinken bewahren. Da die Boje flach im Inneren der Vorrichtung liegt, können ihr Sonne und Regen nichts anhaben. Safe Guard ist sehr platzsparend zu montieren.

Safe Guard is a type of water rescue device. The device, with the life buoy inside, is installed at the top of riverside fences. The rescuer can lift the top of the device and throw it to the drowning person. Shortly after the flat life buoy touches the water, it will automatically be inflated with gas. After the drowning person gets hold of the buoy, the rescuer can pull back the rope linked to the buoy, helping the person get out of the water. As the buoy is installed inside of fences, it not only prevents the life buoy from damage by the sun and rain but also saves more space for the public.

PRODUCT
Kacha
Digitalkamera
Digital camera

DESIGN
Lite-On Technology Corp.
Taipei, Taiwan
Jiangnan University
Linyuzi Zhang, Xuanwei Li, Lu Lu
Jiangsu Province, China

MANUFACTURER
Lite-On Technology Corp.
Taipei, Taiwan

Die intuitive Bedienung der Digitalkamera Kacha macht das Fotografieren zum reinsten Vergnügen. Durch ihre rahmenartige Gestaltung und Vertiefung in der Mitte kann der Nutzer genau das fotografieren, was er direkt durch den Kamerarahmen sieht. Ohne konventionellen Sucher hat Kacha ein viel leichteres Gehäuse und ist deutlich einfacher zu bedienen als herkömmliche Digitalkameras. Man fotografiert sozusagen direkt mit den Augen, in Harmonie mit dem natürlichen menschlichen Verhalten.
Die Kamera erhält beim Getragenwerden mechanische Bewegungsenergie. Dieses Produkt ermöglicht umweltfreundliches Fotografieren auf einfachste Art und Weise.

Kacha is a digital camera that makes taking photos more intuitive and fun. With a frame-like appearance and a hollow center, users can take photos of what they see by pulling out the frame and look out directly through it. Instead of using a view finder like conventional DCs, Kacha simplifies the operation and makes the body of the camera much lighter. People can use their eyes to take photos directly in keeping with natural human behavior. Furthermore, it can be powered mechanical energy from people's body movements while carrying the camera. This special camera presents a simple and environmentally-friendly way of taking pictures.

PRODUCT
Smart Chair
Elektrischer Rollstuhl
Electric wheelchair

DESIGN
Designnext
Seoul, South Korea

MANUFACTURER
Posco
Seoul, South Korea

Im Gegensatz zum standardisierten und unzugänglichen Design der allgemeinen medizinischen Geräte zielt der Smart Chair auf die leichte Zugänglichkeit ab. Jeder soll ihn benutzen können. Der Stuhl wurde mit der Absicht entworfen, dass die Behinderten in aller Welt mit normalen Menschen glücklich leben sollen. Der Smart Chair besteht aus Magnesium zur Reduzierung des Gewichts von 110 kg auf 60 kg und hat den ausdehnbaren Rahmen und auch viele Apparate mit dem UX-Konzept, um die Sicherheit und die Speichermöglichkeit auf ein Höchstmaß zu bringen.

In contrast to the standardized and inaccessible design of common medical devices, the design of Smart Chair is set on easy accessibility, in which everyone, including the elderly and the handicapped, can use. It is styled with the motive of the world where the handicapped live happily with regular people. Smart Chair is made of magnesium to reduce the weight from 110 kg to only 60 kg, built with the extension frame structure, and has UX-concept-applied convenient appliances to maximize safety and storability. Smart Chair can decrease society's stereotypes of the handicapped and become a futuristic suggestion of individual transportation method.

iF INDUSTRIE FORUM DESIGN E.V.

MITGLIEDERLISTE | SATZUNG DES VEREINS
LIST OF MEMBERS | ARTICLES OF ASSOCIATION

VORSTÄNDE / *BOARD*

1. Vorsitzender / 1st Chairman

Ernst Raue
Senior Advisor Deutsche Messe AG
Messegelände
30521 Hannover
Germany
www.messe.de

Christoph Böninger
Böcklinstraße 54
80638 München
Germany
www.auerberg.eu

Prof. Fritz Frenkler
f/p design GmbH
Mauerkicherstraße 4
81679 München
Germany
www.fp-design.com

Susanne Schmidhuber
SCHMIDHUBER
Nederlinger Straße 21
80638 München
Germany
www.schmidhuber.de

Boris Kochan
KOCHAN & PARTNER GmbH
Strategie | Kommunikation | Design
Hirschgartenallee 25
80639 München
Germany
www.kochan.de

GESCHÄFTSFÜHRENDER VORSTAND / *MANAGING DIRECTOR*

Ralph Wiegmann
iF Industrie Forum Design e.V.
Bahnhofstrasse 8
30159 Hannover
Germany
www.ifdesign.de

EHRENMITGLIEDER / *HONORARY MEMBERS*

Herbert H. Schultes
Rodelbahnstraße 1
82256 Fürstenfeldbruck
Germany

Knut Bliesener
Im Haspelfelde 31
30173 Hannover
Germany

Prof. Herbert Lindinger
Brahmstraße 3
30175 Hannover
Germany

Sepp D. Heckmann
Schopenhauerstraße 12
30625 Hannover
Germany

UNTERNEHMEN / *CORPORATE MEMBERS*

AL-KO Geräte GmbH
Ichenhauser Straße 14
89359 Kötz
Germany
www.al-ko.de

Artemide GmbH
Hans-Böckler-Straße 2
58730 Fröndenberg
Germany
www.artemide.de

B / S / H Bosch und Siemens Hausgeräte GmbH
Carl-Wery-Straße 34
81793 München
Germany
www.bsh-group.de

BASF SE
Designfabrik E-KTE/IF - F206, Zi. 563
E-KTE/IF - F 206, Zi. 563
67056 Ludwigshafen
Germany
www.basf.com

Blomus GmbH
Zur Hubertushalle 4
59846 Sundern
Germany
www.blomus.com

BMW AG
Knorrstraße 147
80788 München
Germany
www.bmwgroup.com

BREE Collection GmbH & Co. KG
Gerberstraße 3
30916 Isernhagen
www.bree.de
Germany

Carpet Concept
Objekt-Teppichboden GmbH
Bunzlauer Straße 7
33719 Bielefeld
Germany
www.carpet-concept.de

CLAGE GmbH
Pirolweg 1-5
21337 Lüneburg
Germany
www.clage.de

Crown Gabelstapler GmbH & Co. KG
Moosacher Straße 52
80809 München
Germany
www.crown.com/de

Daimler AG
Mercedes-Benz Cars Develpoment
Werk 059, HPC X800
71059 Sindelfingen
Germany
www.daimler.com

designaffairs GmbH
Balanstraße 73
81541 München
Germany
www.designaffairs.com

Deutsche Messe AG
Messegelände
30521 Hannover
Germany
www.messe.de

Die Neue Sammlung, Pinakothek der Moderne
Türkenstraße 15
80333 München
Germany
www.die-neue-sammlung.de

EnBW AG
Messen und Events
Obere Stegwiesen 29
88400 Biberach
Germany
www.enbw.com

EnBW AG
Marketing und Koordination
Durlacher Allee 93
76131 Karlsruhe
Germany
www.enbw.com

Expotechnik Heinz Soschinski GmbH
Aarstraße 176
65232 Taunusstein
Germany
www.expotechnik.com

FESTO AG & Co. KG
Leiter Design Coordination
Ruiter Straße 82
73734 Esslingen
Germany
www.festo.com

Gira Giersiepen GmbH & Co. KG
Dahlienstraße
42477 Radevormwald
Germany
www.gira.de

Grohe AG
Design Studio
Feldmühleplatz 15
40545 Düsseldorf
Germany
www.grohe.com

häfelinger + wagner design gmbh
Türkenstraße 55-57
80799 München
Germany
www.hwdesign.de

Hansgrohe AG
Auestraße 5-9
77761 Schiltach
Germany
www.hansgrohe.com

HBK Braunschweig
Johannes-Selenka-Platz 1
38118 Braunschweig
Germany
 www.hbk-bs.de

HEWI Heinrich Wilke GmbH
Postfach 1260
34442 Bad Arolsen
Germany
www.hewi.de

Hiller Objektmöbel GmbH & Co. KG
Kippenheimer Straße 6
77971 Kippenheim
Germany
www.hiller-moebel.de

IBM Deutschland GmbH
IBM-Allee 1
71139 Ehningen
Germany
www.ibm.com/de

interstil - Diedrichsen GmbH
Liebigstraße 1-3
33803 Steinhagen
Germany
www.interstil.de

Interstuhl Büromöbel GmbH & Co. KG
Brühlstraße 21
72469 Meßstetten-Tieringen
Germany
www.interstuhl.de

Isaria Corporate Design AG
Gewerbepark Aich 7-9
85667 Oberpframmern
Germany
www.isaria.com

JAB Teppiche Heinz Anstoetz KG
Dammheider Straße 67
32052 Herford
Germany
www.jab.de

Kermi GmbH
Pankofen-Bahnhof 1
94447 Plattling
Germany
www.kermi.de

Kochan & Partner GmbH
Strategie | Kommunikation | Design
Hirschgartenallee 25
80639 München
Germany
www.kochan.de

Köttermann GmbH & Co. KG
Industriestraße 2-10
31311 Uetze
Germany
www.kottermann.com

KWC AG
Hauptstraße 57
5726 Unterkulm
Switzerland
www.kwc.ch

LOEWE OPTA GmbH
Leiter Design/Designmanagement
Industriestraße 11
96317 Kronach
Germany
www.loewe.de

MeisterSinger GmbH & Co. KG
Hafenweg 46
48155 Münster
Germany
www.meistersinger.de

MüllerKälber GmbH
Daimlerstraße 2
71546 Aspach
Germany
www.muellerkaelber.de

Niedersächsisches Ministerium
für Wirtschaft, Technologie u. Verkehr
Friedrichswall 1
30159 Hannover
Germany
www.mw.niedersachsen.de

Nils Holger Moormann GmbH
An der Festhalle 2
83229 Aschau
Germany
www.moormann.de

OCTANORM-Vertriebs-GmbH
für Bauelemente
Raiffeisenstraße 39
70794 Filderstadt
Germany
www.octanorm.de

Oventrop GmbH & Co. KG
Paul-Oventrop-Straße 1
59939 Olsberg
Germany
www.oventrop.de

Philips GmbH
UB Consumer Lifestyle
Lübeckertordamm 5
20099 Hamburg
Germany
www.philips.de

PLANMECA OY
Asentajankatu 6
00880 Helsinki
Finland
www.planmeca.com

Poggenpohl Möbelwerke GmbH
Poggenpohl Straße 1
32051 Herford
Germany
www.poggenpohl.de

REALTIME TECHNOLOGY (RTT)
Rosenheimer Straße 145
81671 München
Germany
www.rtt.ag

Schendel & Pawlaczyk Messebau GmbH
Im Derdel 3
48167 Münster
Germany
www.schendel-pawlaczyk.de

Schneider Electric GmbH
Gothaer Str. 29
40880 Ratingen
Germany
www.schneider-electric.com

SCHULTE Duschkabinenbau KG
Lockweg 81
59846 Sundern
Germany
www.schulte.de

Sedus Stoll AG
Brückenstraße 15
79761 Waldshut-Tiengen
Germany
www.sedus.de

Seibel Designpartner GmbH
Industriestraße 5
40822 Mettmann
Germany
www.seibel-designpartner.de

Sennheiser Electronic GmbH & Co. KG
Am Labor 1
30900 Wedemark
Germany
www.sennheiser.com

Siemens AG
Abt. CC MC1
Wittelsbacherplatz 2
80333 München
Germany
www.siemens.com

SKYLOTEC GmbH
Im Bruch 11-15
56567 Neuwied
Germany
www.skylotec.de

SMA Solar Technology AG
Sonnenallee 1
34266 Niestetal
Germany
www.sma.de

Steelcase Werndl AG
Georg-Aicher-Straße 7
83026 Rosenheim
Germany
www.steelcase-werndl.de

Storck Bicycle GmbH
Rudolfstraße 1
65510 Idstein
Germany
www.storck-bicycle.de

TRILUX GmbH + Co KG
Heidestraße 4
59759 Arnsberg
Germany
www.trilux.de

Vauth-Sagel
Systemtechnik GmbH & Co. KG
Neue Straße 27
33034 Brakel-Erkeln
Germany
www.vauth-sagel.de

Viessmann Werke GmbH Co. KG
Viessmannstraße 1
35108 Allendorf/Eder
Germany
www.viessmann.de

Volkswagen AG
Volkswagen Design
Brieffach 1701, Berliner Ring 2
38436 Wolfsburg
Germany
www.volkswagen.de

wiege Entwicklungs GmbH
Hauptstraße 81
31848 Bad Münder
Germany
www.wiege.com

Wilkhahn
Wilkening + Hahne GmbH + Co. KG.
Fritz Hahne Straße 8
31848 Bad Münder
Germany
www.wilkhahn.de

WINI Büromöbel GmbH & Co. KG
Auhagenstraße 79
31863 Coppenbrügge
Germany
www.wini.de

wodtke GmbH
Rittweg 55-57
72070 Tübingen-Hirschau
Germany
www.wodtke.com

Yokogawa Electric Corporation
2-9-32 naka-cho
Mushashino-shi, Tokyo, 180-8750
Japan
www.yokogawa.com

Zumtobel Lighting GmbH
Schweizer Straße 30
6850 Dornbirn
Austria
www.zumtobel.de

DESIGNER O. DESIGNBÜROS / DESIGN STUDIOS OR DESIGNER

3-point concepts GmbH
Prinzessinnenstr. 1
10969 Berlin
Germany
www.3pc.de

aka buna design consult
Nonnbergstiege 1
5020 Salzburg
Austria
www.akabuna.at

ArGe Design braucht Täter
c/o id 3 Michael Gehlen
Ägidiusstraße 1
50937 Köln
Germany
www.martin-neuhaus.com

artcollin
Goethestraße 28
80336 München
Germany
www.artcollin.de

ArteFakt Pohl Fiegl
Liebigstraße 50 - 52
64293 Darmstadt
Germany
www.artefakt.de

at-design
Flugplatzstraße 111
90768 Fürth
Germany
www.atdesign.de

Avidus Consulting
Wielandstraße 1
65187 Wiesbaden
Germany
www.avidus-consulting.com

bayern design forum e.V.
Luitpoldstraße 3
90402 Nürnberg
Germany
www.bayern-design.de

B:SIGN Design & Communications GmbH
Ellernstraße 36
30175 Hannover
Germany
www.bsign.de

Braake Design
Turnierstraße 3
70599 Stuttgart
Germany
www.braake.com

brodbeck design
Schillerstraße 40 c
80336 München
Germany
www.brodbeckdesign.de

D´ART Visuelle Kommunikation GmbH
Adlerstraße 41
70199 Stuttgart
Germany
www.dartwork.de

design studio hartmut s. engel
Monreposstraße 7
71634 Ludwigsburg
Germany

Design Tech
Zeppelinstraße 53
72119 Ammerbuch
Germany
www.designtechschmid.de

Deutscher Designer Club e.V.
Große Fischestraße 7
60311 Frankfurt am Main
Germany
www.ddc.de

DIV Deutscher Industrieverlag GmbH
Arnulfstr. 124
80636 München
www.di-verlag.de

DRWA Das Rudel Werbeagentur
Erbprinzenstraße 11
79098 Freiburg
Germany
www.drwa.de

f/p design GmbH
Mauerkicherstraße 4
81679 München
Germany
www.f-p-design.com

Fuenfwerken Design AG
Taunusstraße 52
65183 Wiesbaden
Germany

FRACKENPOHL POULHEIM GMBH
Luxemburger Str. 72
50674 Köln
Germany
www.frackenpohl-poulheim.de

GDC Design
Kaiserstraße 168-170
90763 Fürth
Germany
www.gdc-design.de

GUTE GESELLSCHAFT FÜR STRATEGIE, DESIGN UND KOMMUNIKATION MBH
Grafenberger Allee 126
40237 Düsseldorf
Germany
www.gutegesellschaft.com

H H Schultes Design Studio
Rodelbahnstraße 1
82256 Fürstenfeldbruck
Germany

i / i / d Institut für Integriertes Design
an der HfK Bremen
Am Speicher XI, Abtlg.7, Boden 3
28217 Bremen
Germany
www.iidbremen.de

identis GmbH
Bötzinger Straße 36
79111 Freiburg
Germany
www.identis.de

INOID DesignGroup
Reutlingerstraße 114
70597 Stuttgart
Germany
www.inoid.de

Interbrand
Kirchenweg 5
8008 Zürich
Switzerland
www.interbrand.com

MEDIADESIGN HOCHSCHULE
für Design und Informatik
Claudius-Keller-Straße 7
81669 München
Germany
www.mediadesign.de

.molldesign
Turmgasse 7
73525 Schwäbisch Gmünd
Germany
www.molldesign.de

mormedi
Plaza Republica Argentina 3
28002 Madrid
Spain
www.momedi.com

Nova Design Co., Ltd.
Tower C, 8F, No. 96, Sec. 1, Xintai 5th Rd.
Xizh City
Taipei Country 221
Taiwan
www.e-novadesign.com

OCO-Design O. K. Nüsse
An der Kleimannbrücke 79
48157 Münster
Germany
www.oco-design.de

Olaf Hoffmann Industrial Design
Metzstraße 14 b
81667 München
Germany
www.olaf-hoffmann-design.de

Philips International BV Philips Design
Building HWD
Emmasingel 24
5600 MD Eindhoven
The Netherlands
www.philips.nl

Pilotfish GmbH
Schleissheimer Straße 6
80333 München
Germany
www.pilotfish.eu

Polvan Design Ltd.
Cemil Topuzlu cad. 79/2 Caddebostan
34170 Istanbul
Turkey

PROMOTIONAL iDEAS Werbeagentur GmbH
Hessenring 76
61348 Bad Homburg
Germany
www.promotionalideas.de

rahe+rahe design
Konsul-Smidt-Straße 8c
28217 Bremen
Germany

Rokitta Produkt & Markenästhetik
Kölner Straße 38 a
45481 Mühlheim an der Ruhr
Germany

SCHOLZ & VOLKMER GmbH
Schwalbacher Straße 72
65183 Wiesbaden
Germany
www.s-v.de

Spirit Design Consulting & Services GmbH
Silbergasse 8
1190 Wien
Austria
www.spiritdesign.com

Strategy&Marketing Institute GmbH
Lange-Hop-Straße 19
30559 Hannover
Germany

Taipei Base Design Center
1F.,No.4,Ln.176,Sec.1,Da'an Rd.,Da'an Dist.
Taipei City 106
Taiwan
www.asia-bdc.com

TRICON Design AG
Bahnhofstraße 26
72138 Kirchentellinsfurt
Germany
www.tricon-design.de

Ueberholz GmbH
Warndtstraße 7
42285 Wuppertal
Germany
www.ueberholz.de

UNIPLAN GmbH & Co. KG
Schanzenstraße 39 a/b
51063 Köln
Germany
www.uniplan.com

VDID/DDV
Markgrafenstraße 15
10969 Berlin
Germany
www.vidid.de

Weinberg & Ruf
Produktgestaltung
Martinsstraße 5
70794 Filderstadt
Germany
www.weinberg-ruf.de

PRIVATPERSONEN / *INDIVIDUAL MEMBERS*

Thomas Bade
Im Knick 9
31655 Stadthagen
Germany

Olaf Barski
Hermannstraße 15
60318 Frankfurt
Germany
www.barskidesign.com

Thomas Biswanger
Probierlweg 47
85049 Ingolstadt
Germany
www.thomasbiswanger.de

Christoph Böninger
Auerberg 1
83730 Fischbachau
Germany
www.auerberg.eu

Gerd Bulthaup
Chamissostraße 1
81925 München
Germany

Prof. Dr. Gerdum Enders
Terrasse 19
34117 Kassel
Germany

Christoph Eschke
Admiralitätstraße 10
20459 Hamburg
Germany
www.ebnerstolz.de

Holger Fricke
Loogestieg 19
20249 Hamburg
Germany

Andreas Gantenhammer
Meerbuscher Straße 64-78
40670 Meerbusch
Germany
www.gantenhammer.de

Michael Grüter
Hainholzstraße 17
31558 Hagenburg
Germany

Annette Häfelinger
Johannisplatz 7
81677 München
Germany

Peter Hartmann
Fasaneriestraße 10
80636 München
Germany
www.h-bc.de

Josef Hasberg
Lokenbach 8 - 10
51491 Overath
Germany

Bibs Hosak-Robb
Mendelssohnstraße 31
81245 München
Germany
www.bibs-design.de

K. Michael Kühne
Kampstraße 96
22113 Osteinbeck
Germany
www.creacon.de

Sebastian Le Peetz
Osterstraße 43 a
30159 Hannover
Germany

Hildegund Lichtwark
Lommertzweg 20
41569 Rommerskirchen
Germany

Johannes Loer
Luisenstraße 24
59379 Selm-Bork
Germany
www.metamorphdesignwerk.de

Kai Miethig
P.O. Box 11224, Wind Tower, 6th Floor
Diplomatic Area, Manama
Bahrain
www.bg-ca.com

Seyed Mansour Pour Mohseni Shakib
No.281- Yasseman Alley-Manzariyeh-Namjo St.
41936 Rasht
Iran

Seyed Mahdi Pour Mohseni Shakib
No.281- Yasseman Alley-Manzariyeh-Namjo St.
41936 Rasht
Iran

Christoph Rohrer
Roecklplatz 3
80469 München
Germany
www.kms-team.de

Karina Rudolph
Friedrichstraße 11
78050 VS - Villingen
Germany
www.schoenformerei.de

HD Schellnack
Mintropstraße 61
45329 Essen
Germany
www.nodesign.com

Eberhard Schlegel
Am Kapellenweg 4
88525 Dürmentingen
Germany
www.schlegel.biz

Prof. Gunnar Spellmeyer
c/o Fachhochschule Hannover Expo Plaza 2
30539 Hannover
Germany
www.mixxd.com

Andreas Thierry
Arthur-Kutscher-Platz 1 / VII
80802 München
Germany

Peter Thonet
Michael-Thonet-Straße 1
35066 Frankenberg
Germany
www.thonet.de

Prof. Martin Topel
Fuhlrottstraße 10, Gebäude I, Ebene 16, Raum 76
42119 Wuppertal
Germany
www.visionlabs.org

Roland Wagner
Tullstraße 19
77933 Lahr
Germany
www.wagner-system.de

Gabriel Weber
Orffstraße 35
80637 München
Germany
www.rausweber.de

SATZUNG DES VEREINS „iF – INDUSTRIE FORUM DESIGN E. V."

§ 1   Name und Sitz des Vereins

1. Der Verein trägt den Namen „iF – Industrie Forum Design e. V.".
2. iF – Industrie Forum Design ist im Vereinsregister eingetragen.
3. Der Verein hat seinen Sitz in Hannover.

§ 2   Zweck des Vereins

Der Verein verfolgt den Zweck der Förderung und Akzeptanz von Design als Teil der Wertschöpfungskette und als kulturelles Element der Gesellschaft. Die bewusste Gestaltung von Produkten und Lebensräumen für den privaten und öffentlichen Bereich sowie von benutzerfreundlichen Softwareanwendungen betrachtet der Verein als seine gesellschaftspolitische und kulturelle Aufgabe. Vereinsziele sind:

1. Die Anerkennung der Designleistung zur Erreichung von Unternehmenszielen und zur Sicherung von wirtschaftlichem Erfolg;
2. Die Organisation von Wettbewerben, Ausstellungen, Konferenzen, Vortragsveranstaltungen und weiteren Aktivitäten;
3. Die Veröffentlichung von Publikationen als Grundlage für Diskussionen;
4. Die Stärkung des Bewusstseins für Design in der Öffentlichkeit;
5. Das Angebot eines Forums zur Kommunikation auf neutraler Ebene;

Der Verein ist mit seinen Aktivitäten regional, national und international präsent.

§ 3   Geschäftsjahr

Das Geschäftsjahr ist das Kalenderjahr.

§ 4   Mitgliedschaft

1. Jede natürliche oder juristische Person kann Mitglied im iF e. V. werden. Der schriftliche Aufnahmeantrag wird von der Geschäftsführung geprüft und von ihr entschieden – in Zweifelsfällen beschließt der Vorstand mit einfacher Mehrheit über die Aufnahme des Mitglieds. Die Ablehnung der Aufnahme braucht nicht begründet zu werden.
2. Der Verein hat neben Mitgliedern auch Ehrenmitglieder. Ehrenmitglieder sind Persönlichkeiten, die sich im besonderen Maße um die Förderung und das Ansehen des „iF – Industrie Forum Design e. V." Verdienste erworben haben. Sie können durch einstimmigen Beschluss der Mitgliederversammlung zu Ehrenmitgliedern ernannt werden und haben in der Mitgliederversammlung kein Stimmrecht.
3. Die Mitgliedschaft endet durch
   a) Austritt, der dem Verein gegenüber zu erklären ist. Der Austritt kann nur durch schriftliche Erklärung zum Ende eines jeden Geschäftsjahres mit dreimonatiger Frist erklärt werden,
   b) Ausschluss aus dem Verein, über den der Vorstand einstimmig beschließt,
   c) Tod eines Mitglieds.

§ 5   Organe

Die Organe des Vereins sind:

1. die Mitgliederversammlung
2. der Vorstand
3. die Geschäftsführung.

§ 6   Mitgliederversammlung

1. Die Mitgliederversammlung ist zuständig für:
   a) Entgegennahme des Jahresberichts des Vorstandes und des Berichts der Rechnungsprüfer,
   b) Wahl des Vorstands,
   c) Entlastung des Vorstands und der Geschäftsführung,
   d) Satzungsänderungen,
   e) Auflösung des Vereins,
   f) Verwendung des Vermögens bei Auflösung des Vereins,
   g) die Verwendung des jährlichen Gewinnvortrages bzw. die Behandlung eines Verlustes,
   h) Entscheidung über neue Aktivitäten des Vereins,
   i) Festsetzung des Jahresmitgliedsbeitrages,
   j) Wahl der Ehrenmitglieder.
2. Jährlich ist eine ordentliche Mitgliederversammlung durchzuführen, zu der alle Mitglieder des Vereins eingeladen werden und in der insbesondere über das abgelaufene Geschäftsjahr, über den Rechnungsabschluss und das Ergebnis der Rechnungsprüfung zu berichten ist.
3. Die Mitgliederversammlung wird vom Vorsitzenden des Vorstandes mit einer Frist von mindestens einer Woche schriftlich unter Angabe der Tagesordnung einberufen. Die Tagesordnung der Mitgliederversammlung setzt der Vorsitzende des Vorstandes oder ein anderes von ihm benanntes Vorstandsmitglied fest. Anträge einzelner Mitglieder zur Tagesordnung können nachträglich auf die Tagesordnung gesetzt werden, wenn die Mitgliederversammlung es einstimmig beschließt.
4. Außerordentliche Mitgliederversammlungen können jederzeit vom Vorsitzenden des Vorstandes einberufen werden, wenn ein wichtiger Grund vorliegt. Die Einberufung muss erfolgen, wenn dies von mindestens ⅓ der Mitglieder schriftlich beantragt wird. Die Einberufungsfrist beträgt 2 Tage. In Eilfällen können die Einladungen telefonisch oder per Fax erfolgen.
5. Die Mitgliederversammlung wird von dem Vorsitzenden des Vorstandes, im Falle seiner Verhinderung durch ein von ihm bestimmtes anderes Vorstandsmitglied geleitet.
6. Die ordnungsgemäß einberufene Mitgliederversammlung ist beschlussfähig, wenn außer dem Versammlungsleiter mindestens drei weitere stimmberechtigte Mitglieder anwesend sind.

7. Jedes Mitglied hat in der Mitgliederversammlung eine Stimme. Beschlüsse der Mitgliederversammlung werden mit einfacher Mehrheit der bei der Abstimmung anwesenden stimmberechtigten Mitglieder gefasst, soweit diese Satzung nicht etwas anderes bestimmt. Ein Beschluss über die Verwendung des Gewinnvortrages bzw. die Behandlung eines Verlustes bedarf einer Mehrheit von 80% der bei der Abstimmung anwesenden stimmberechtigten Mitglieder. Stimmberechtigte Mitglieder können sich in der Mitgliederversammlung vertreten lassen, wobei auch die Übertragung des Stimmrechts auf den Vertreter zulässig ist. Bei Stimmengleichheit entscheidet die Stimme des Versammlungsleiters.

8. Eilbeschlüsse können im Umlaufverfahren schriftlich gefasst werden.

9. Zu einem Beschluss über eine Änderung der Satzung ist eine Mehrheit von ¾ der Stimmen der erschienenen stimmberechtigten Mitglieder erforderlich.

10. Die gefassten Beschlüsse werden in einem Protokoll erfasst, das vom Protokollführer und dem Leiter der Mitgliederversammlung unterschrieben werden muss. Jedem Mitglied ist eine Niederschrift des Protokolls der Mitgliederversammlung zuzustellen.

§ 7 Vorstand

1. Der Vorstand des Vereins besteht aus dem 1. Vorsitzenden sowie maximal sechs weiteren Mitgliedern. Die Vorstandsmitglieder werden von den Mitgliedern auf die Dauer von vier Jahren gewählt. Sie verbleiben bis zur Neuwahl im Amt. Die Wahlen können aus wichtigem Grund auf der Mitgliederversammlung widerrufen werden.

2. Der Verein wird gerichtlich und außergerichtlich im Rahmen des Vereinszwecks durch den 1. Vorsitzenden vertreten. Der 1. Vorsitzende ist berechtigt, für Einzelaufgaben Dritten Vollmacht zu erteilen.

3. Der Vorstand unterstützt die Geschäftsführung bei der Leitung des Vereins und beschließt über alle Vereinsangelegenheiten, soweit diese nicht der Mitgliederversammlung vorbehalten sind. Der Vorstand kann weitere zur Verwaltung des Vereins erforderlichen Personen wählen und entscheidet über sämtliche Einnahmen und Ausgaben des Vereins.

4. Über Aktivitäten besonderer Art und die Höhe der damit verbundenen Kosten beschließen nach Vorlage des Vorstandes die Mitglieder in der Mitgliederversammlung.

5. Die Mitgliederversammlung kann dem Vorstand eine Geschäftsordnung geben, nach der die Geschäfte des Vereins zu führen sind.

§ 8 Geschäftsführung

Der Vorstand bestellt eine Geschäftsführung. Diese führt die laufenden Aufgaben des Vereins nach Richtlinien des Vorstands durch. Sie ist auch zur Entscheidung über die Aufnahmeanträge der neuen Mitglieder bevollmächtigt. Die Geschäftsführung hat den Vorstand über alle Vereinsangelegenheiten von Bedeutung zu unterrichten. Sie ist an die Weisungen des Vorstandes gebunden und hat den Vorstand in allen wichtigen Angelegenheiten vorher zu konsultieren.

§ 9 Mitgliedsbeiträge

Der Jahresmitgliederbeitrag wird durch die Mitgliederversammlung bestimmt und staffelt sich zur Zeit wie folgt:

– Unternehmen: mindestens   600,– Euro
– Designer / Designbüros: mindestens   300,– Euro
– Privatpersonen: mindestens   150,– Euro.

§ 10 Revision

Mit der Rechnungsprüfung wird die Revision der Deutsche Messe AG bzw. eine Wirtschaftsprüfungsgesellschaft beauftragt. Über das Revisionsergebnis ist in der ordentlichen Mitgliederversammlung zu berichten.

§ 11 Auflösung des Vereins

1. Ein Beschluss auf Auflösung des Vereins bedarf einer Mehrheit von ¾ der stimmberechtigten Mitglieder, wobei die Mitgliederversammlung nur beschlussfähig ist, wenn mindestens ⅔ der stimmberechtigten Mitglieder anwesend sind.

2. Bei Auflösung oder Aufhebung des Vereins oder bei Wegfall des jetzigen Zwecks fällt das Vermögen, soweit es die eingezahlten Kapitalanteile der Mitglieder und den gemeinen Wert der von den Mitgliedern geleisteten Sacheinlagen übersteigt, an eine Körperschaft des öffentlichen Rechts zwecks Verwendung für kulturelle oder soziale Zwecke. Beschlüsse über die künftige Verwendung des Vermögens dürfen erst nach Einwilligung des Finanzamtes ausgeführt werden.

3. Die die Auflösung beschließende Mitgliederversammlung entscheidet über die Verwendung des Vereinsvermögens mit ¾ Mehrheit.

§ 12 Überschüsse, Ausgaben, Buchführung

1. Etwaige Gewinne des Vereins dürfen nur für steuerbegünstigte Zwecke der Satzung verwendet werden. Die Mitglieder erhalten keine Gewinnanteile und in ihrer Eigenschaft als Mitglieder auch keine sonstigen Zuwendungen aus Mitteln des Vereins.

2. Es darf keine Person durch Verwaltungsaufgaben, die dem Zweck des Vereins fremd sind, mittels unverhältnismäßig hoher Vergütungen begünstigt werden.

3. Der Nachweis für die Mittelverwendung ist durch eine ordnungsgemäße Buchführung zu gewährleisten.

Hannover, 5. Juni 2008

Ernst Raue
Vorsitzender

ARTICLES OF ASSOCIATION OF "iF – INDUSTRIE FORUM DESIGN E. V."

ARTICLE 1. NAME AND REGISTERED OFFICE OF THE ASSOCIATION

1. The name of the Association is "iF – Industrie Forum Design e. V.".
2. iF – Industrie Forum Design is listed in the Register of Associations (Vereinsregister).
3. The Association's registered office is in Hannover, Germany.

ARTICLE 2. OBJECT OF THE ASSOCIATION

The object of the Association is to support and gain acceptance for design as a link in the value chain and as a cultural component of society. The Association considers the targeted design of products, public and private living spaces, and user-friendly software applications as constituting its own civic and cultural mission. The Association aims to:

1. Recognize design achievements that help companies achieve their business goals and cement their economic success
2. Organize competitions, exhibitions, conferences, lectures, and other events
3. Issue publications to serve as the basis for discussions
4. Bolster the public's awareness of design
5. Provide a forum for objective dialogue on design-related issues.

The Association's activities give it a regional, national, and international presence.

ARTICLE 3. FINANCIAL YEAR

The financial year corresponds to the calendar year.

ARTICLE 4. MEMBERSHIP

1. Any natural person or legal entity may become a member of the Association. Executive Management shall examine and decide on membership applications, which are to be submitted in writing. In cases where Executive Management is unsure, the Board of Management shall decide on whether to grant membership by means of a simple majority vote. The Association is not required to justify a negative decision on membership.
2. In addition to members, the Association also consists of honorary members. Honorary members are individuals who have been particularly meritorious in their support of "iF – Industrie Forum Design". They may be elected to honorary membership by way of a unanimous resolution passed at the General Meeting. They are not entitled to vote at the General Meeting.
3. Membership shall end
    a) Through resignation, which must be declared to the Association in writing. This declaration requires a minimum of three months' advance notice before the end of the financial year, and takes effect at the end of the financial year.
    b) By way of expulsion upon a unanimous resolution by the Board of Management.
    c) At the time of a member's death.

ARTICLE 5. OFFICIAL BODIES

The Association's official bodies are:

1. The General Meeting
2. The Board of Management
3. Executive Management.

ARTICLE 6. GENERAL MEETING

1. The General Meeting is responsible for:
    a) Receiving the reports of the Board of Management and the independent auditors
    b) Electing the Board of Management
    c) Approving the actions of the Board of Management and the Executive Management
    d) Changing the Articles of Association
    e) Dissolving the Association
    f) Using the Association's assets in the event that it should be dissolved
    g) Using the annual profits or handling of any loss
    h) Setting the annual membership fee
    i) Electing honorary members
2. A regular General Meeting will be held annually. All members of the Association shall be invited to attend the General Meeting. The agenda of the regular General Meeting will, in particular, include reports on the preceding financial year, on the Association's financial statements, and on the results of the auditing of accounts.
3. General Meeting shall be called in writing by the Chairperson of the Board of Management, with a minimum of one week's advance notice and with such notice containing a meeting agenda. The agenda of the General Meeting is set by the Chairperson of the Board of Management or by another member of the Board of Management appointed by the Chairperson. Topics requested by individual members may be added to the agenda if the General Meeting gives its unanimous consent.
4. The Chairperson of the Board of Management may call an extraordinary General Meeting if an important reason exists for doing so. A meeting of this kind must be called if it has been requested in writing by at least one third of all members. Two day's advance notice is required. In urgent cases, invitations may be transmitted by telephone or fax.
5. General Meetings shall be presided over by the Chairperson of the Board of Management or, in the event that he or she should be prevented from doing so, by another member of the Board of Management appointed by the Chairperson.
6. A General Meeting that has been properly called has a quorum if, in addition to the individual presiding over the Meeting, at least three other members in possession of voting rights are present.

7. Each member has one vote at the General Meeting. Unless otherwise stipulated in these Articles, resolutions of the General Meeting shall be passed by way of a simple majority of those members present and entitled to vote. Passing a resolution on the appropriation of profit carried forward or the treatment of a loss requires a majority of 80 percent among the voting members present. Members entitled to vote may appoint a proxy to attend the General Meeting in their place, including a proxy voting right. In the of a tie, the deciding vote shall be cast by the individual presiding over the Meeting.

8. Urgent resolutions may be passed by round-robin procedure.

9. Resolutions on amendments to the Articles of Association shall require a three-quarters majority vote by the attending members who are eligible to vote.

10. Approved resolutions must be recorded in writing and signed by both the individual presiding over the Meeting and the keeper of the minutes. All members shall receive a copy of the minutes of the General Meeting.

ARTICLE 7. BOARD OF MANAGEMENT

1. The Association's Board of Management consists of the Chairperson and a maximum of six other members. The members of the Board of Management will be elected by the members of the Association for a term of four years. They shall remain in office until new elections take place. Elections may be revoked at General Meetings for good cause.

2. The Association will be represented in and out of court by the Chairperson of the Board of Management, who shall be permitted to delegate a power of attorney to third persons in individual cases.

3. The Board of Management shall support Executive Management in the running of the Association and shall decide on all matters concerning the Association, providing that the right to such decision-making is not reserved by the General Meeting. The Board of Management may elect other individuals required to assume administrative tasks and will decide on all of the Association's income and expenditures.

4. At the General Meeting, the members will decide on special activities and related expenditures as presented by the Board of Management.

5. The General Meeting may provide the Board of Management with rules of procedure governing the Association's operation.

ARTICLE 8. EXECUTIVE MANAGEMENT

The Board of Management shall appoint the executive management, which will be charged with executing the ongoing tasks of the Association in accordance with the guidelines issued by the Board of Management. Executive Management is authorized to make decisions on membership applications for new members. Executive Management shall inform the Board of Management about all significant matters affecting the Association. Executive Management shall follow all instructions issued by the Board of Management and shall consult the Board of Management in advance regarding all important matters.

ARTICLE 9. MEMBERSHIP FEES

The annual membership fee will be set at the General Meeting and is currently as follows:

– Companies:	600 Euro minimum
– Designers and design studios:	300 Euro minimum
– Individuals:	150 Euro minimum.

ARTICLE 10. AUDITING

Accounting control will be assigned to Deutsche Messe AG's auditing department or to an independent auditor. The results of auditing will be reported at the regular General Meeting.

ARTICLE 11. DISSOLUTION OF THE ASSOCIATION

1. A resolution to dissolve the Association shall require a three-fourths majority vote by the members who are entitled to vote, provided that at least two thirds of the members entitled to vote are present at the General Meeting.

2. Upon dissolution or annulment of the Association or in the event that the current object of the Association should cease to be applicable, any assets exceeding the capital shares deposited by the members and the fair market value of non-cash capital contributions made by members shall go to a public corporation that will use the assets for cultural or community welfare purposes. Resolutions on the future application of such assets may only be acted upon subsequent to consent thereto by the tax authorities.

3. The General Meeting which resolves to dissolve the Association shall pass a resolution on the application of the Association's assets by way of a three-fourths majority vote.

ARTICLE 12. PROFITS, EXPENDITURES, ACCOUNTING

1. Any profits produced by the Association shall be used exclusively for the tax-privileged purposes of these Articles of Association. Members shall not receive shares of profit, nor shall they, in their capacity as members, receive any other forms of bestowal from Association funds.

2. No individual may be favored by receiving disproportionately high remuneration for administrative tasks not in keeping with the object of the Association.

3. Proof that the Association's funds are being used properly shall be guaranteed by way of adequate and orderly accounting procedures.

Hannover, June 5, 2008

Ernst Raue
Chairman

iF PARTNER AND SPONSORS 2013

iF official partner

Allianz deutscher Designer
Germany

Packaging Connections
India

Bundesverband Digitale Wirtschaft
Germany

raumPROBE
Germany

China Industrial Designers Association
Taiwan

Taiwan External Trade Development Council
Taiwan

Haute Innovation
Material and Technology
Germany

Taiwan Design Center
Taiwan

Korea Institue of Design Promotion
South Korea

National Institute of Design India
India

Werben & Verkaufen
Fachmagazin für Marketing und Kommunikation
Germany

Ideen und Know-How
für Design, Werbung, Medien
Fachmagazin für Kreative
Germany

Das Online-Magazin für Industriedesign
und Innovation
Germany

GOLD Sponsors iF concept design award

Hansgrohe SE
Germany

iF International Forum Design GmbH
Germany

LG Hausys, Ltd.
South Korea

Samsung Electronics Co., Ltd.
South Korea

Volkswagen AG
Germany

BRONZE Sponsor iF concept design award

event it AG
Germany

Beratungsunternehmen
für gesellschaftlichen Wandel
B.G.W GmbH
Germany

Media partner iF concept design award

Yanko Design
Canada

583

BOB Package Style Group Co., Ltd.
Seoul, South Korea
http://bobdesign.co.kr
▲ vol. 1: 117
● vol. 1: 117

Bodo Warden Product Design
Mönchengladbach, Germany
http://bw-dc.de
● vol. 1: 259

Böker Messer-Manufaktur
Solingen, Germany
www.boeker-solingen.de
▲ vol. 2: 174
● vol. 2: 174

Bosch Sicherheitssysteme GmbH
Grasbrunn, Germany
www.bosch-sicherheitssysteme.de
▲ vol. 1: 195

Bosch Thermotechnik GmbH Werk Lollar
Lollar, Germany
www.bosch-thermotechnik.de
▲ vol. 2: 337

Braake Design
Stuttgart, Germany
www.braake.com
● vol. 2: 466, 530

Brabantia International B. V.
Valkenswaard, Netherlands
www.brabantia.com
▲ vol. 2: 175

brains4design GmbH
München, Germany
www.brains4design.com
● vol. 2: 22, 323

BRANDIS Industrial Design
Nürnberg, Germany
http://brandis-design.de
● vol. 2: 260

Brandoffice GmbH
München, Germany
www.brandoffice.com
● vol. 1: 230

Braun Design
Kronberg i. T., Germany
www.braun.com
● vol. 1: 106, 169

Breimann & Bruun Garten- und
Landschaftsarchitekten
Hamburg, Germany
www.breimann-bruun.de
● vol. 2: 350

B/R/K Vertriebs-GmbH
Wuppertal, Germany
www.brk-germany.com
▲ vol. 2: 169

Brother Industries, Ltd.
Nagoya, Japan
www.brother.com
▲ vol. 1: 388, 418 – 423
● vol. 1: 388, 418 – 423
▲ vol. 2: 23
● vol. 2: 23

Brunner GmbH
Rheinau, Germany
www.brunner-group.com
▲ vol. 1: 554

BSH Home Appliances (China) Co., Ltd.
Nanjing, China
www.bsh-group.com
▲ vol. 2: 176, 177, 253

BUCK
Belgrade, Serbia
www.buck.rs
▲ vol. 2: 24

Budde Industrie Design GmbH
Münster, Germany
www.budde-design.de
● vol. 2: 536, 539

BUFFALO Inc.
Nagoya, Japan
www.buffalo-asia.com
▲ vol. 1: 424, 425
● vol. 1: 424, 425

Buffon Wang
Taipei, Taiwan
● vol. 2: 551

Bull Electric Co., Ltd.
Cixi, China
www.gongniu.cn
▲ vol. 1: 555

Burkhard Vogtherr
Mulhouse, France
www.vogtherr.com
● vol. 1: 563

büro+staubach gmbh
Berlin, Germany
www.buero-staubach.de
● vol. 1: 74

busk + hertzog
London, United Kingdom
www.busk-hertzog.com
● vol. 2: 377

Busse Design & Engineering
Elchingen, Germany
www.busse-design-ulm.de
● vol. 2: 484

BW Bielefelder Werkstätten
Bielefeld, Germany
www.bielefelder-werkstaetten.de
▲ vol. 2: 116

B&W Group Ltd.
Steyning, United Kingdom
www.bwgroup.com
▲ vol. 1: 189
● vol. 1: 189

C

Campeggi S. R. L.
Anzano del Parco, Italy
www.campeggisrl.it
▲ vol. 2: 117

Canon Inc.
Tokyo, Japan
www.canon.com
▲ vol. 1: 196 – 199, 426 – 428
● vol. 1: 196 – 199, 426 – 428

Canyon Bicycles GmbH
Koblenz, Germany
www.canyon.com
▲ vol. 1: 96, 118
● vol. 1: 96

CARL MERTENS Besteckfarbrik GmbH
Solingen, Germany
www.carl-mertens.com
▲ vol. 2: 178

Carl Zeiss AG
Oberkochen, Germany
www.zeiss.de
▲ vol. 1: 174, 200 – 203

Carsten Gollnick Design
Berlin, Germany
www.gollnick-design.de
● vol. 2: 178

Casablanca Leuchten GmbH
Offenbach, Germany
www.casablanca-leuchten.de
▲ vol. 2: 25

Cyphics
Seoul, South Korea
http://cyphics.com
● vol. 2: 430

D

DAB Pumps S. p. A.
Mestrino (PD), Italy
www.dabpumps.com
▲ vol. 2: 464
● vol. 2: 464

Dadam Design Associates Inc.
Seoul, South Korea
www.dadam.com
● vol. 2: 360, 434

DAELIM DOBIDOS
Incheon, South Korea
www.dlt.co.kr
▲ vol. 2: 294
● vol. 2: 294

Daelim Trading Co., Ltd.
Incheon, South Korea
▲ vol. 2: 295
● vol. 2: 295

DAEWOO E & C Co.
Seoul, South Korea
www.daewooenc.co.kr
● vol. 2: 338

D&A Experiences
Helsinki, Finland
www.dear-experiences.com
● vol. 1: 380

DAI-Labor / TU Berlin
Berlin, Germany
www.dai-labor.de
▲ vol. 2: 557
● vol. 2: 557

Daimler AG
Sindelfingen, Germany
www.daimler.com
▲ vol. 1: 83
● vol. 1: 83
▲ vol. 2: 558
● vol. 2: 558

Darfon Electronics Corp.
Gueishan, Taoyuan, Taiwan
www.darfon.com
▲ vol. 1: 440
● vol. 1: 440

Dataflex International
Krimpen a / d IJssel, Netherlands
www.dataflex-int.com
▲ vol. 1: 560
● vol. 1: 560

DATRON AG
Mühltal, Germany
www.datron.de
▲ vol. 2: 462
● vol. 2: 462

Day & Day Trading Corp.
Taipei, Taiwan
www.toastliving.com
▲ vol. 2: 182

DCA
Warwick, United Kingdom
www.dca-design.com
● vol. 2: 431

Decameron Design
São Paulo, Brazil
www.decamerondesign.com.br
▲ vol. 2: 118
● vol. 2: 118

defortec GmbH design for technology
Tübingen / Dettenhausen, Germany
http://defortec.de
● vol. 2: 479

Dell Inc.
Round Rock, TX, United States of
America
www.dell.com
▲ vol. 1: 390, 441 – 444

Dell Inc.
Experience Design Group
Round Rock, TX,
United States of America
www.dell.com
● vol. 1: 390, 441 – 444

Delphin Design GbR
Thomas Wagner, Dirk Loff
Berlin, Germany
www.delphin-design.de
● vol. 2: 138, 139, 281

DELTA LIGHT N. V.
Wevelgem, Belgium
www.deltalight.com
▲ vol. 2: 27 – 29
● vol. 2: 27 – 29

Dental Photonics, Inc.
Walpole, MA, United States of America
www.dentalphotonics.com
▲ vol. 2: 397

Design 3
Hamburg, Germany
www.design3.de
● vol. 2: 292

designaffairs GmbH
Erlangen, Germany
München, Germany
www.designaffairs.com
● vol. 1: 89
● vol. 2: 337, 424

design büro groiss peter
Laakirchen, Austria
www.dbgp.at
● vol. 2: 47

Design dada associates
Seoul, South Korea
www.dada-da.com
▲ vol. 2: 375
● vol. 2: 375

Design Form Technik
Triesenberg, Liechtenstein
www.design-form-technik.com
● vol. 2: 500

Designit Aarhus
Aarhus C, Denmark
http://designit.com
● vol. 2: 386

Designit Copenhagen
Copenhagen NV, Denmark
http://designit.com
● vol. 2: 166

Designit Munich
München, Germany
http://designit.com
● vol. 1: 213, 214, 300, 327

Designit Oslo
Oslo, Norway
http://designit.com
● vol. 1: 315

DESIGN K2L
Seoul, South Korea
http://designk2l.com
● vol. 2: 356

designkonzentrat
Köln, Germany
www.designkonzentrat.de
● vol. 2: 258

Design Mu
Seoul, South Korea
● vol. 2: 343

Acrylic Design,Backlight Effect

GADMEI

Always Beside You

Gadmei Electronics Technology Co.,Ltd which was founded in Aug.1999 specializes in R&D, manufacturing and marketing.

Gadmei focuses on designing and manufacturing 3 series of products: Desktop Digital Media series, Portable Digital Media series and IT Media series, which include Smart Pal, DPF, MID, Power Bank, Cloud TV Box and so on.

www.gadmei.com

Smart Pal

MID

DPF

lixtec GmbH
Regau, Austria
www.lixtec.com
▲ vol. 2: 47

LKK Design (Shenzhen) Co., Ltd.
Shenzhen, China
www.lkkdesign.com
● vol. 1: 194

Loewe AG
Kronach, Germany
www.loewe.tv
▲ vol. 1: 180, 230

Loewe Design
Kronach, Germany
www.loewe.de
● vol. 1: 180

Logitech Europe
Lausanne, Switzerland
www.logitech.com
▲ vol. 1: 493

Logitech Gateway
Newark, NJ, United States of America
www.logitech.com
▲ vol. 1: 231, 494

Lomak Industrial Co., Ltd.
Hong Kong
www.lomak.com
▲ vol. 2: 48
● vol. 2: 48

LORCH Schweißtechnik GmbH
Auenwald-Mittelbrüden, Germany
www.lorch.biz
▲ vol. 2: 497

Lumicenter Lighting
São José dos Pinhais, Brazil
www.lumicenter.com
▲ vol. 2: 49
● vol. 2: 49

LUNAR
San Francisco, CA, United States of
America
www.lunar.com
● vol. 1: 559

Luxuni GmbH
Leer, Germany
www.luxuni.de
▲ vol. 2: 50, 51

M

M1 – Sporttechnik GmbH & Co. KG
Großhelfendorf, Germany
www.m1-sporttechnik.de
▲ vol. 1: 131
● vol. 1: 131

MADA Marx Datentechnik GmbH
Villingen-Schwenningen, Germany
www.mada.de
▲ vol. 2: 349
● vol. 2: 349

ma design GmbH & Co. KG
Kiel, Germany
● vol. 1: 276

Maginidesign Studio
Milano, Italy
www.emanuelemagini.it
● vol. 2: 117

maKe design
Darmstadt, Germany
● vol. 2: 303

Maltani lighting
Seoul, South Korea
www.taewon.co.kr
▲ vol. 2: 52
● vol. 2: 52

Mapa GmbH
Zeven, Germany
www.nuk.de
www.mapa.de
▲ vol. 1: 132
● vol. 1: 132
▲ vol. 2: 410
● vol. 2: 410

Marco Goffi
Milano, Italy
http://marcogoffi.com
● vol. 2: 552

MARCO HEMMERLING
Studio for Spatial Design
Köln, Germany
www.marcohemmerling.com
● vol. 2: 120

Marken-Design Gaggenau
München, Germany
www.gaggenau.com
● vol. 2: 212

Marna Inc.
Tokyo, Japan
www.marna-inc.co.jp
▲ vol. 2: 235 – 238
● vol. 2: 235 – 238

MARTINELLI LUCE S. p. A.
Lucca, Italy
www.martinelliluce.it
▲ vol. 2: 53
● vol. 2: 53

marwin productdesign
München, Germany
www.marwin-productdesign.de
● vol. 1: 547

MAS Design Products Ltd.
Dorset, United Kingdom
www.mas-design.com
● vol. 1: 133

Matteo Thun & Partners
Milano, Italy
www.matteothun.com
● vol. 2: 302

Matuschek Design & Management
Aalen, Germany
www.matuschekdesign.de
● vol. 2: 485

medi GmbH & Co. KG
Bayreuth, Germany
www.medi.de
▲ vol. 2: 411
● vol. 2: 411

Medion AG
Essen, Germany
www.medion.com
▲ vol. 1: 232, 495, 496
● vol. 1: 232, 495, 496

medwork medical products
and services GmbH
Höchstadt, Germany
www.medwork.com
▲ vol. 2: 412

Meister Inc.
Seoul, South Korea
www.mandofootloose.com
▲ vol. 1: 133

Memmert GmbH & Co. KG
Schwabach, Germany
www.memmert.com
▲ vol. 2: 413

Metalligence Technology Corp.
New Taipei, Taiwan
www.metalligence.com
▲ vol. 2: 414
● vol. 2: 414

Sartorius
Corporate Administration GmbH
Göttingen, Germany
www.sartorius.com
● vol. 2: 432

Sartorius
Weighing Technology GmbH
Göttingen, Germany
www.sartorius.com
▲ vol. 2: 432

Scanomat A/S
Kokkedal, Denmark
www.scanomat.com
▲ vol. 1: 580
● vol. 1: 580

Schindler Design
Wolfurt, Austria
www.schindler-design.de
● vol. 1: 304

Schirrmacher Product Design
Landsberg, Germany
www.schirrmacher-product-design.de
● vol. 2: 471, 472

Schmitz-Leuchten GmbH & Co. KG
Arnsberg, Germany
www.schmitz-leuchten.de
▲ vol. 2: 88, 89

Schmitz-Werke GmbH & Co. KG
Emsdetten, Germany
www.markilux.com
▲ vol. 2: 359

Schneider Schreibgeräte GmbH
Schramberg, Germany
www.schneiderpen.com
▲ vol. 1: 581

SDI CORPORATION
ChangHua, Taiwan
http://stationery.sdi.com.tw
▲ vol. 1: 582
● vol. 1: 582

seca gmbh & co. kg.
Hamburg, Germany
www.seca.com
▲ vol. 2: 390

Seiko Epson Corporation
Shiojiri-shi, Nagano-ken, Japan
www.epson.com
● vol. 1: 272, 519 – 524, 583
▲ vol. 1: 272, 519 – 524, 583

Selic Industriedesign
Augsburg, Germany
www.selic.de
● vol. 2: 444, 456 – 458, 494

Selle Italia
Casella d'Asolo (TV), Italy
www.selleitalia.com
▲ vol. 1: 151
● vol. 1: 151

Semiline Co., Ltd.
Seoul, South Korea
www.semipos.com
▲ vol. 1: 525

Senao Networks, Inc. (EnGenius)
Taoyuan, Taiwan
www.engeniusnetworks.com
▲ vol. 1: 526
● vol. 1: 526

Sennheiser electronic GmbH & Co. KG
Wedemark, Germany
http://sennheiser.com
www.sennheiser.de
▲ vol. 1: 273 – 276
● vol. 1: 276

Serge Cornelissen BVBA
Roeselare, Belgium
www.sergecornelissen.com
● vol. 2: 88

Seymourpowell
London, United Kingdom
www.seymourpowell.com
● vol. 1: 478

SHADELAB S. R. L.
Motta di Livenza, Italy
http://shadelab.it
▲ vol. 2: 132

Shanghai BLLC Environment Technology
Co., Ltd.
Shanghai, China
www.bllc.com.cn
▲ vol. 2: 506
● vol. 2: 506

Sharp Corporation
Osaka, Japan
www.sharp.co.jp
▲ vol. 1: 365
● vol. 1: 365

Shea + Latone
East Greenville, PA, United States of
America
www.shealatone.com
● vol. 1: 550

Shenzhen Baojia Battery Tech Co., Ltd.
Shenzhen, China
www.mipow.com
▲ vol. 1: 152, 153
● vol. 1: 152, 153

Shenzhen CIGA Design Co., Ltd.
Shenzhen, China
http://ciga.com.cn
▲ vol. 2: 90
● vol. 2: 90

Shenzhen Great-Time Vision Marketing
& Planning Co., Ltd.
Shenzhen, China
www.cocotemam.com
▲ vol. 1: 366
● vol. 1: 366

Shenzhen Imay Design Co., Ltd.
Shenzhen, China
http://imaydesign.com
● vol. 1: 277

Shenzhen Koonlung Technology Co., Ltd.
Shenzhen, China
www.koonlung.net
▲ vol. 1: 277

Shenzhen Rapoo Technology Co., Ltd.
Shenzhen, China
www.rapoo.com
▲ vol. 1: 527
● vol. 1: 527

ShenZhen Renice Technology Co., Ltd.
ShenZhen, China
www.renice-tech.com
▲ vol. 1: 367

Shimadzu Corporation
Kyoto, Japan
www.shimadzu.com
● vol. 2: 507

Shimadzu Mectem, Inc.
Shiga, Japan
www.shimadzu-mectem.com
▲ vol. 2: 507

Ship and Ocean Industries R & D Center
New Taipei, Taiwan
www.soic.org.tw
▲ vol. 2: 551

The new Secura®
Riskless weighing in regulated areas.

Stefano Sandonà
Selvazzano Dentro (PD), Italy
www.sandonadesign.it
● vol. 2: 121

Stefan Schöning Studio
Antwerpen, Belgium
www.stefanschoning.com
● vol. 2: 31

stephan gahlow produktgestaltung
Hamburg, Germany
www.gahlow.de
● vol. 2: 498

Storck Bicycle GmbH
Idstein, Germany
www.storck-bicycle.de
▲ vol. 1: 157 – 159
● vol. 1: 157, 158

Studio 1:1 Jarosław Szymański
Gdańsk, Poland
http://studio1do1.pl
● vol. 2: 341

Studio Aisslinger
Berlin, Germany
www.aisslinger.de
● vol. 2: 330, 333 – 336

Studio Carlotta de Bevilacqua
Milan, Italy
www.debevilacqua.com
● vol. 2: 21

Studio Domo Inc.
Taipei, Taiwan
www.studiodomo.net
▲ vol. 2: 136

Studio Hannes Wettstein AG
Zürich, Switzerland
www.studiohanneswettstein.com
● vol. 1: 169

Studio Mario Mazzer
Conegliano, Italy
www.mariomazzer.it
● vol. 2: 132

Studio Oeding GmbH
Hamburg, Germany
www.studio-oeding.com
● vol. 1: 85

Studio Urquiola
Milano, Italy
www.patriciaurquiola.com
● vol. 2: 108

Sulzer Mixpac AG
Haag, Switzerland
www.sulzerchemtech.com
▲ vol. 2: 436

Sunny Optical Technology Co.,Ltd.
Yuyao, China
www.sunnyoptical.com
▲ vol. 1: 238

Supfina Grieshaber GmbH & Co. KG
Wolfach, Germany
www.supfina.com
▲ vol. 2: 516

Swareflex GmbH
Vomp, Austria
www.swareflex.com
▲ vol. 2: 92
● vol. 2: 92

SYNTHESIS Design Partner
Pieter Kuschel e. K.
Breckerfeld, Germany
www.synthesis-design.de
● vol. 2: 169

Sysmex Corporation
Nishi-ku, Kobe, Japan
www.sysmex.co.jp
▲ vol. 2: 437

T

TAC design Inc.
Osaka, Japan
www.tac-design.com
● vol. 2: 501

taliaYsebastian ID
Wien, Austria
www.taliaysebastian.com
● vol. 2: 410

Tangram Design Lab., Inc.
Seoul, South Korea
www.tangramdesignlab.com
▲ vol. 1: 297, 377
● vol. 1: 297, 377

TCL Multimedia Technology Holdings Ltd.
Shenzhen, China
http://multimedia.tcl.com
▲ vol. 1: 298, 299
● vol. 1: 298, 299

TD Tech Ltd.
Beijing, China
www.td-tech.com
▲ vol. 1: 378
● vol. 1: 378

TEAGUE
Seattle, WA, United States of America
www.teague.com
● vol. 1: 76
● vol. 2: 167

TEAK Cultue & Creative Co., Ltd.
Hangzhou, China
● vol. 1: 126
● vol. 2: 561

TEAM 7 Natürlich Wohnen GmbH
Ried im Innkreis, Austria
www.team7.at
▲ vol. 2: 137
● vol. 2: 137

TEAMS Design
Esslingen, Germany
Shanghai, China
www.teamsdesign.com
● vol. 1: 195

Technogym
Cesena, Italy
www.technogym.com
▲ vol. 1: 160
● vol. 1: 160

TEKTRO TECHNOLOGY CORPORATION
TEKTRO R&D
Changhua, Taiwan
www.tektro.com
▲ vol. 1: 161
● vol. 1: 161

TESTA MOTARI – Design Manufaktur
Johanngeorgenstadt, Germany
● vol. 1: 547

TGS Design Consultancy
Shenzhen, China
● vol. 1: 349

The Brand Union GmbH
Hamburg, Germany
thebrandunion.de
● vol. 2: 59

Thermaltake Technology Co., Ltd.
Taipei, Taiwan
www.thermaltake.com.tw
www.thermaltakeusa.com
▲ vol. 1: 396, 535 – 537

Thermokon Sensortechnik GmbH
Mittenaar, Germany
www.thermokon.de
▲ vol. 2: 361
● vol. 2: 361

Thomas Trauth Design GmbH
Lorch, Germany
thomas-trauth-design.de
● vol. 1: 162

Thonet GmbH
Frankenberg, Germany
www.thonet.de
▲ vol. 2: 138 – 140

Thule AB
Malmö, Sweden
http://thulegroup.com
www.thule.com
▲ vol. 1: 90, 91, 163, 164
● vol. 1: 90, 91, 163

Tiptel.com GmbH
Business Solutions
Ratingen, Germany
www.tiptel.com
▲ vol. 1: 379
● vol. 1: 379

TOAST Living
Taipei, Taiwan
www.toastliving.com
● vol. 2: 182

Tobias Grau GmbH
Rellingen, Germany
www.tobias-grau.com
▲ vol. 2: 93, 94
● vol. 2: 93, 94

Tons Lightology Inc.
New Taipei City, Taiwan
www.tons.com.tw
▲ vol. 2: 95
● vol. 2: 95

Tools Design
Copenhagen, Denmark
www.toolsdesign.com
● vol. 1: 121, 332
● vol. 2: 210, 559

Toout
Hangzhou, China
● vol. 1: 301

TopGun/Tforce/Ubike
Yuan Lin Town, Changhua, Taiwan
www.ubike-tech.com
▲ vol. 1: 165
● vol. 1: 165

Toshiba Corporation
Tokyo, Japan
www.toshiba.co.jp
● vol. 1: 538, 539
● vol. 2: 158, 279, 280

Toshiba Corporation
Digital Products & Services Company
Tokyo, Japan
www.toshiba.co.jp
▲ vol. 1: 538, 539

Toshiba
Home Appliances Corporation
Tokyo, Japan
www.toshiba.co.jp
▲ vol. 2: 158, 279, 280

Toshiba Tec Corporation
Tokyo, Japan
www.toshibatec.co.jp/en
▲ vol. 1: 540
● vol. 1: 540

TP-LINK Design
Nanshan, Shenzhen, China
www.tp-link.com
● vol. 1: 542
▲ vol. 1: 542, 544

TPV technology Ltd.
New Taipei City, Taiwan
www.tpv-tech.com
▲ vol. 1: 545
● vol. 1: 545

Trendglas Jena GmbH
Jena, Germany
www.trendglas-jena.com
▲ vol. 2: 281

Tribecraft AG Design Team
Zürich, Switzerland
www.tribecraft.ch
● vol. 2: 367

TRILUX GmbH & Co. KG
Arnsberg, Germany
www.trilux.de
▲ vol. 2: 96

TSUBAKI KABELSCHLEPP GmbH
Wenden-Gerlingen, Germany
http://kabelschlepp.de
▲ vol. 2: 517
● vol. 2: 517

Tt Design
Taipei, Taiwan
www.ttdesignworks.com
● vol. 1: 536

Tung Tzu Industrial Co., Ltd.
YongKang Dist., Tainan City, Taiwan
www.babyace.com.tw
▲ vol. 1: 166
● vol. 1: 166

Two+Group
New Taipei City, Taiwan
www.aideoffice.com
● vol. 2: 346, 408

txtr GmbH
Berlin, Germany
http://txtr.com
▲ vol. 1: 546

U

UBIK Philippe Starck Network
Paris, France
www.starck.com
● vol. 1: 480

Union Design & Development Corp.
Taipei, Taiwan
www.uddc.com.tw
● vol. 2: 450, 451

United Navigation GmbH
Ostfildern, Germany
www.united-navigation.com
▲ vol. 1: 300
● vol. 1: 300

Uniview
Hangzhou, China
www.uniview.com.cn
▲ vol. 1: 301
● vol. 1: 301

Uros Oy
Oulu, Finland
www.uros.com
▲ vol. 1: 380

UVEX ARBEITSSCHUTZ GmbH
Fürth, Germany
www.uvex-safety.com
▲ vol. 2: 518, 519

V

Vaillant GmbH
Remscheid, Germany
www.vaillant.de
▲ vol. 2: 362

Valerie Trauttmansdorff
Wien, Austria
● vol. 2: 422

Zweibrüder Optoelectronics
GmbH & Co. KG
Solingen, Germany
www.zweibrueder.com
▲ vol. 2: 101, 102
● vol. 2: 101, 102

zweigrad GmbH & Co. KG
Hamburg, Germany
www.zweigrad.de
● vol. 2: 463, 545